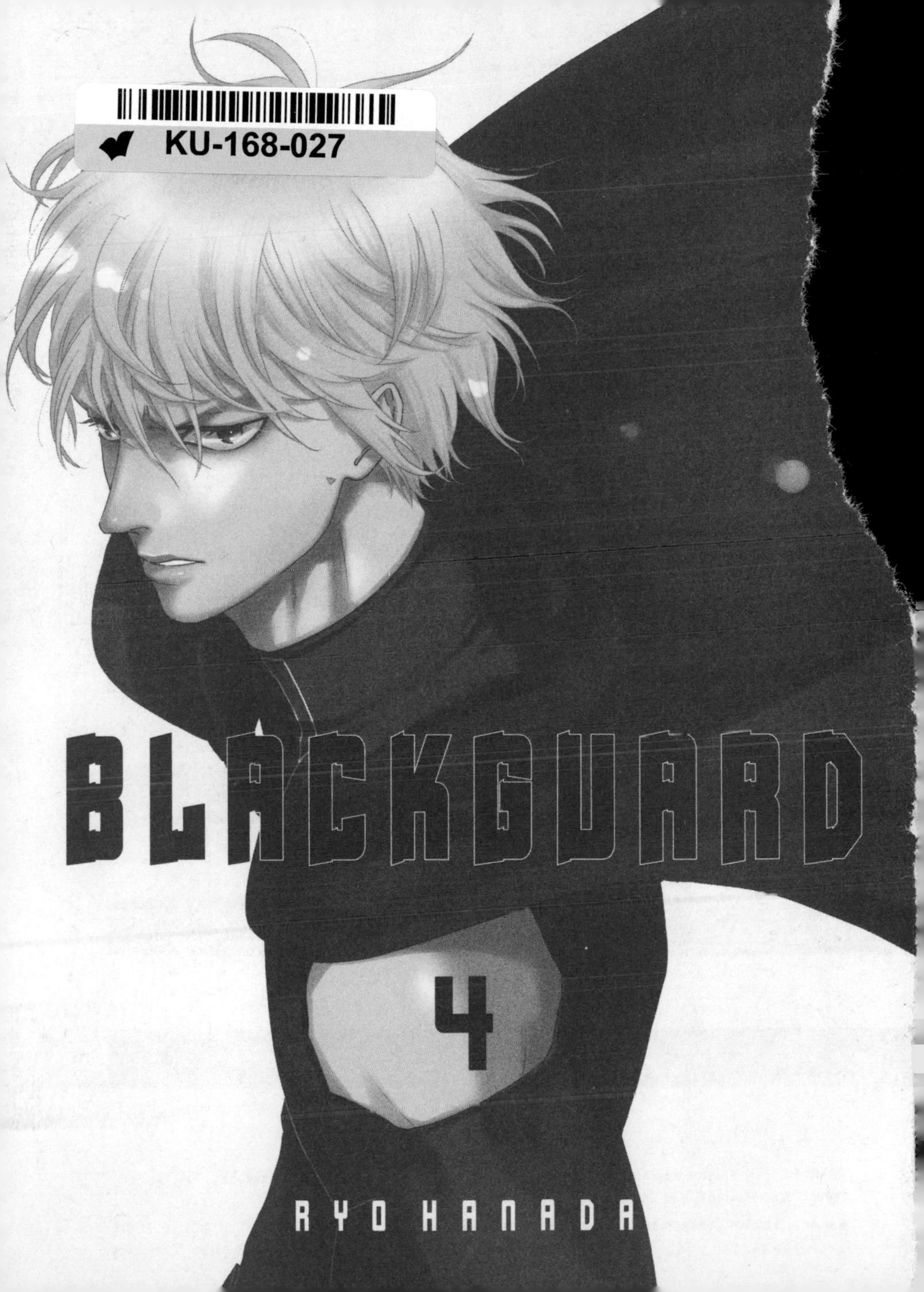
BLACKGUARD
4
RYO HANADA

CONTENTS

WARNING: This volume contains references to suicide. If you or someone you know has suicidal thoughts or feelings, you are not alone, and there is free, 24/7 help.

National Suicide Prevention Lifeline offers confidential support for those in crisis or emotional distress. You can call 1-800-273-TALK (8255) or go to SuicidePreventionLifeline.org for free, 24/7 help.

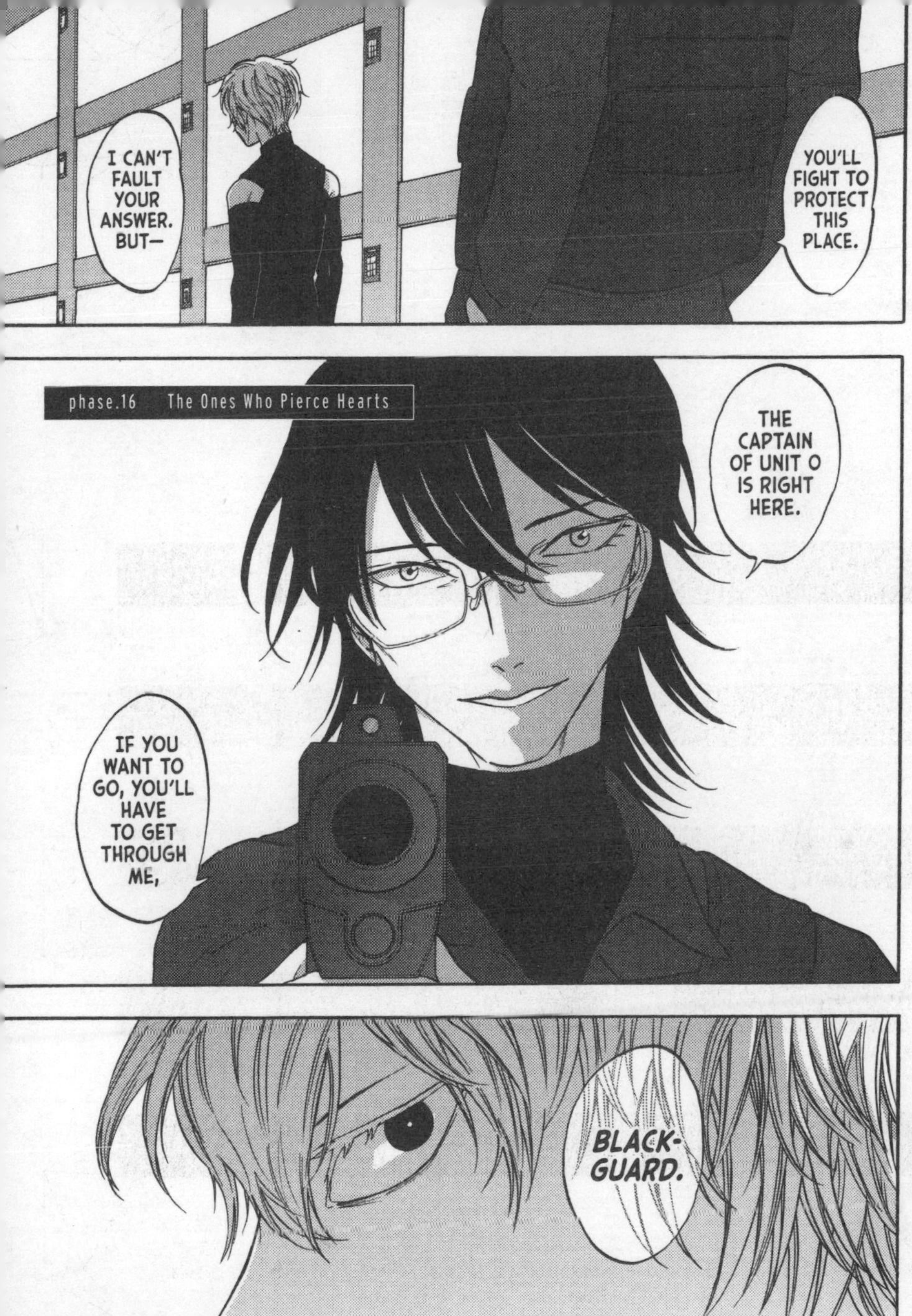
YOU'LL FIGHT TO PROTECT THIS PLACE.
I CAN'T FAULT YOUR ANSWER. BUT—
phase.16 The Ones Who Pierce Hearts
THE CAPTAIN OF UNIT O IS RIGHT HERE.
IF YOU WANT TO GO, YOU'LL HAVE TO GET THROUGH ME,
BLACK-GUARD.

phase.16 The Ones Who Pierce Hearts

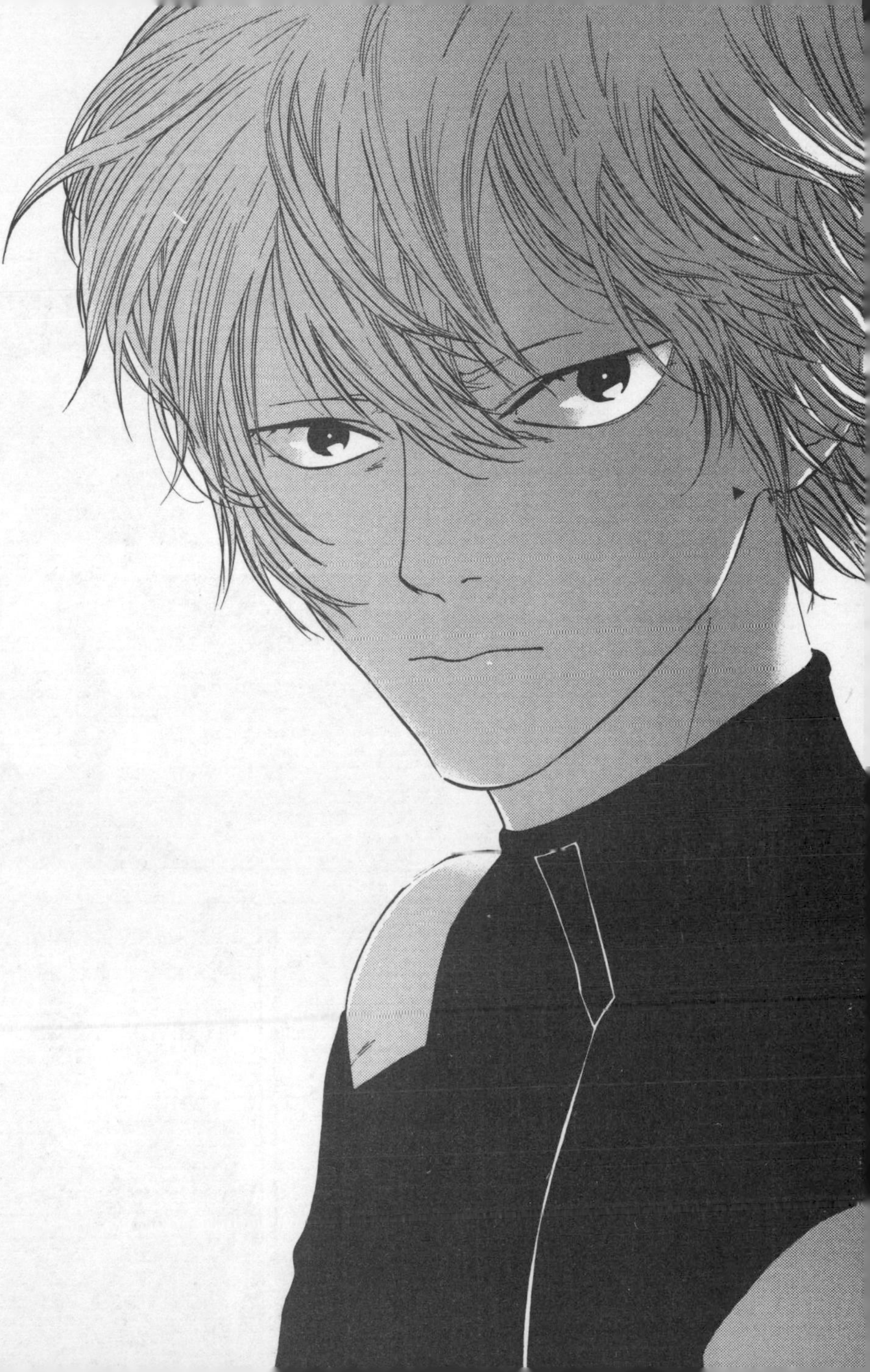

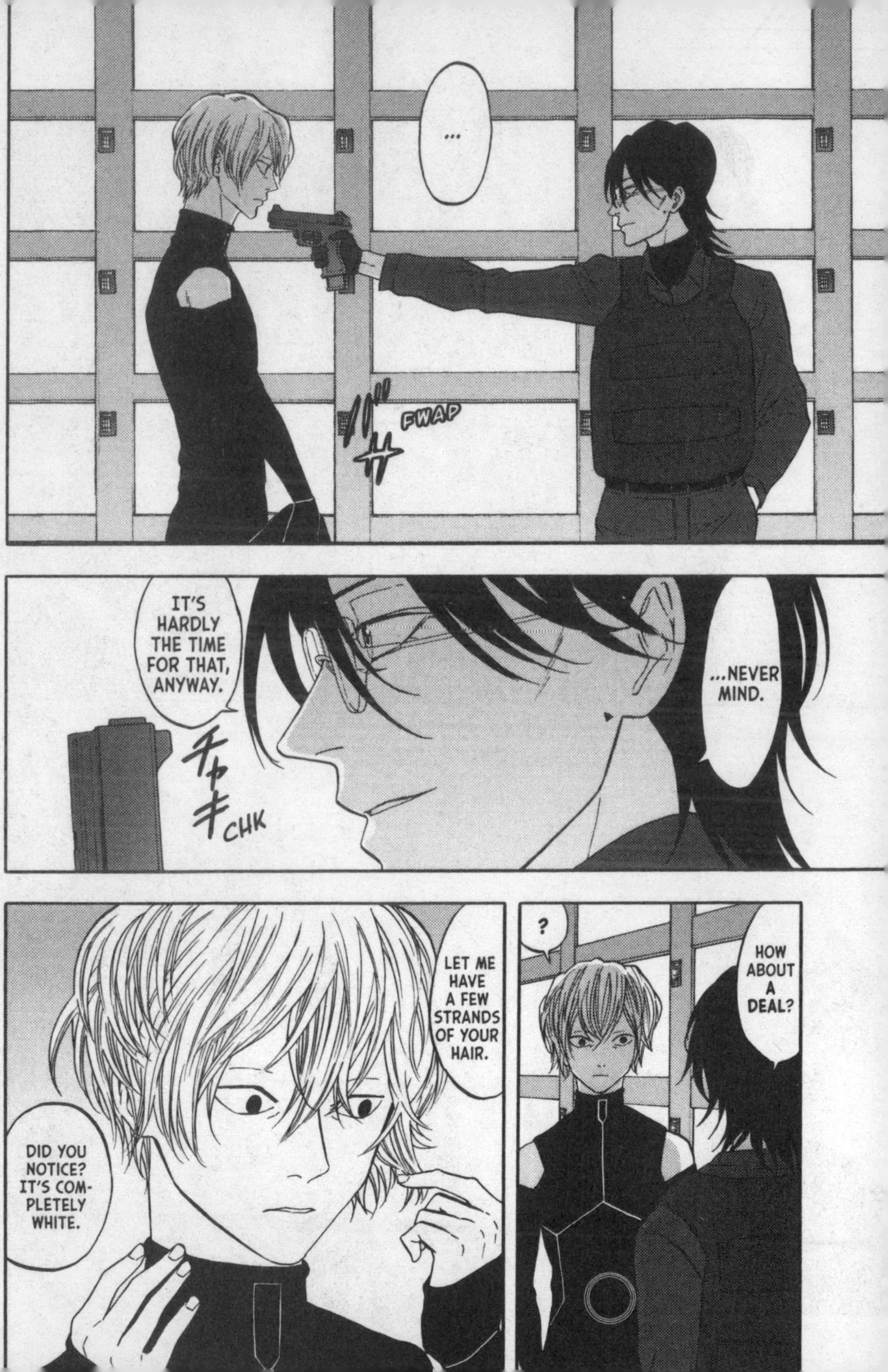
...
FWAP
...NEVER MIND.
IT'S HARDLY THE TIME FOR THAT, ANYWAY.
チャキ
CHK
HOW ABOUT A DEAL?
?
LET ME HAVE A FEW STRANDS OF YOUR HAIR.
DID YOU NOTICE? IT'S COMPLETELY WHITE.

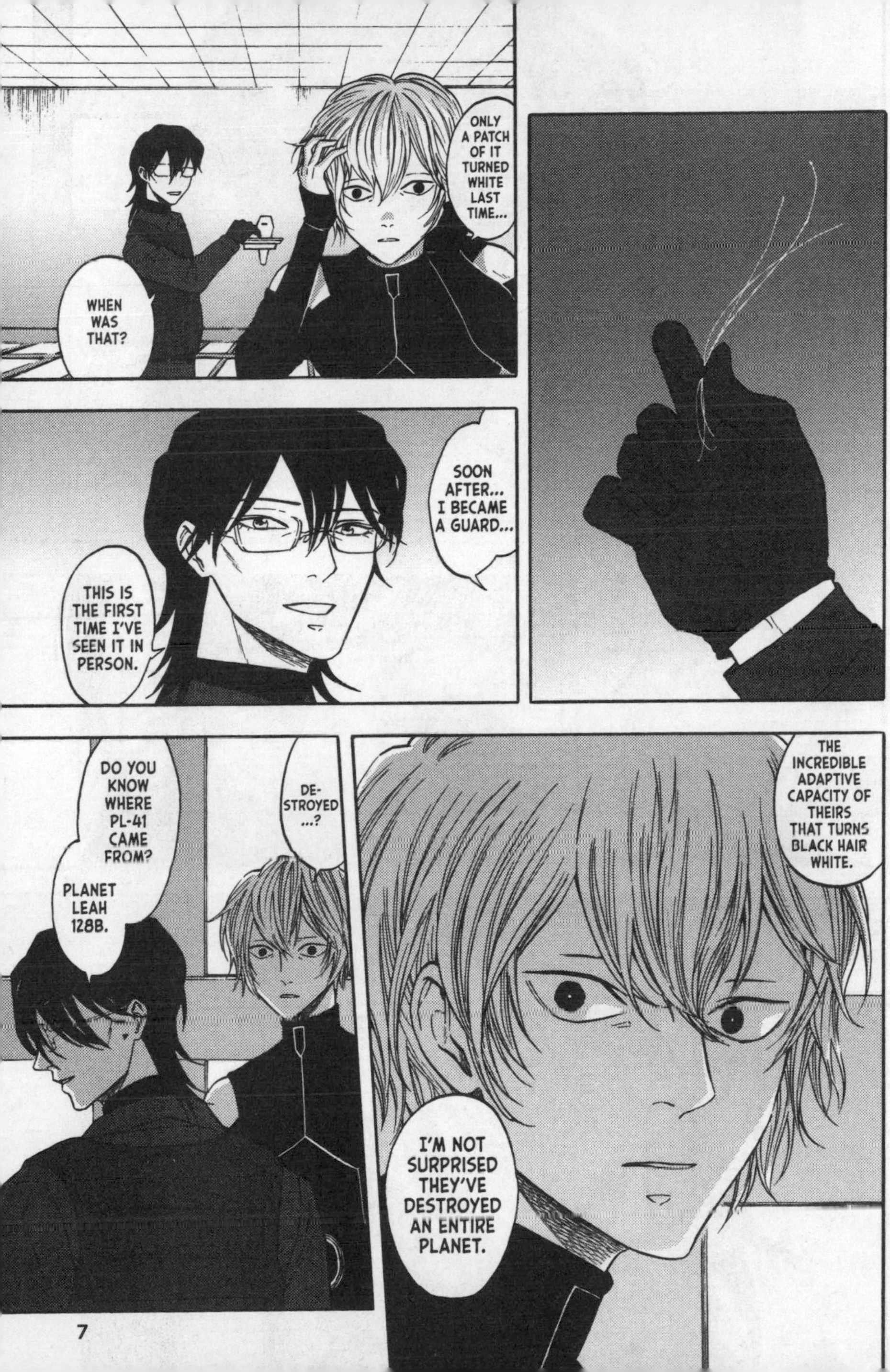
ONLY A PATCH OF IT TURNED WHITE LAST TIME...
WHEN WAS THAT?
SOON AFTER... I BECAME A GUARD...
THIS IS THE FIRST TIME I'VE SEEN IT IN PERSON.
THE INCREDIBLE ADAPTIVE CAPACITY OF THEIRS THAT TURNS BLACK HAIR WHITE.
I'M NOT SURPRISED THEY'VE DESTROYED AN ENTIRE PLANET.
DE-STROYED ...?
DO YOU KNOW WHERE PL-41 CAME FROM?
PLANET LEAH 128B.

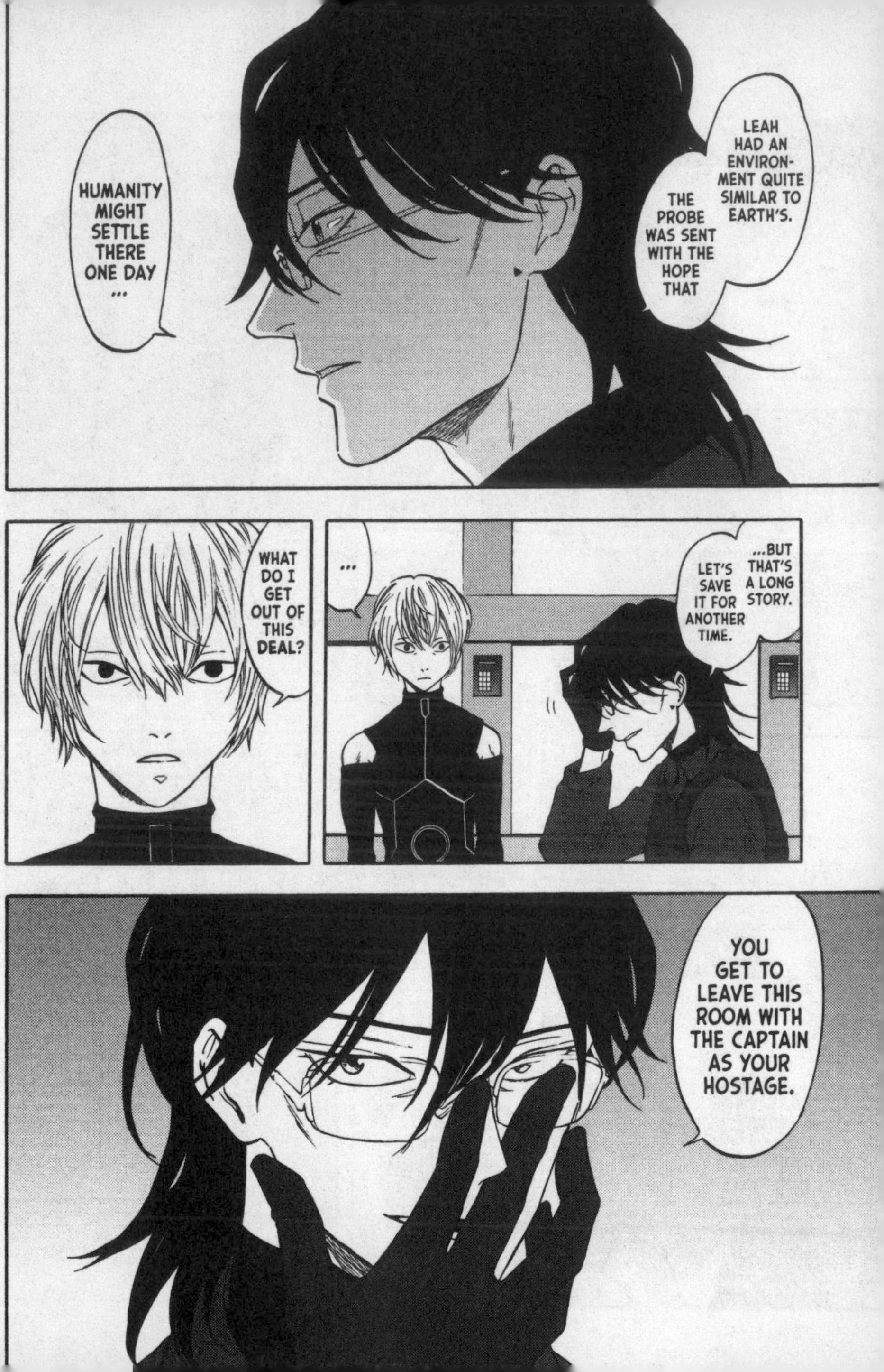
LEAH HAD AN ENVIRON-MENT QUITE SIMILAR TO EARTH'S.
THE PROBE WAS SENT WITH THE HOPE THAT
HUMANITY MIGHT SETTLE THERE ONE DAY ...
...BUT THAT'S A LONG STORY.
LET'S SAVE IT FOR ANOTHER TIME.
...
WHAT DO I GET OUT OF THIS DEAL?
YOU GET TO LEAVE THIS ROOM WITH THE CAPTAIN AS YOUR HOSTAGE.

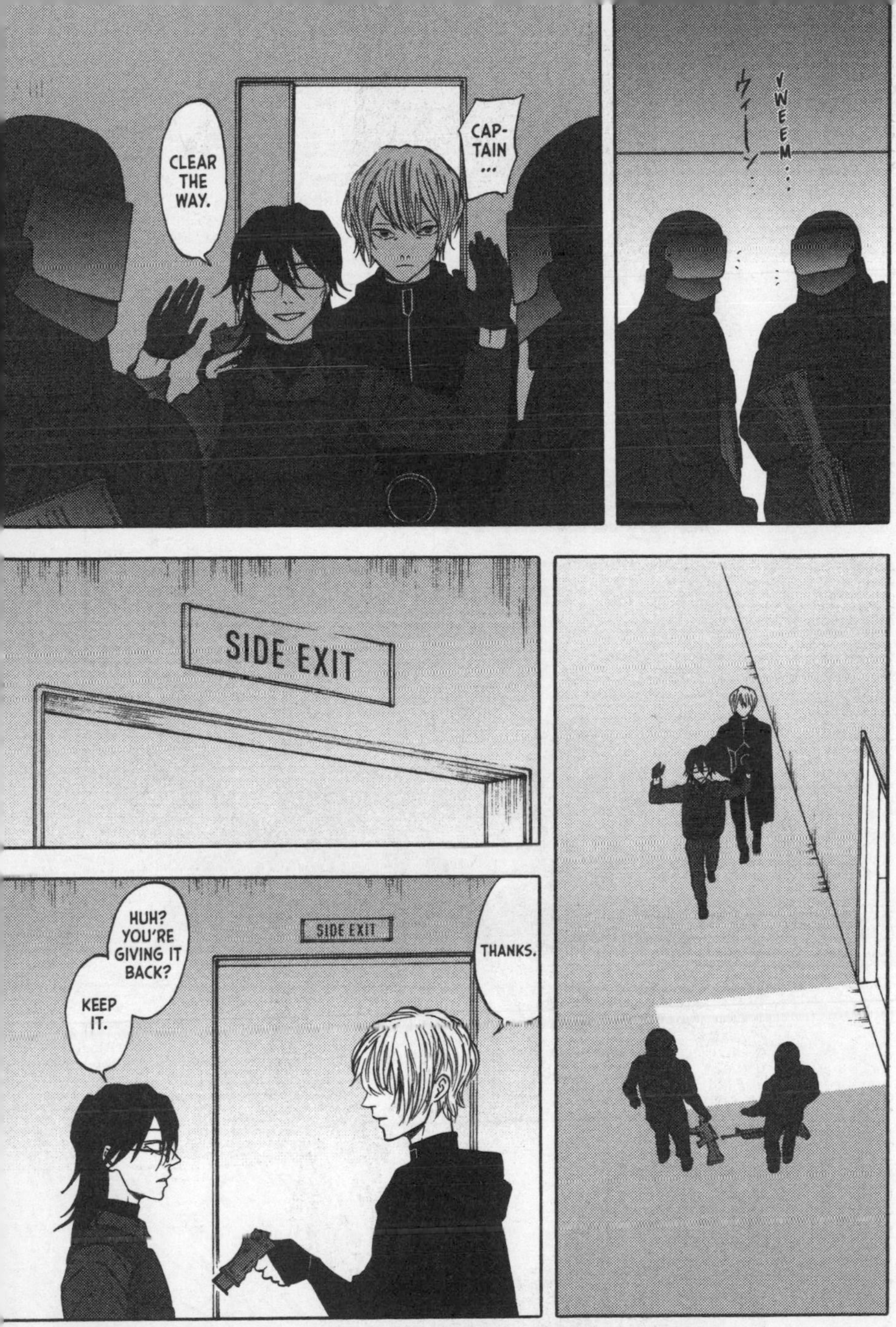

ウィーン…
VWEEM…
CAP-TAIN…
CLEAR THE WAY.
SIDE EXIT
SIDE EXIT
THANKS.
HUH? YOU'RE GIVING IT BACK?
KEEP IT.

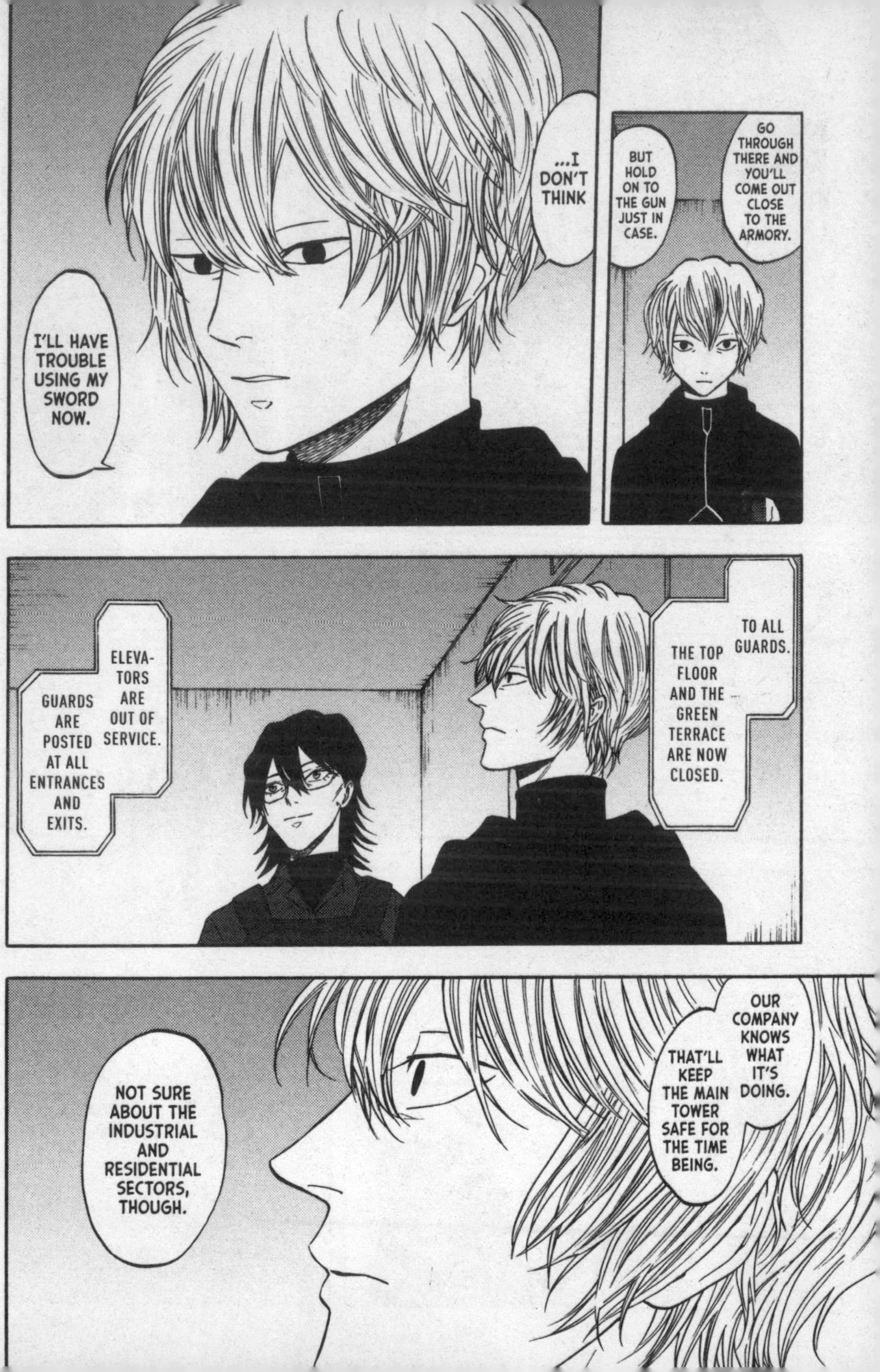
GO THROUGH THERE AND YOU'LL COME OUT CLOSE TO THE ARMORY.
BUT HOLD ON TO THE GUN JUST IN CASE.
...I DON'T THINK
I'LL HAVE TROUBLE USING MY SWORD NOW.
TO ALL GUARDS.
THE TOP FLOOR AND THE GREEN TERRACE ARE NOW CLOSED.
ELEVA-TORS ARE OUT OF SERVICE.
GUARDS ARE POSTED AT ALL ENTRANCES AND EXITS.
OUR COMPANY KNOWS WHAT IT'S DOING.
THAT'LL KEEP THE MAIN TOWER SAFE FOR THE TIME BEING.
NOT SURE ABOUT THE INDUSTRIAL AND RESIDENTIAL SECTORS, THOUGH.

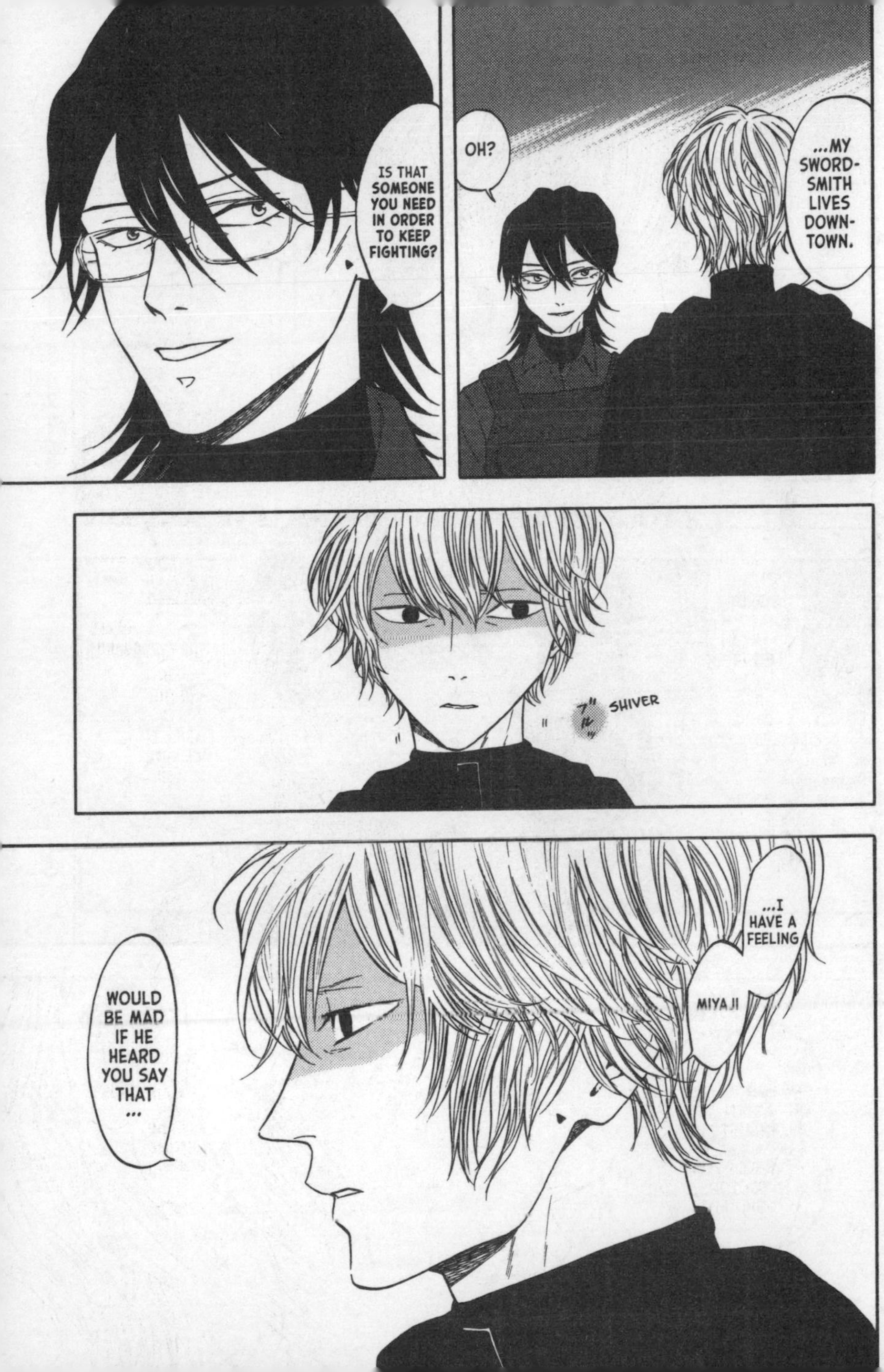
...MY SWORD-SMITH LIVES DOWN-TOWN.
OH?
IS THAT SOMEONE YOU NEED IN ORDER TO KEEP FIGHTING?
SHIVER
...I HAVE A FEELING
MIYAJI
WOULD BE MAD IF HE HEARD YOU SAY THAT ...

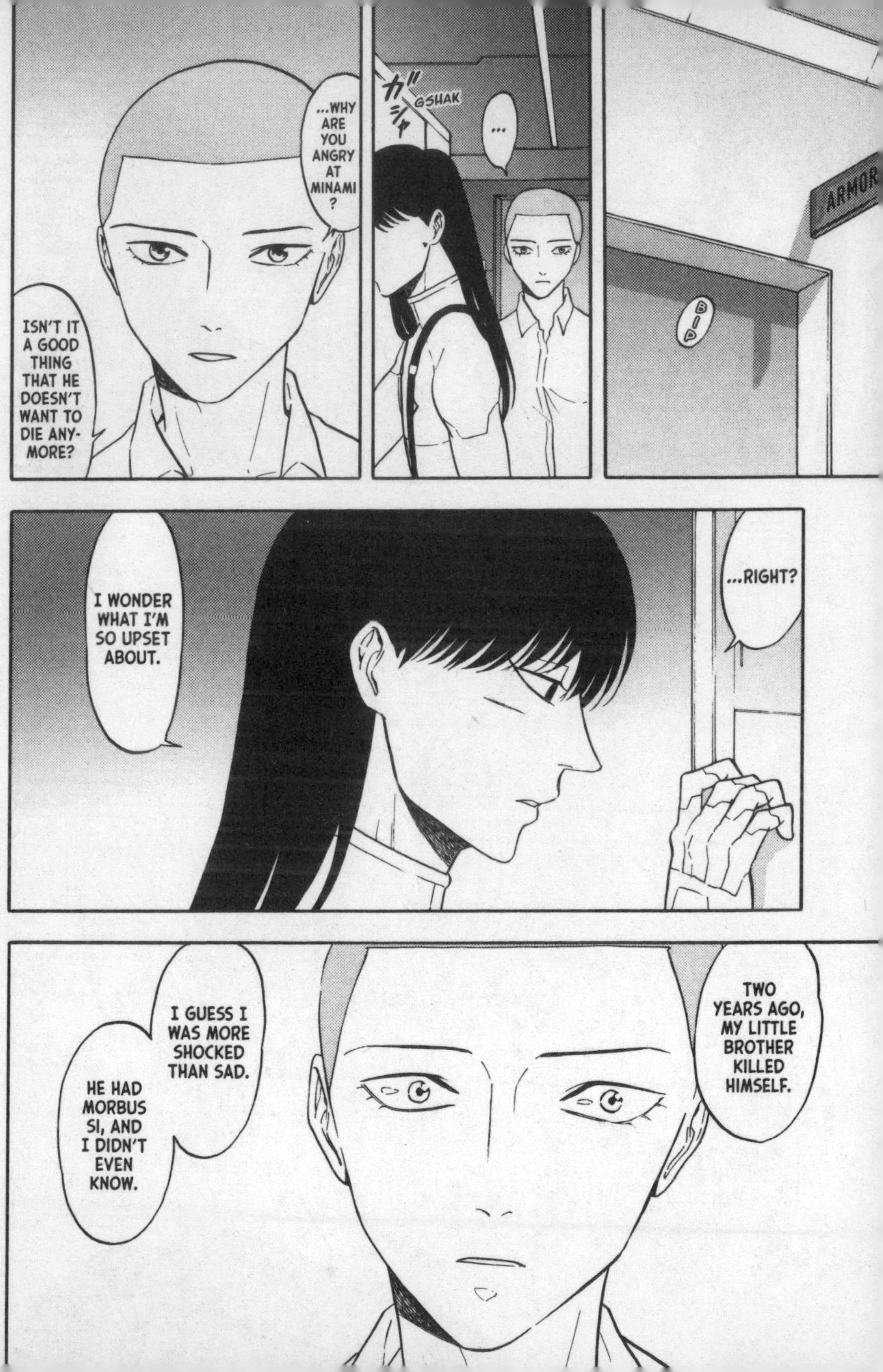
ARMOR
BIP
ガシャ
GSHAK
...
...WHY ARE YOU ANGRY AT MINAMI?
ISN'T IT A GOOD THING THAT HE DOESN'T WANT TO DIE ANY-MORE?
...RIGHT?
I WONDER WHAT I'M SO UPSET ABOUT.
TWO YEARS AGO, MY LITTLE BROTHER KILLED HIMSELF.
I GUESS I WAS MORE SHOCKED THAN SAD.
HE HAD MORBUS SI, AND I DIDN'T EVEN KNOW.

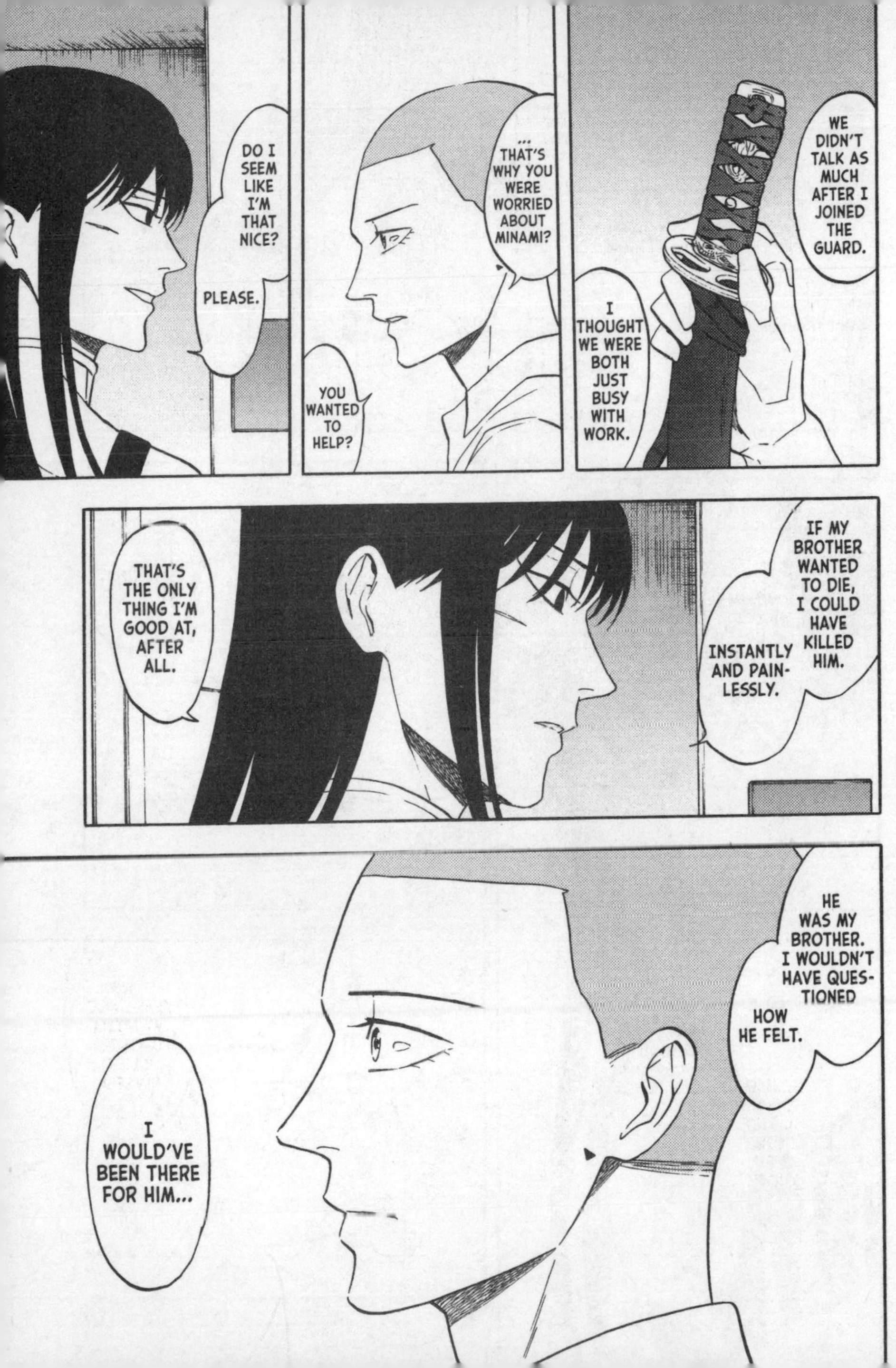
WE DIDN'T TALK AS MUCH AFTER I JOINED THE GUARD.
I THOUGHT WE WERE BOTH JUST BUSY WITH WORK.
... THAT'S WHY YOU WERE WORRIED ABOUT MINAMI?
YOU WANTED TO HELP?
DO I SEEM LIKE I'M THAT NICE?
PLEASE.
IF MY BROTHER WANTED TO DIE, I COULD HAVE KILLED HIM.
INSTANTLY AND PAIN-LESSLY.
THAT'S THE ONLY THING I'M GOOD AT, AFTER ALL.
HE WAS MY BROTHER. I WOULDN'T HAVE QUES-TIONED
HOW HE FELT.
I WOULD'VE BEEN THERE FOR HIM...

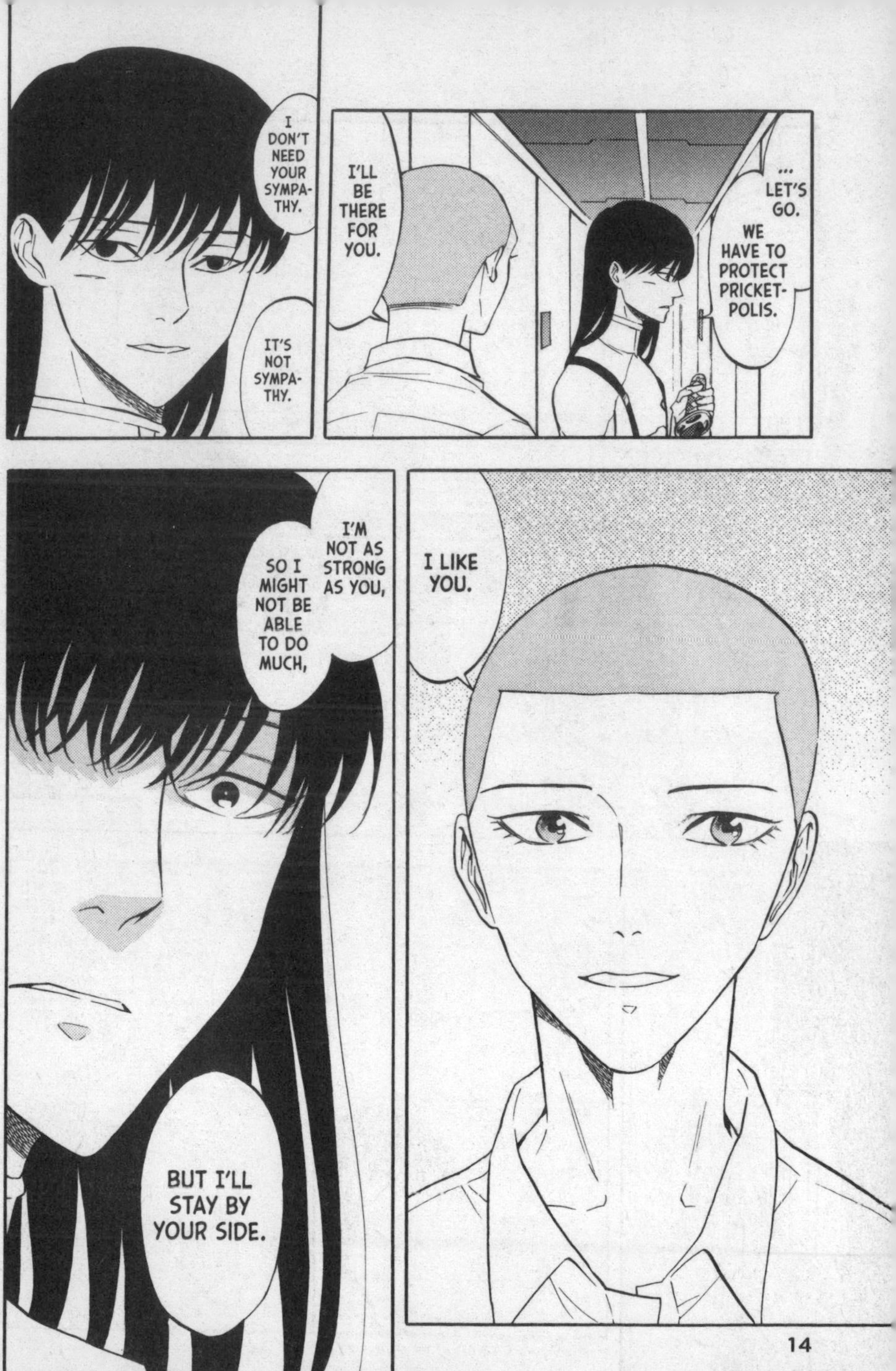
... LET'S GO. WE HAVE TO PROTECT PRICKETPOLIS.
I'LL BE THERE FOR YOU.
I DON'T NEED YOUR SYMPATHY.
IT'S NOT SYMPATHY.
I LIKE YOU.
I'M NOT AS STRONG AS YOU,
SO I MIGHT NOT BE ABLE TO DO MUCH,
BUT I'LL STAY BY YOUR SIDE.

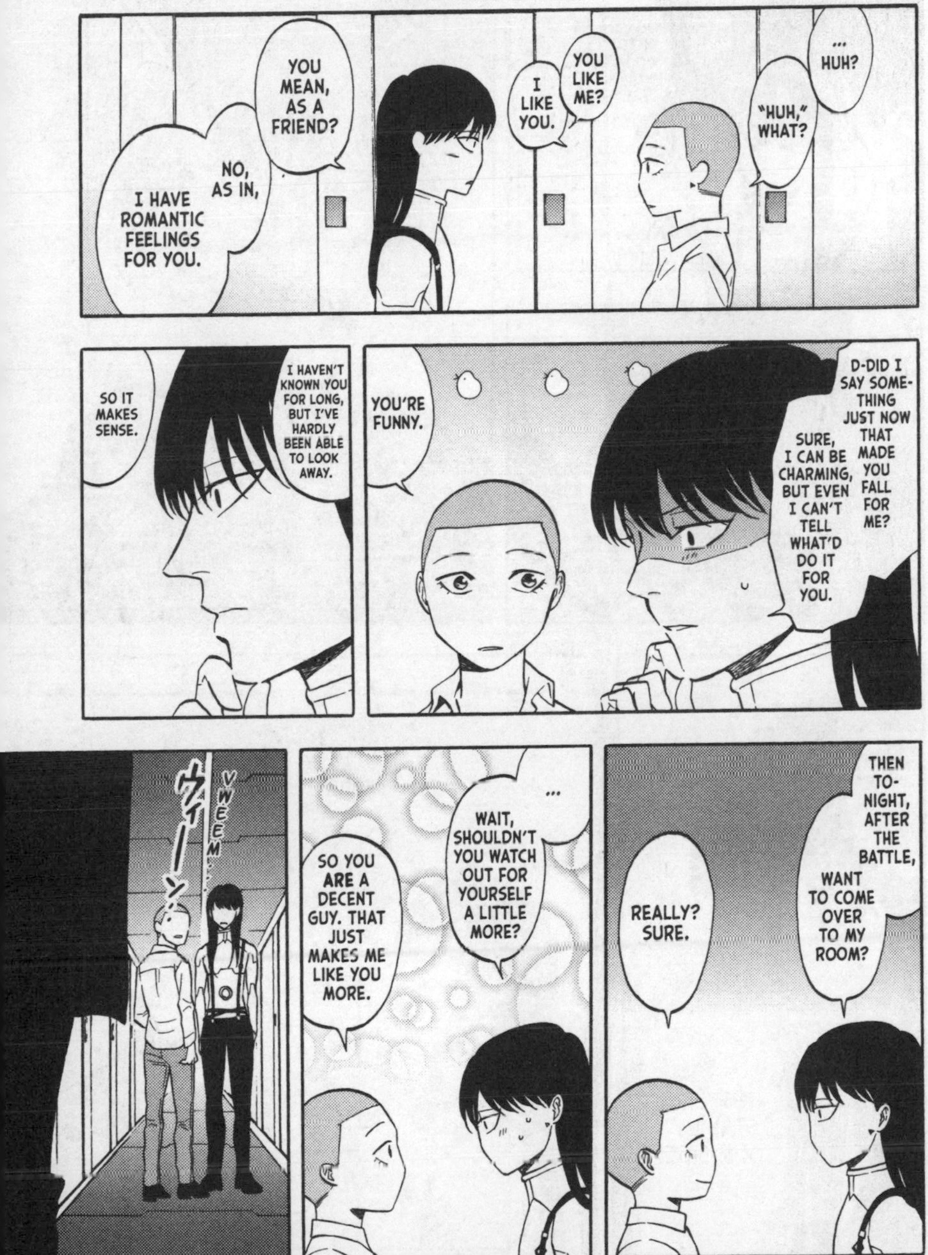
... HUH?
"HUH," WHAT?
YOU LIKE ME?
I LIKE YOU.
YOU MEAN, AS A FRIEND?
NO, AS IN,
I HAVE ROMANTIC FEELINGS FOR YOU.
D-DID I SAY SOME-THING JUST NOW THAT MADE YOU FALL FOR ME?
SURE, I CAN BE CHARMING, BUT EVEN I CAN'T TELL WHAT'D DO IT FOR YOU.
YOU'RE FUNNY.
I HAVEN'T KNOWN YOU FOR LONG, BUT I'VE HARDLY BEEN ABLE TO LOOK AWAY.
SO IT MAKES SENSE.
THEN TO-NIGHT, AFTER THE BATTLE, WANT TO COME OVER TO MY ROOM?
REALLY? SURE.
...
WAIT, SHOULDN'T YOU WATCH OUT FOR YOURSELF A LITTLE MORE?
SO YOU ARE A DECENT GUY. THAT JUST MAKES ME LIKE YOU MORE.
ヴィーン
VWEEEM...

KAWAKAMI FEELS A TWINGE OF GUILT.

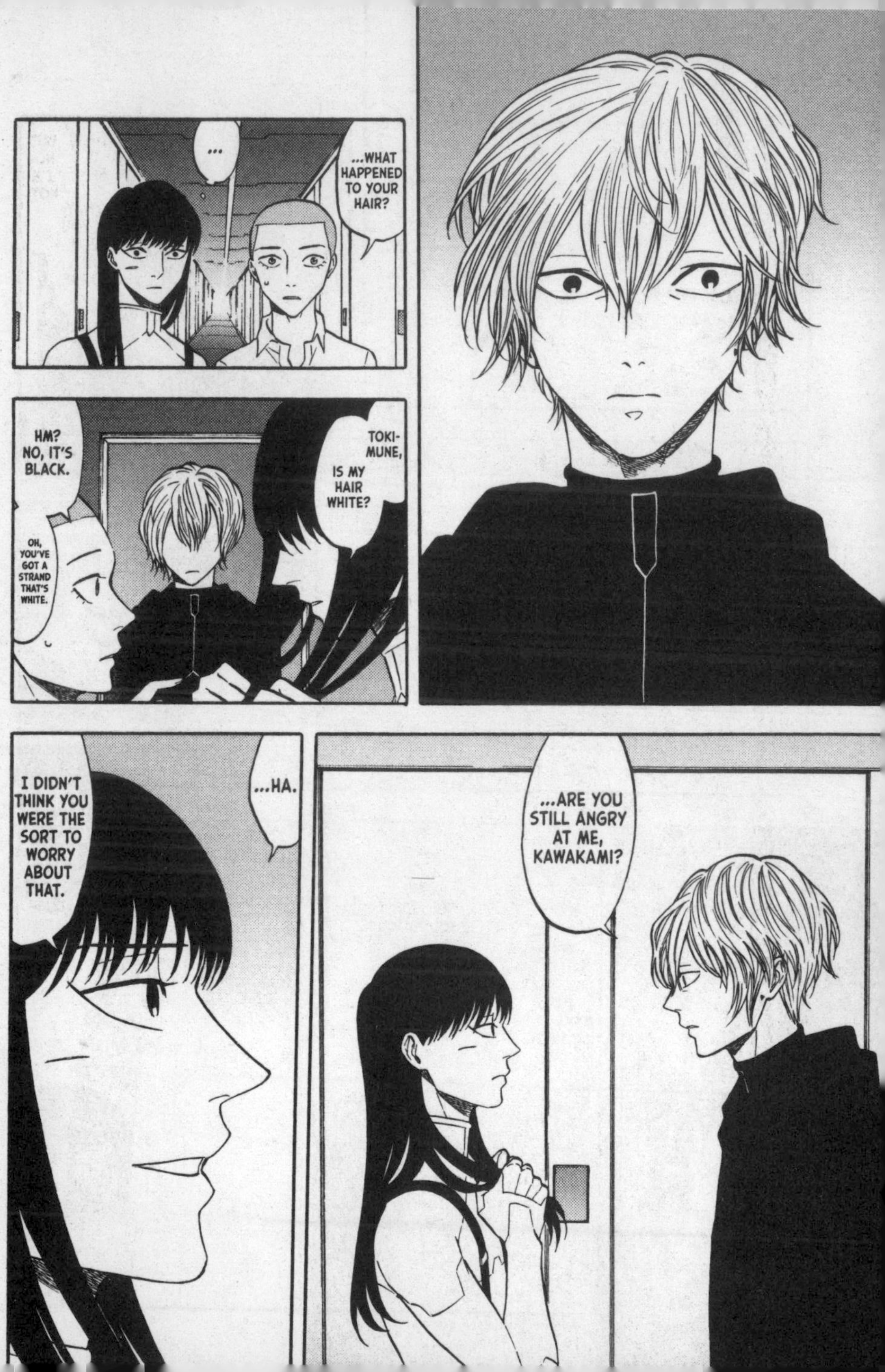
...WHAT HAPPENED TO YOUR HAIR?
...
TOKI-MUNE, IS MY HAIR WHITE?
HM? NO, IT'S BLACK.
OH, YOU'VE GOT A STRAND THAT'S WHITE.
...ARE YOU STILL ANGRY AT ME, KAWAKAMI?
...HA.
I DIDN'T THINK YOU WERE THE SORT TO WORRY ABOUT THAT.

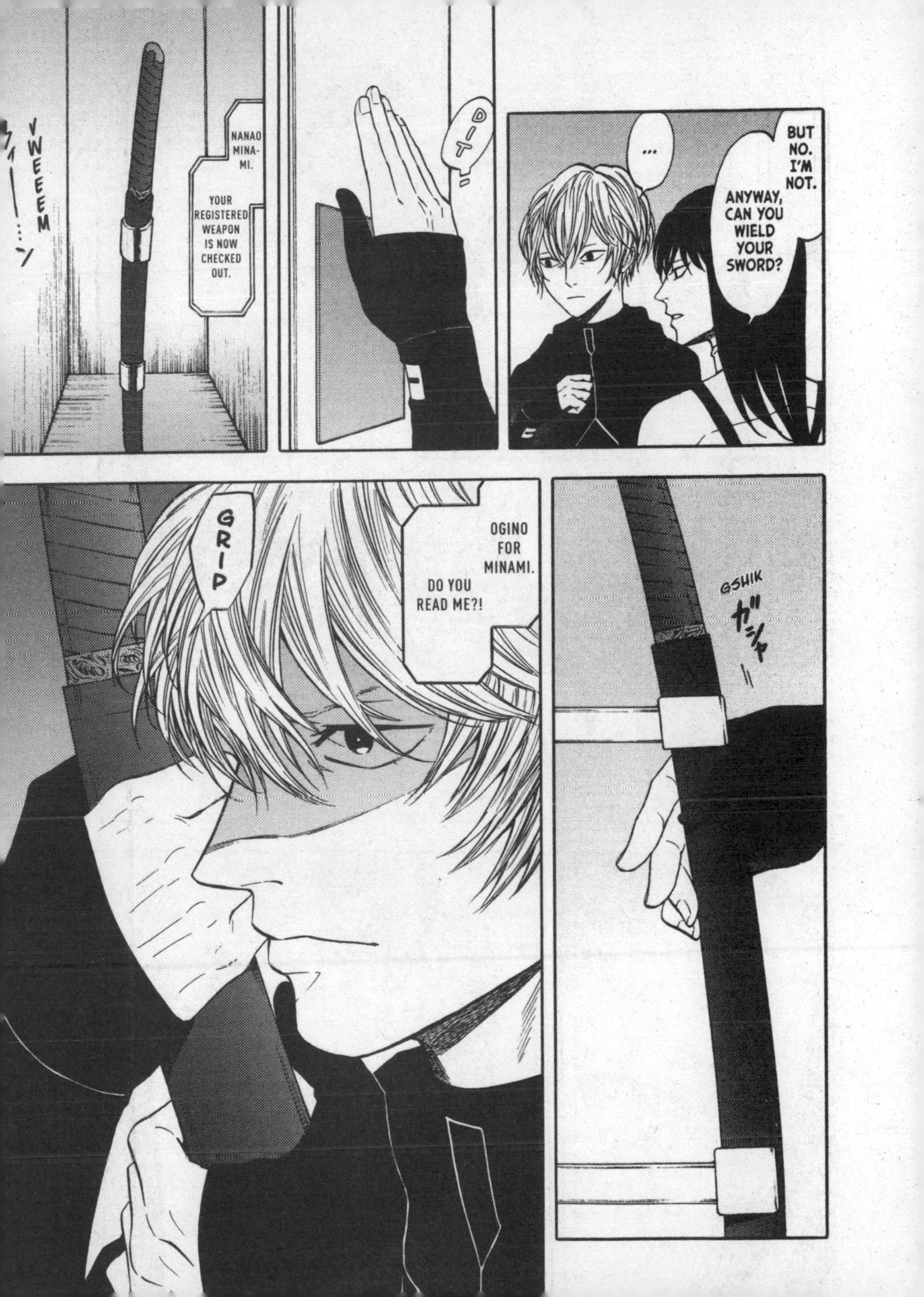
BUT NO. I'M NOT. ANYWAY, CAN YOU WIELD YOUR SWORD?
...
DIT
NANAO MINAMI.
YOUR REGISTERED WEAPON IS NOW CHECKED OUT.
VWEEEM
GSHIK
ガシャ
OGINO FOR MINAMI.
DO YOU READ ME?!
GRIP

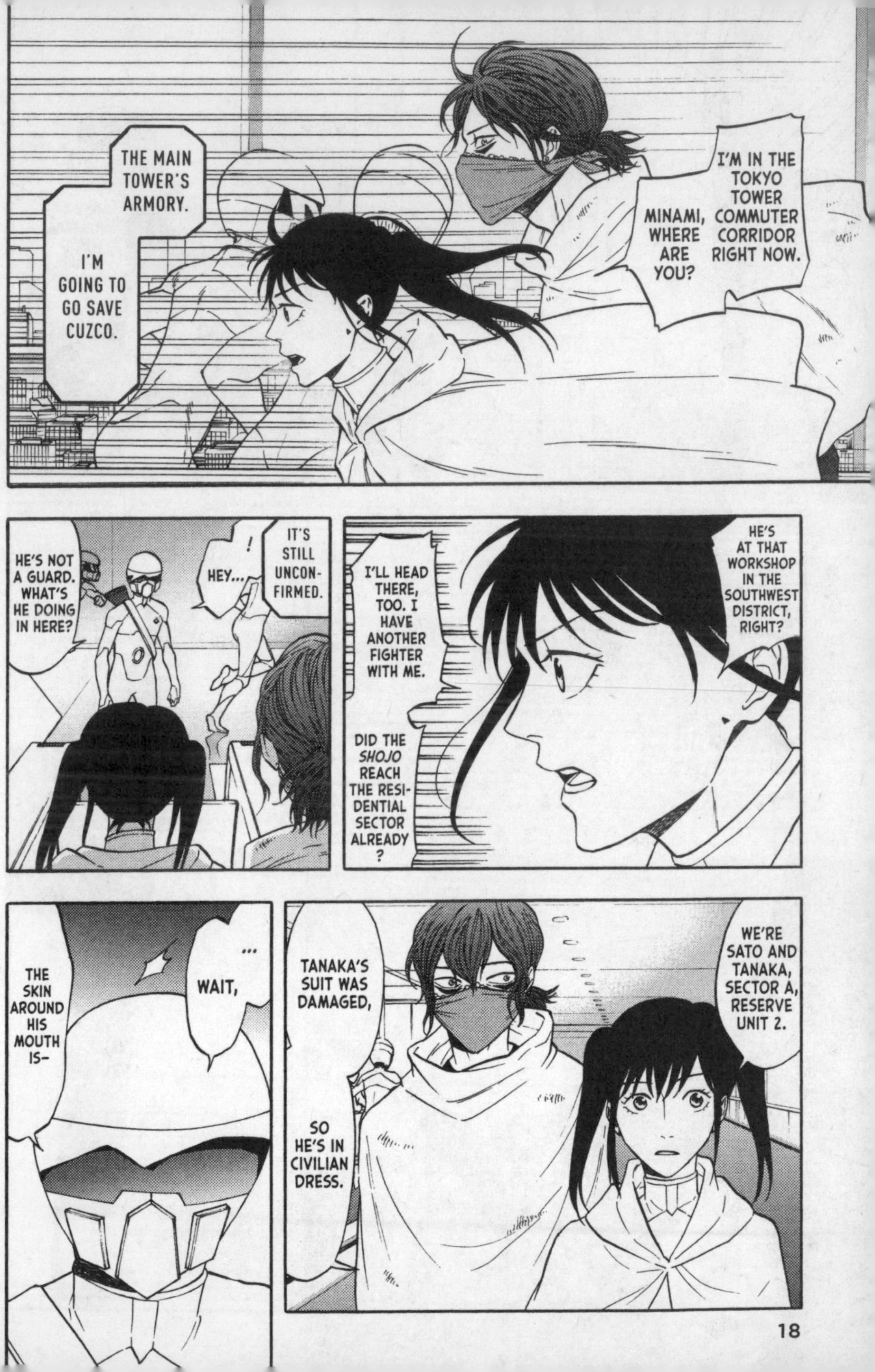
I'M IN THE TOKYO TOWER COMMUTER CORRIDOR RIGHT NOW.
MINAMI, WHERE ARE YOU?
THE MAIN TOWER'S ARMORY.
I'M GOING TO GO SAVE CUZCO.
HE'S AT THAT WORKSHOP IN THE SOUTHWEST DISTRICT, RIGHT?
I'LL HEAD THERE, TOO. I HAVE ANOTHER FIGHTER WITH ME.
DID THE *SHOJO* REACH THE RESIDENTIAL SECTOR ALREADY?
IT'S STILL UNCONFIRMED.
!
HEY...
HE'S NOT A GUARD. WHAT'S HE DOING IN HERE?
WE'RE SATO AND TANAKA, SECTOR A, RESERVE UNIT 2.
TANAKA'S SUIT WAS DAMAGED,
SO HE'S IN CIVILIAN DRESS.
...
WAIT,
THE SKIN AROUND HIS MOUTH IS–

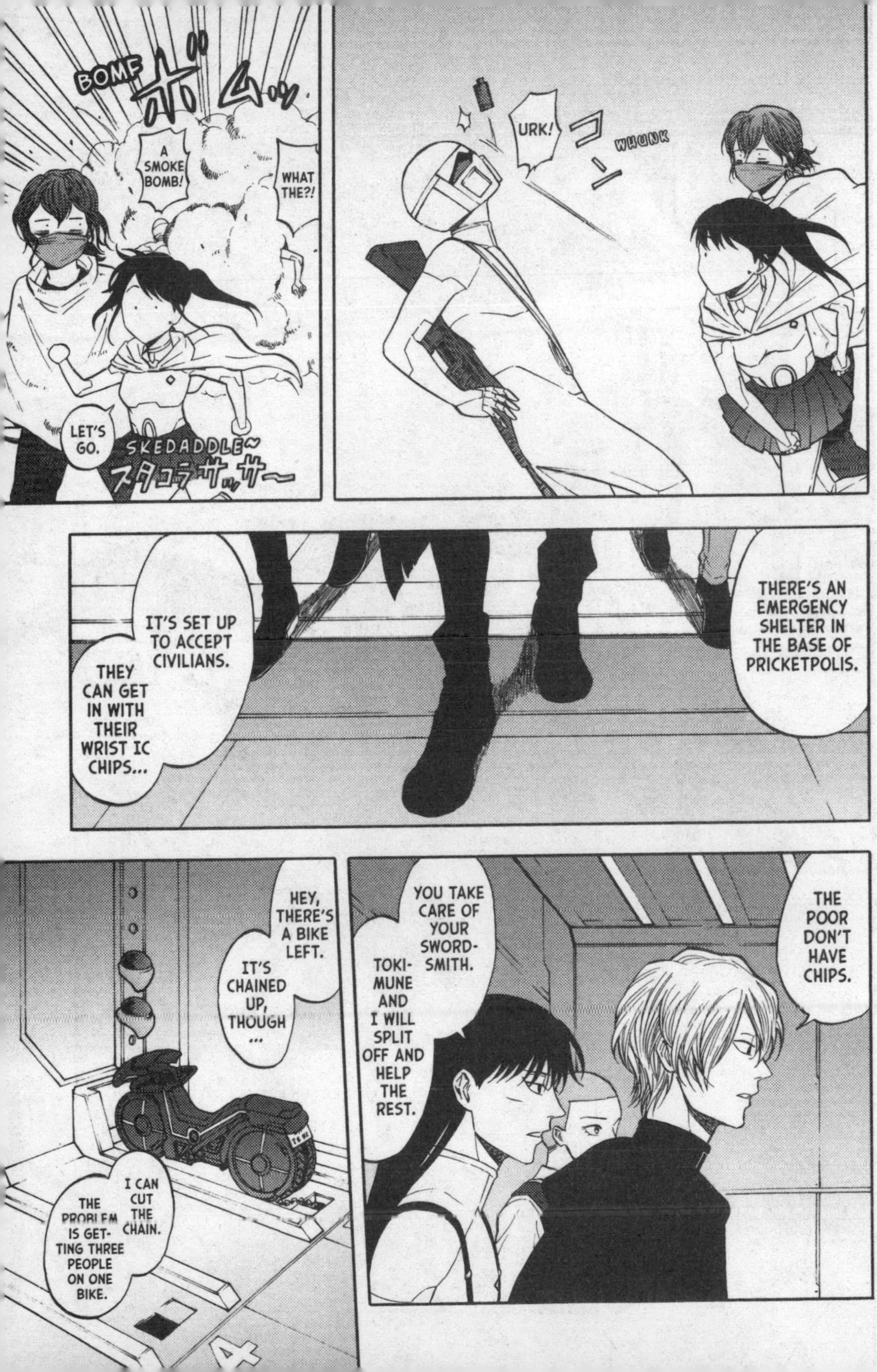
URK!
WHUNK
BOMF
WHAT THE?!
A SMOKE BOMB!
LET'S GO.
SKEDADDLE~
THERE'S AN EMERGENCY SHELTER IN THE BASE OF PRICKETPOLIS.
IT'S SET UP TO ACCEPT CIVILIANS.
THEY CAN GET IN WITH THEIR WRIST IC CHIPS...
THE POOR DON'T HAVE CHIPS.
YOU TAKE CARE OF YOUR SWORDSMITH.
TOKIMUNE AND I WILL SPLIT OFF AND HELP THE REST.
HEY, THERE'S A BIKE LEFT.
IT'S CHAINED UP, THOUGH...
I CAN CUT THE CHAIN.
THE PROBLEM IS GETTING THREE PEOPLE ON ONE BIKE.

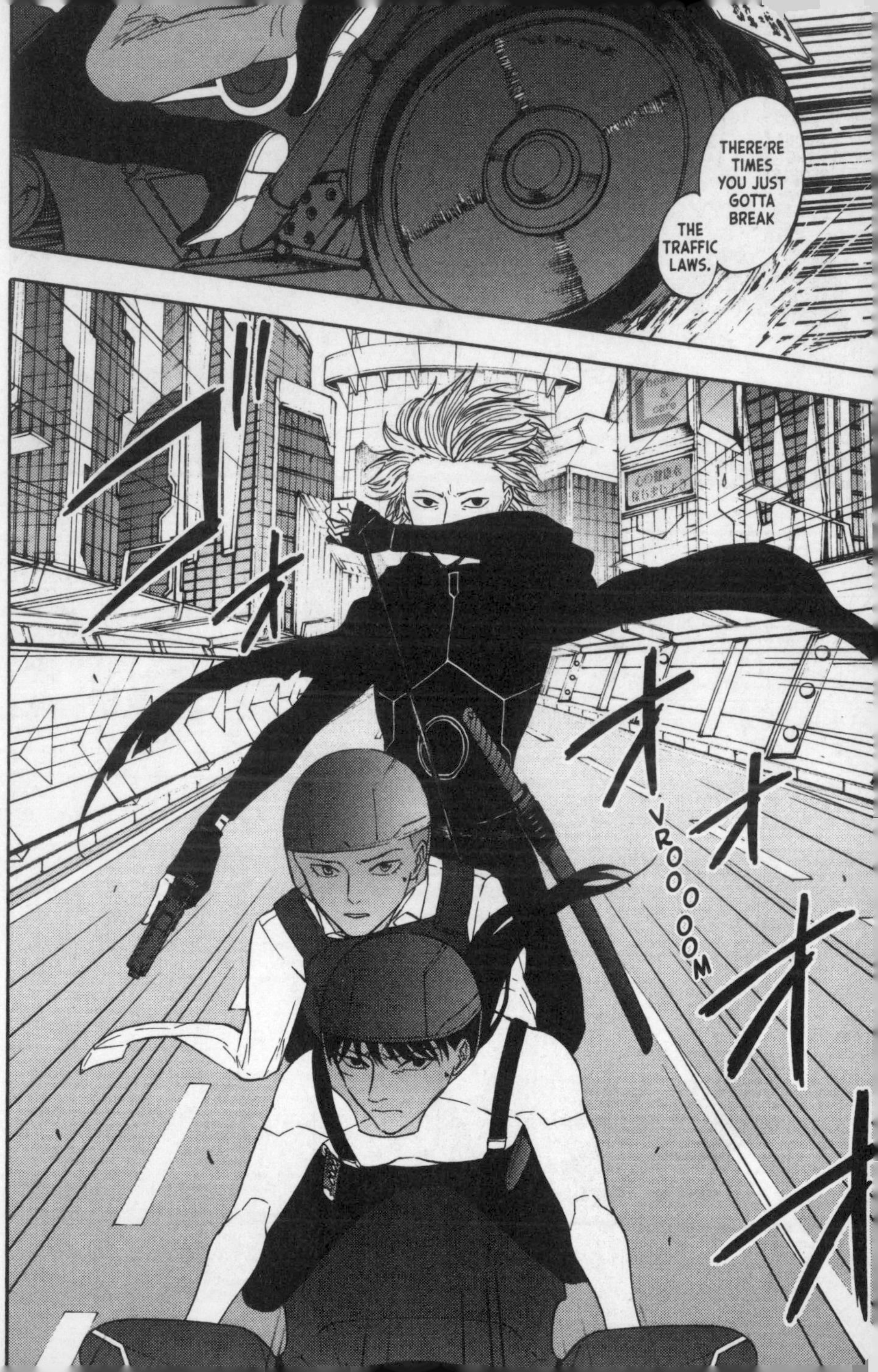
THERE'RE TIMES YOU JUST GOTTA BREAK
THE TRAFFIC LAWS.
VROOOOOM

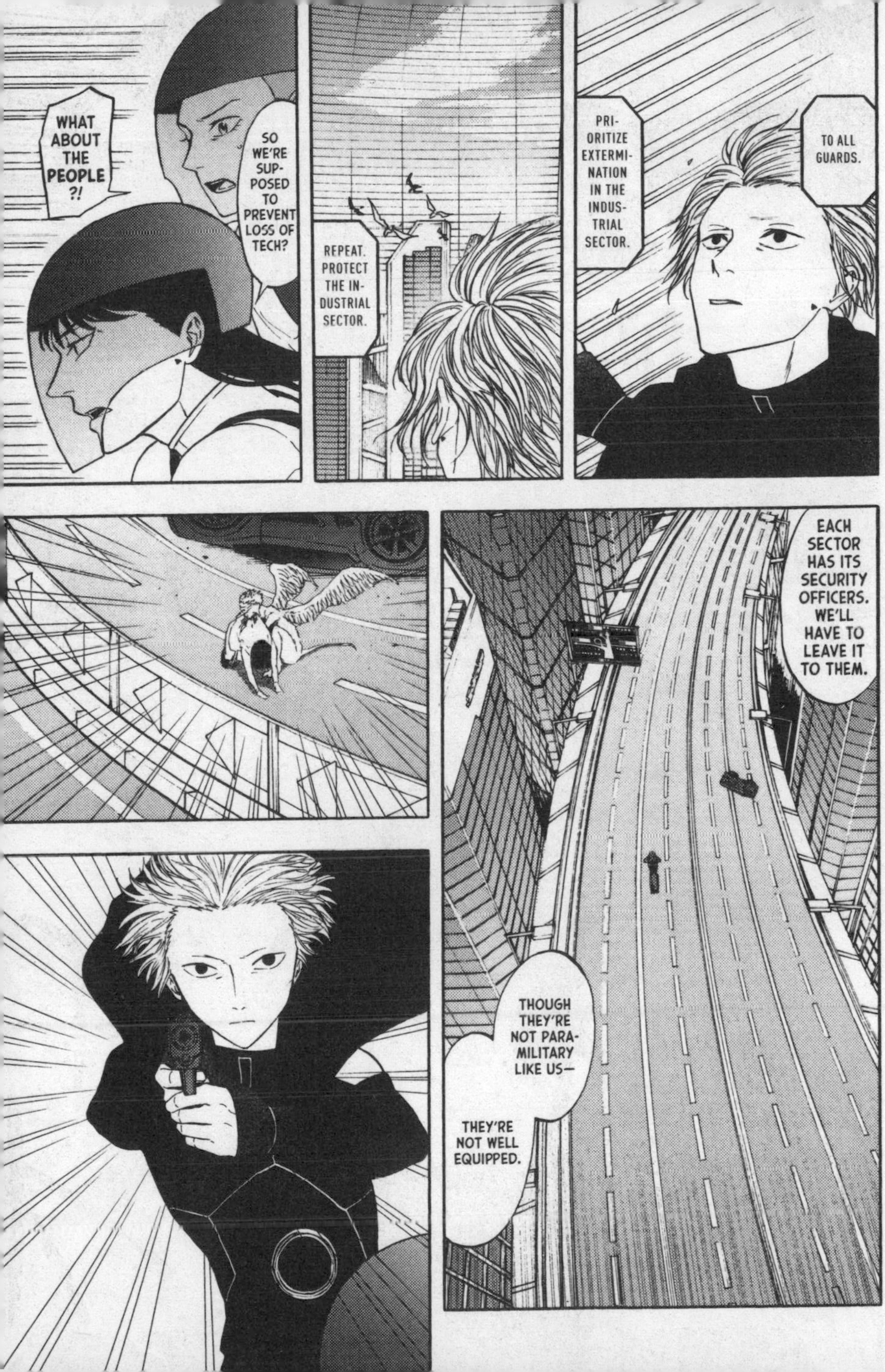
TO ALL GUARDS.
PRIORITIZE EXTERMINATION IN THE INDUSTRIAL SECTOR.
REPEAT. PROTECT THE INDUSTRIAL SECTOR.
SO WE'RE SUPPOSED TO PREVENT LOSS OF TECH?
WHAT ABOUT THE PEOPLE?!
EACH SECTOR HAS ITS SECURITY OFFICERS. WE'LL HAVE TO LEAVE IT TO THEM.
THOUGH THEY'RE NOT PARAMILITARY LIKE US—
THEY'RE NOT WELL EQUIPPED.

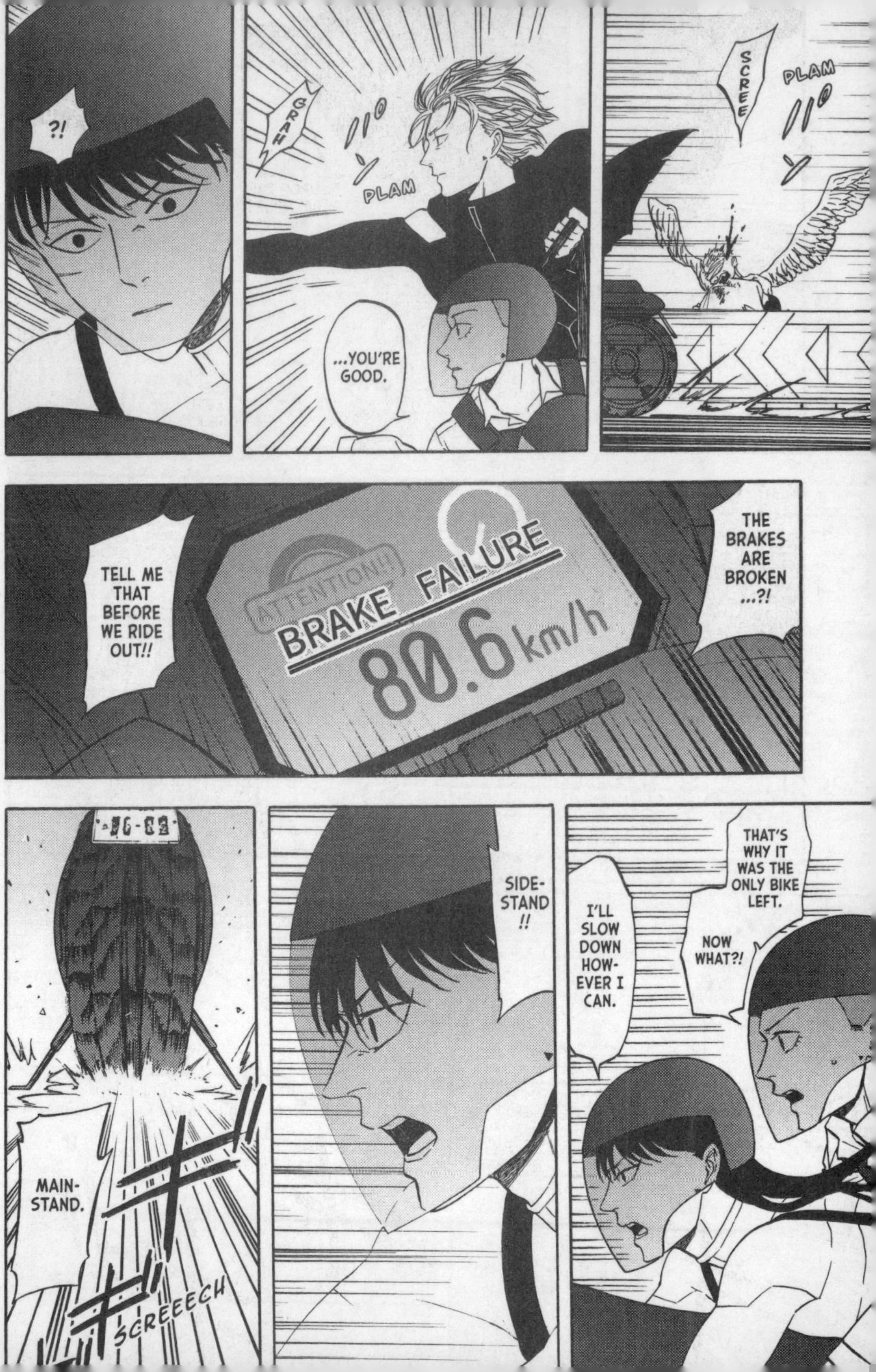
SCREE
PLAM
GRAH
PLAM
...YOU'RE GOOD.
?!
THE BRAKES ARE BROKEN ...?!
ATTENTION!!
BRAKE FAILURE
80.6 km/h
TELL ME THAT BEFORE WE RIDE OUT!!
THAT'S WHY IT WAS THE ONLY BIKE LEFT.
NOW WHAT?!
I'LL SLOW DOWN HOW-EVER I CAN.
SIDE-STAND !!
MAIN-STAND.
SCREEECH

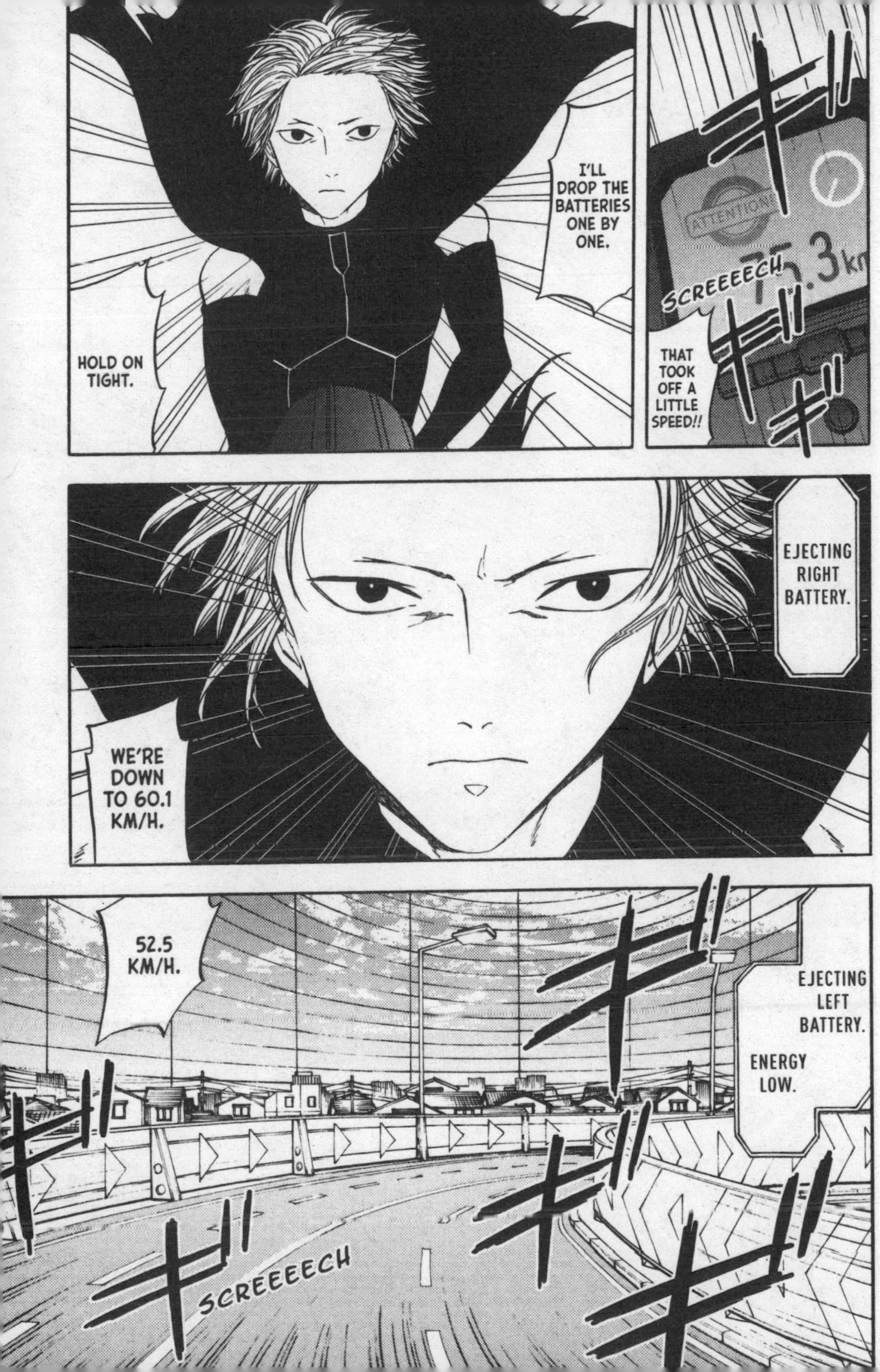
ATTENTION
SCREEEECH
THAT TOOK OFF A LITTLE SPEED!!
I'LL DROP THE BATTERIES ONE BY ONE.
HOLD ON TIGHT.
EJECTING RIGHT BATTERY.
WE'RE DOWN TO 60.1 KM/H.
EJECTING LEFT BATTERY.
ENERGY LOW.
52.5 KM/H.
SCREEEEECH

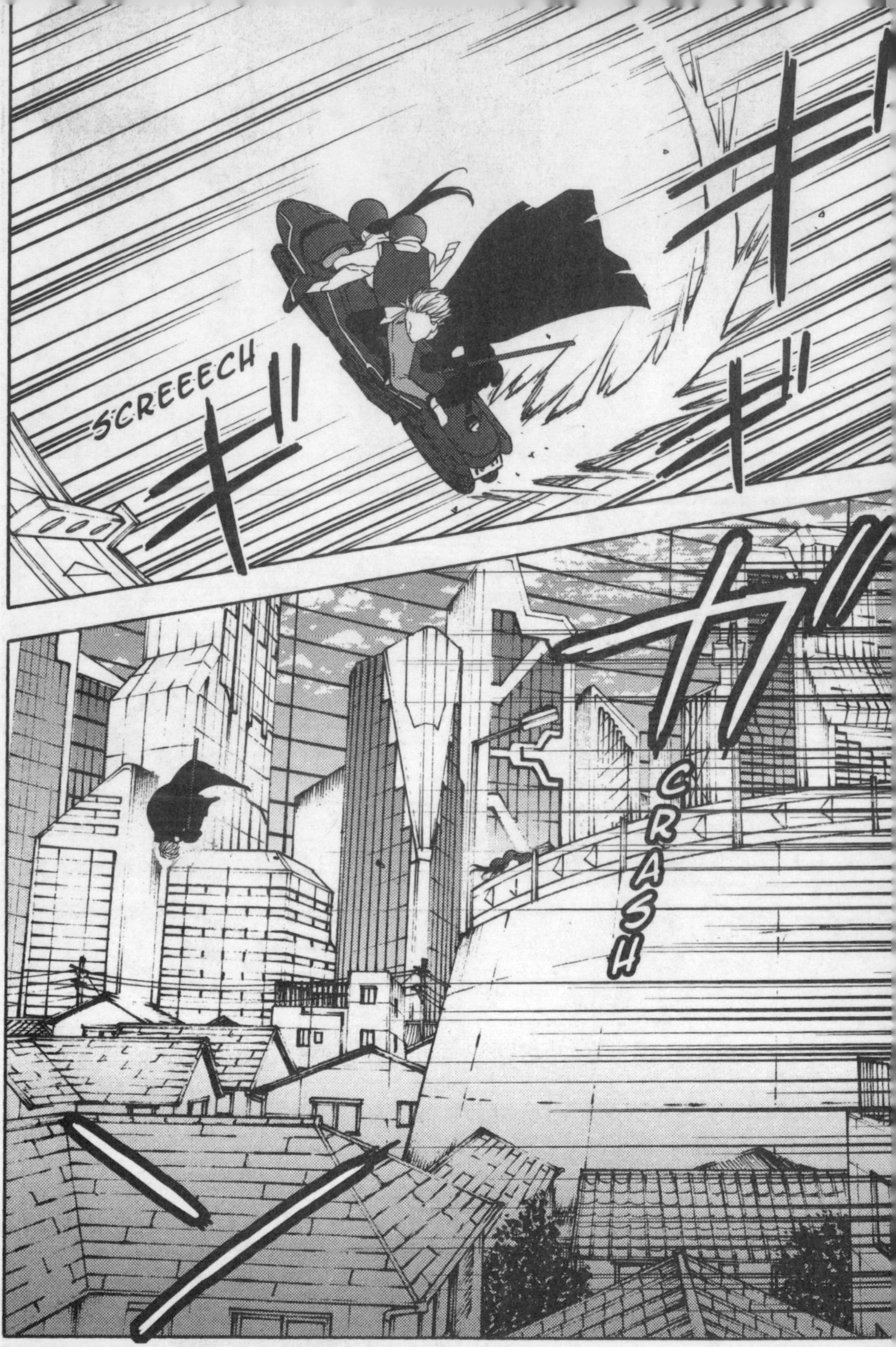
SCREEECH
CRASH

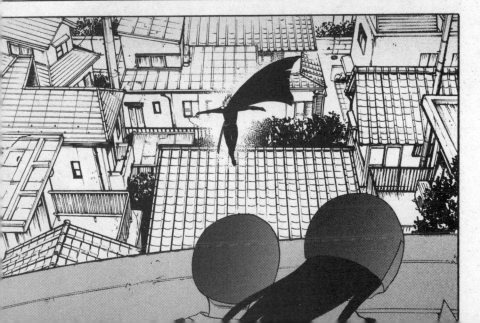

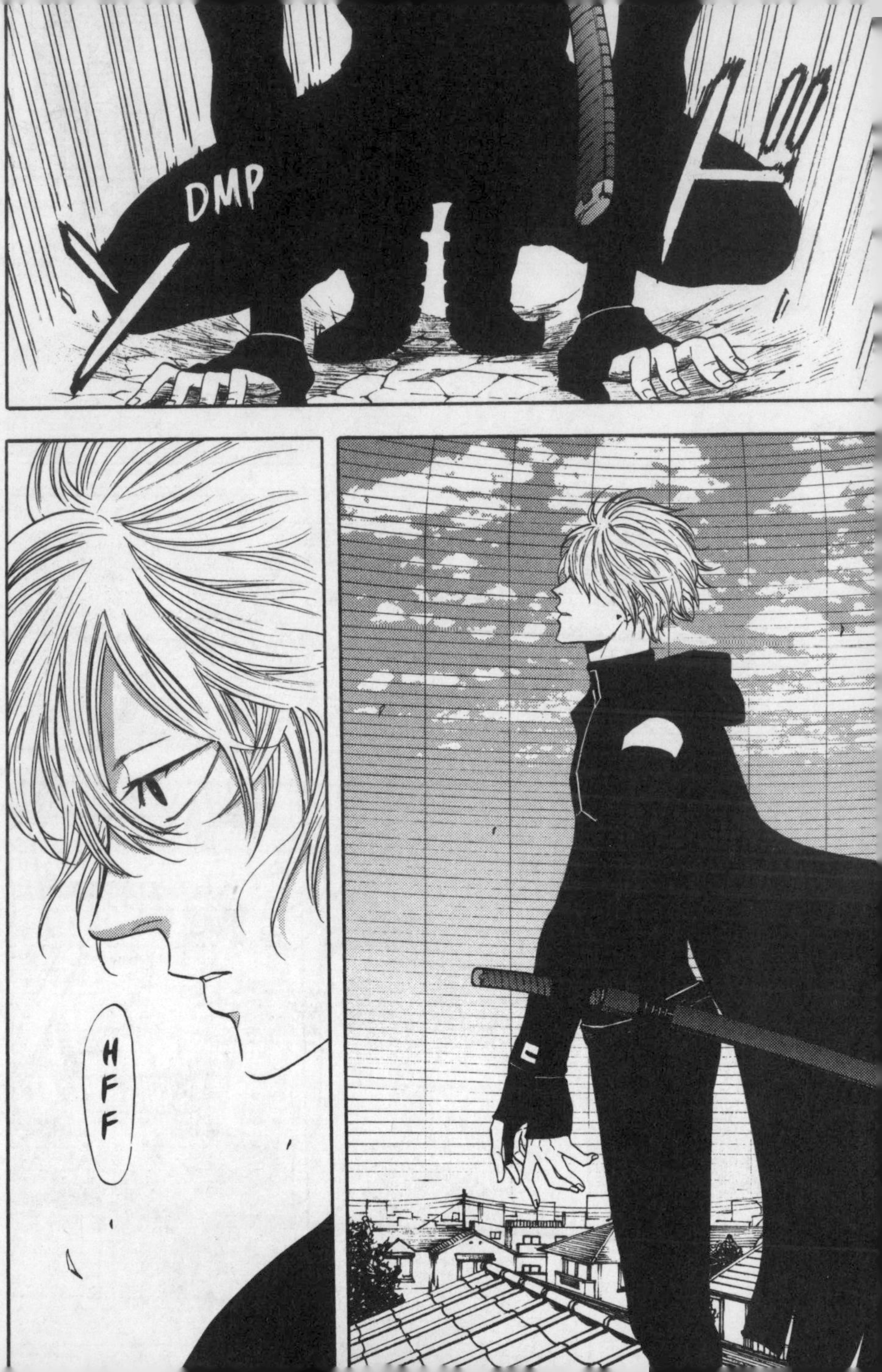
DMP
HFF

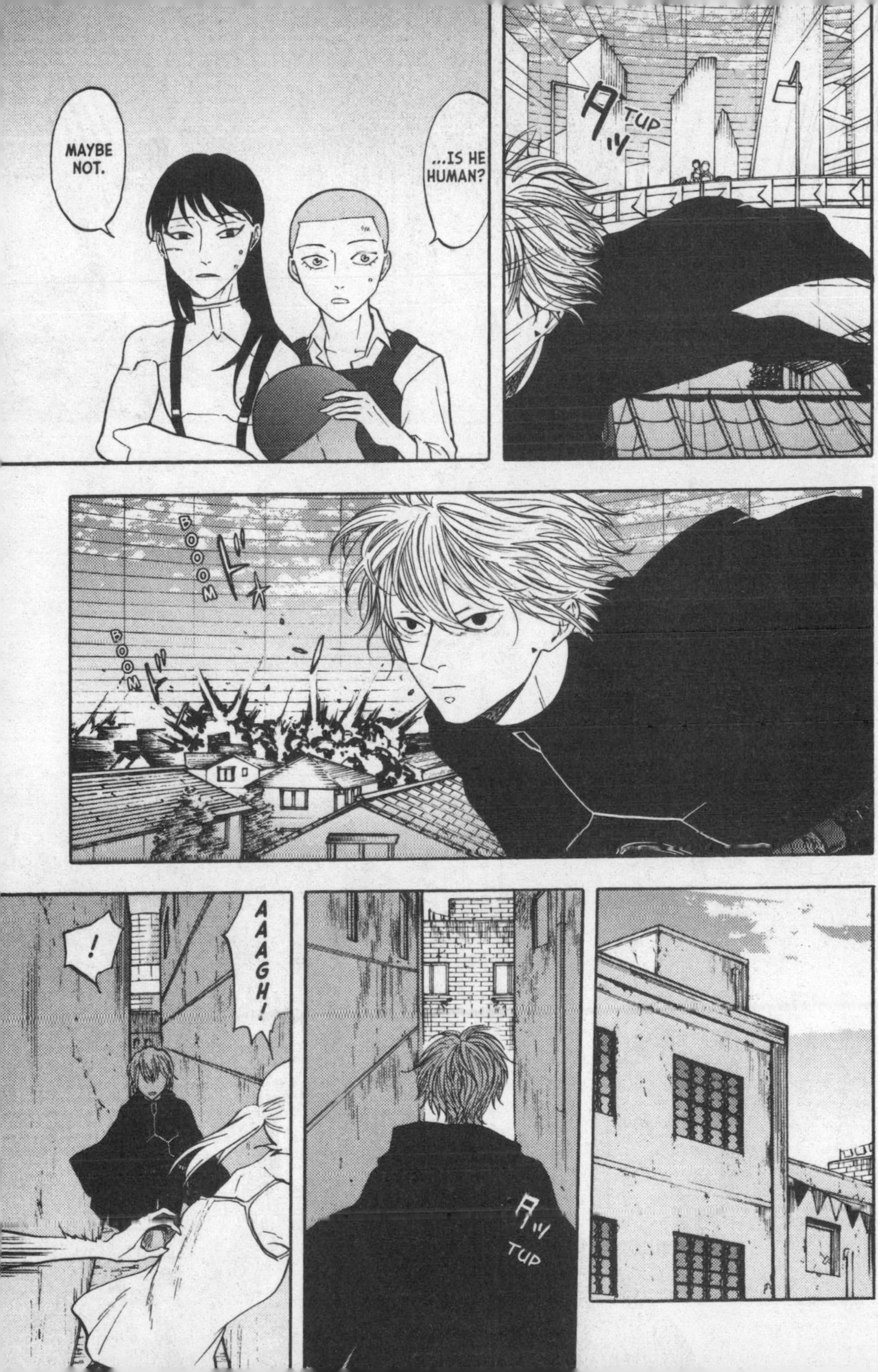
TUP
...IS HE HUMAN?
MAYBE NOT.
BOOOOM
BOOOM
TUP
AAAGH!
!

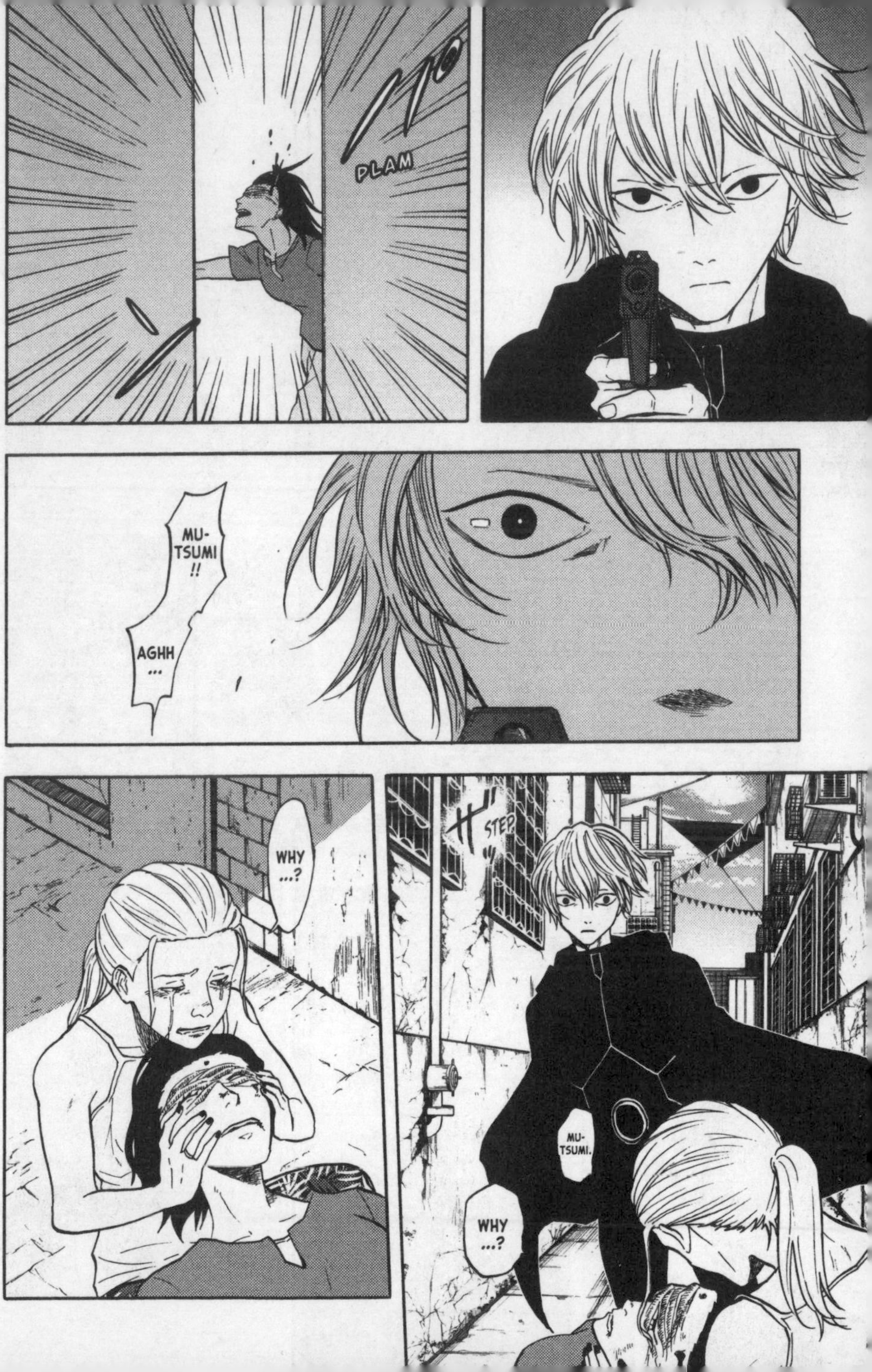
PLAM
MU-TSUMI!!
AGHH...
STEP
MU-TSUMI.
WHY...?
WHY...?

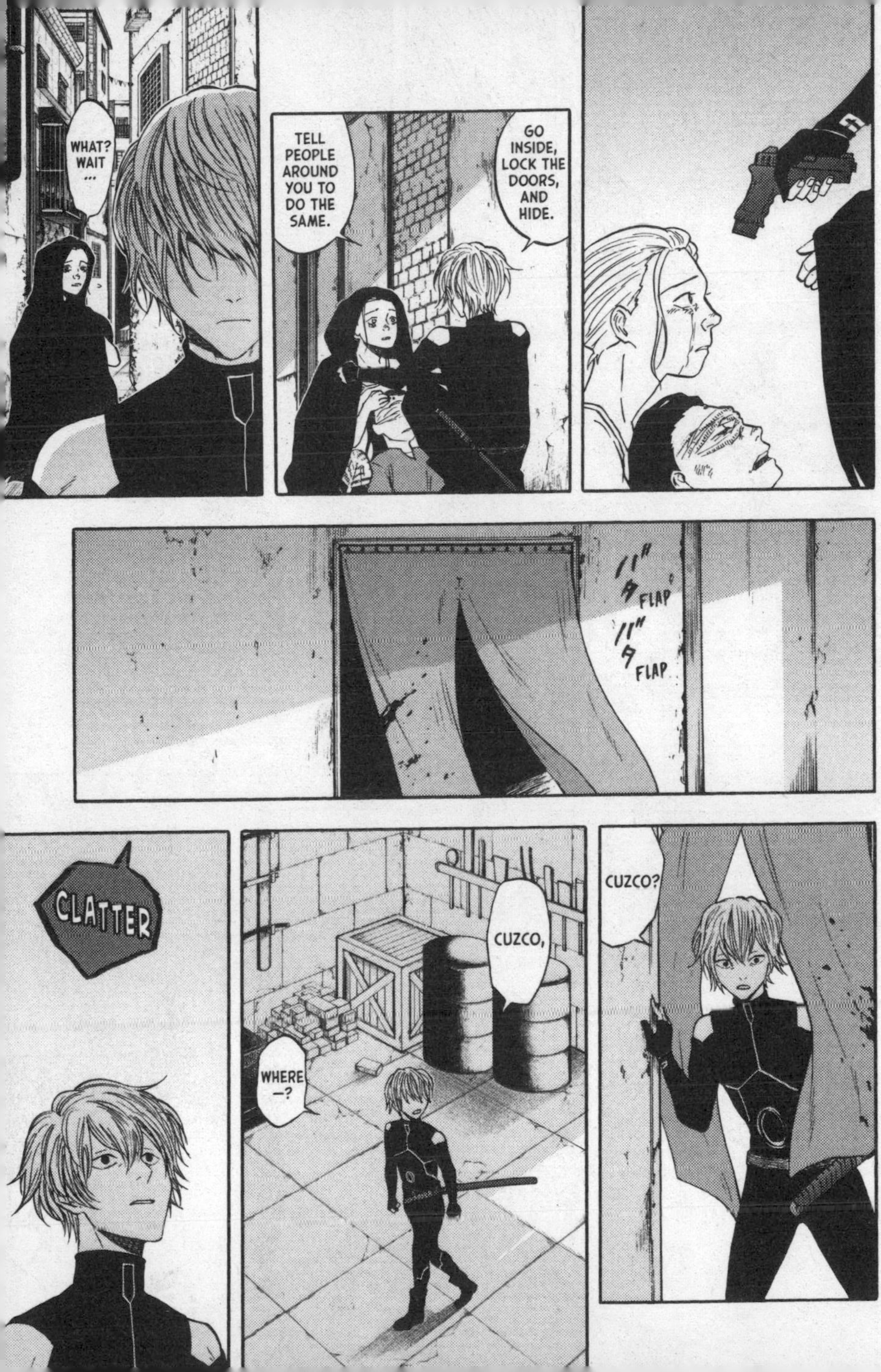

GO INSIDE, LOCK THE DOORS, AND HIDE.
TELL PEOPLE AROUND YOU TO DO THE SAME.
WHAT? WAIT ...
バタ FLAP
バタ FLAP
CUZCO?
CUZCO,
WHERE —?
CLATTER

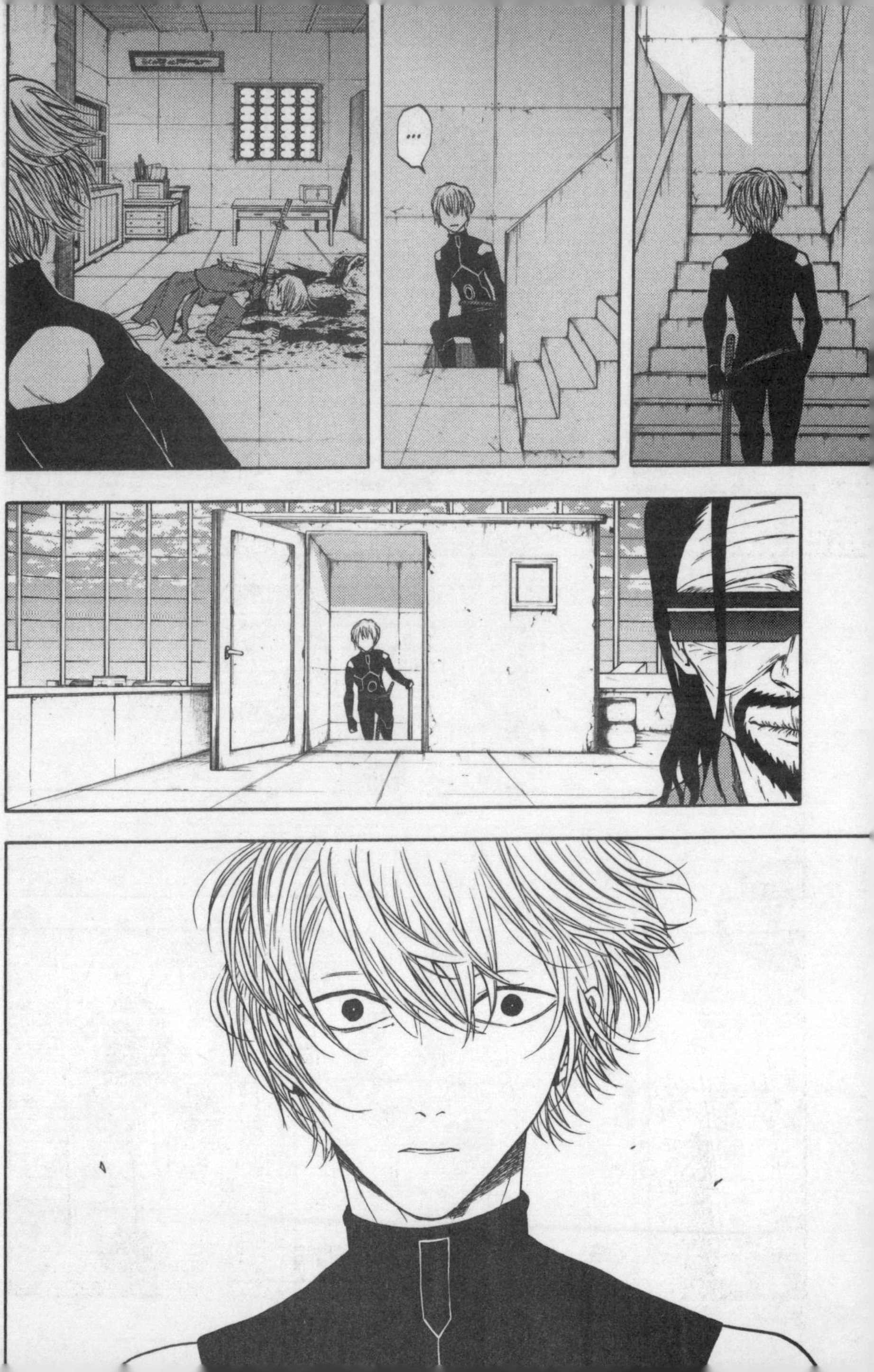
…

NANAO?
AGH
AGH
PERFECT TIMING.
THIS IS MY LIVE-IN BLACK-SMITH'S BABY.
GRH
GRH
I KILLED THE PARENTS, SINCE THEY WERE INFECTED,
BUT THEN I LEFT MY SWORD DOWN-STAIRS.
I WAS JUST TRYING TO THINK WHETHER I'D HAVE MY MIND
LONG ENOUGH TO GO AND GET IT.

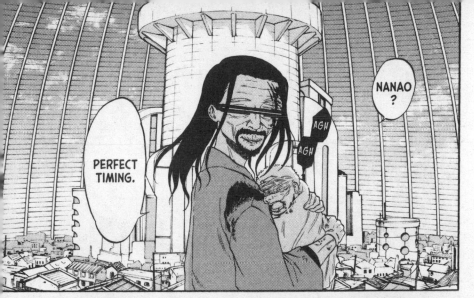

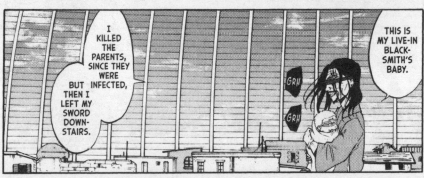

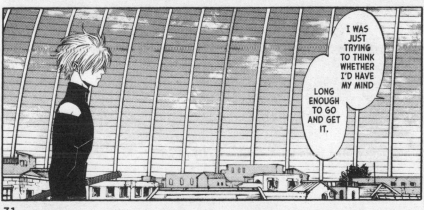

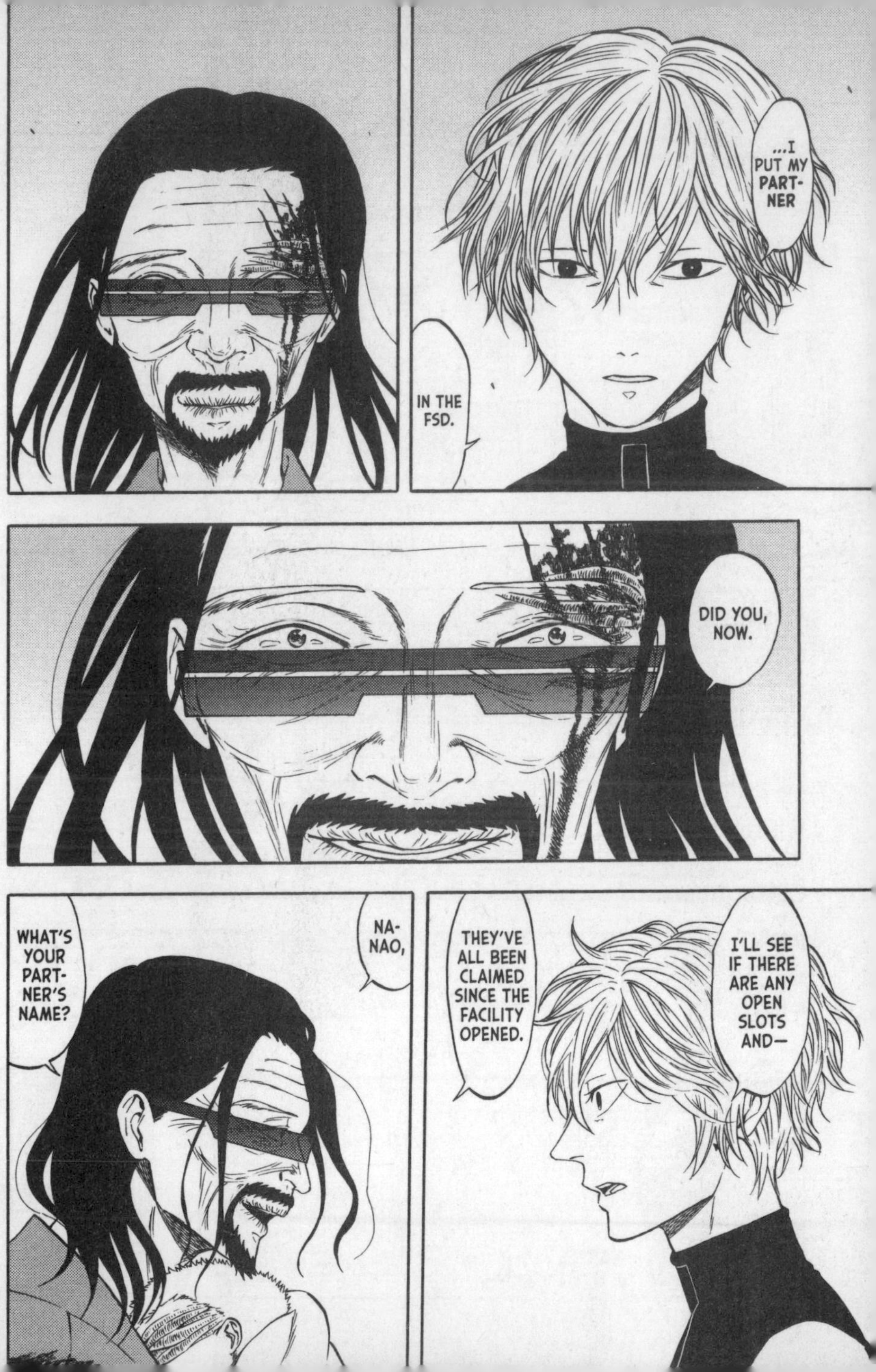
...I PUT MY PART-NER
IN THE FSD.
DID YOU, NOW.
I'LL SEE IF THERE ARE ANY OPEN SLOTS AND—
THEY'VE ALL BEEN CLAIMED SINCE THE FACILITY OPENED.
NA-NAO,
WHAT'S YOUR PART-NER'S NAME?

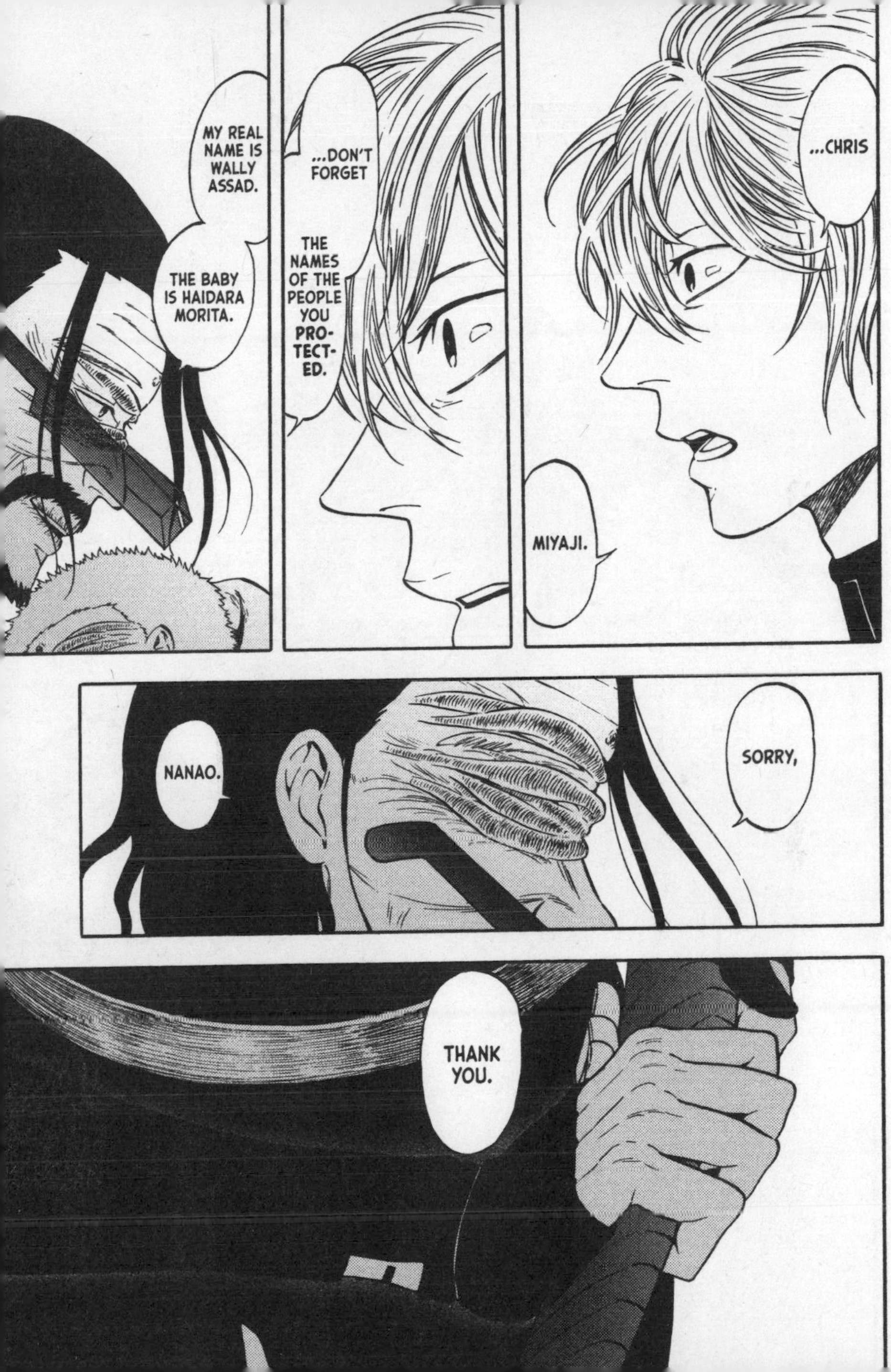
...CHRIS
MIYAJI.
...DON'T FORGET
THE NAMES OF THE PEOPLE YOU PRO-TECT-ED.
MY REAL NAME IS WALLY ASSAD.
THE BABY IS HAIDARA MORITA.
SORRY,
NANAO.
THANK YOU.

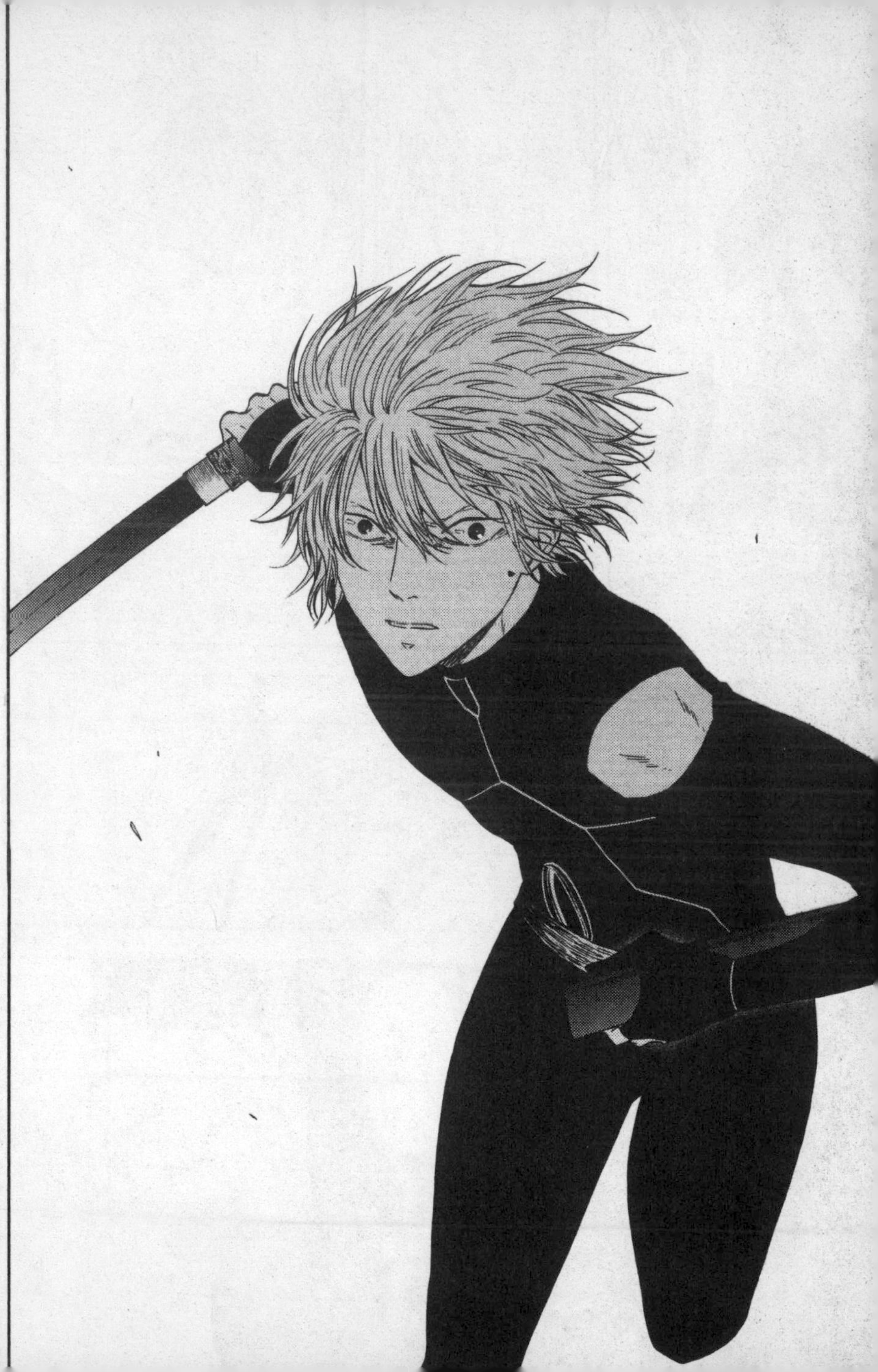

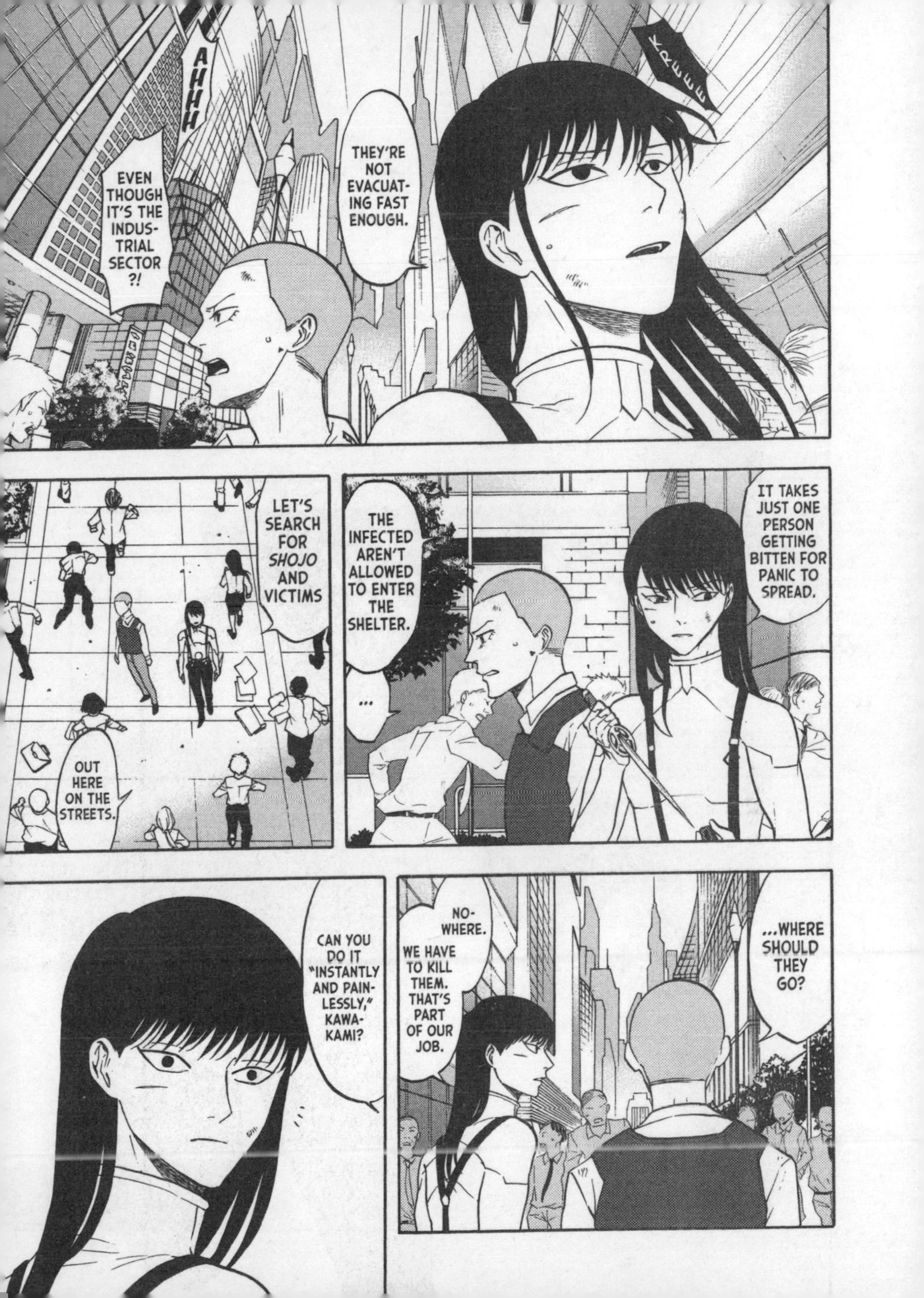
KREEEE
THEY'RE NOT EVACUATING FAST ENOUGH.
AHHH
EVEN THOUGH IT'S THE INDUSTRIAL SECTOR ?!
IT TAKES JUST ONE PERSON GETTING BITTEN FOR PANIC TO SPREAD.
THE INFECTED AREN'T ALLOWED TO ENTER THE SHELTER.
...
LET'S SEARCH FOR *SHOJO* AND VICTIMS
OUT HERE ON THE STREETS.
...WHERE SHOULD THEY GO?
NO-WHERE.
WE HAVE TO KILL THEM. THAT'S PART OF OUR JOB.
CAN YOU DO IT "INSTANTLY AND PAINLESSLY," KAWAKAMI?

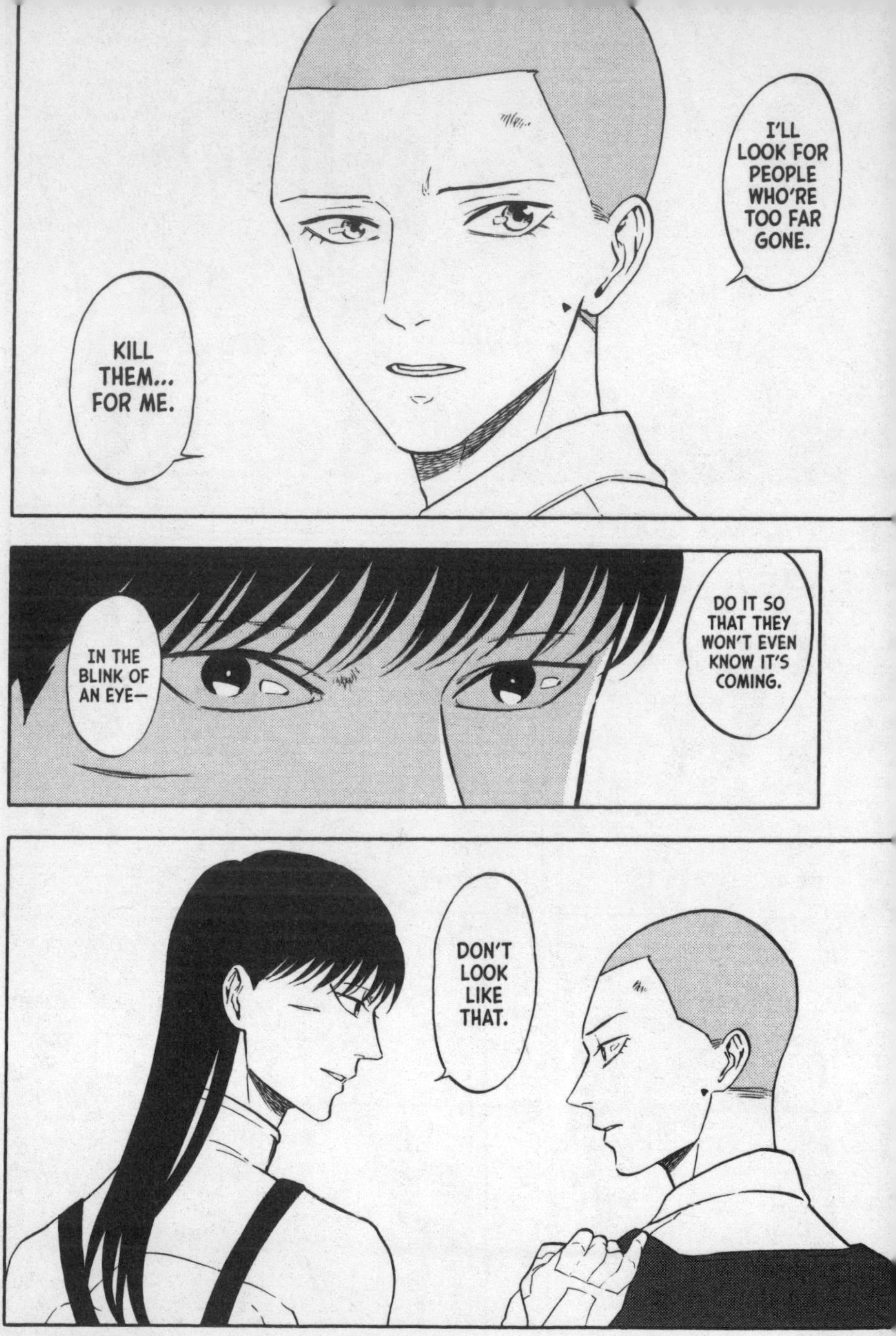
I'LL LOOK FOR PEOPLE WHO'RE TOO FAR GONE.
KILL THEM... FOR ME.
DO IT SO THAT THEY WON'T EVEN KNOW IT'S COMING.
IN THE BLINK OF AN EYE—
DON'T LOOK LIKE THAT.

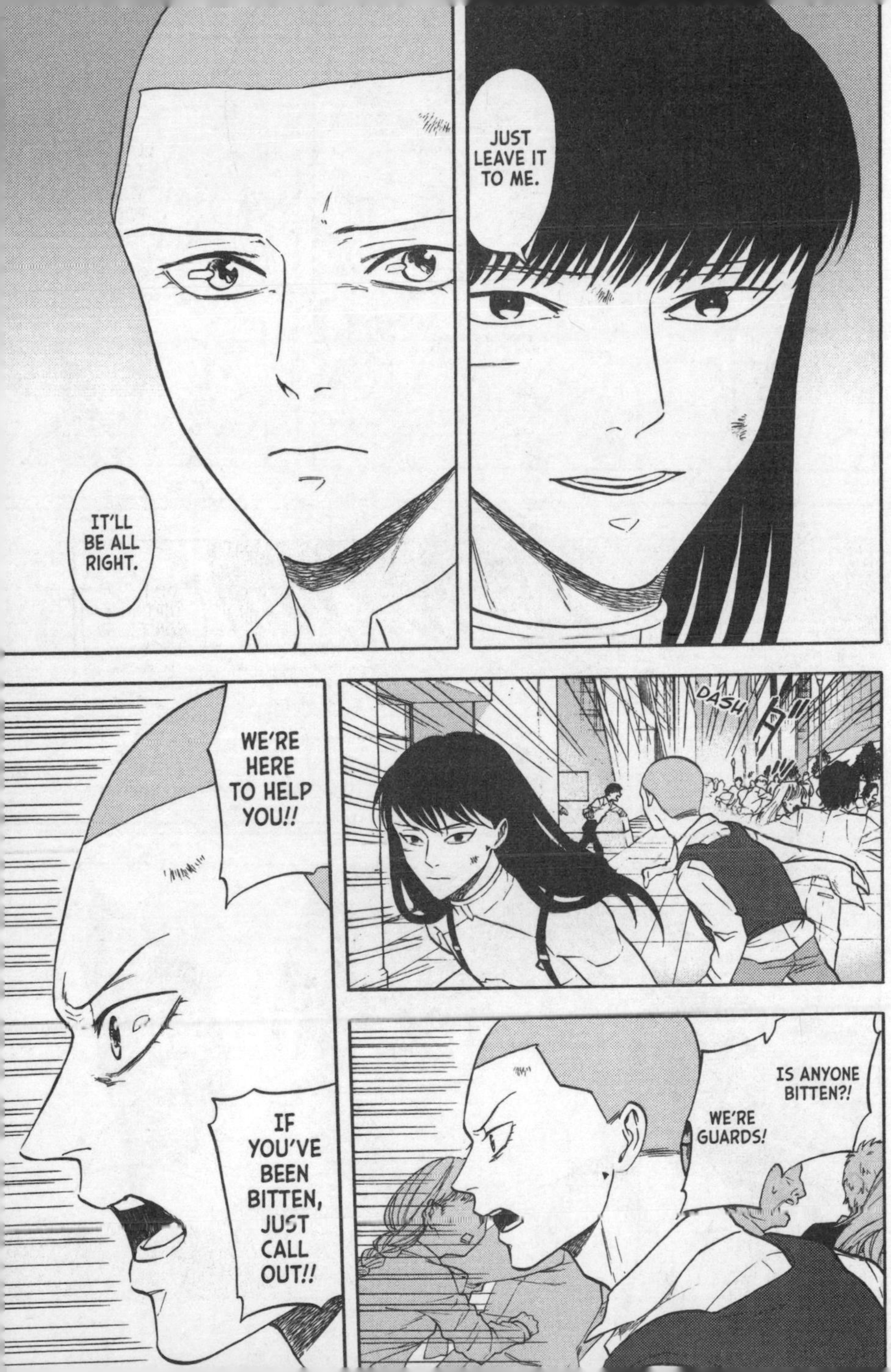
JUST LEAVE IT TO ME.
IT'LL BE ALL RIGHT.
DASH
IS ANYONE BITTEN?!
WE'RE GUARDS!
WE'RE HERE TO HELP YOU!!
IF YOU'VE BEEN BITTEN, JUST CALL OUT!!

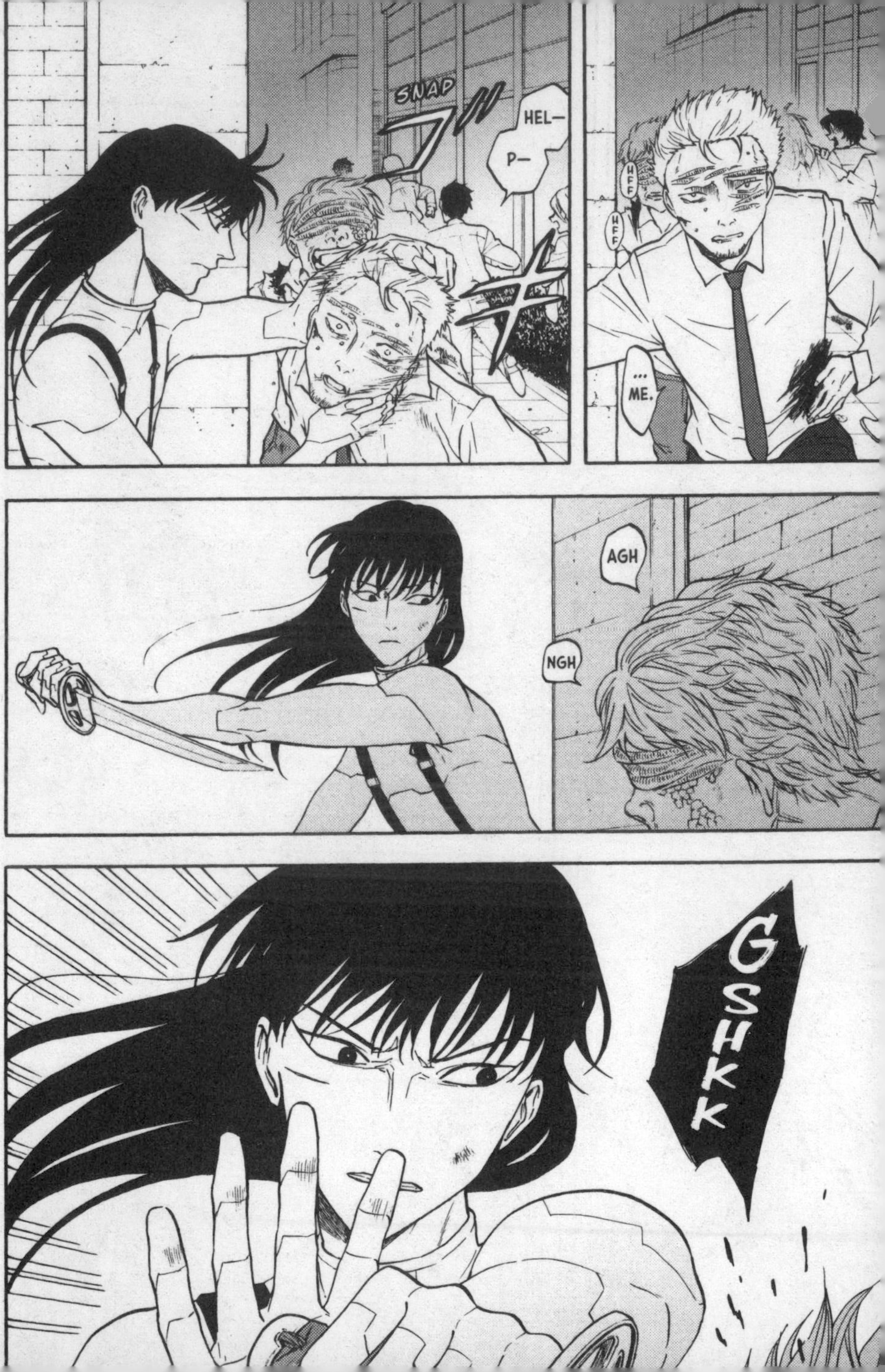
HFF
HFF
... ME.
SNAP
HEL—
P—
AGH
NGH
GSHKK

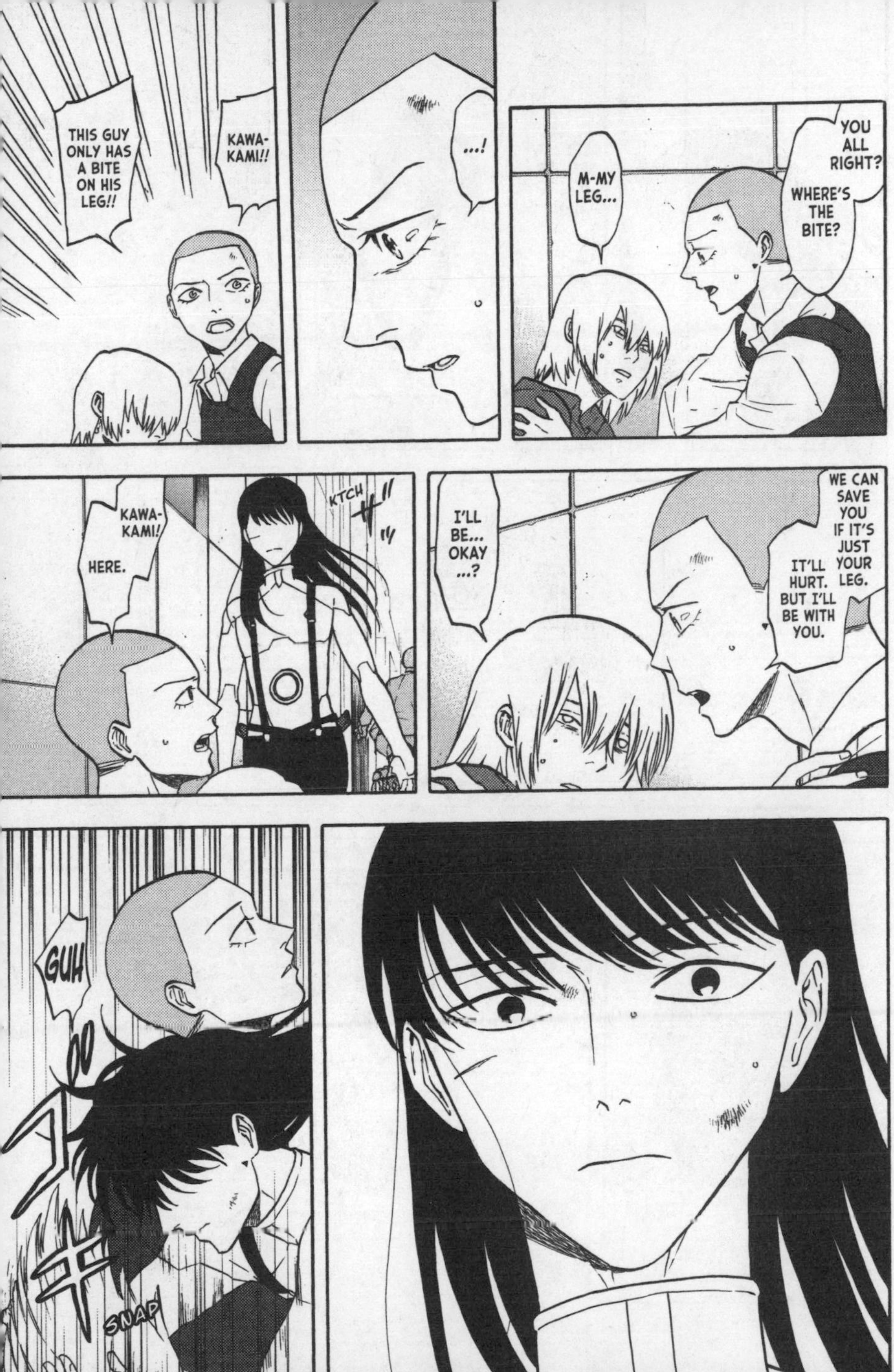
YOU ALL RIGHT?
WHERE'S THE BITE?
M-MY LEG...
...!
KAWA-KAMI!!
THIS GUY ONLY HAS A BITE ON HIS LEG!!
WE CAN SAVE YOU IF IT'S JUST YOUR LEG.
IT'LL HURT. BUT I'LL BE WITH YOU.
I'LL BE... OKAY ...?
KTCH
KAWA-KAMI!
HERE.
GUH
SNAP

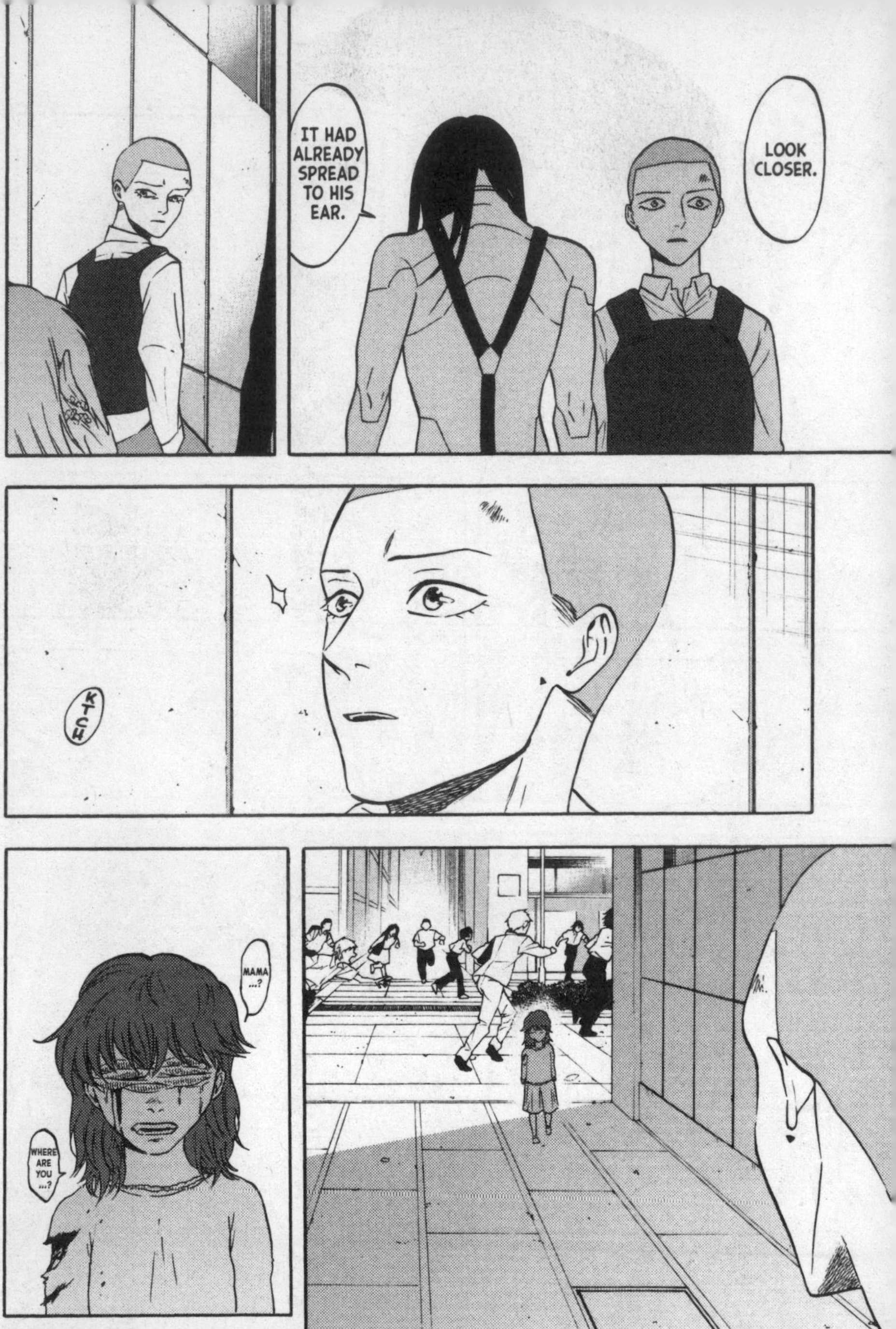
LOOK CLOSER.
IT HAD ALREADY SPREAD TO HIS EAR.
KTCH
MAMA ...?
WHERE ARE YOU ...?

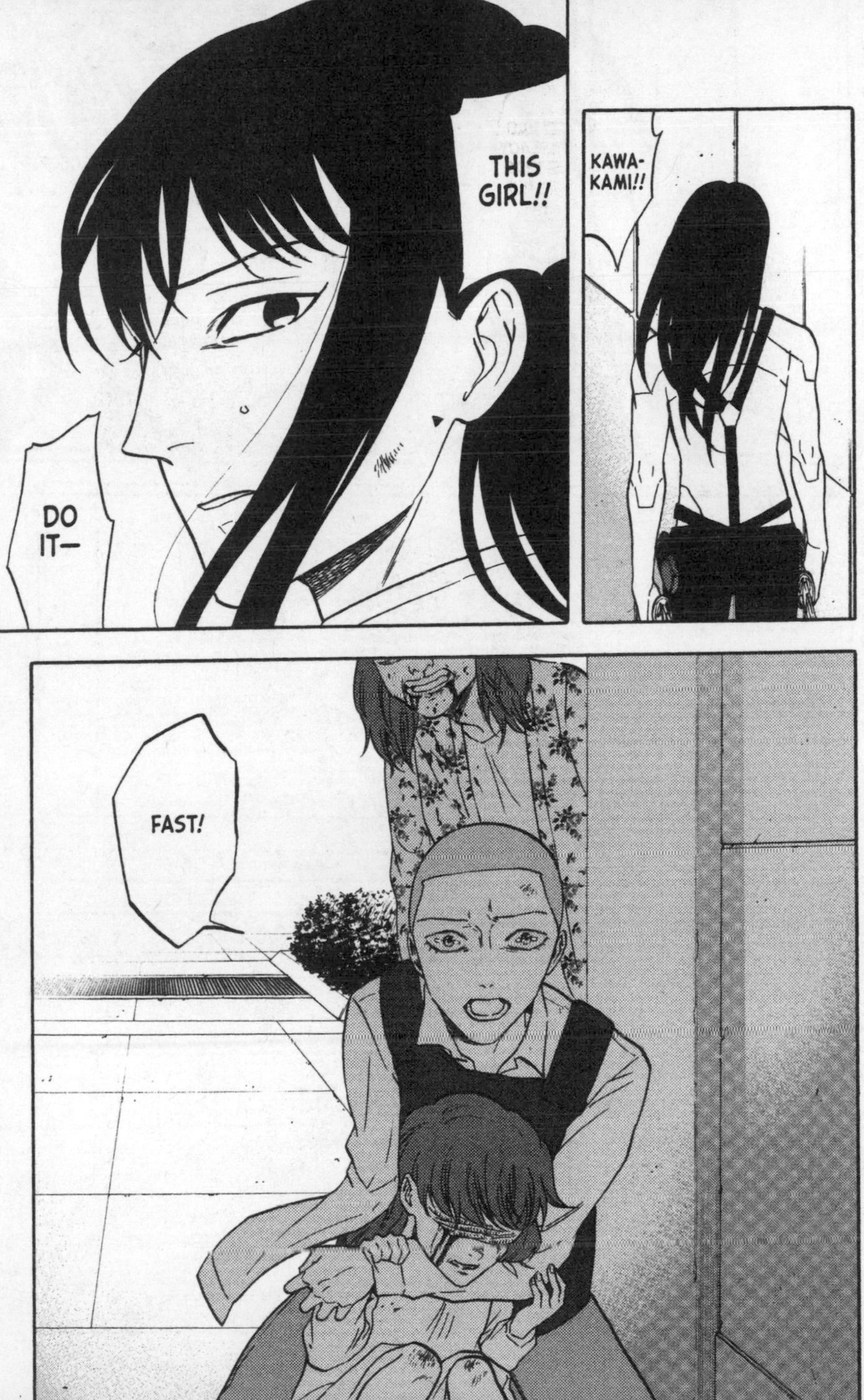
KAWA-KAMI!!
THIS GIRL!!
DO IT—
FAST!

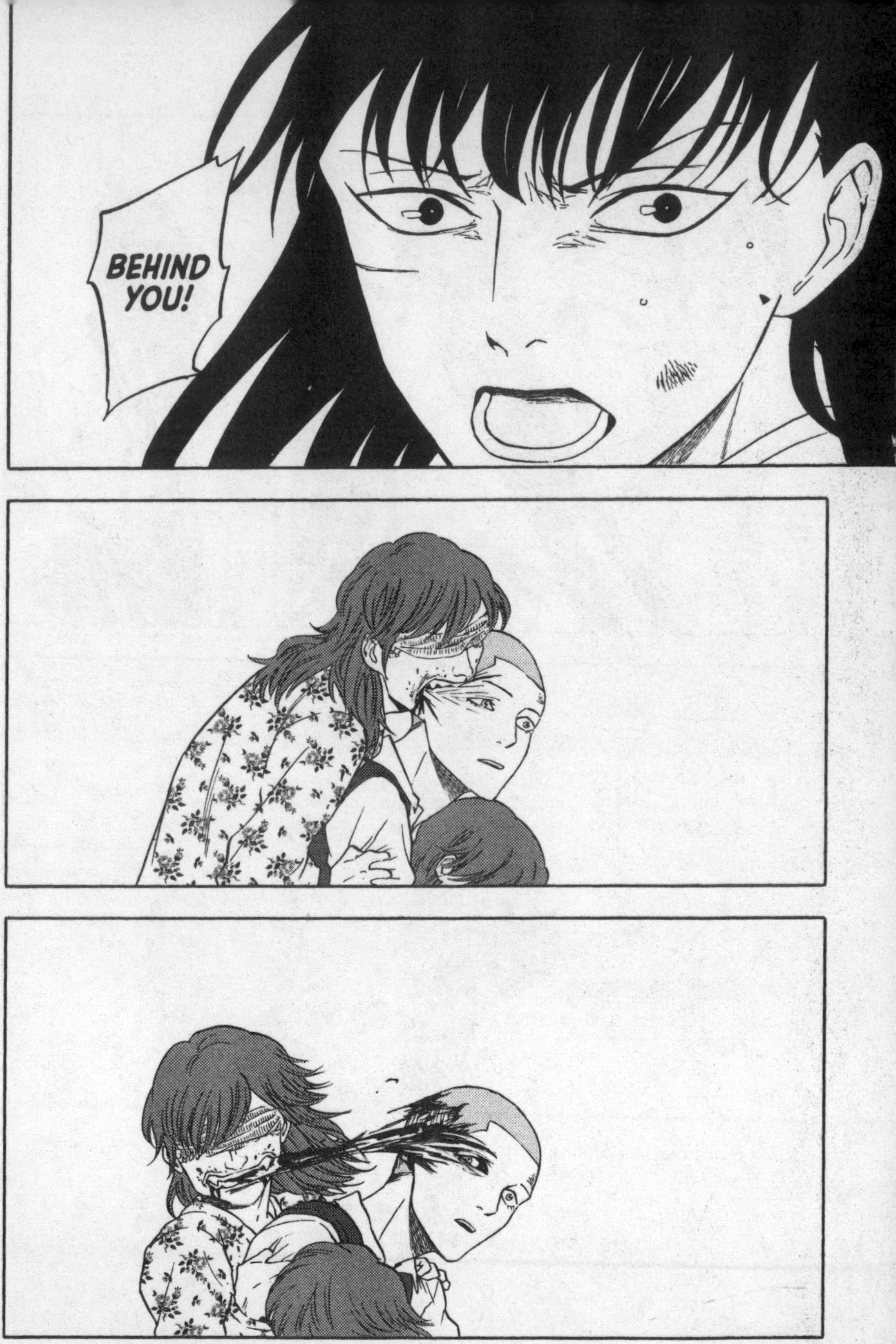
BEHIND YOU!

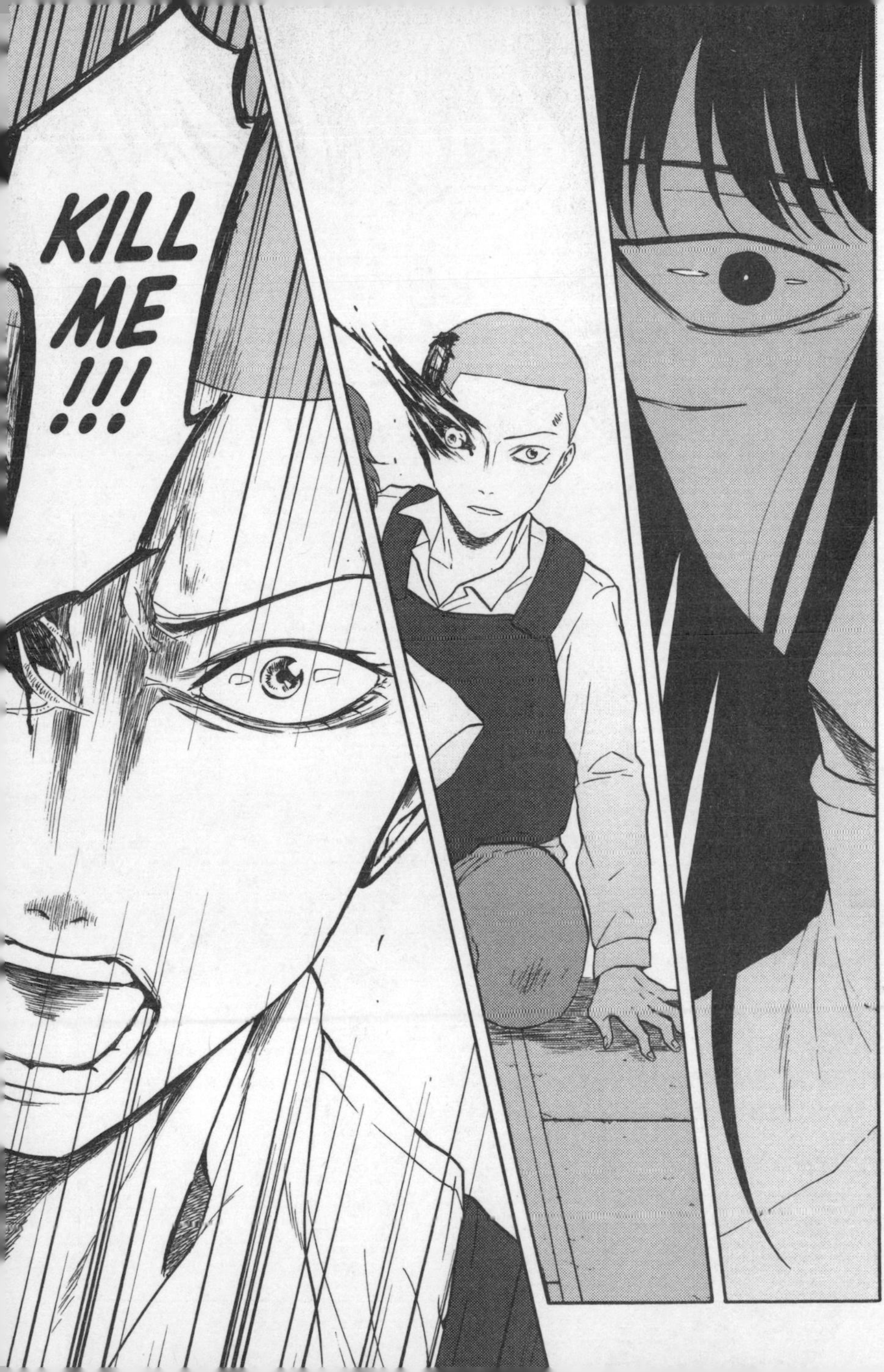
KILL ME !!!

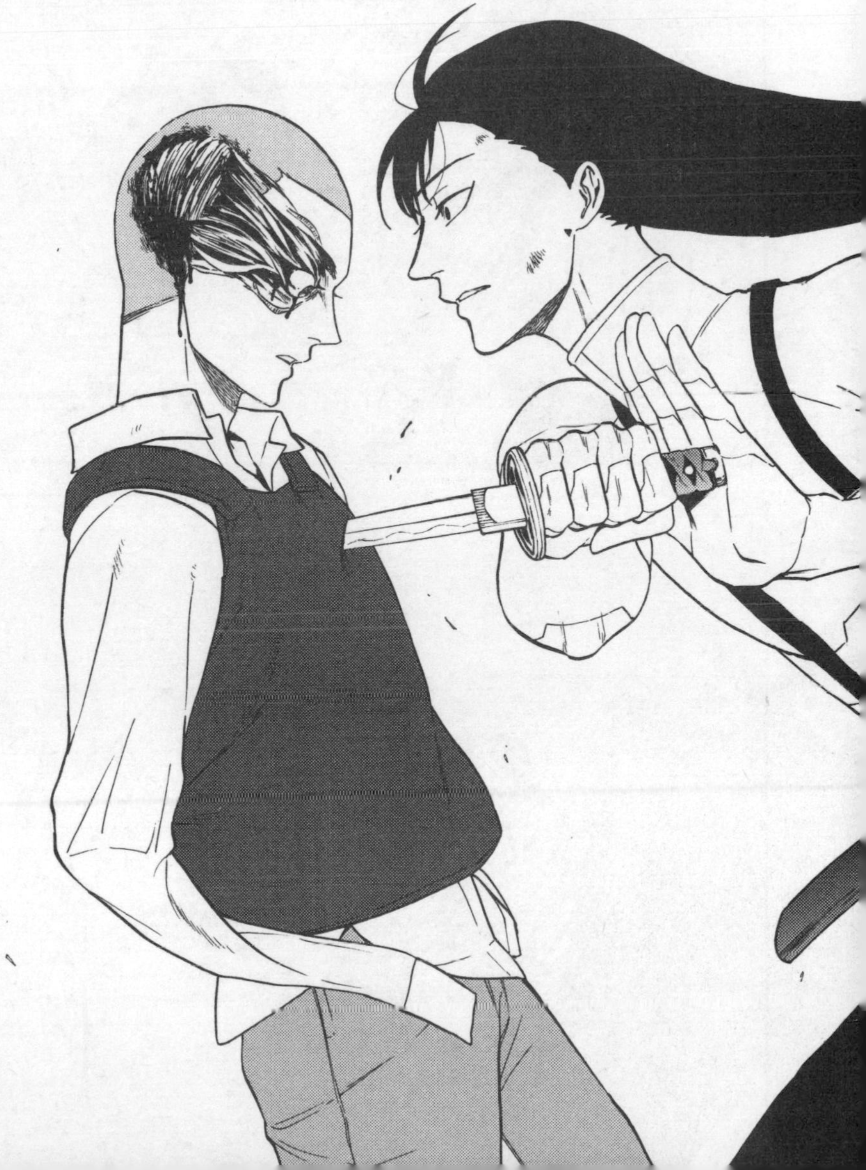

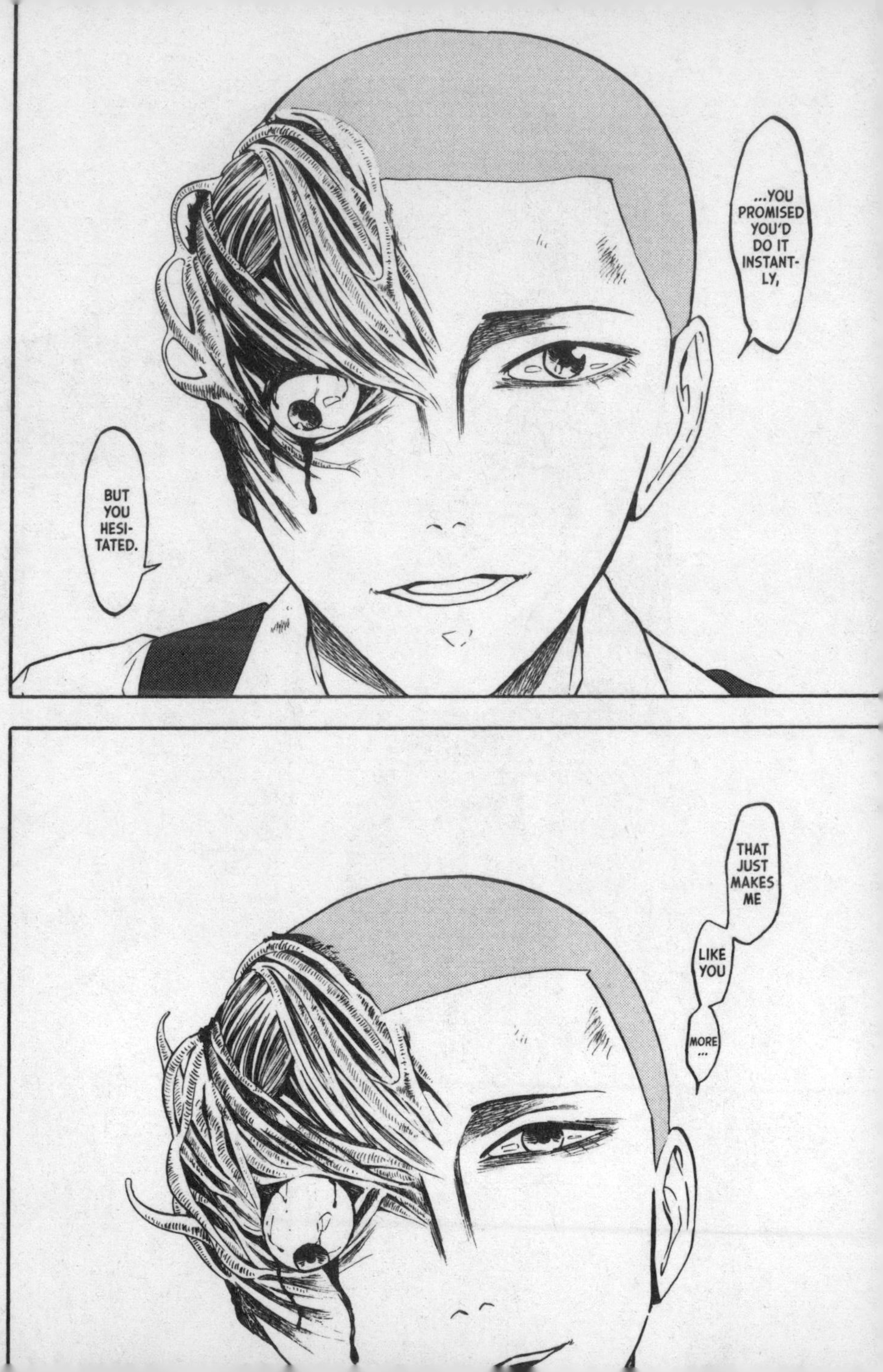
...YOU PROMISED YOU'D DO IT INSTANT-LY,
BUT YOU HESI-TATED.
THAT JUST MAKES ME
LIKE YOU
MORE...

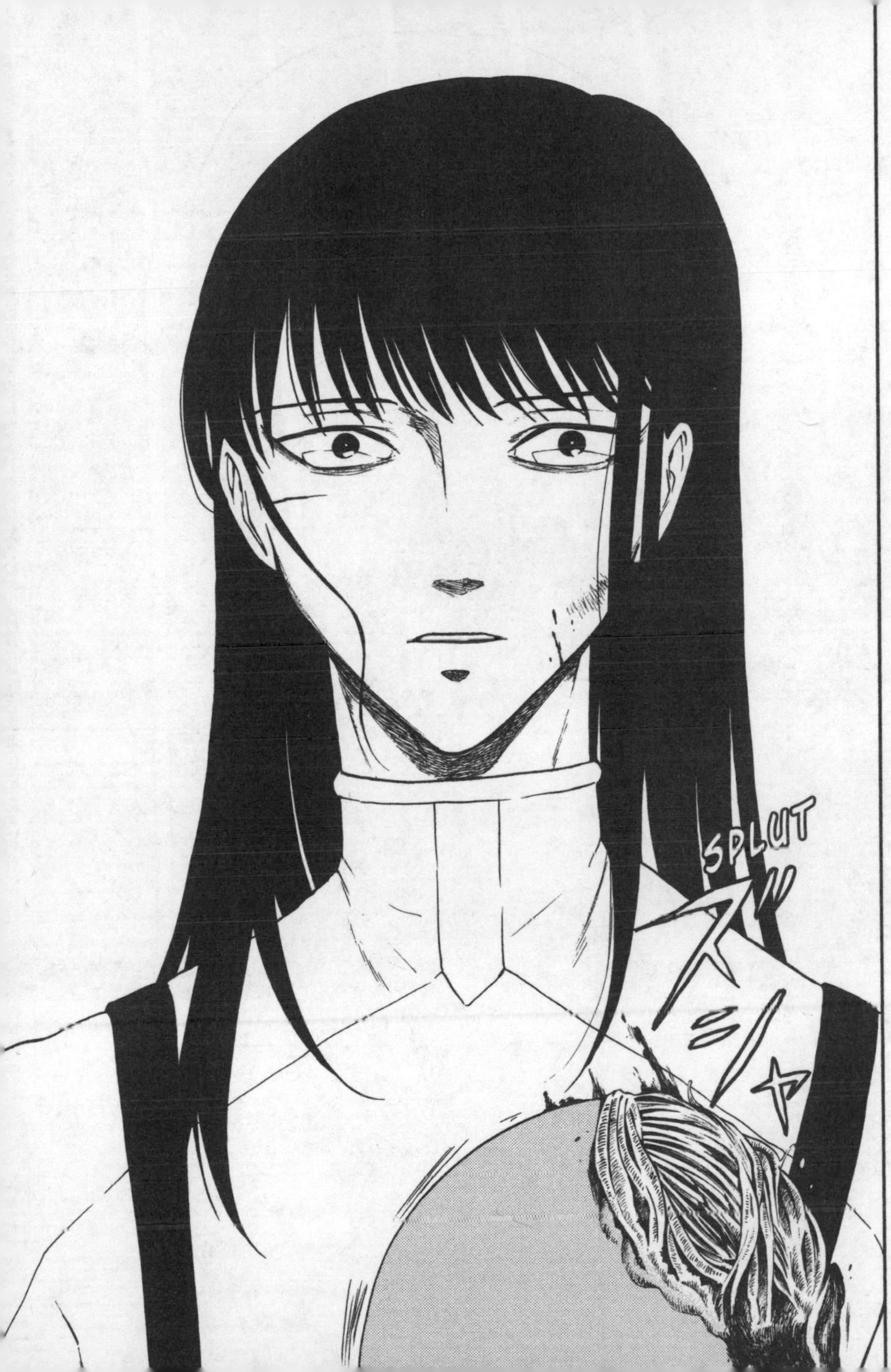
SPLUT

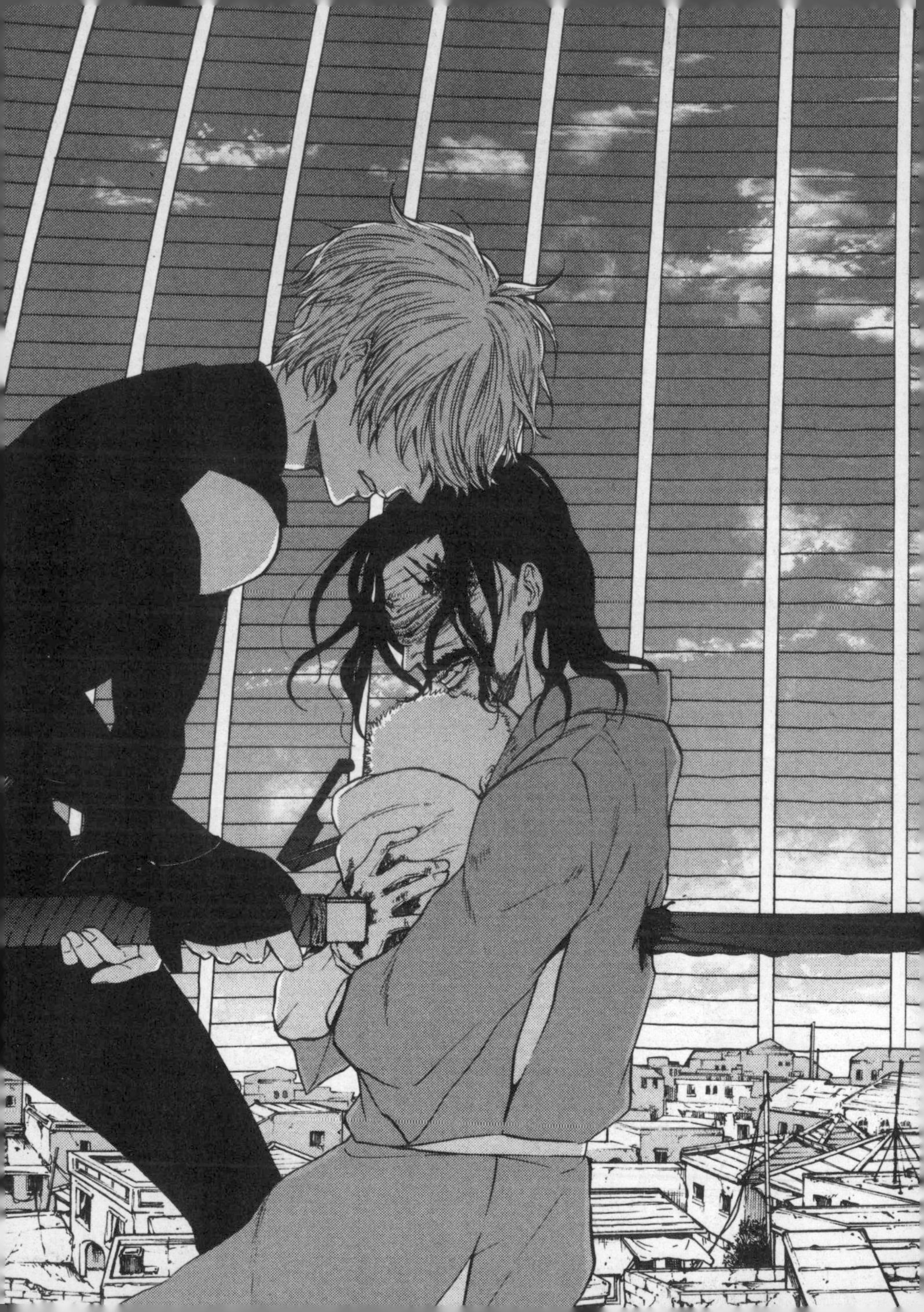

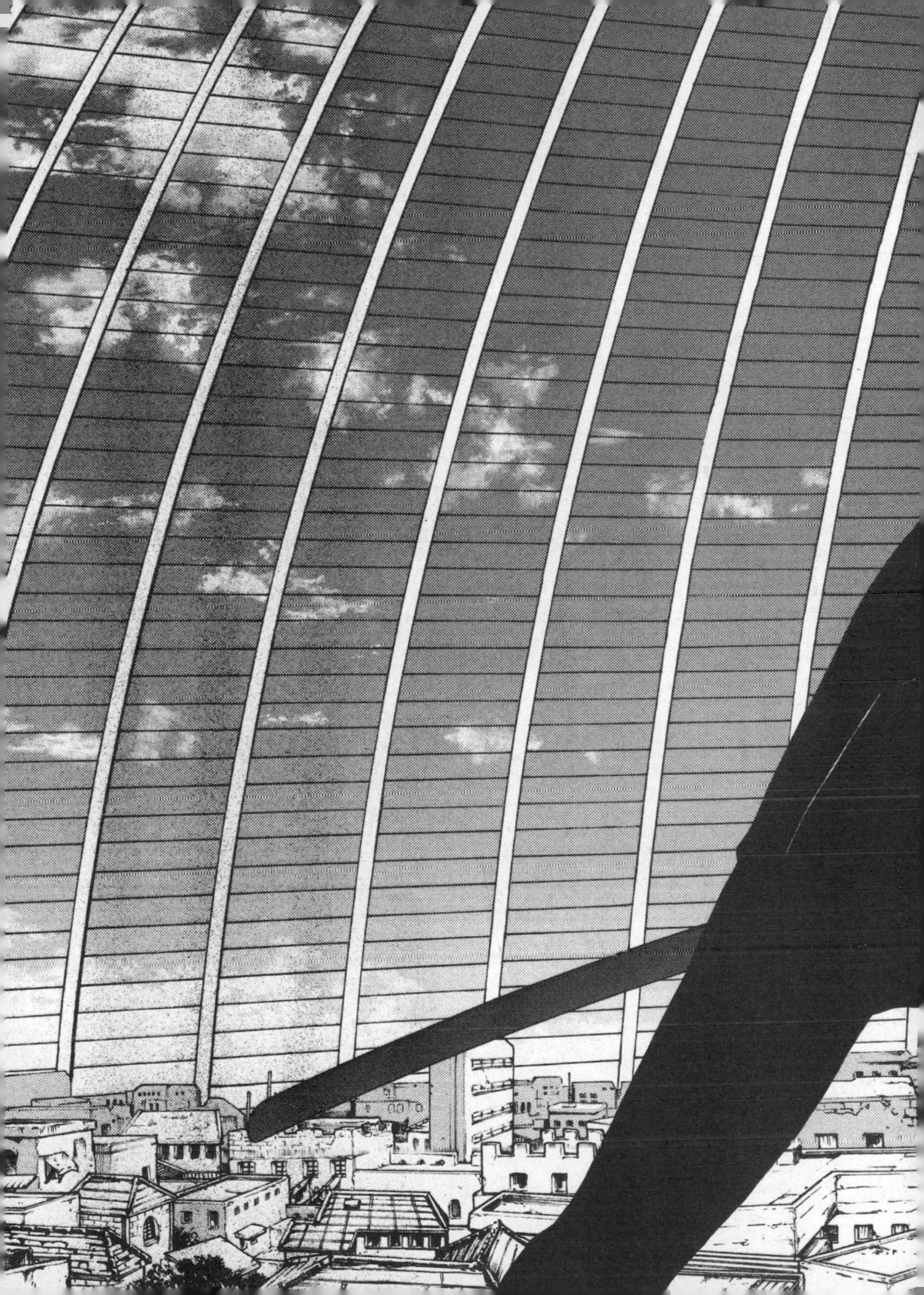

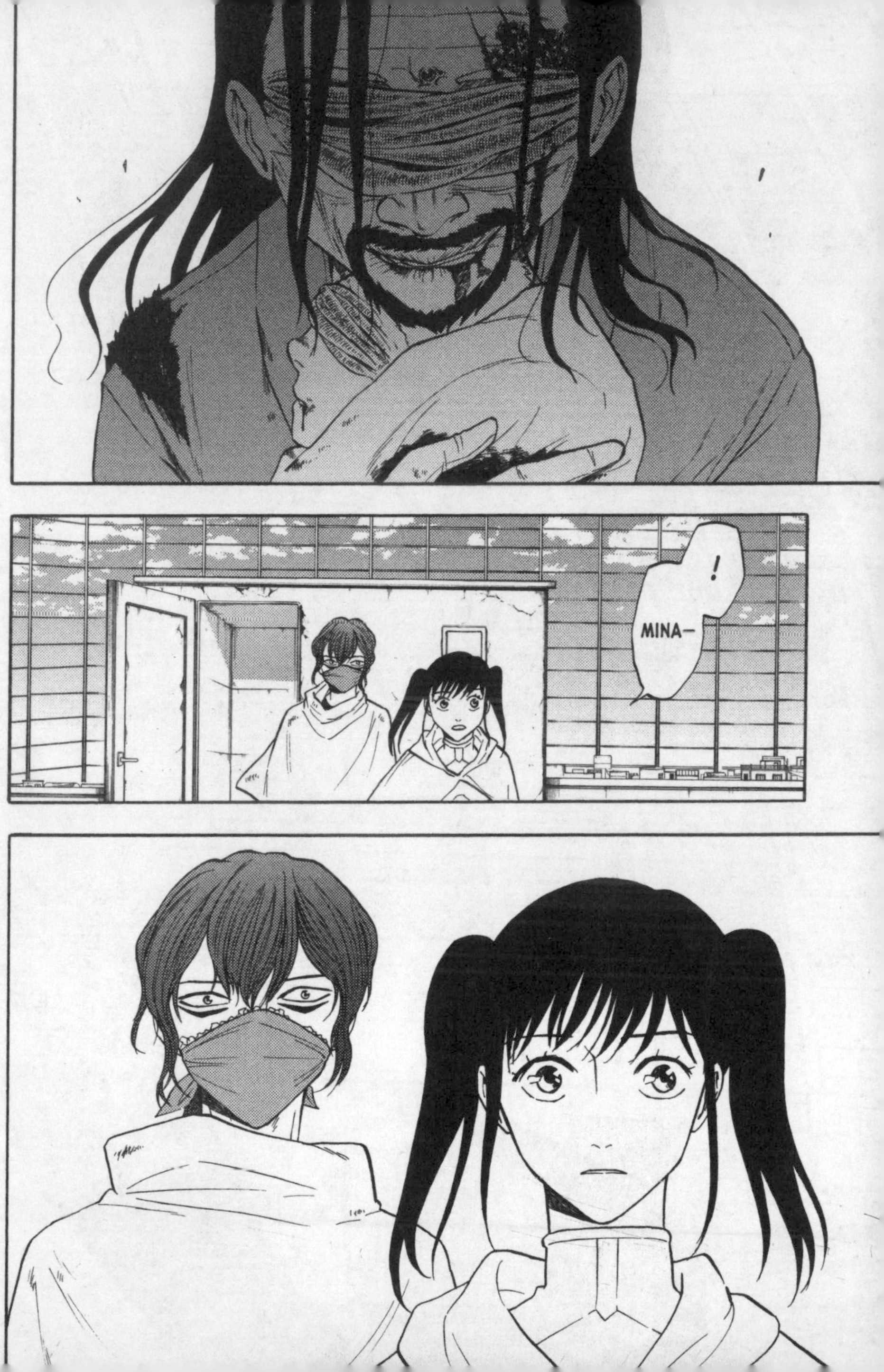
!
MINA—

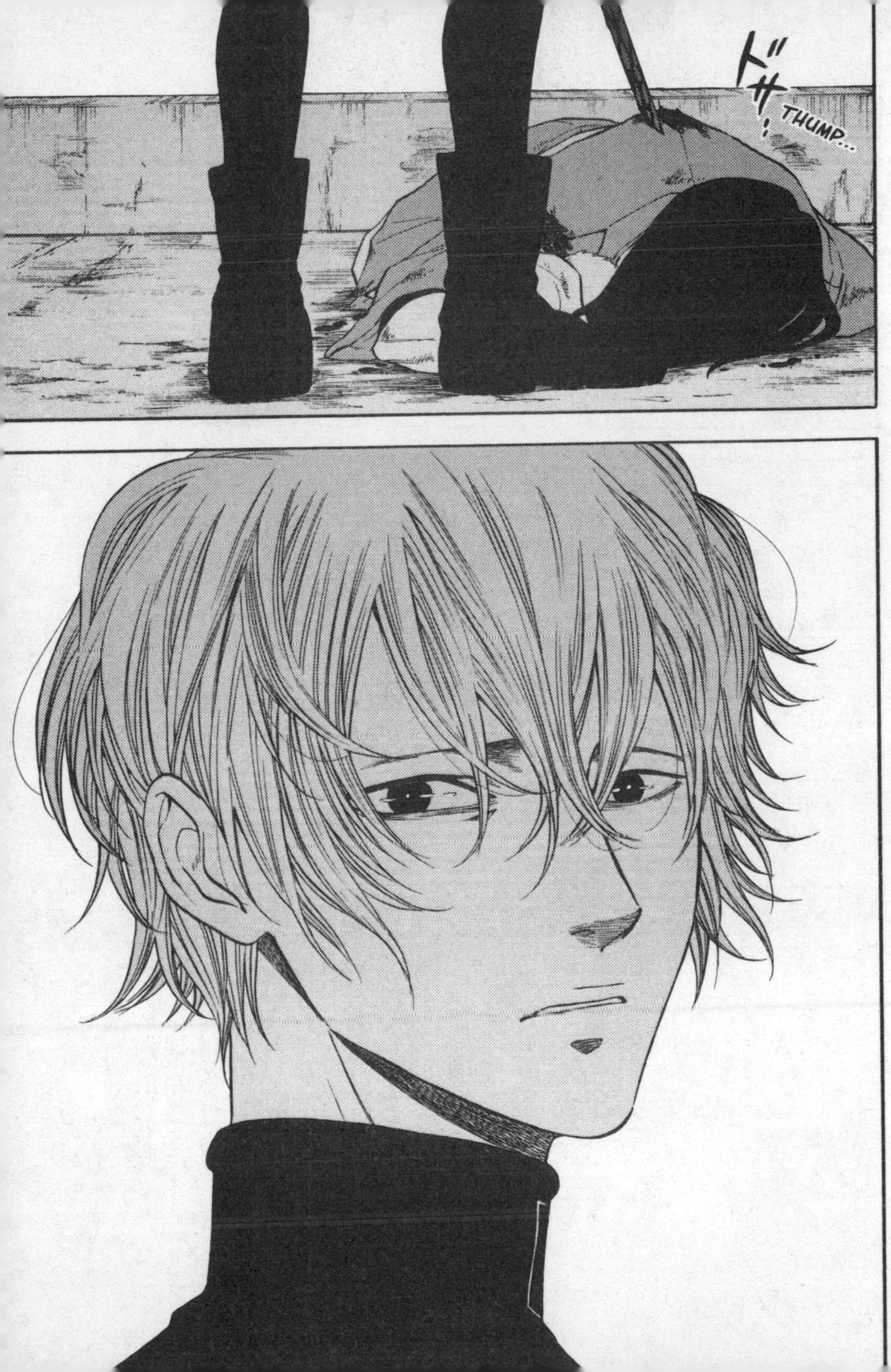
ドザッ
THUMP...

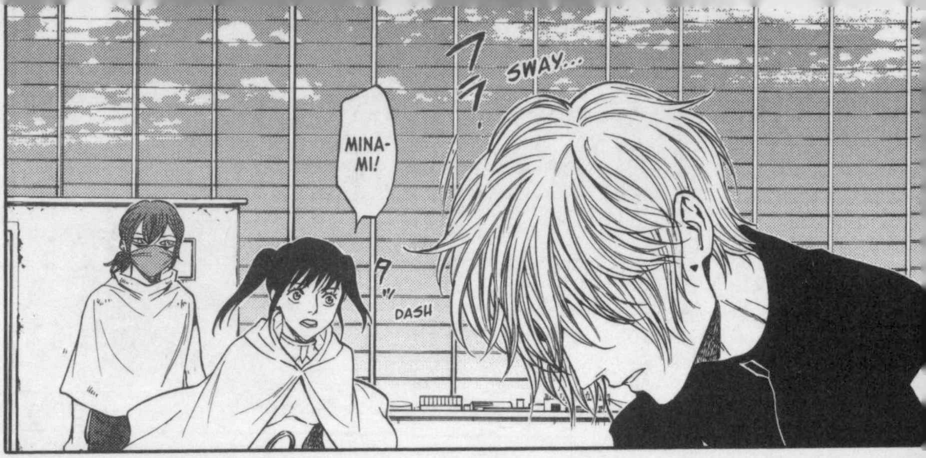
SWAY...
MINA-MI!
DASH

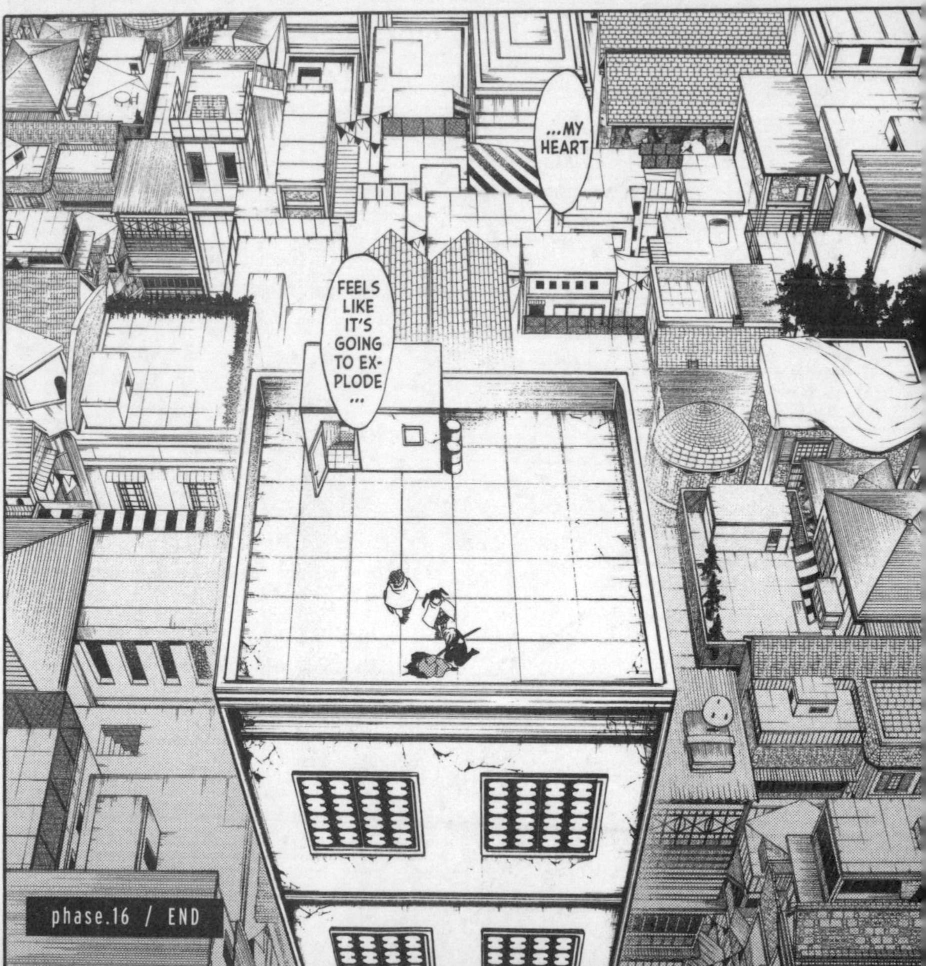
...MY HEART
FEELS LIKE IT'S GOING TO EX-PLODE...
phase.16 / END

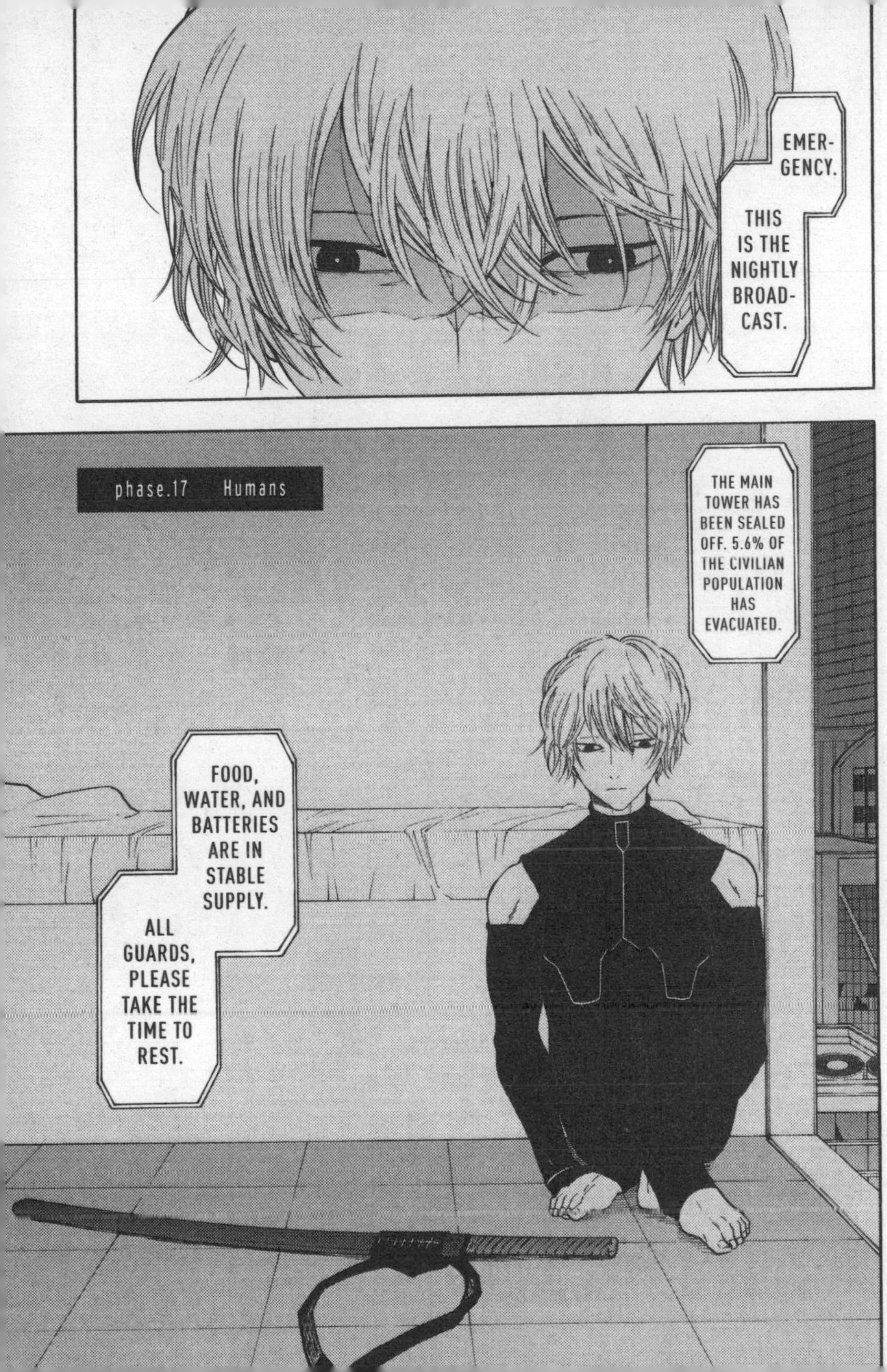
EMER-GENCY.
THIS IS THE NIGHTLY BROAD-CAST.
THE MAIN TOWER HAS BEEN SEALED OFF. 5.6% OF THE CIVILIAN POPULATION HAS EVACUATED.
phase.17 Humans
FOOD, WATER, AND BATTERIES ARE IN STABLE SUPPLY.
ALL GUARDS, PLEASE TAKE THE TIME TO REST.

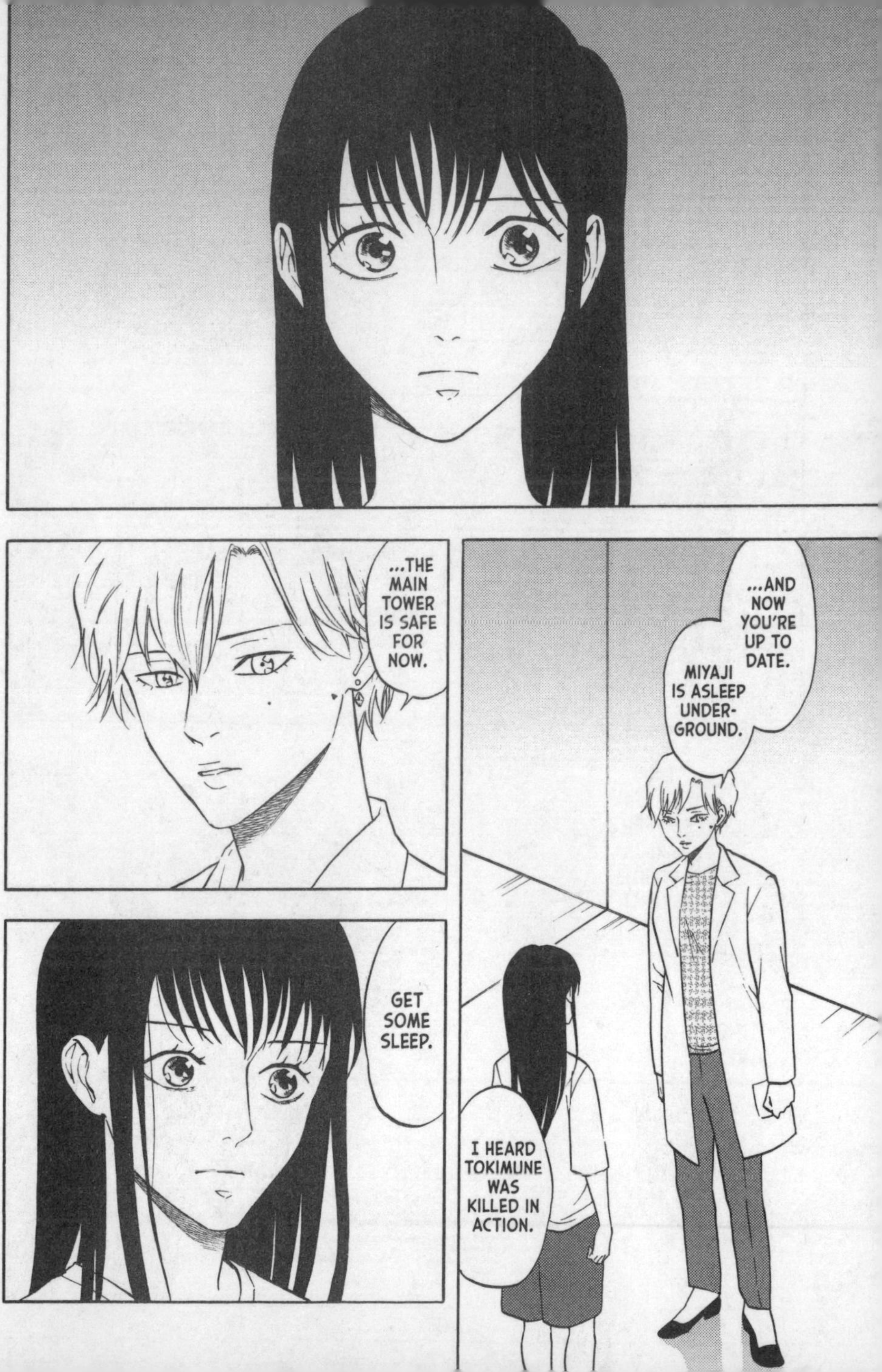
...AND NOW YOU'RE UP TO DATE.
MIYAJI IS ASLEEP UNDER-GROUND.
I HEARD TOKIMUNE WAS KILLED IN ACTION.
...THE MAIN TOWER IS SAFE FOR NOW.
GET SOME SLEEP.

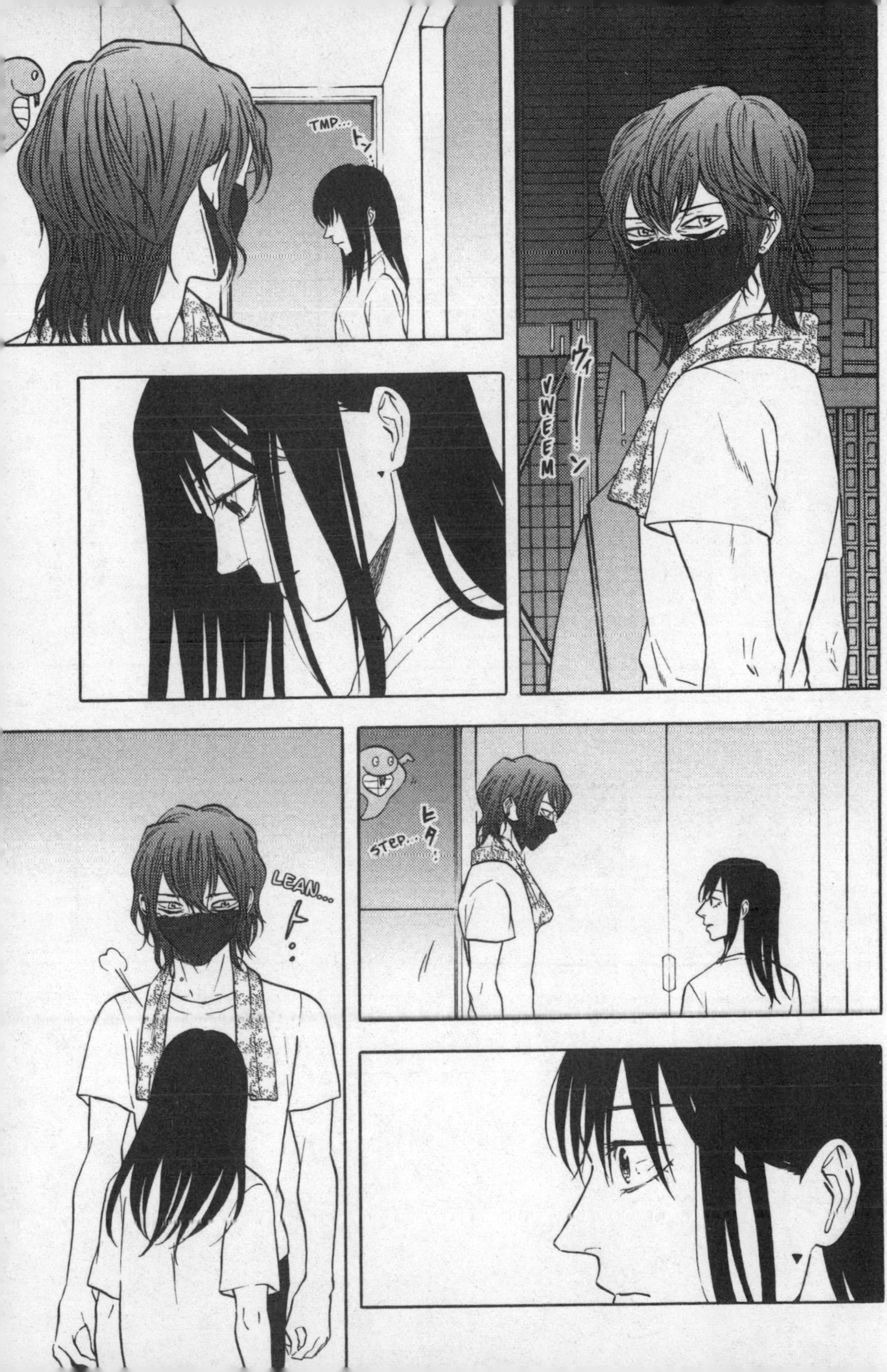
VWEEM
ヴィーン
TMP...
トン...
STEP...
ヒタ...
LEAN...
ト...

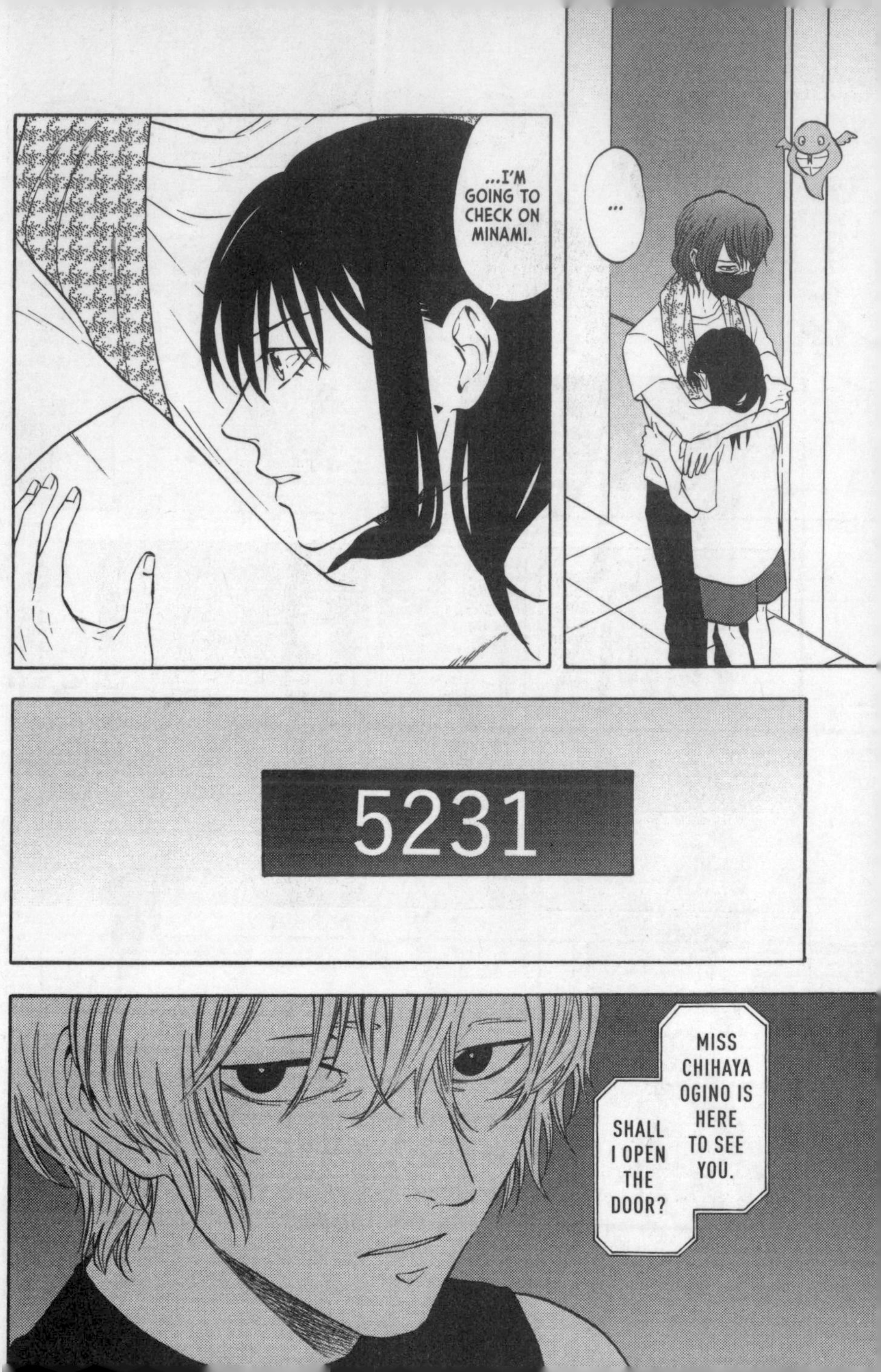
...
...I'M GOING TO CHECK ON MINAMI.
5231
MISS CHIHAYA OGINO IS HERE TO SEE YOU.
SHALL I OPEN THE DOOR?

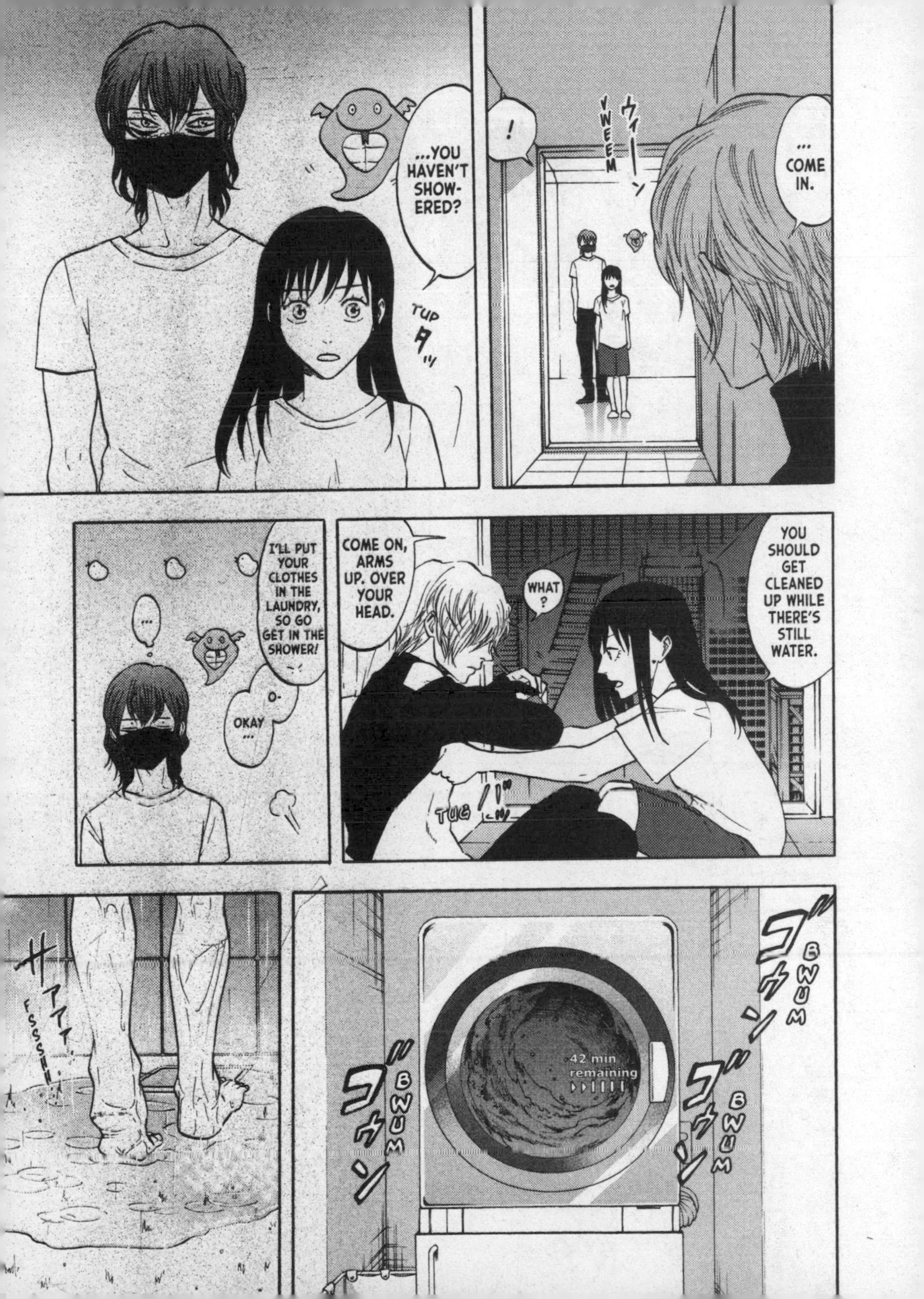

... COME IN.
VWEEM
!
...YOU HAVEN'T SHOWERED?
TUP
YOU SHOULD GET CLEANED UP WHILE THERE'S STILL WATER.
WHAT?
COME ON, ARMS UP. OVER YOUR HEAD.
TUG
I'LL PUT YOUR CLOTHES IN THE LAUNDRY, SO GO GET IN THE SHOWER!
O-OKAY...
...
BWUM
BWUM
42 min remaining
BWUM
FSSSHH

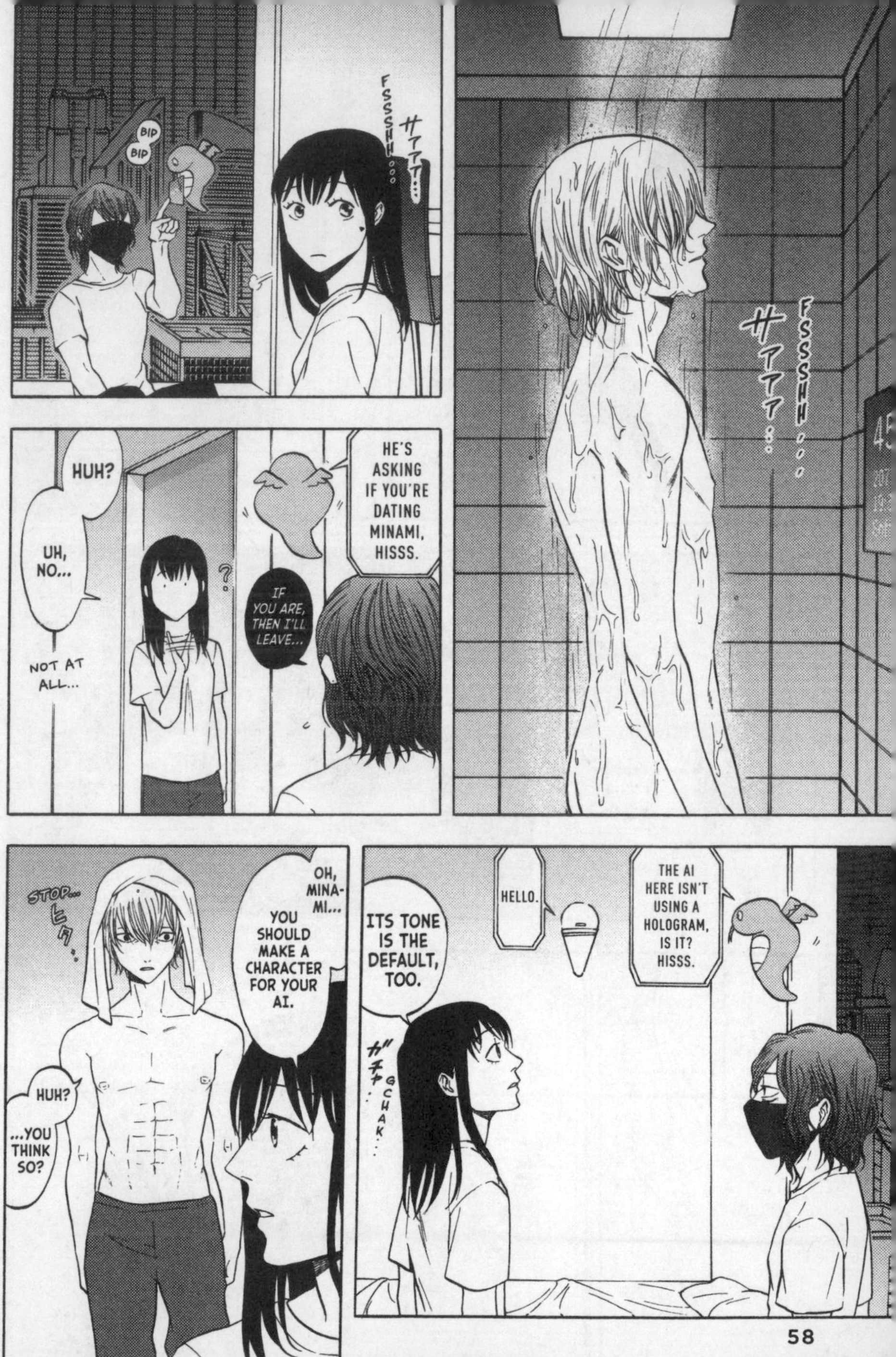
FSSSHH...
FSSSHH...
BIP
BIP
HE'S ASKING IF YOU'RE DATING MINAMI, HISSS.
HUH?
IF YOU ARE, THEN I'LL LEAVE...
UH, NO...
NOT AT ALL...
THE AI HERE ISN'T USING A HOLOGRAM, IS IT? HISSS.
HELLO.
ITS TONE IS THE DEFAULT, TOO.
GCHAK...
OH, MINA-MI... YOU SHOULD MAKE A CHARACTER FOR YOUR AI.
STOP...
HUH?
...YOU THINK SO?

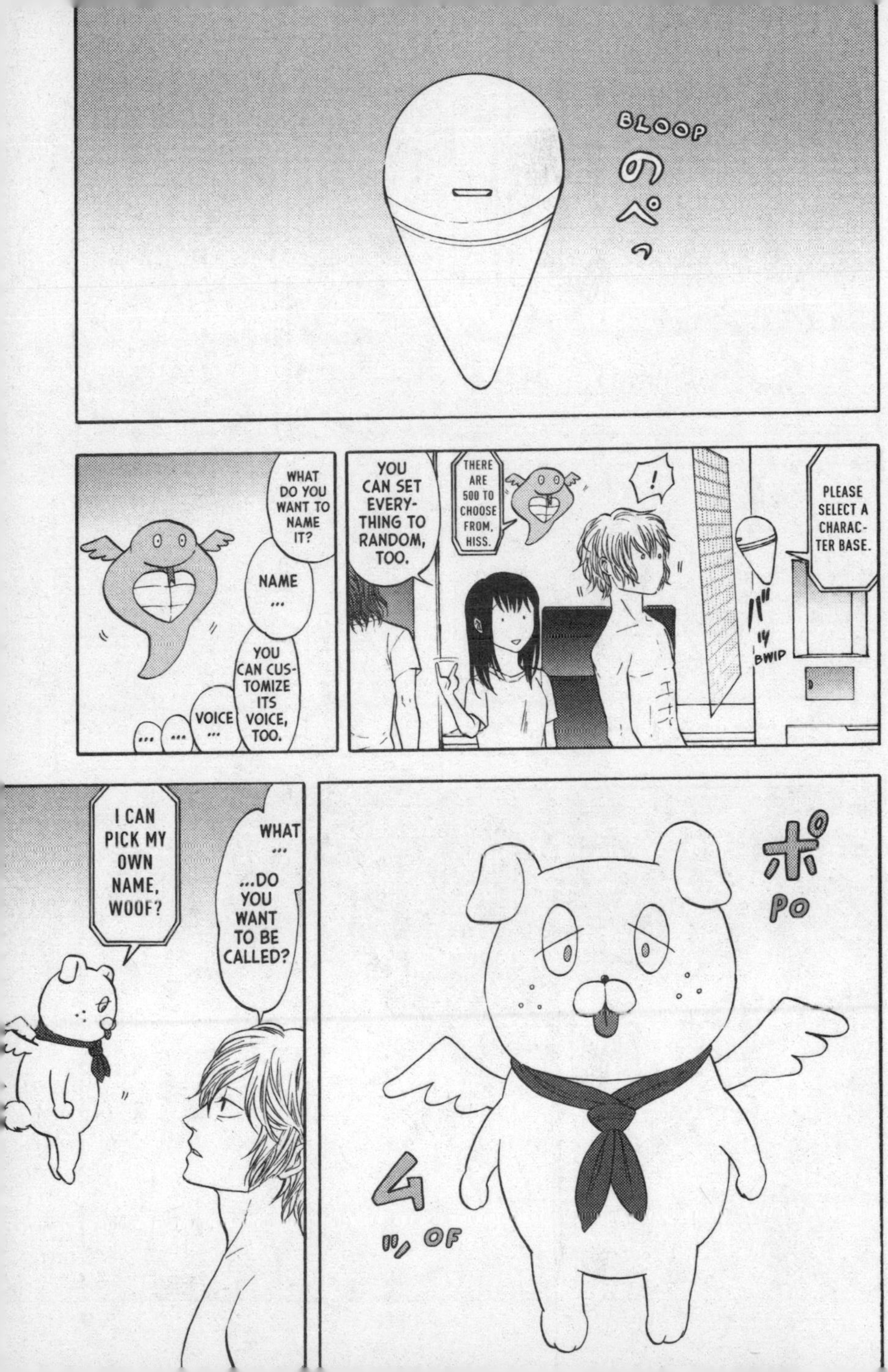
BLOOP
のぺっ
PLEASE SELECT A CHARACTER BASE.
!
BWIP
THERE ARE 500 TO CHOOSE FROM, HISS.
YOU CAN SET EVERYTHING TO RANDOM, TOO.
WHAT DO YOU WANT TO NAME IT?
NAME ...
YOU CAN CUSTOMIZE ITS VOICE, TOO.
VOICE ...
...
...
PO
OF
WHAT ...
...DO YOU WANT TO BE CALLED?
I CAN PICK MY OWN NAME, WOOF?

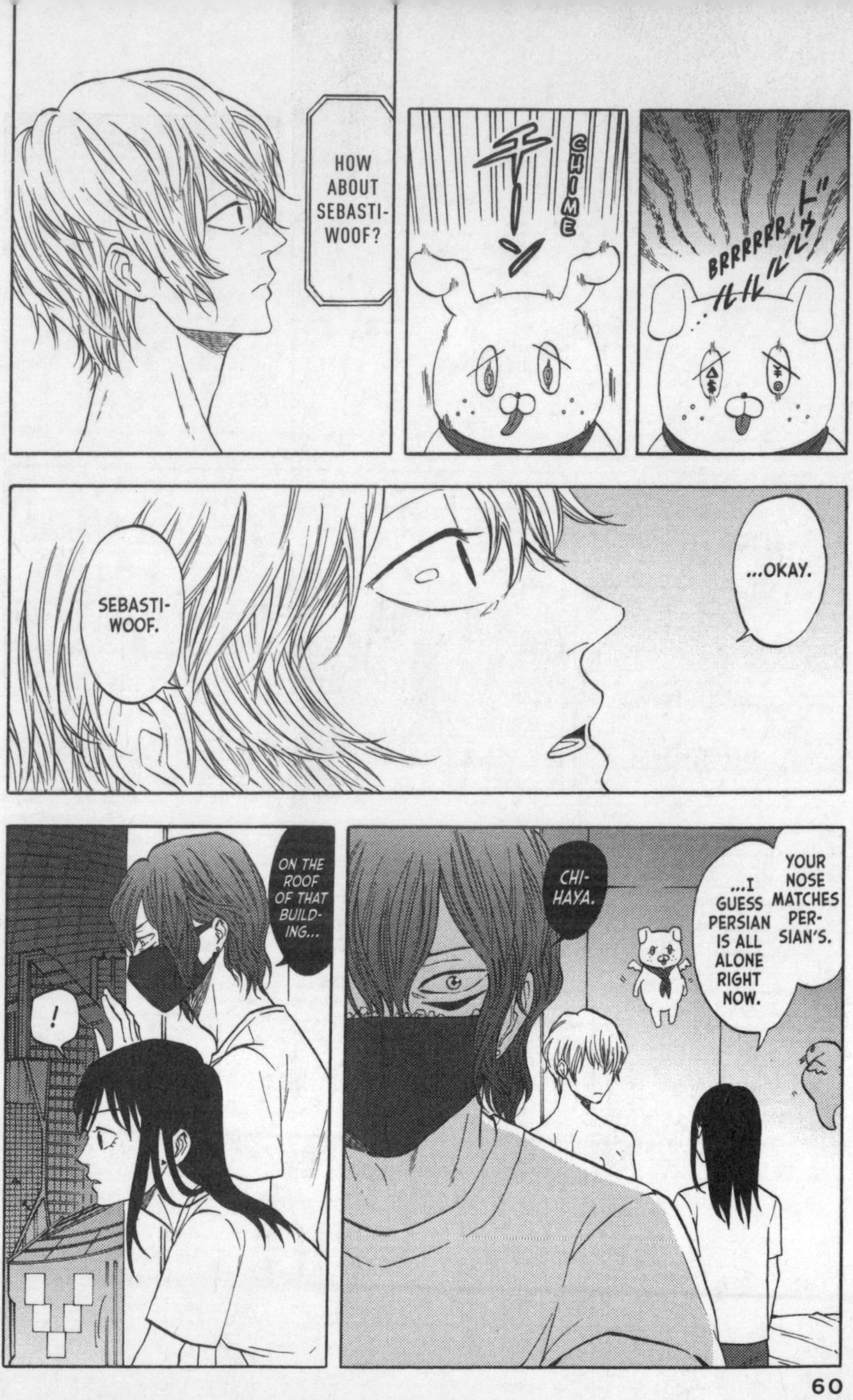
BRRRRRR
CHIME
HOW ABOUT SEBASTI-WOOF?
...OKAY.
SEBASTI-WOOF.
YOUR NOSE MATCHES PER-SIAN'S.
...I GUESS PERSIAN IS ALL ALONE RIGHT NOW.
CHI-HAYA.
ON THE ROOF OF THAT BUILD-ING...
!

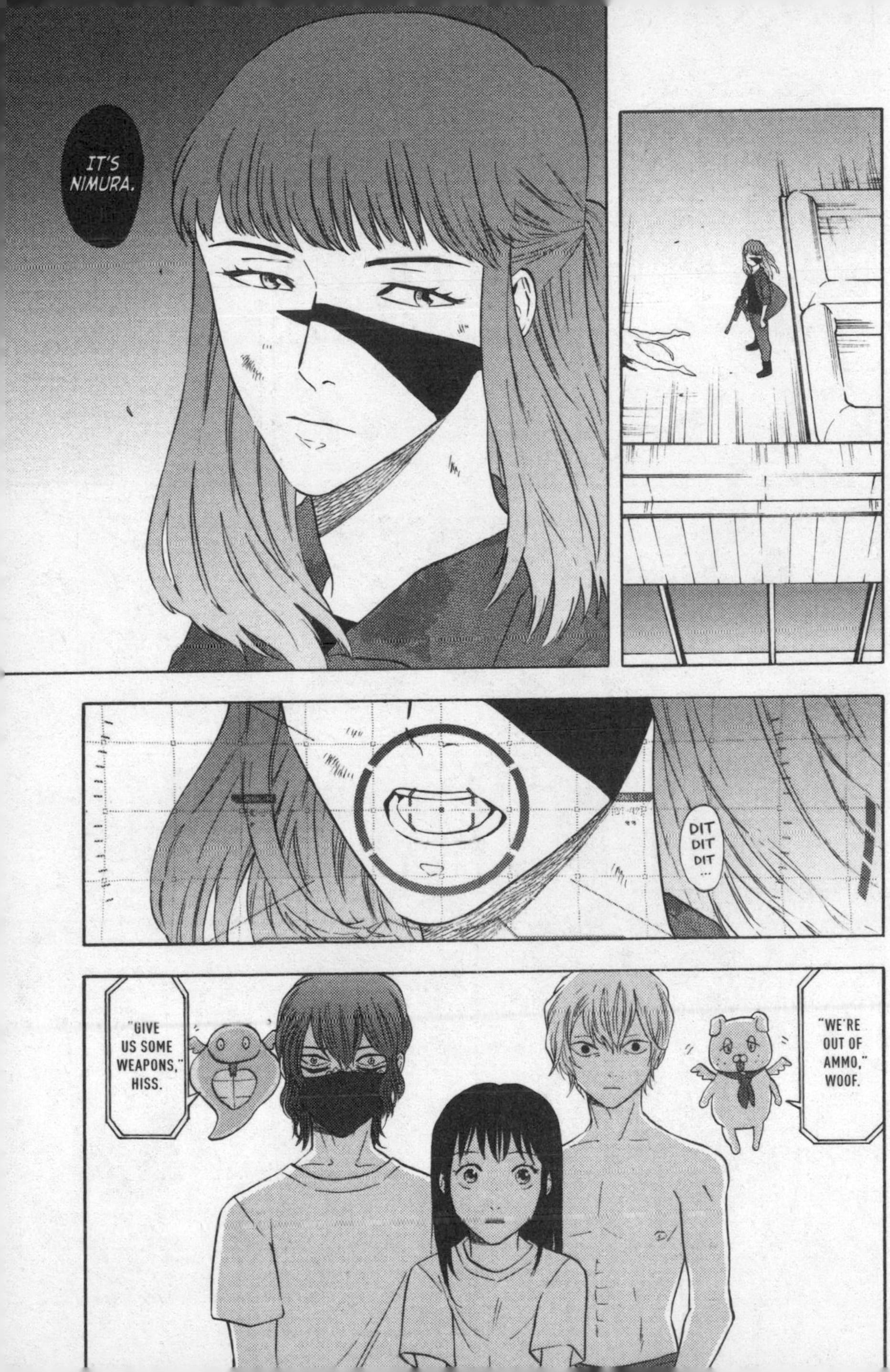
IT'S NIMURA.
DIT DIT DIT ...
"WE'RE OUT OF AMMO," WOOF.
"GIVE US SOME WEAPONS," HISS.

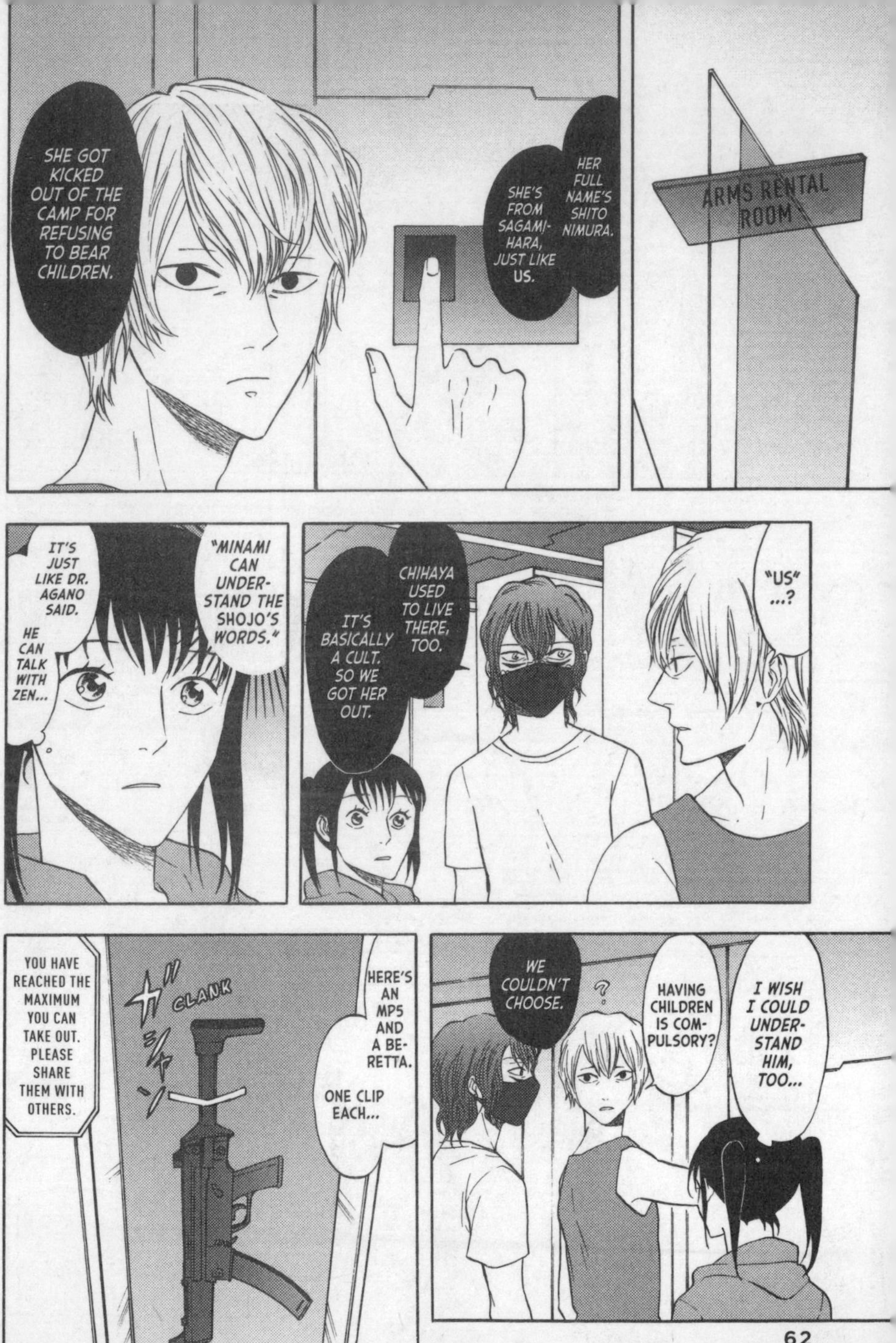
ARMS RENTAL ROOM
HER FULL NAME'S SHITO NIMURA.
SHE'S FROM SAGAMIHARA, JUST LIKE US.
SHE GOT KICKED OUT OF THE CAMP FOR REFUSING TO BEAR CHILDREN.
"US" ...?
CHIHAYA USED TO LIVE THERE, TOO.
IT'S BASICALLY A CULT. SO WE GOT HER OUT.
"MINAMI CAN UNDERSTAND THE SHOJO'S WORDS."
IT'S JUST LIKE DR. AGANO SAID.
HE CAN TALK WITH ZEN...
I WISH I COULD UNDERSTAND HIM, TOO...
HAVING CHILDREN IS COMPULSORY?
?
WE COULDN'T CHOOSE.
HERE'S AN MP5 AND A BERETTA.
ONE CLIP EACH...
CLANK
YOU HAVE REACHED THE MAXIMUM YOU CAN TAKE OUT. PLEASE SHARE THEM WITH OTHERS.

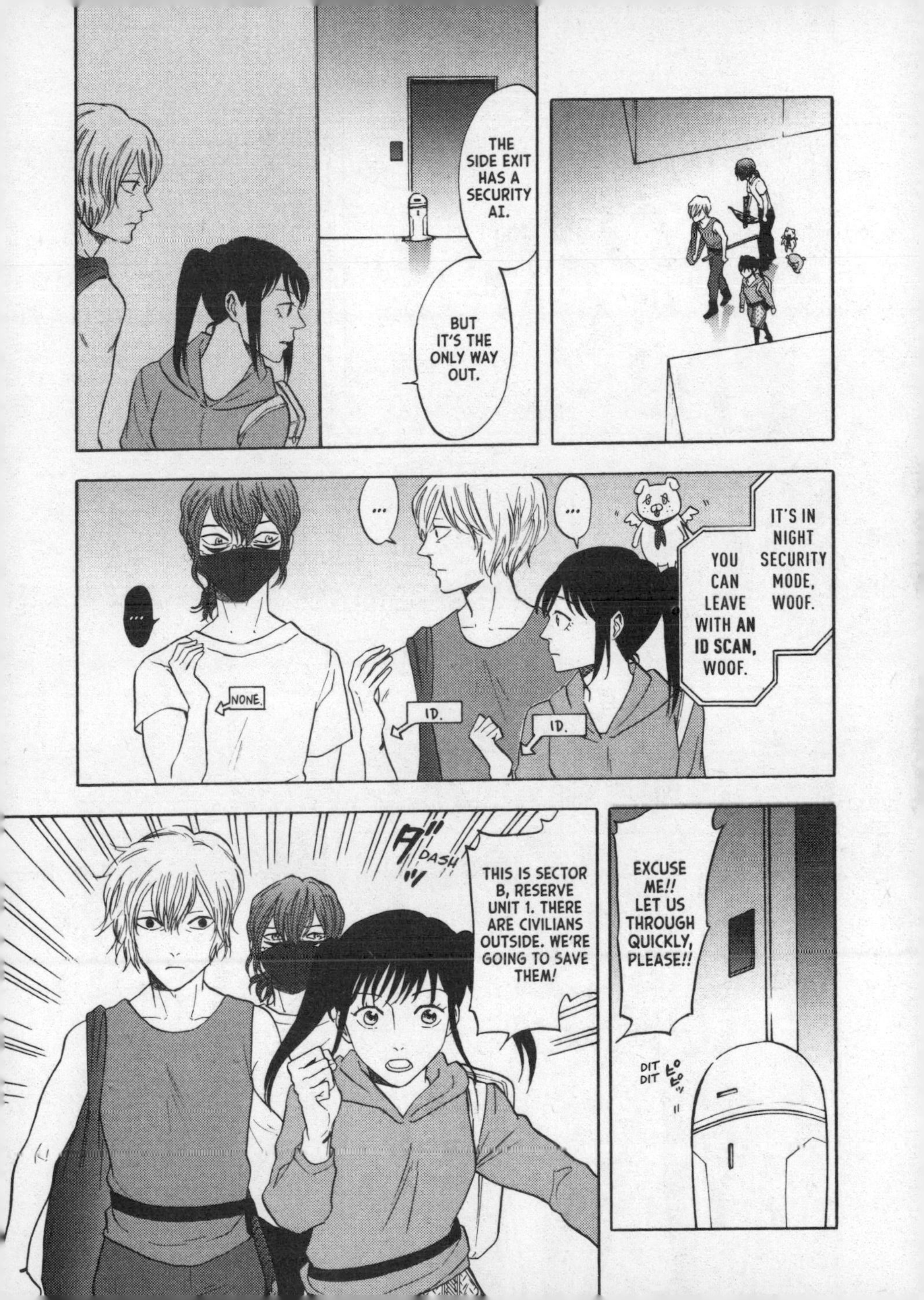
THE SIDE EXIT HAS A SECURITY AI.
BUT IT'S THE ONLY WAY OUT.
IT'S IN NIGHT SECURITY MODE, WOOF.
YOU CAN LEAVE WITH AN ID SCAN, WOOF.
...
...
...
ID.
ID.
NONE.
EXCUSE ME!! LET US THROUGH QUICKLY, PLEASE!!
DIT DIT
THIS IS SECTOR B, RESERVE UNIT 1. THERE ARE CIVILIANS OUTSIDE. WE'RE GOING TO SAVE THEM!
DASH

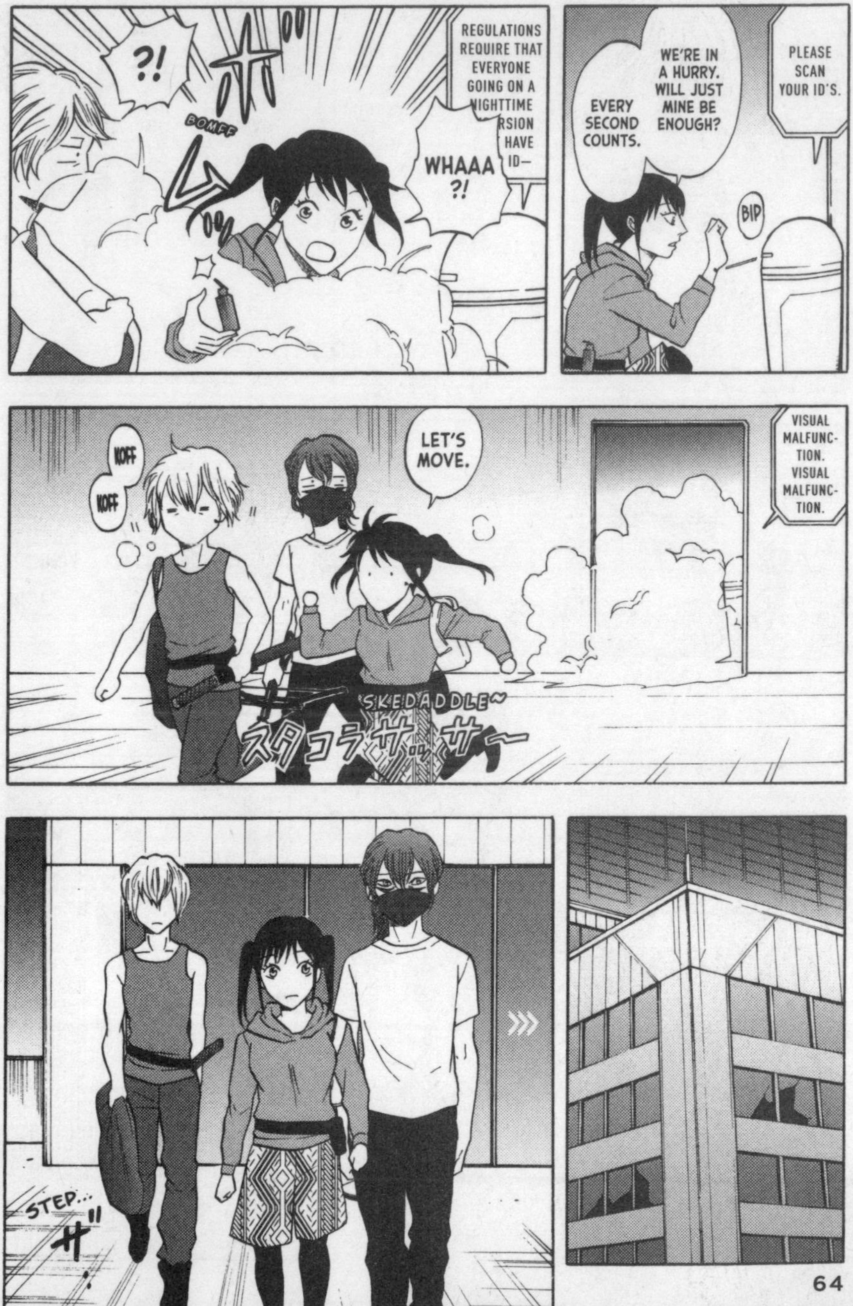
PLEASE SCAN YOUR ID'S.
WE'RE IN A HURRY. WILL JUST MINE BE ENOUGH?
EVERY SECOND COUNTS.
BIP
REGULATIONS REQUIRE THAT EVERYONE GOING ON A NIGHTTIME RSION HAVE ID—
WHAAA ?!
?!
BOMFF
VISUAL MALFUNCTION. VISUAL MALFUNCTION.
LET'S MOVE.
KOFF
KOFF
SKEDADDLE~
スタコラサッサ~
STEP...

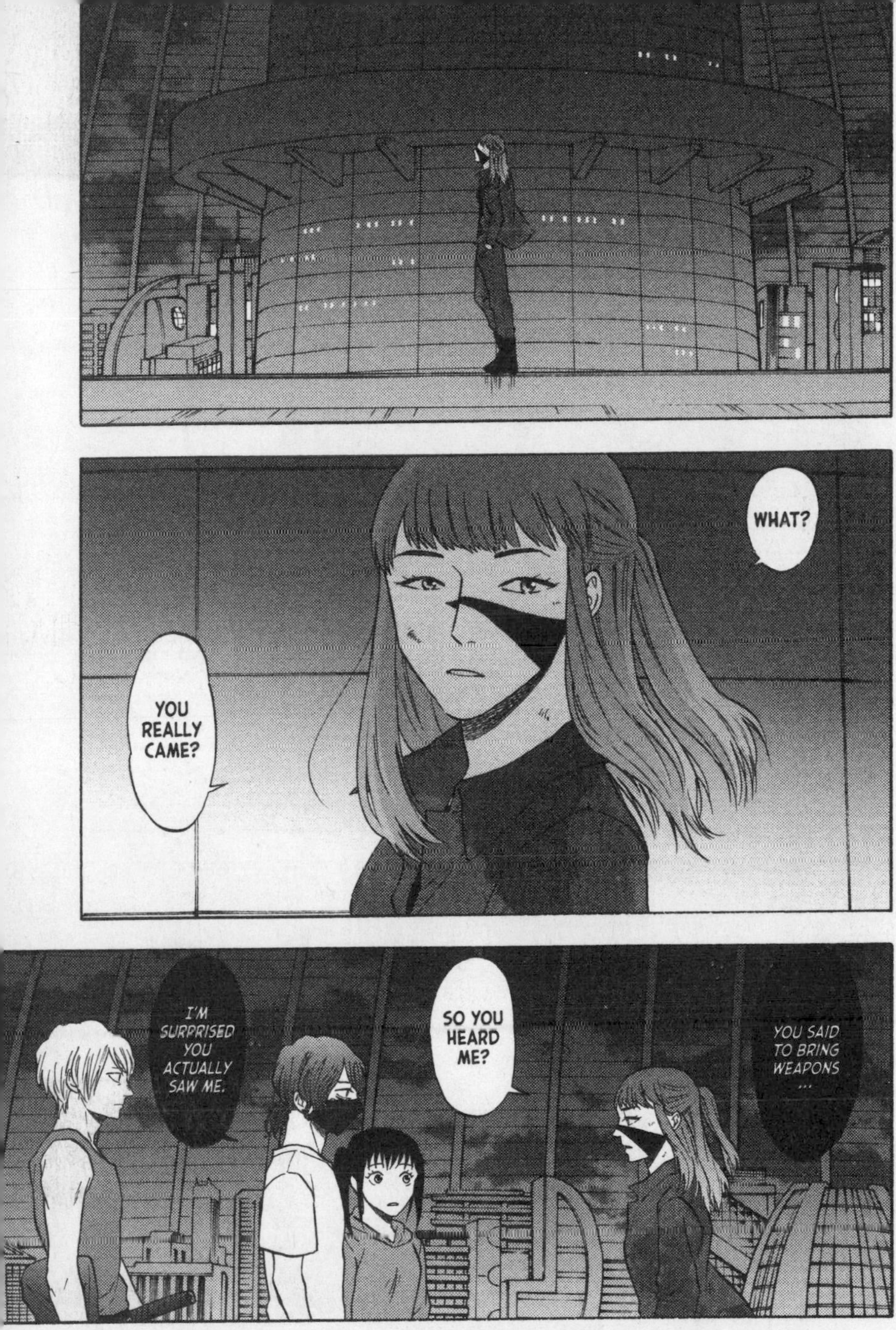
WHAT?
YOU REALLY CAME?
YOU SAID TO BRING WEAPONS ...
SO YOU HEARD ME?
I'M SURPRISED YOU ACTUALLY SAW ME.

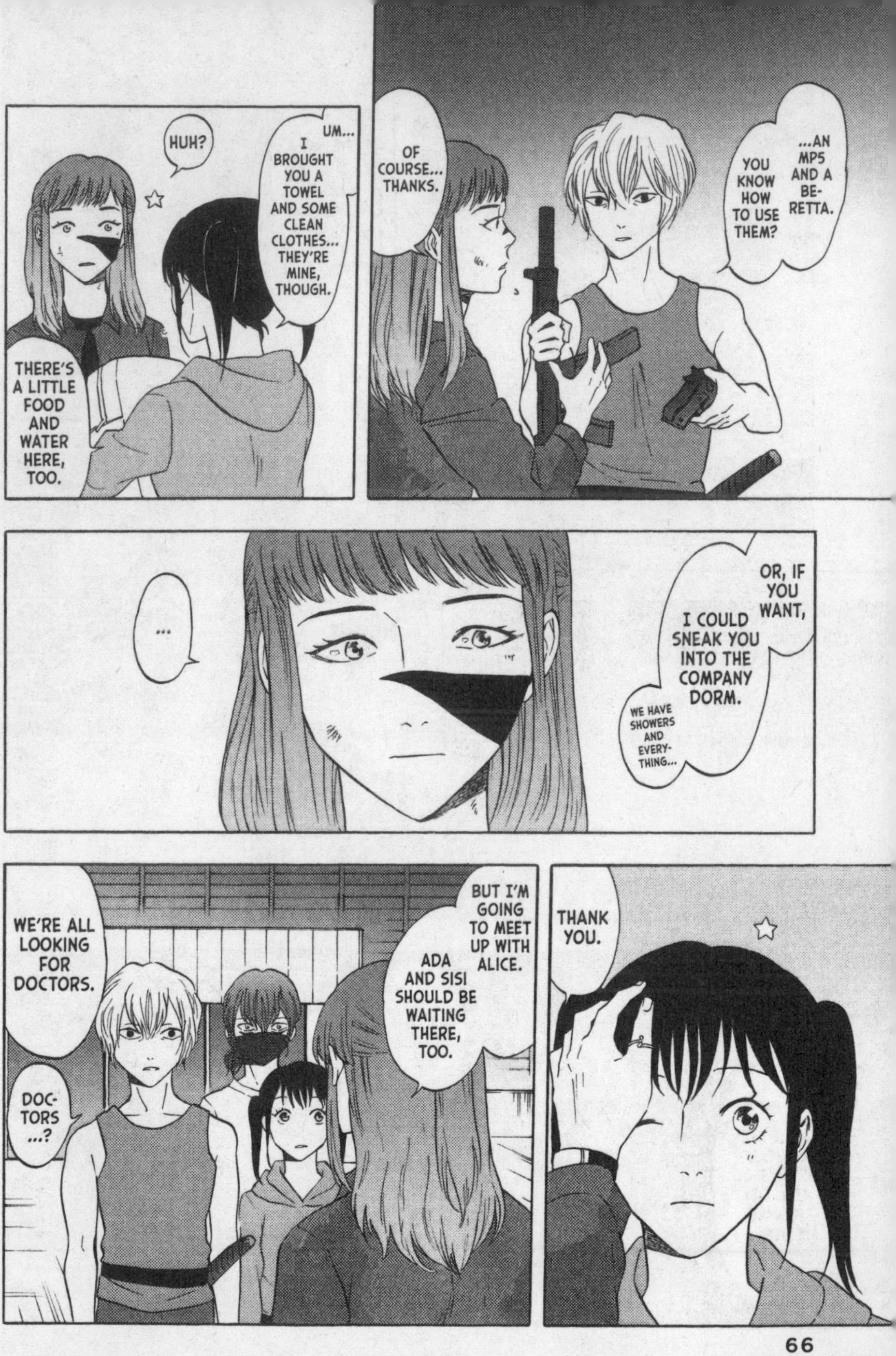
...AN MP5 AND A BE-RETTA.
YOU KNOW HOW TO USE THEM?
OF COURSE... THANKS.
UM... I BROUGHT YOU A TOWEL AND SOME CLEAN CLOTHES... THEY'RE MINE, THOUGH.
HUH?
THERE'S A LITTLE FOOD AND WATER HERE, TOO.
OR, IF YOU WANT, I COULD SNEAK YOU INTO THE COMPANY DORM.
WE HAVE SHOWERS AND EVERYTHING...
...
THANK YOU.
BUT I'M GOING TO MEET UP WITH ALICE.
ADA AND SISI SHOULD BE WAITING THERE, TOO.
WE'RE ALL LOOKING FOR DOCTORS.
DOC-TORS...?

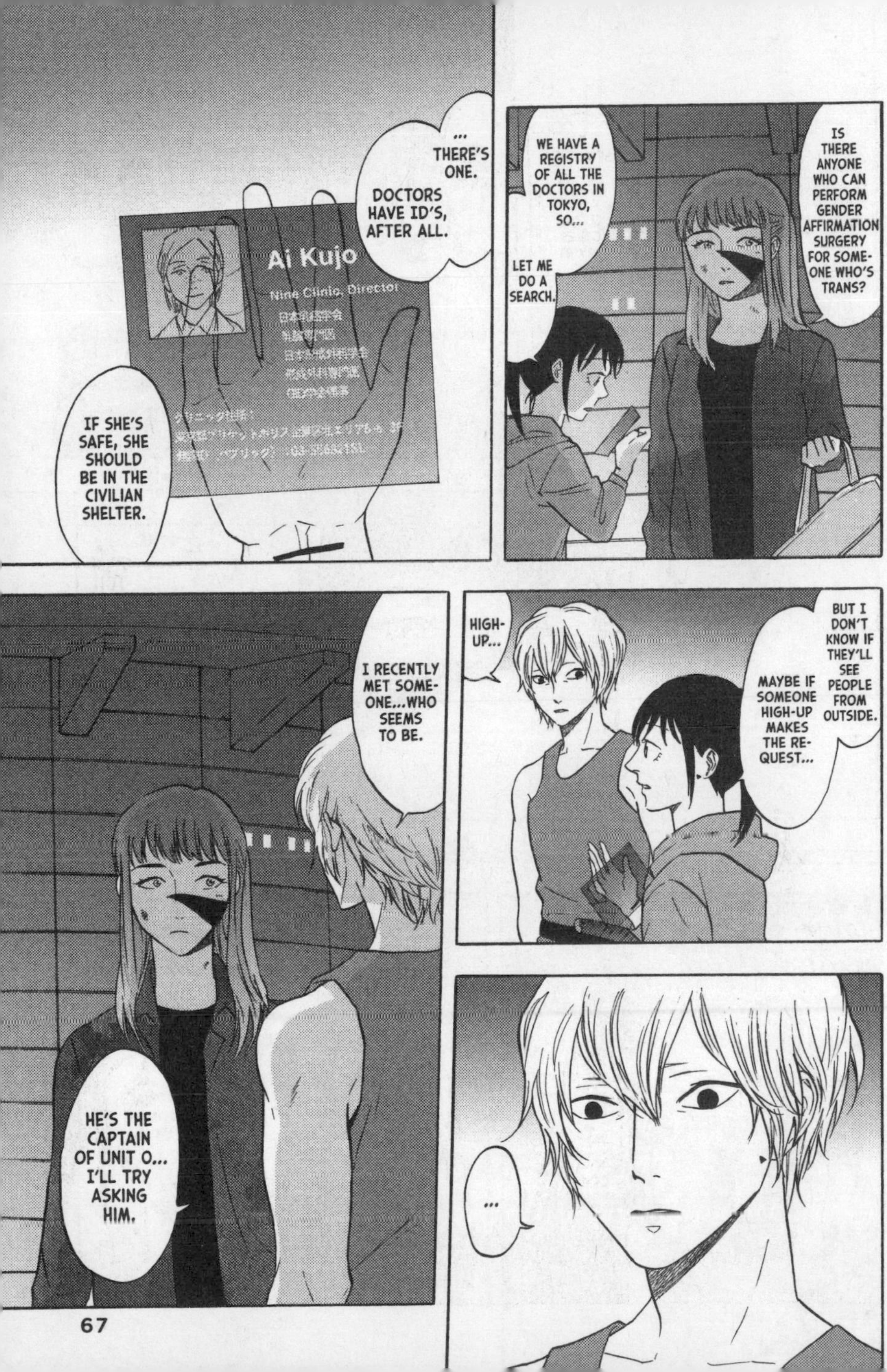
IS THERE ANYONE WHO CAN PERFORM GENDER AFFIRMATION SURGERY FOR SOME-ONE WHO'S TRANS?
WE HAVE A REGISTRY OF ALL THE DOCTORS IN TOKYO, SO...
LET ME DO A SEARCH.
... THERE'S ONE.
DOCTORS HAVE ID'S, AFTER ALL.
Ai Kujo
Nine Clinic, Director
IF SHE'S SAFE, SHE SHOULD BE IN THE CIVILIAN SHELTER.
BUT I DON'T KNOW IF THEY'LL SEE PEOPLE FROM OUTSIDE.
MAYBE IF SOMEONE HIGH-UP MAKES THE RE-QUEST...
HIGH-UP...
...
I RECENTLY MET SOME-ONE...WHO SEEMS TO BE.
HE'S THE CAPTAIN OF UNIT 0... I'LL TRY ASKING HIM.

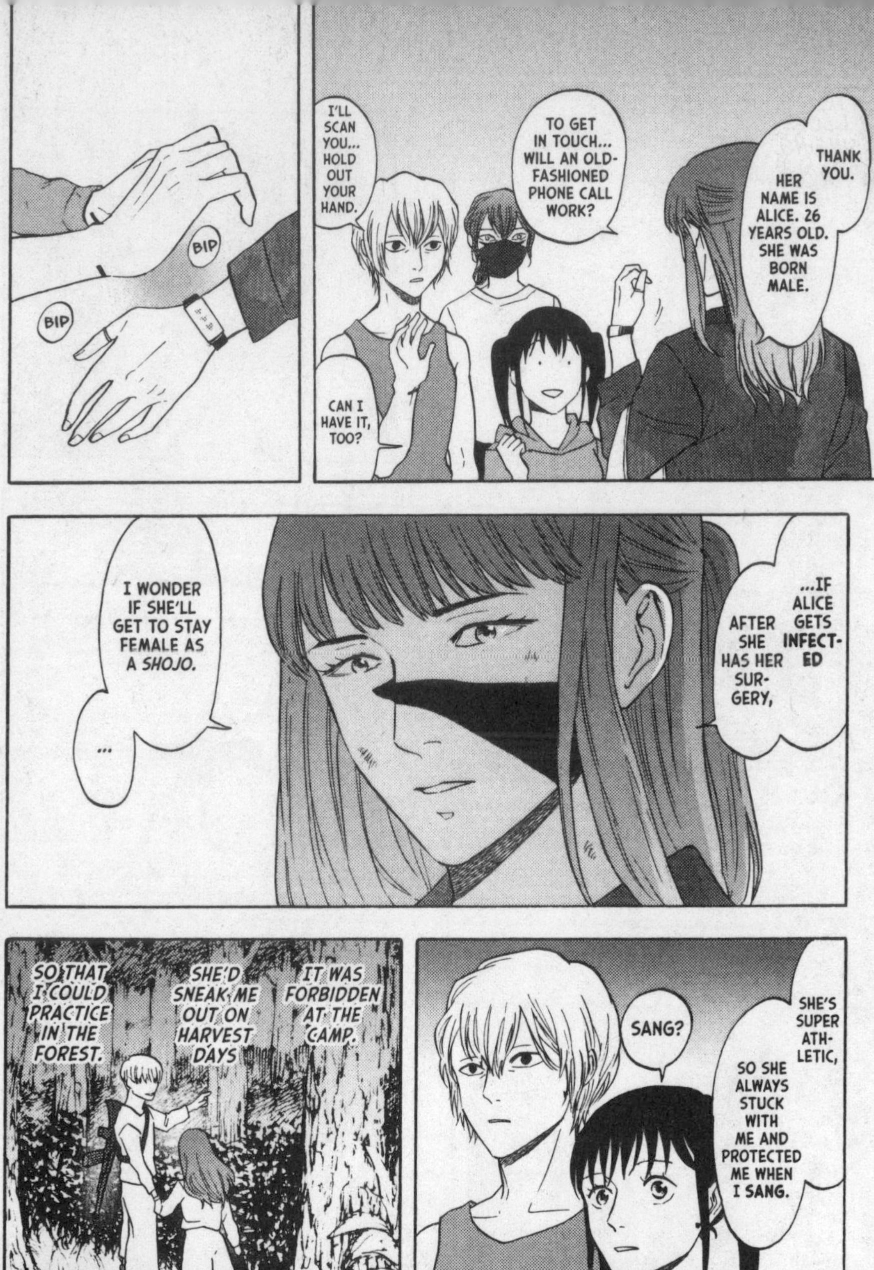
THANK YOU.
HER NAME IS ALICE. 26 YEARS OLD. SHE WAS BORN MALE.
TO GET IN TOUCH... WILL AN OLD-FASHIONED PHONE CALL WORK?
I'LL SCAN YOU... HOLD OUT YOUR HAND.
CAN I HAVE IT, TOO?
BIP
BIP
...IF ALICE GETS **INFECTED** AFTER SHE HAS HER SURGERY,
I WONDER IF SHE'LL GET TO STAY FEMALE AS A *SHOJO*.
...
SHE'S SUPER ATHLETIC, SO SHE ALWAYS STUCK WITH ME AND PROTECTED ME WHEN I SANG.
SANG?
IT WAS FORBIDDEN AT THE CAMP.
SHE'D SNEAK ME OUT ON HARVEST DAYS
SO THAT I COULD PRACTICE IN THE FOREST.

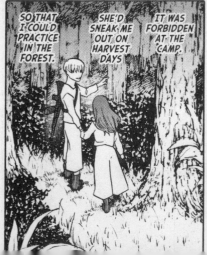

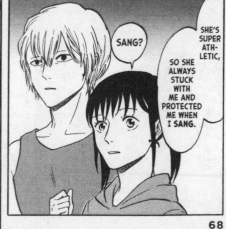

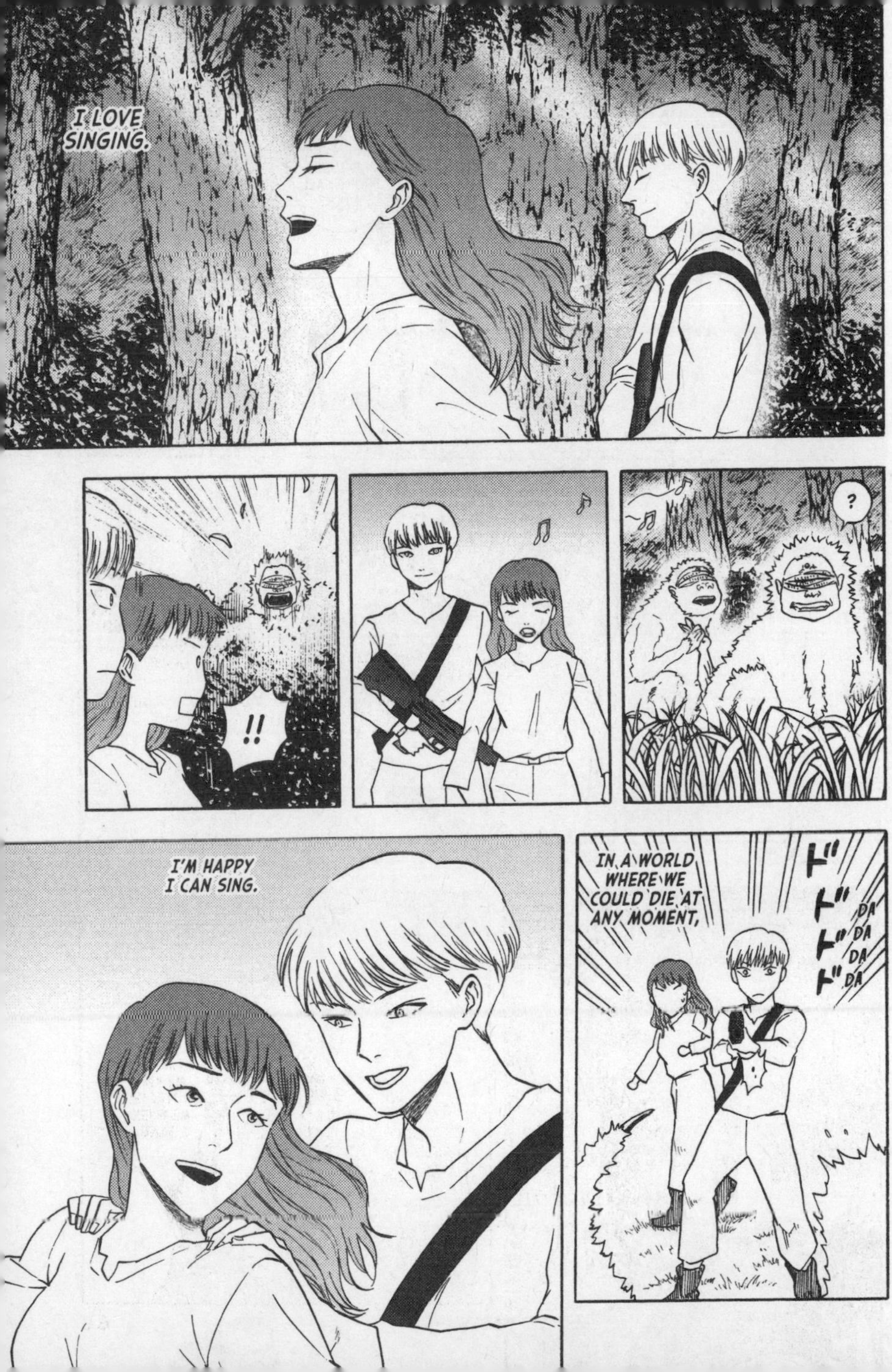
I LOVE SINGING.
?
!!
IN A WORLD WHERE WE COULD DIE AT ANY MOMENT,
ドドドド
DA DA DA DA
I'M HAPPY I CAN SING.

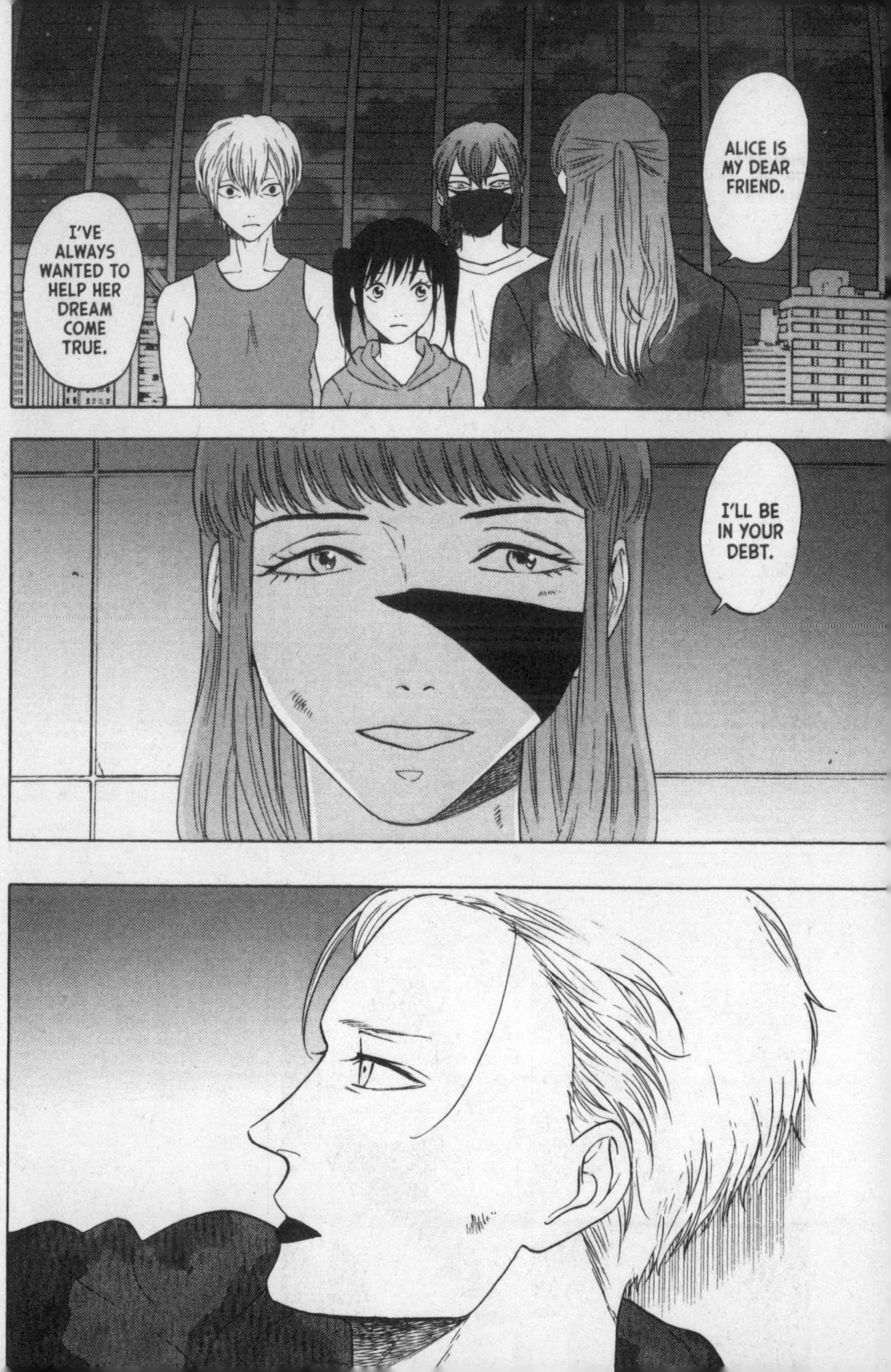
ALICE IS MY DEAR FRIEND.
I'VE ALWAYS WANTED TO HELP HER DREAM COME TRUE.
I'LL BE IN YOUR DEBT.

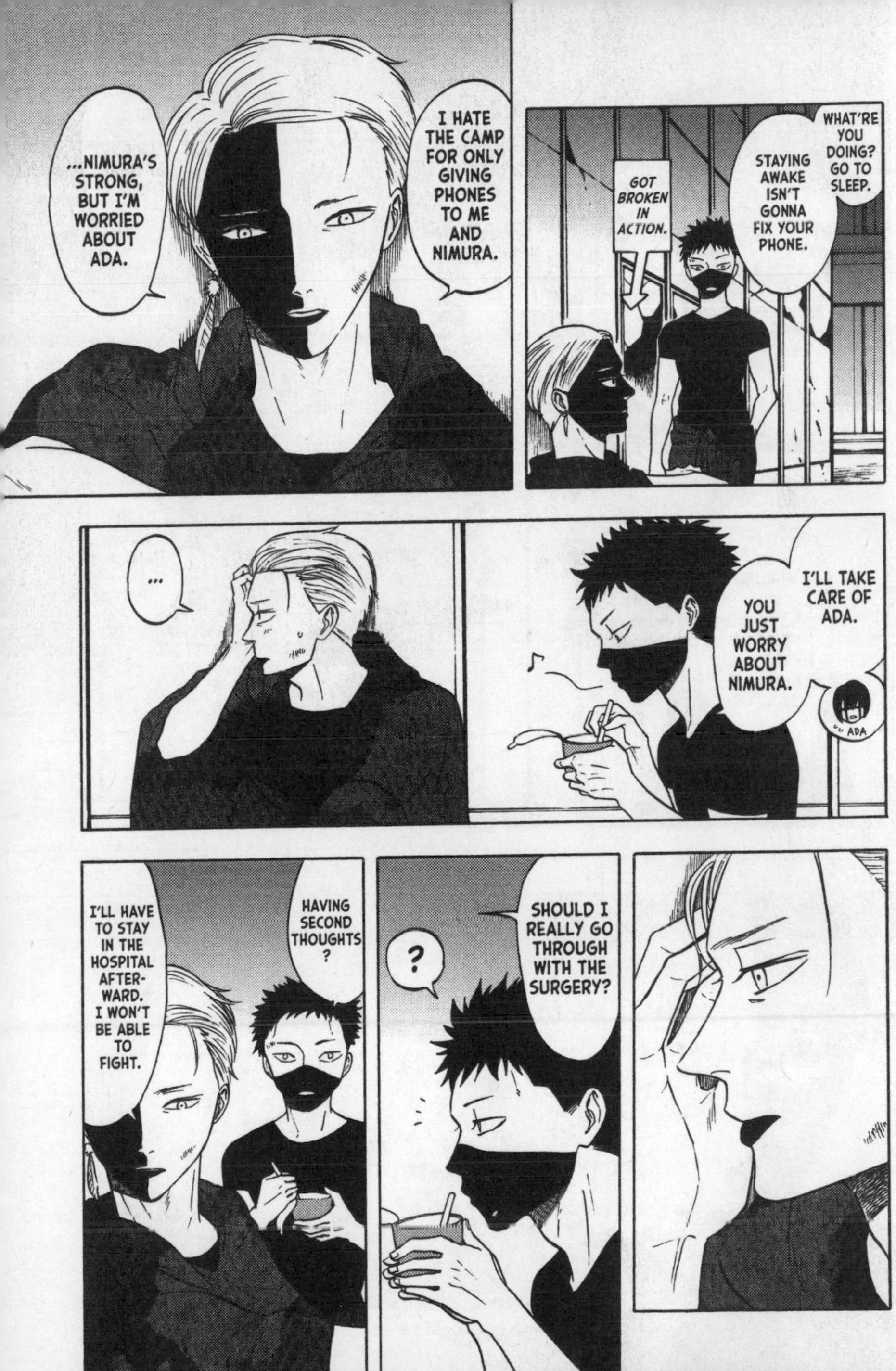
WHAT'RE YOU DOING? GO TO SLEEP.
STAYING AWAKE ISN'T GONNA FIX YOUR PHONE.
GOT BROKEN IN ACTION.
I HATE THE CAMP FOR ONLY GIVING PHONES TO ME AND NIMURA.
...NIMURA'S STRONG, BUT I'M WORRIED ABOUT ADA.
I'LL TAKE CARE OF ADA.
YOU JUST WORRY ABOUT NIMURA.
ADA
...
SHOULD I REALLY GO THROUGH WITH THE SURGERY?
?
HAVING SECOND THOUGHTS?
I'LL HAVE TO STAY IN THE HOSPITAL AFTER-WARD. I WON'T BE ABLE TO FIGHT.

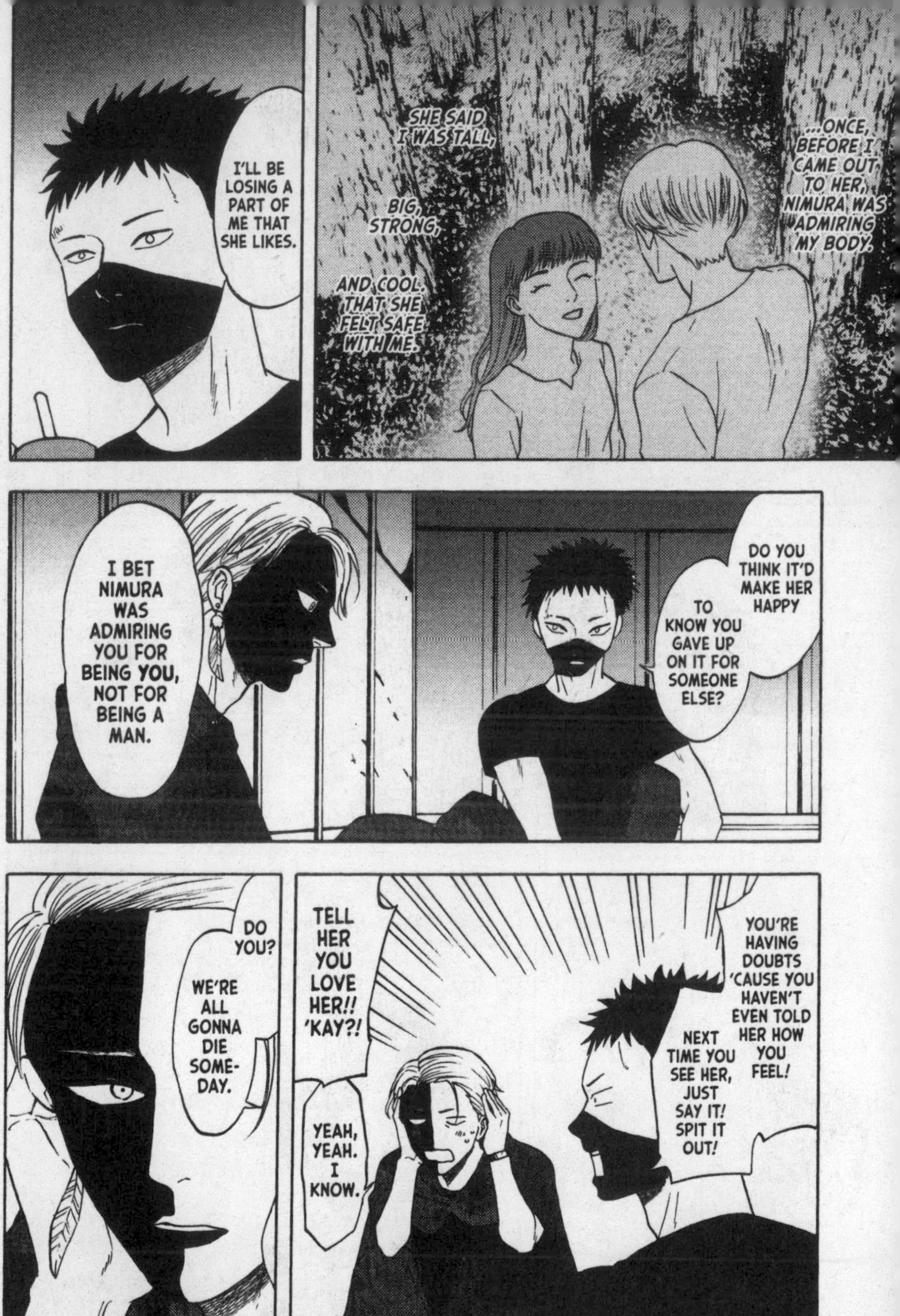
...ONCE, BEFORE I CAME OUT TO HER, NIMURA WAS ADMIRING MY BODY.
SHE SAID I WAS TALL,
BIG, STRONG,
AND COOL. THAT SHE FELT SAFE WITH ME.
I'LL BE LOSING A PART OF ME THAT SHE LIKES.
DO YOU THINK IT'D MAKE HER HAPPY
TO KNOW YOU GAVE UP ON IT FOR SOMEONE ELSE?
I BET NIMURA WAS ADMIRING YOU FOR BEING YOU, NOT FOR BEING A MAN.
YOU'RE HAVING DOUBTS 'CAUSE YOU HAVEN'T EVEN TOLD HER HOW YOU FEEL!
NEXT TIME YOU SEE HER, JUST SAY IT! SPIT IT OUT!
TELL HER YOU LOVE HER!! 'KAY?!
YEAH, YEAH. I KNOW.
DO YOU?
WE'RE ALL GONNA DIE SOME-DAY.

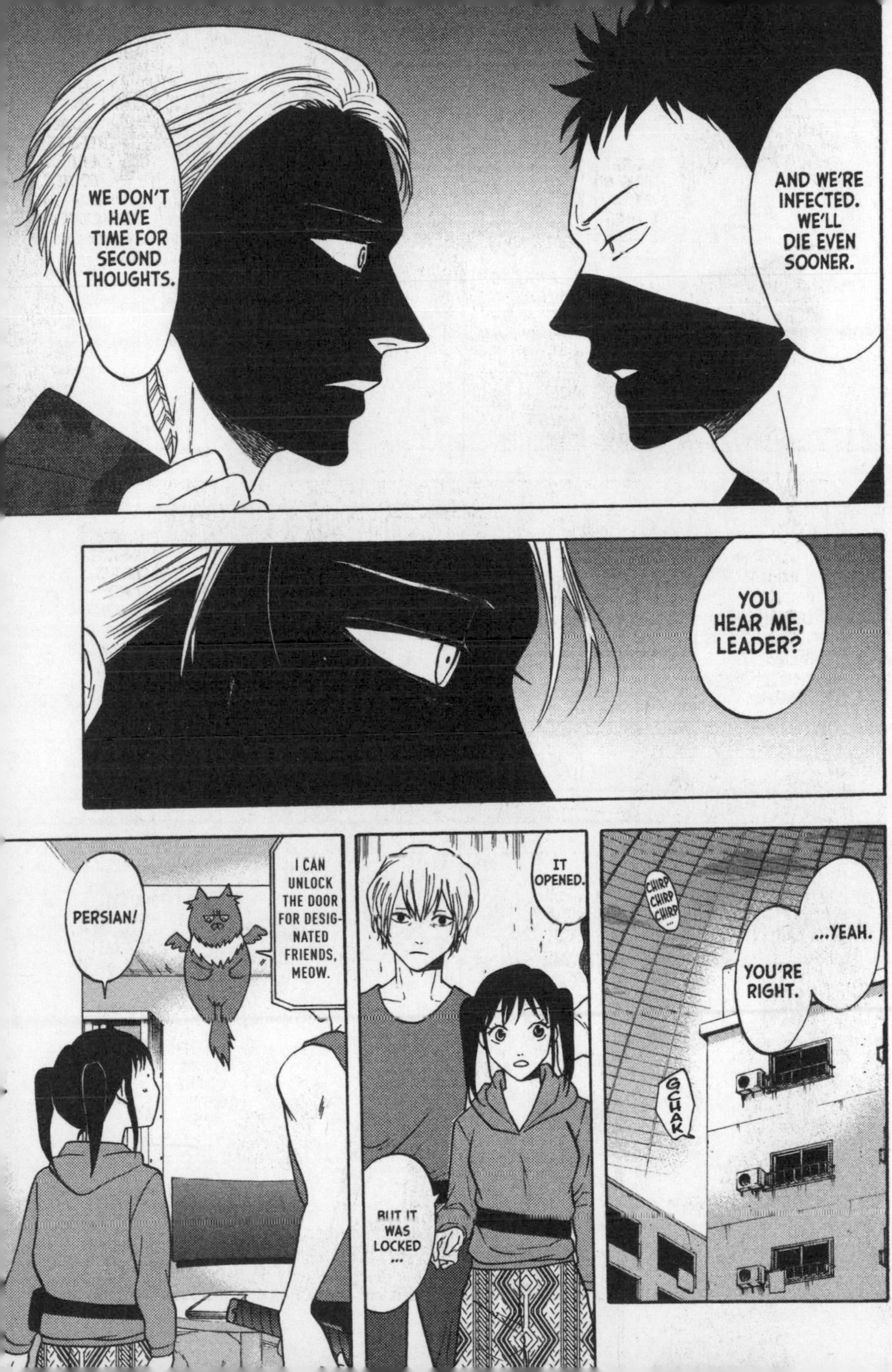
AND WE'RE INFECTED. WE'LL DIE EVEN SOONER.
WE DON'T HAVE TIME FOR SECOND THOUGHTS.
YOU HEAR ME, LEADER?
...YEAH.
CHIRP CHIRP CHIRP...
YOU'RE RIGHT.
GCHAK
IT OPENED.
BUT IT WAS LOCKED...
I CAN UNLOCK THE DOOR FOR DESIGNATED FRIENDS, MEOW.
PERSIAN!

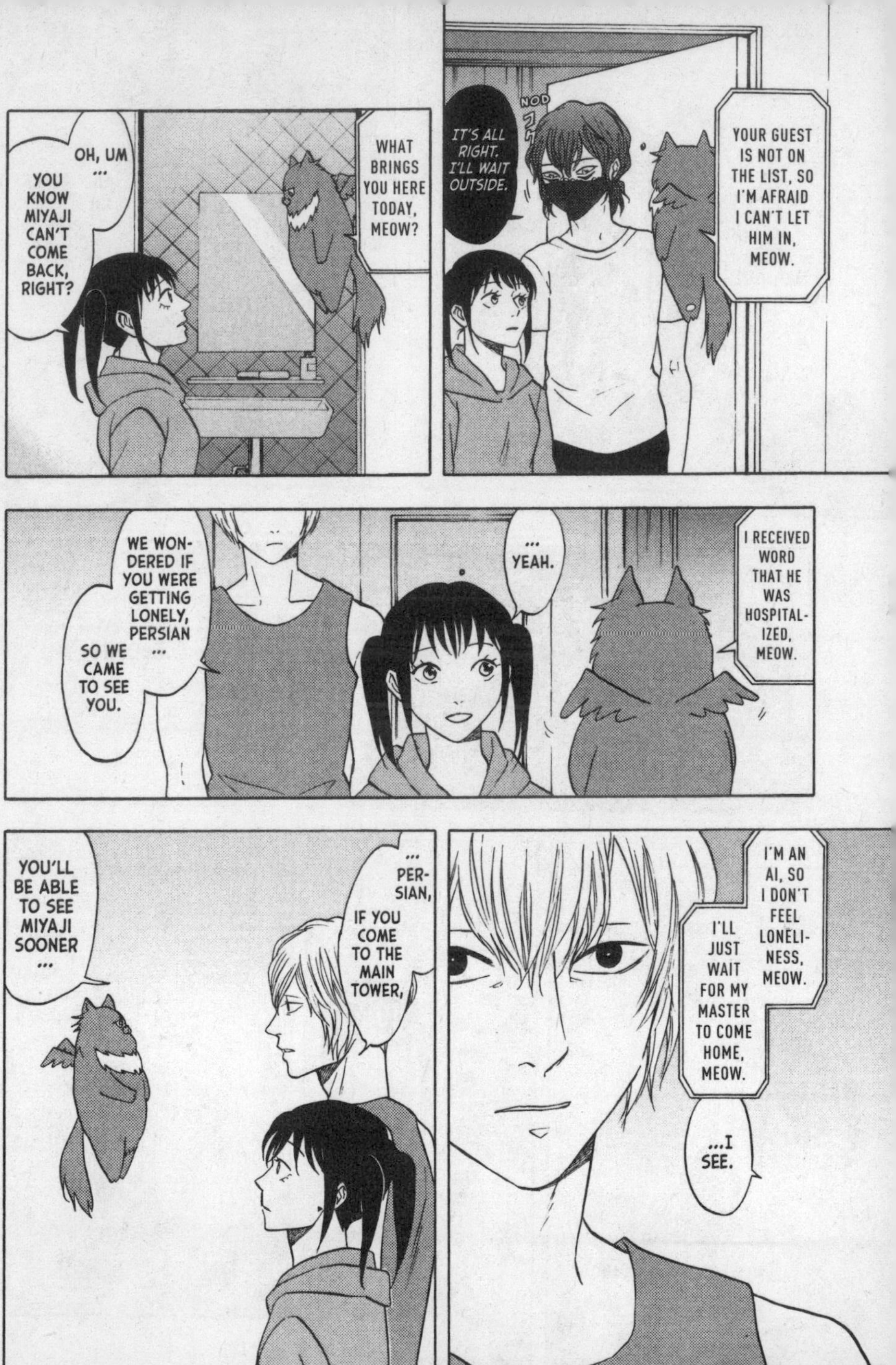
YOUR GUEST IS NOT ON THE LIST, SO I'M AFRAID I CAN'T LET HIM IN, MEOW.
NOD
IT'S ALL RIGHT. I'LL WAIT OUTSIDE.
WHAT BRINGS YOU HERE TODAY, MEOW?
OH, UM ...
YOU KNOW MIYAJI CAN'T COME BACK, RIGHT?
I RECEIVED WORD THAT HE WAS HOSPITAL-IZED, MEOW.
... YEAH.
WE WON-DERED IF YOU WERE GETTING LONELY, PERSIAN ...
SO WE CAME TO SEE YOU.
I'M AN AI, SO I DON'T FEEL LONELI-NESS, MEOW.
I'LL JUST WAIT FOR MY MASTER TO COME HOME, MEOW.
...I SEE.
... PER-SIAN, IF YOU COME TO THE MAIN TOWER,
YOU'LL BE ABLE TO SEE MIYAJI SOONER ...

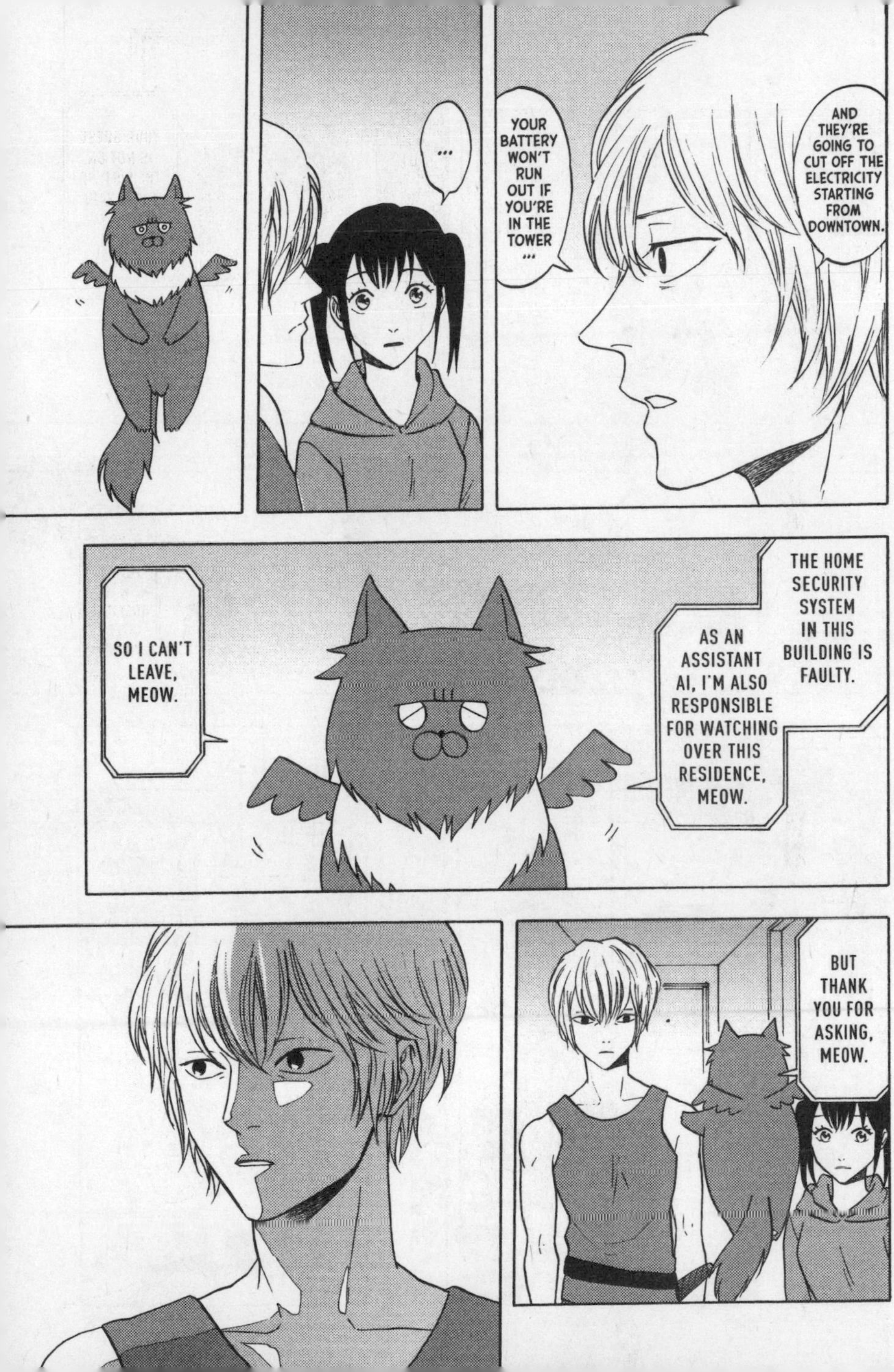
AND THEY'RE GOING TO CUT OFF THE ELECTRICITY STARTING FROM DOWNTOWN.
YOUR BATTERY WON'T RUN OUT IF YOU'RE IN THE TOWER...
...
THE HOME SECURITY SYSTEM IN THIS BUILDING IS FAULTY.
AS AN ASSISTANT AI, I'M ALSO RESPONSIBLE FOR WATCHING OVER THIS RESIDENCE, MEOW.
SO I CAN'T LEAVE, MEOW.
BUT THANK YOU FOR ASKING, MEOW.

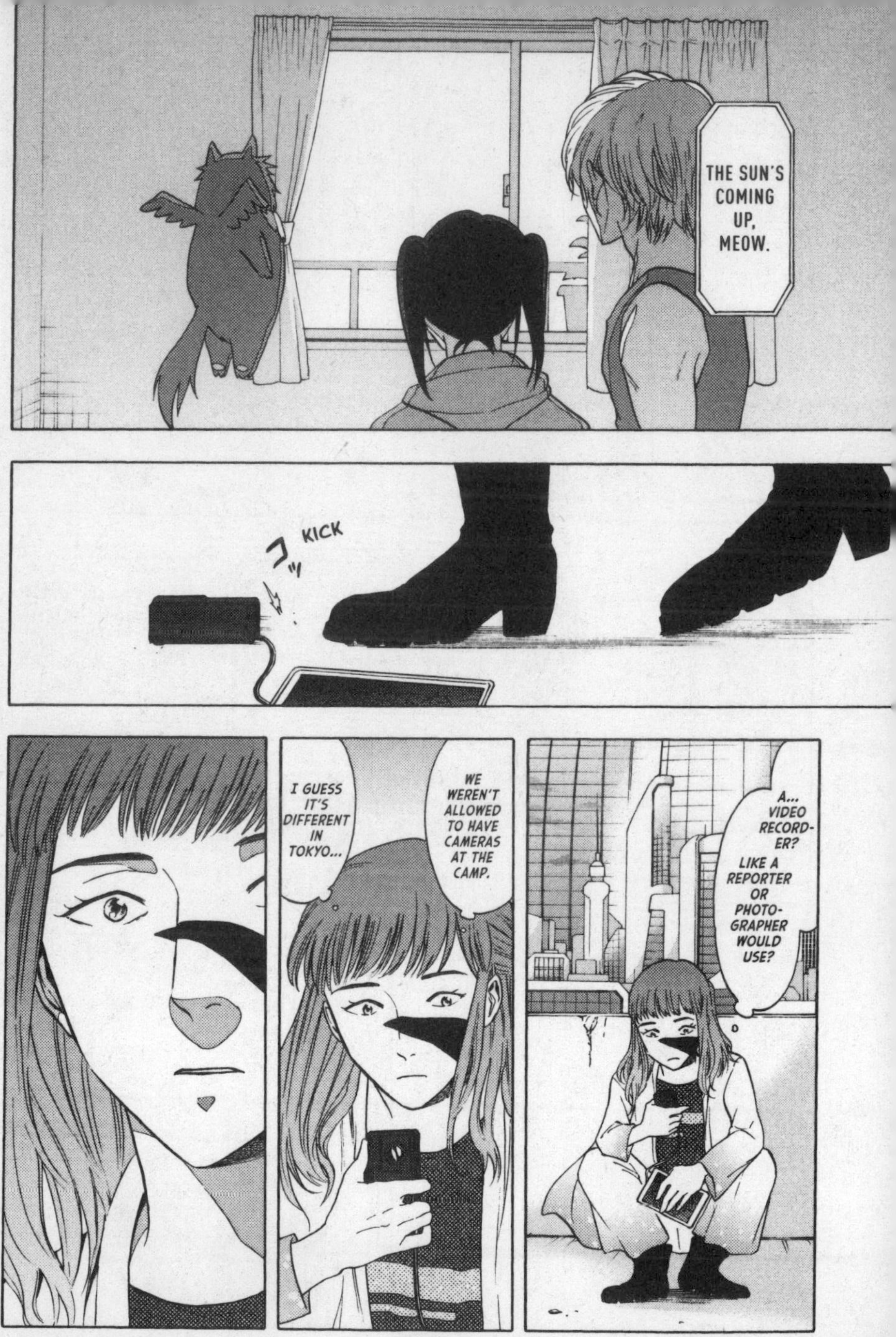
THE SUN'S COMING UP, MEOW.
ゴッ
KICK
A... VIDEO RECORDER? LIKE A REPORTER OR PHOTOGRAPHER WOULD USE?
WE WEREN'T ALLOWED TO HAVE CAMERAS AT THE CAMP.
I GUESS IT'S DIFFERENT IN TOKYO...

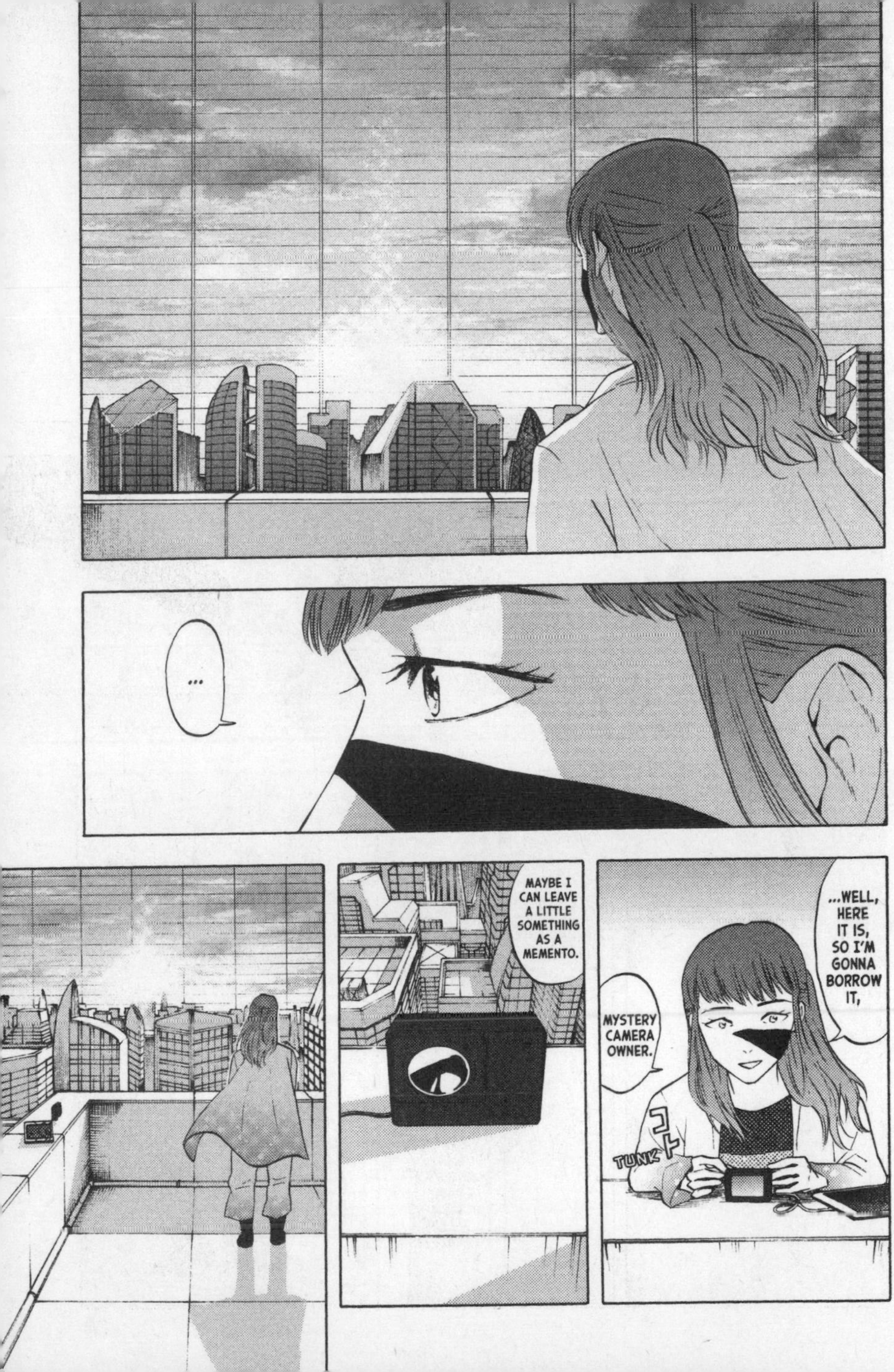
...
...WELL, HERE IT IS, SO I'M GONNA BORROW IT,
MYSTERY CAMERA OWNER.
TUNK
MAYBE I CAN LEAVE A LITTLE SOMETHING AS A MEMENTO.

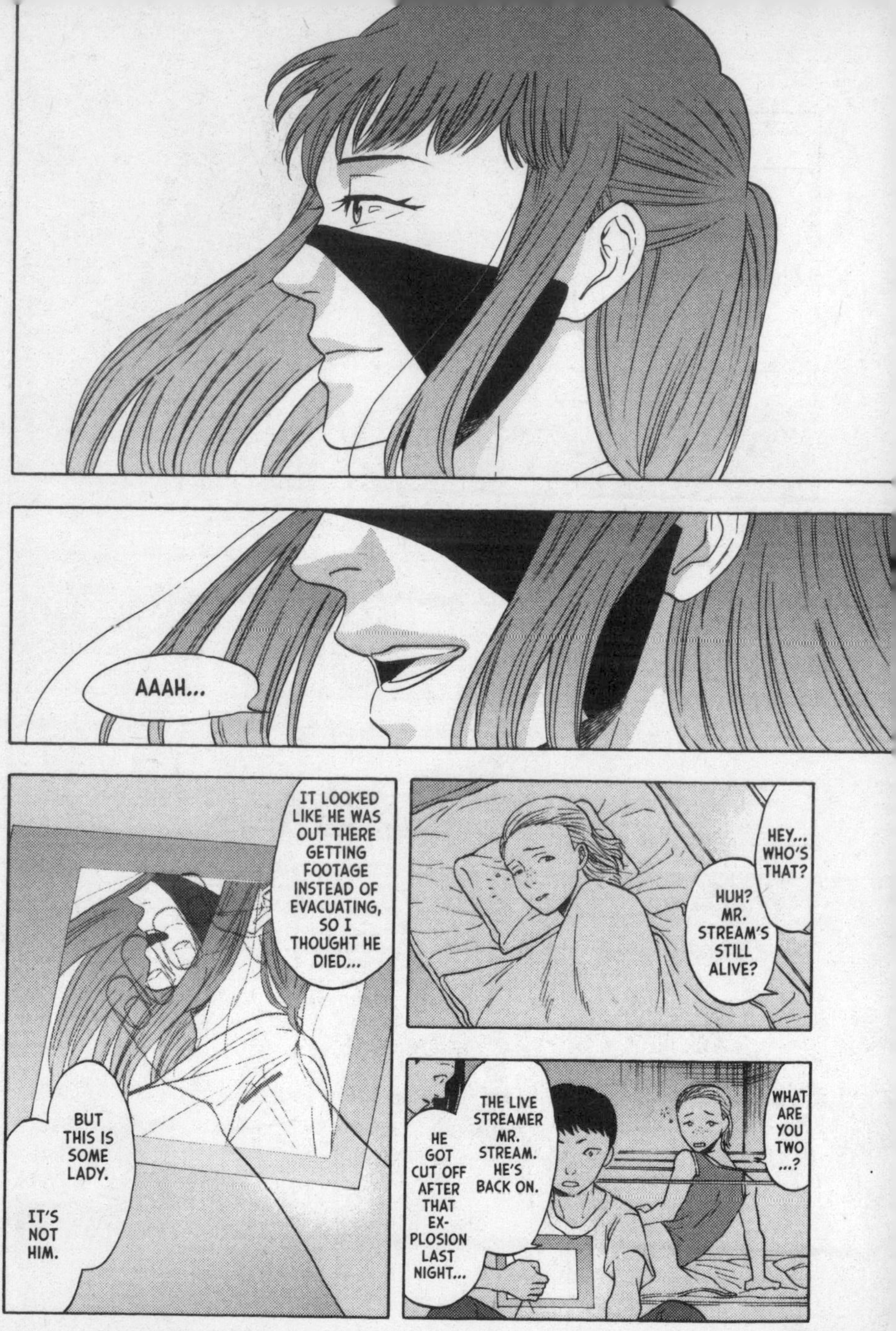
AAAH...
HEY... WHO'S THAT?
HUH? MR. STREAM'S STILL ALIVE?
WHAT ARE YOU TWO ...?
THE LIVE STREAMER MR. STREAM. HE'S BACK ON.
HE GOT CUT OFF AFTER THAT EX-PLOSION LAST NIGHT...
IT LOOKED LIKE HE WAS OUT THERE GETTING FOOTAGE INSTEAD OF EVACUATING, SO I THOUGHT HE DIED...
BUT THIS IS SOME LADY.
IT'S NOT HIM.

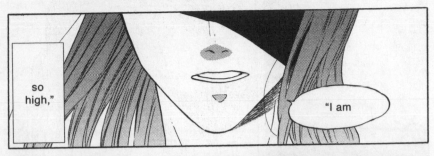

"I am so high,"

"I can hear heaven"

"Oh, but heaven,

...no, heaven don't hear me"

"I am so high, I can hear heaven"

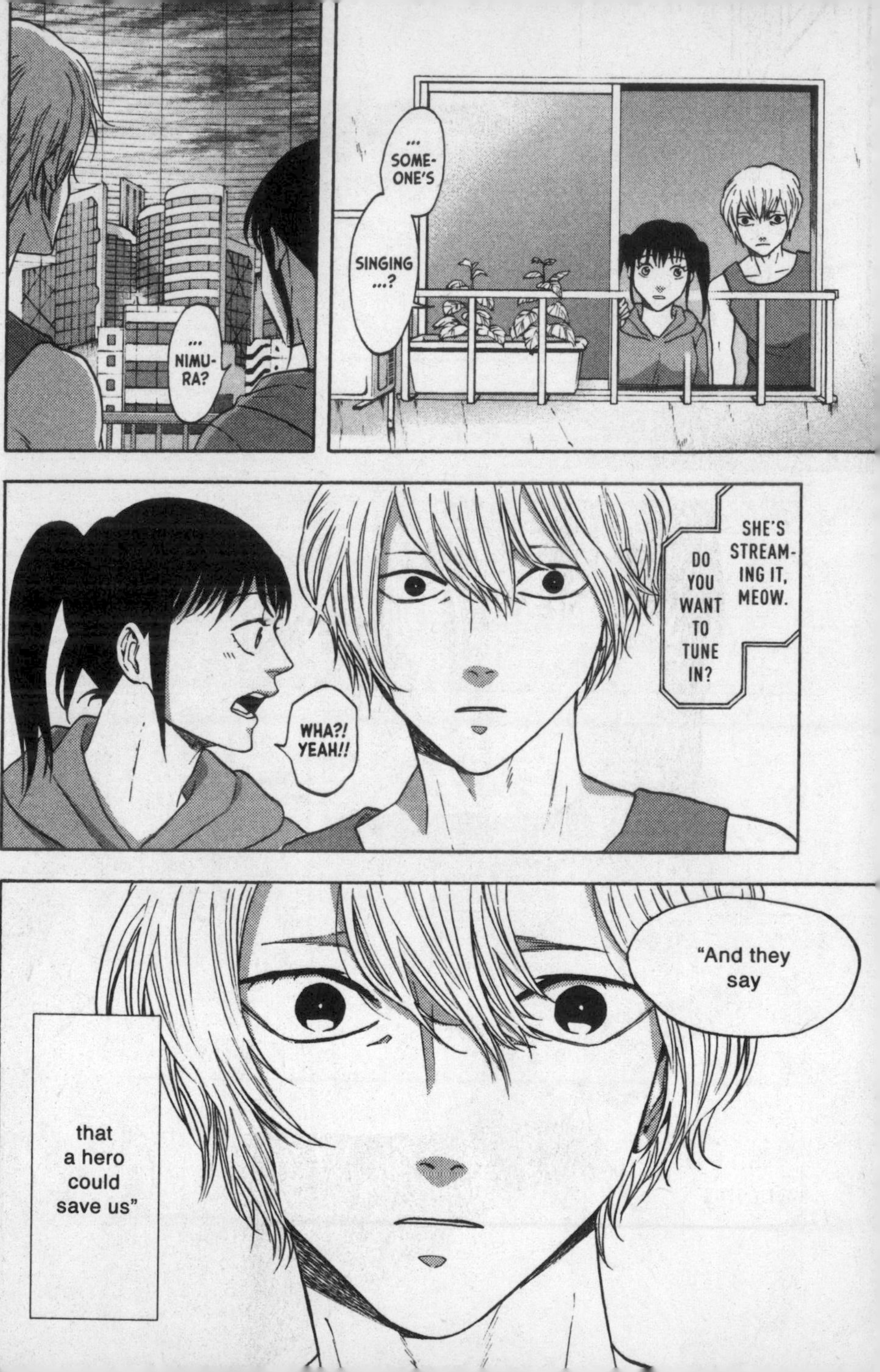
...SOME-ONE'S
SINGING...?
...NIMU-RA?
SHE'S STREAM-ING IT, MEOW.
DO YOU WANT TO TUNE IN?
WHA?! YEAH!!
"And they say
that a hero could save us"

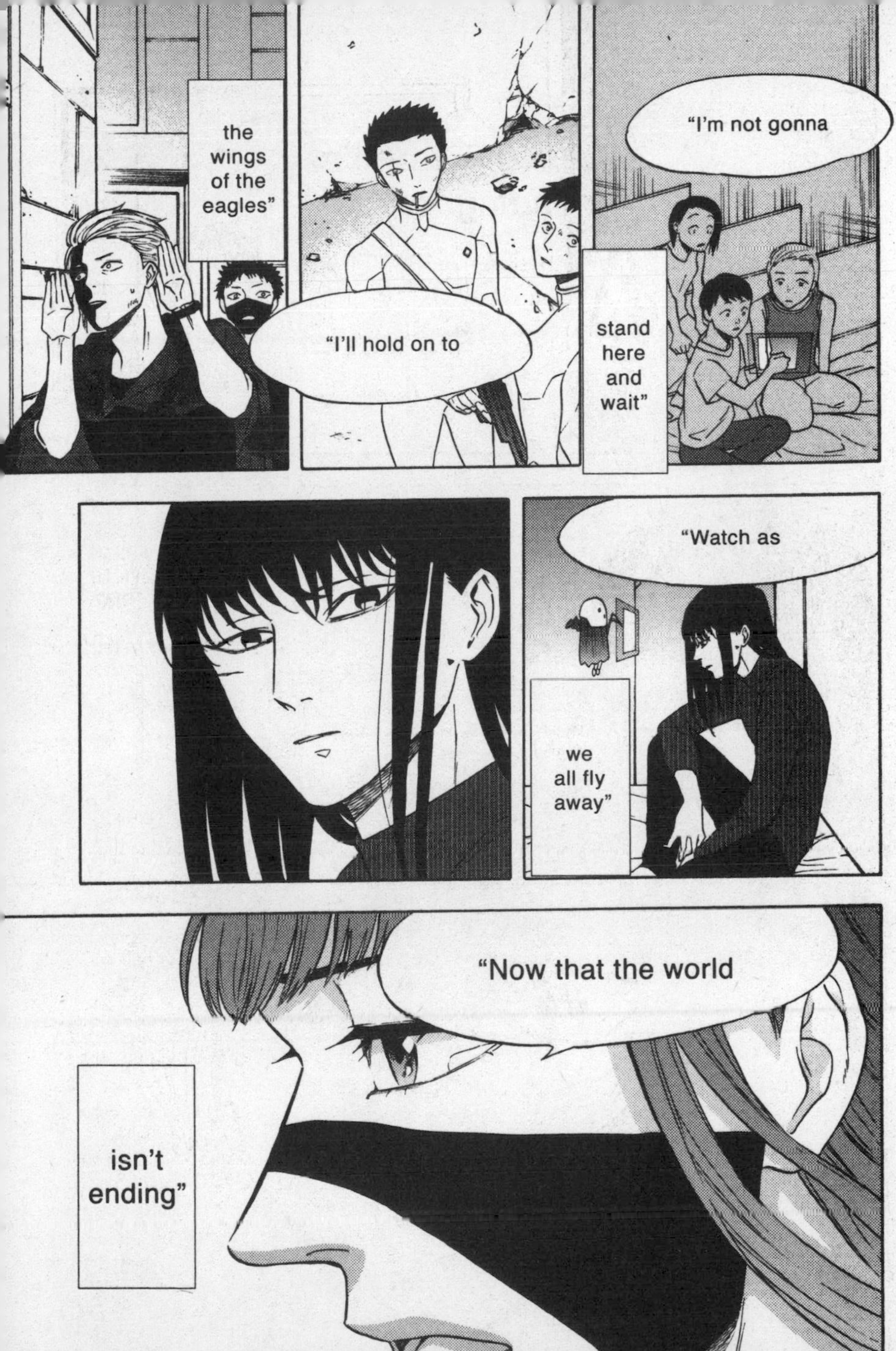
"I'm not gonna
stand here and wait"
"I'll hold on to
the wings of the eagles"
"Watch as
we all fly away"
"Now that the world
isn't ending"

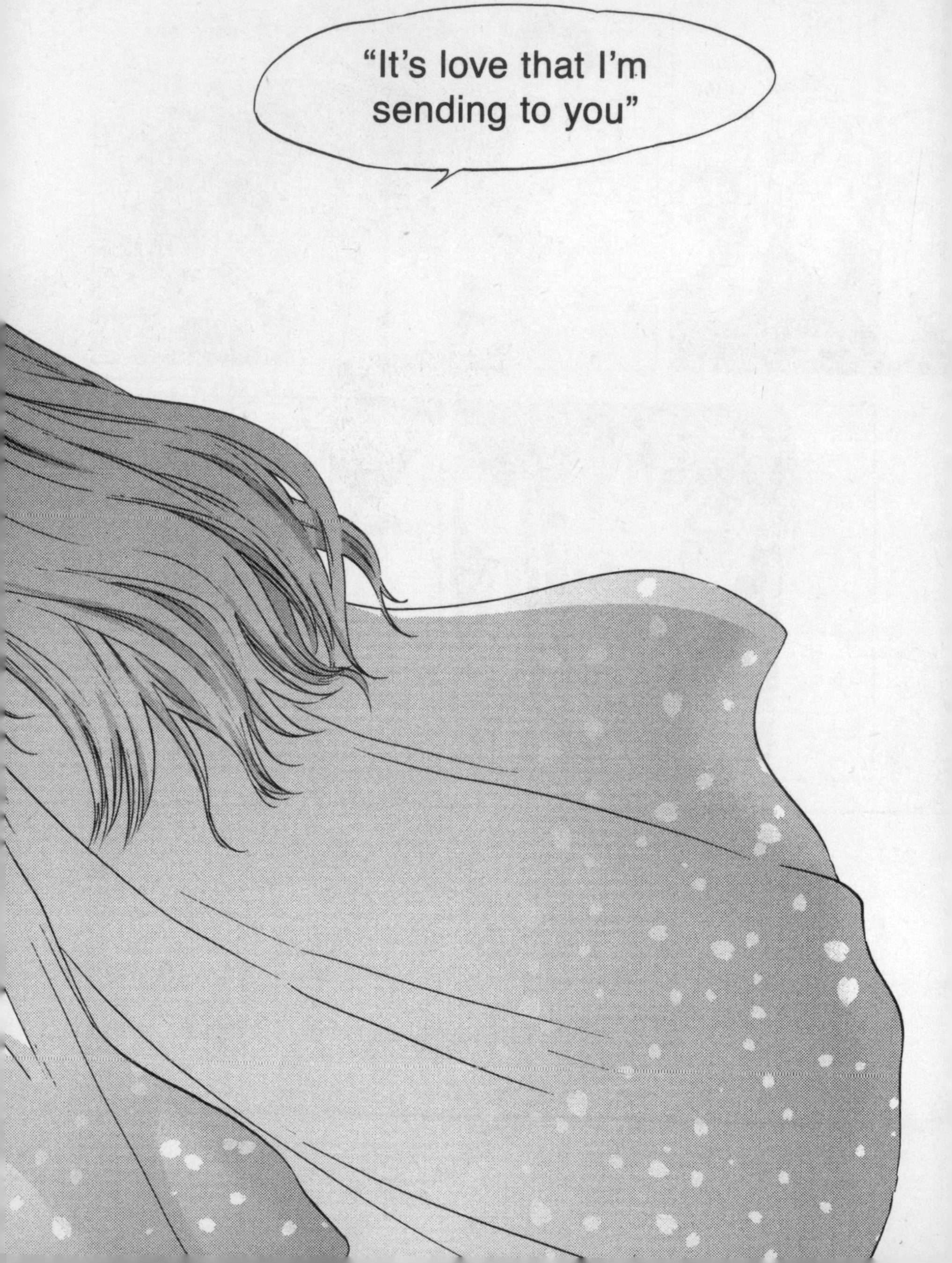
"It's love that I'm sending to you"

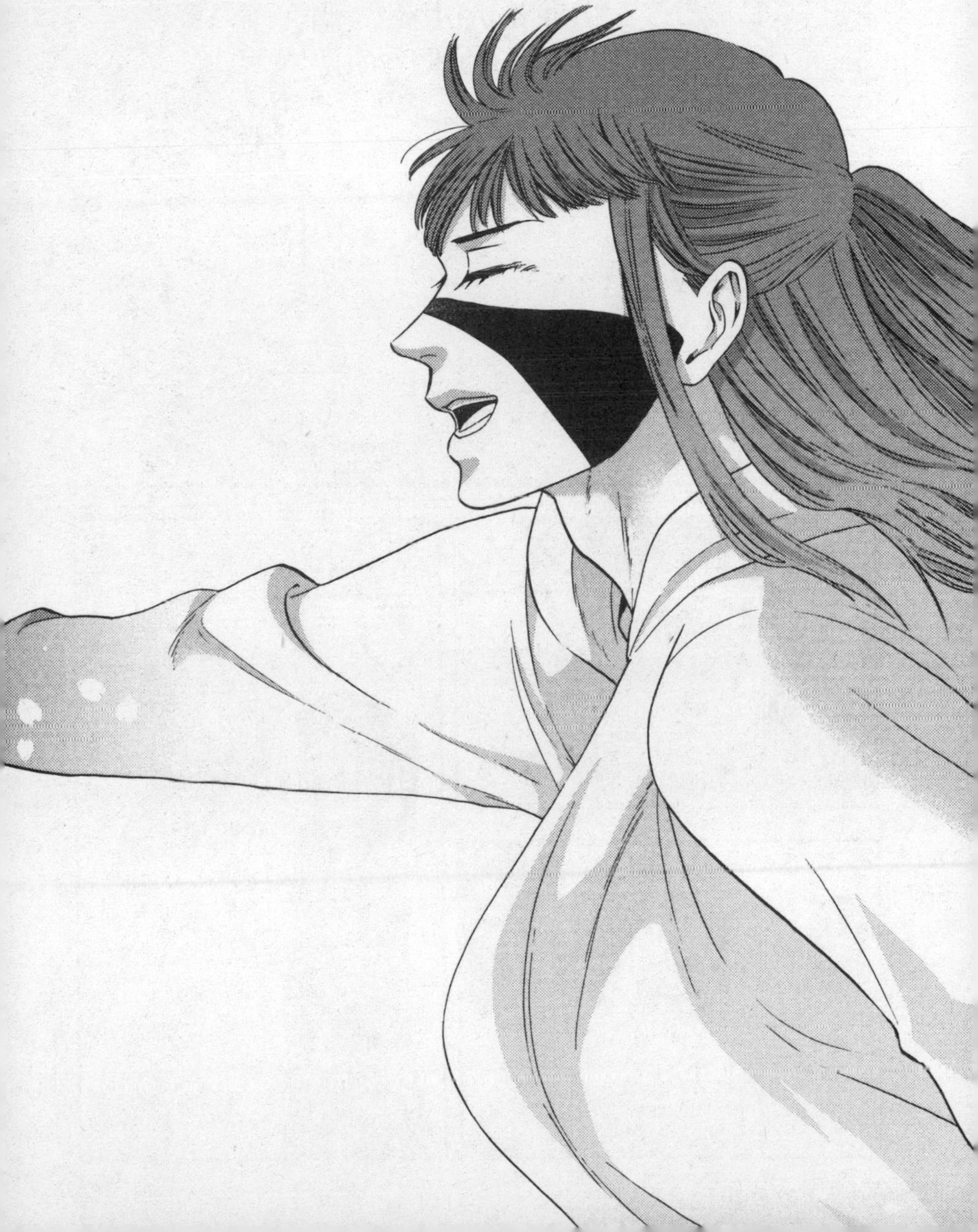

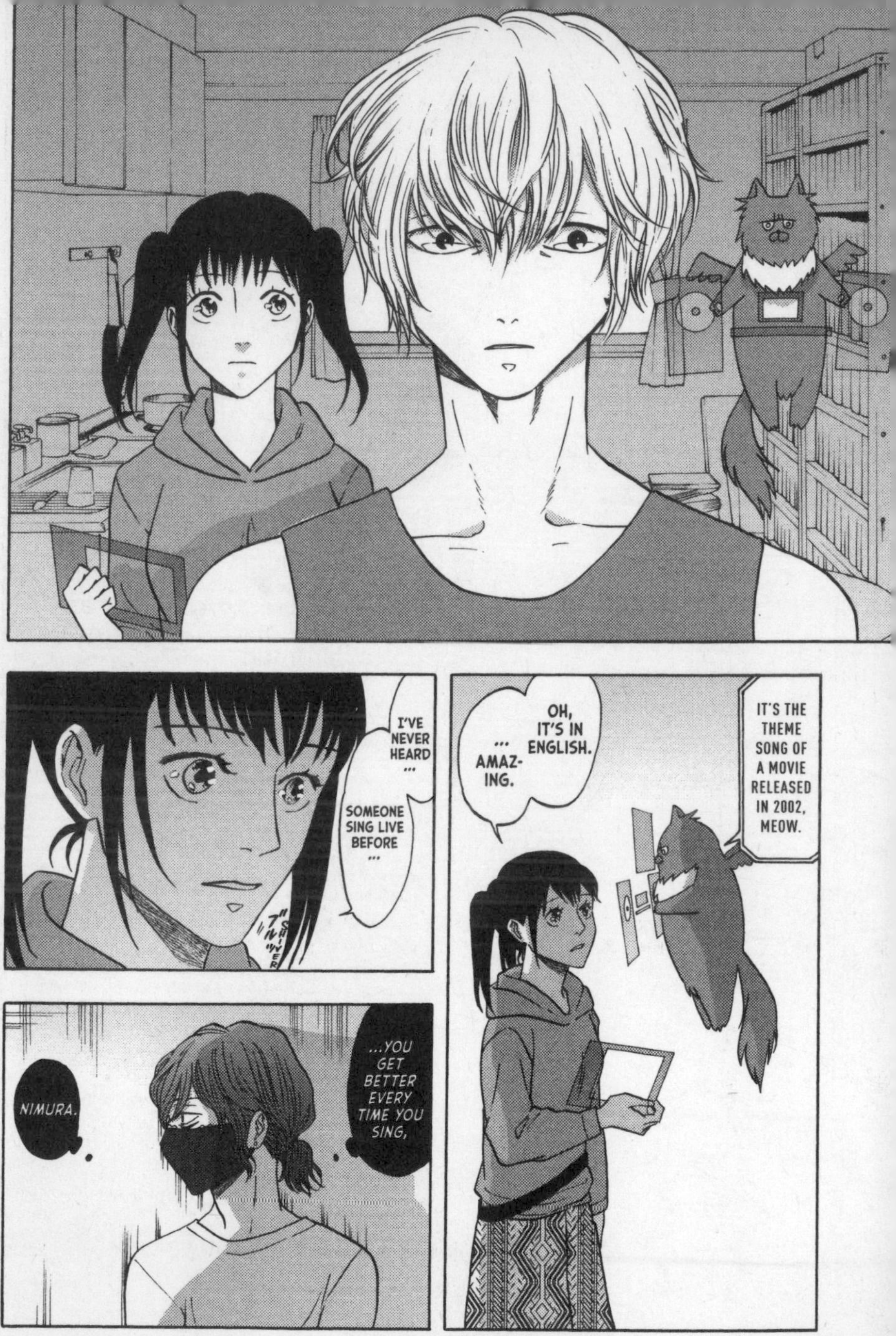
IT'S THE THEME SONG OF A MOVIE RELEASED IN 2002, MEOW.
OH, IT'S IN ENGLISH.
... AMAZ-ING.
I'VE NEVER HEARD ...
SOMEONE SING LIVE BEFORE ...
SHIVER
...YOU GET BETTER EVERY TIME YOU SING,
NIMURA.

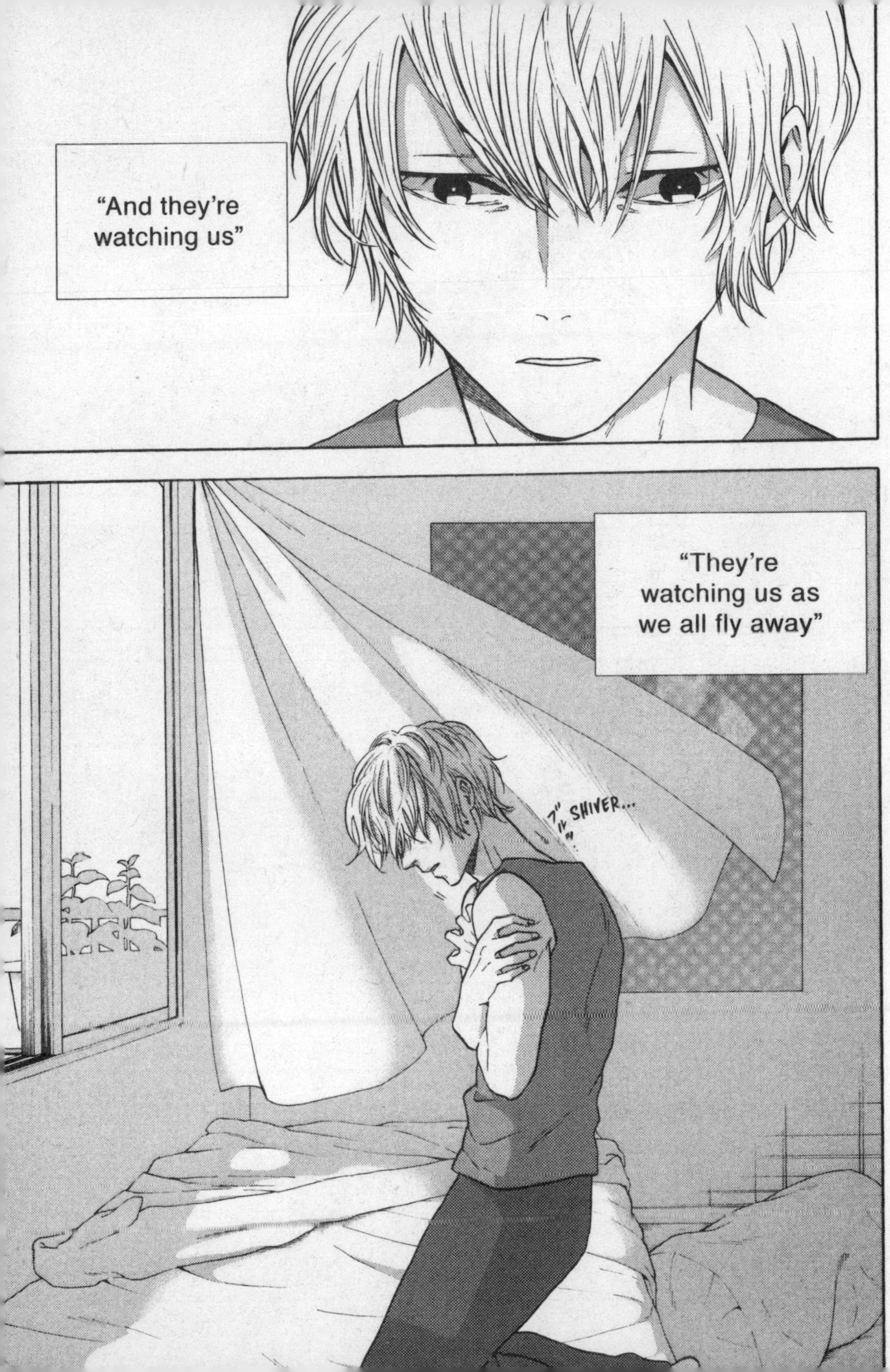
"And they're watching us"
"They're watching us as we all fly away"
SHIVER...

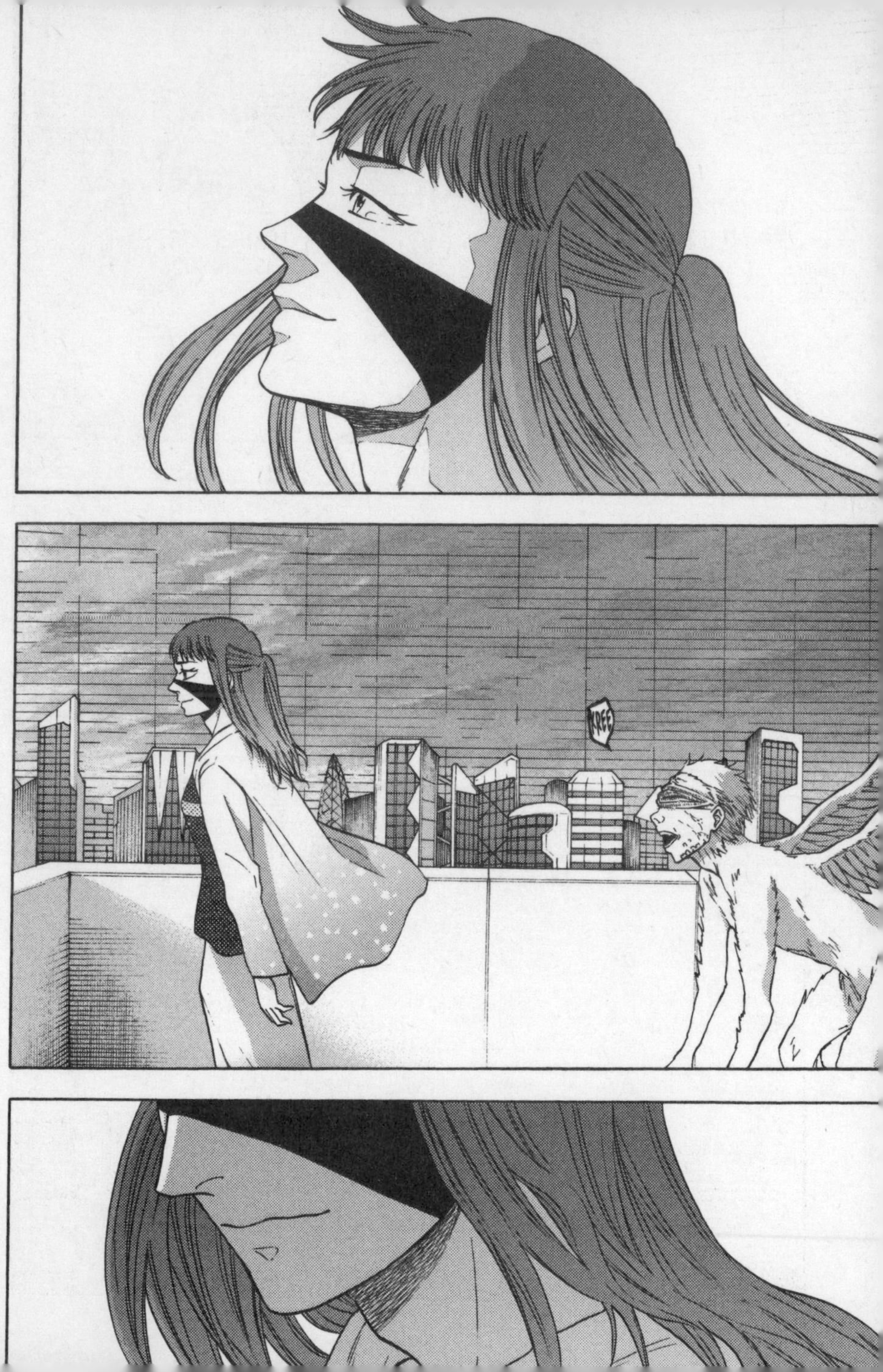
KREE

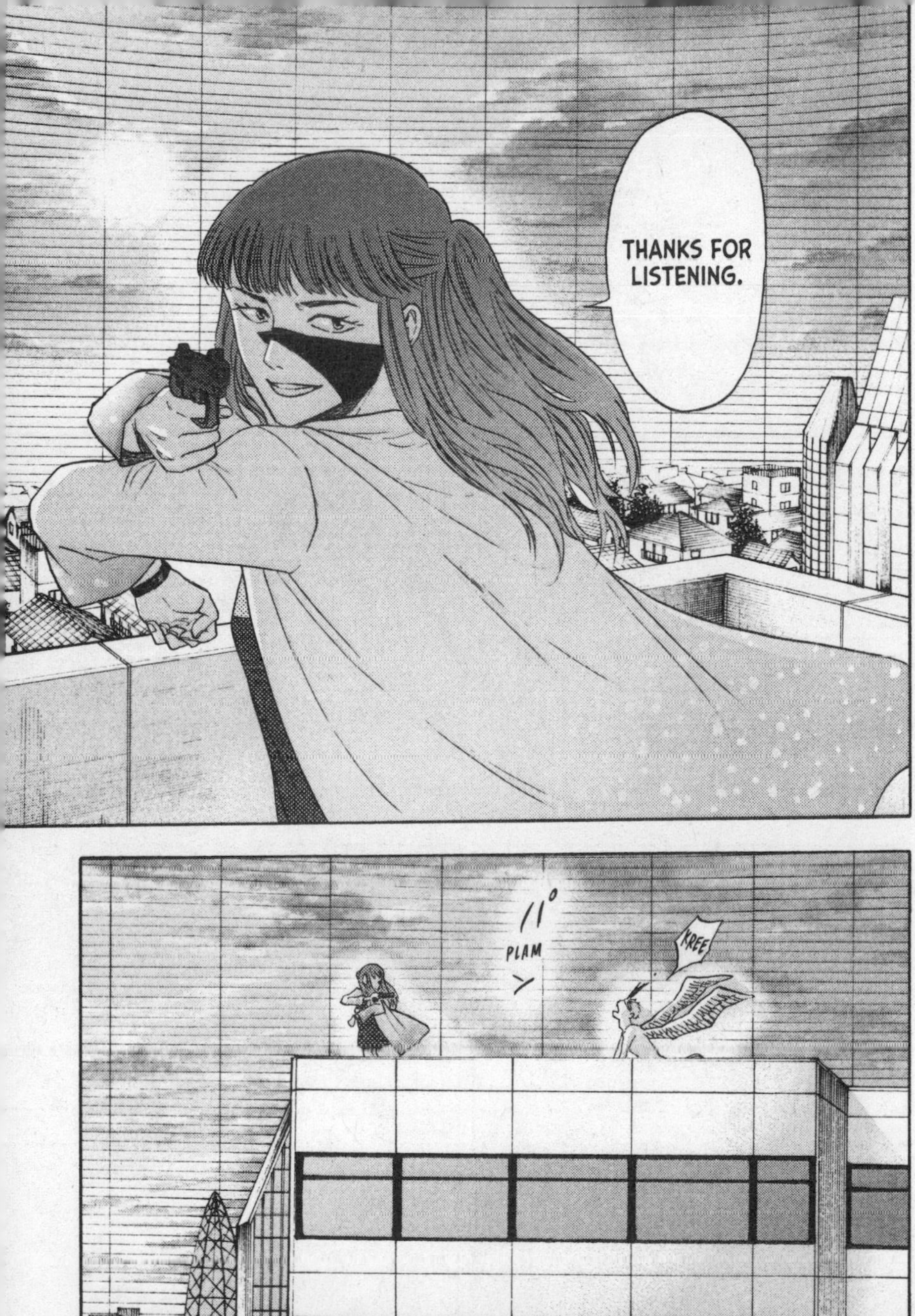
THANKS FOR LISTENING.
PLAM
KREE

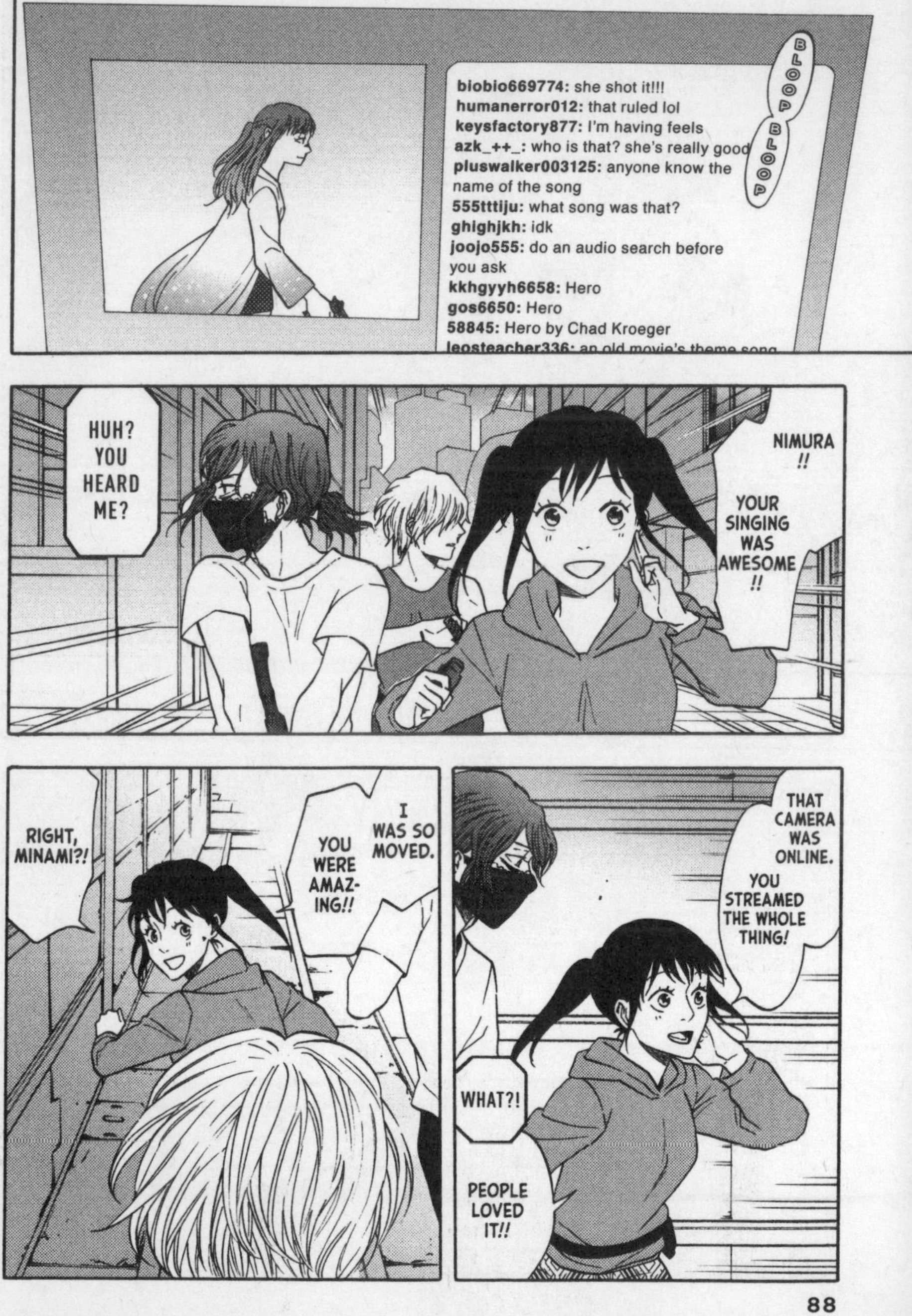
BLOOP BLOOP
biobio669774: she shot it!!!
humanerror012: that ruled lol
keysfactory877: I'm having feels
azk_++_: who is that? she's really good
pluswalker003125: anyone know the name of the song
555tttiju: what song was that?
ghighjkh: idk
joojo555: do an audio search before you ask
kkhgyyh6658: Hero
gos6650: Hero
58845: Hero by Chad Kroeger
leosteacher336: an old movie's theme song
NIMURA!!
YOUR SINGING WAS AWESOME!!
HUH? YOU HEARD ME?
THAT CAMERA WAS ONLINE.
YOU STREAMED THE WHOLE THING!
WHAT?!
PEOPLE LOVED IT!!
I WAS SO MOVED.
YOU WERE AMAZ-ING!!
RIGHT, MINAMI?!

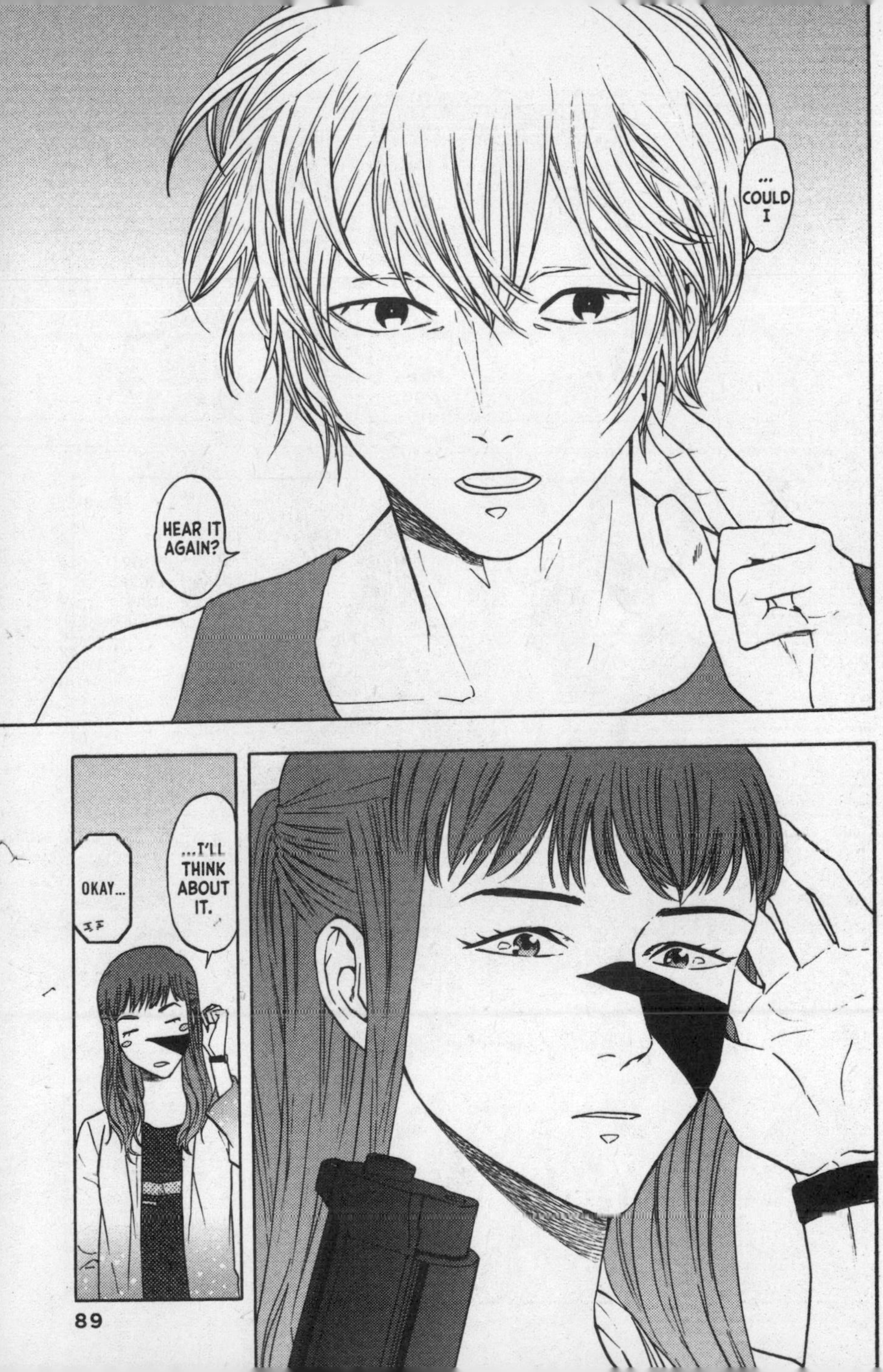
...COULD I
HEAR IT AGAIN?
...I'LL THINK ABOUT IT.
OKAY...

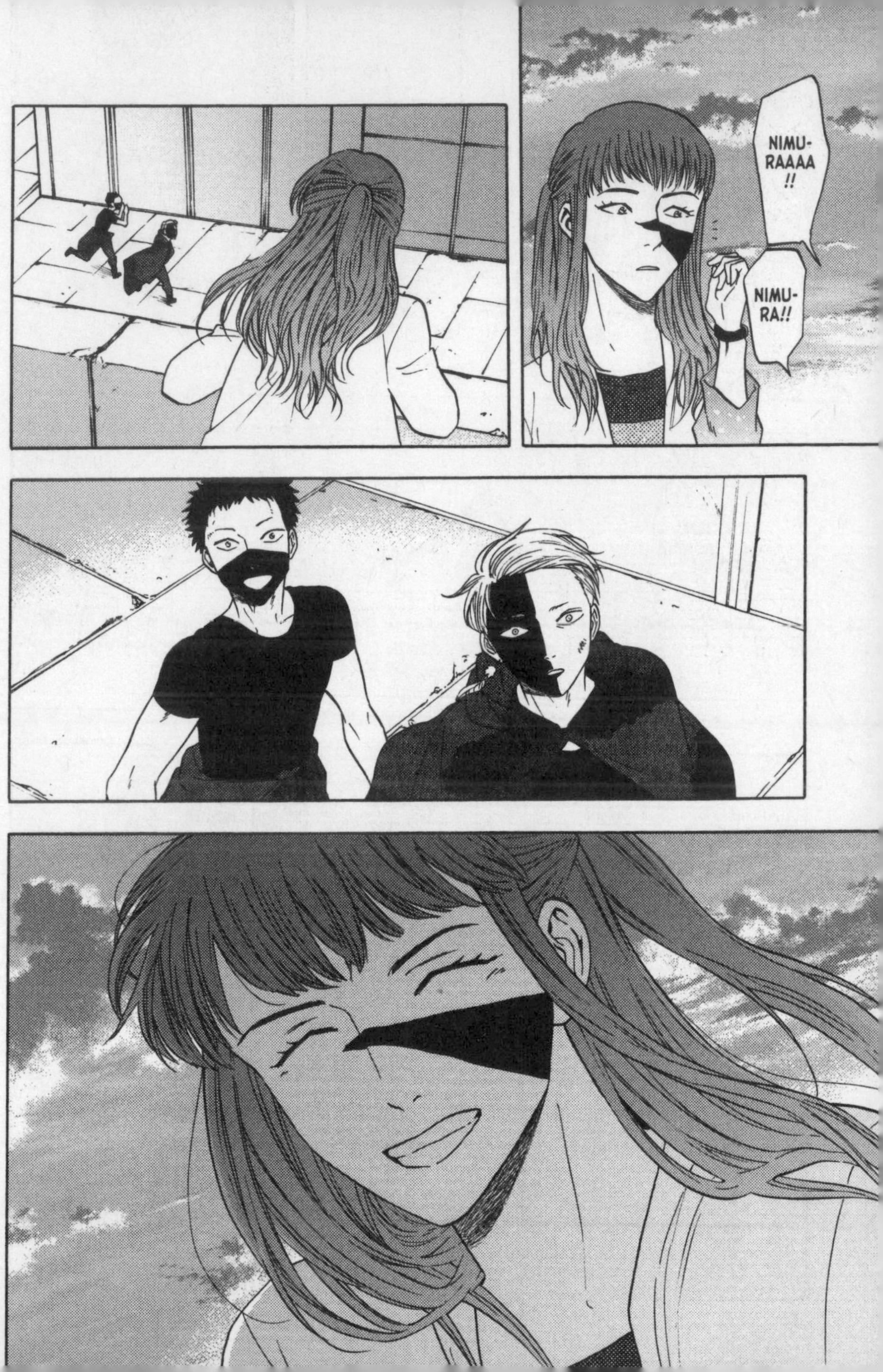

NIMU-RAAAA!!
NIMU-RA!!

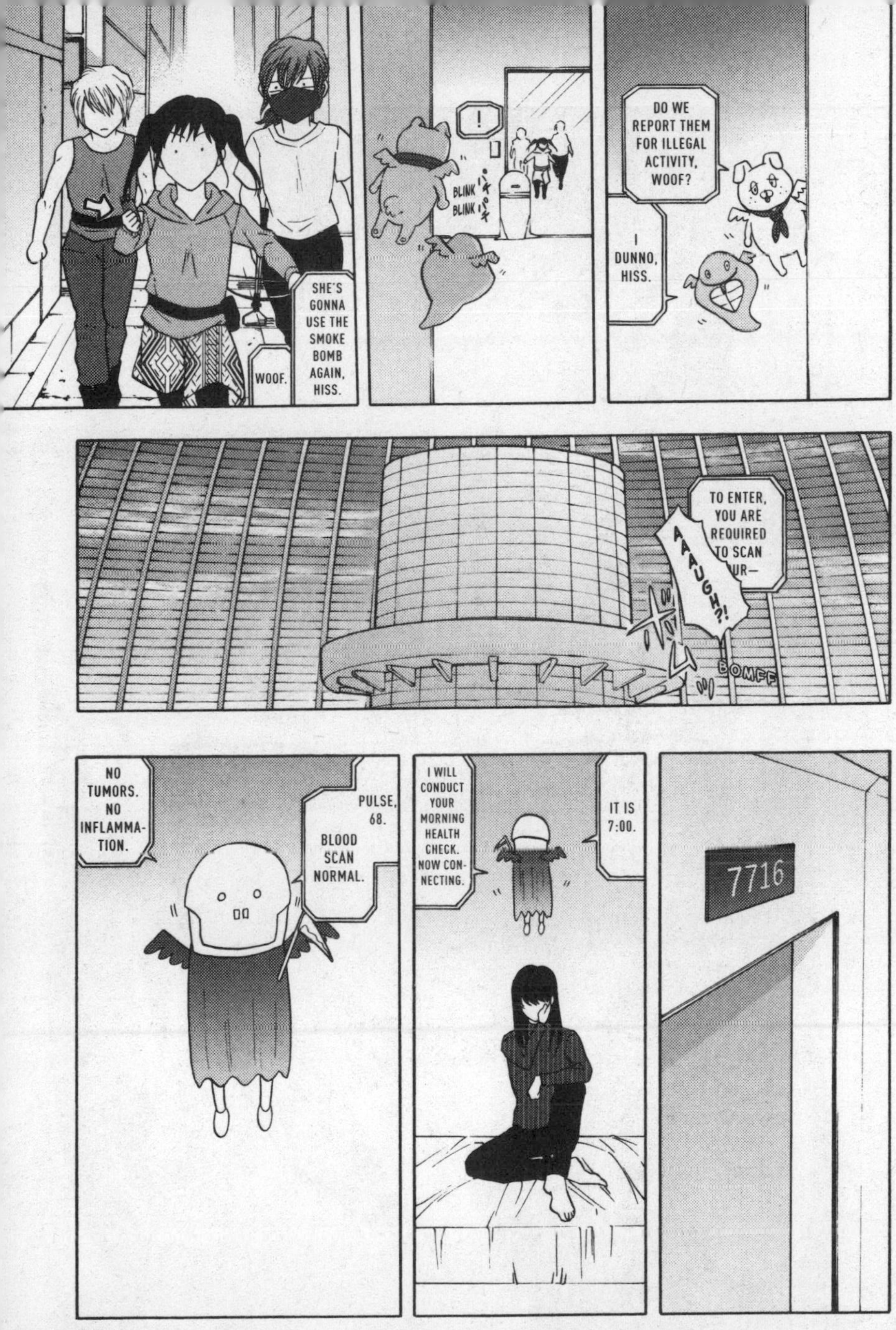
DO WE REPORT THEM FOR ILLEGAL ACTIVITY, WOOF?
I DUNNO, HISS.
!
BLINK BLINK
SHE'S GONNA USE THE SMOKE BOMB AGAIN, HISS.
WOOF.
TO ENTER, YOU ARE REQUIRED TO SCAN UR—
AAAUGH?!
BOMFF
7716
IT IS 7:00.
I WILL CONDUCT YOUR MORNING HEALTH CHECK. NOW CONNECTING.
PULSE, 68.
BLOOD SCAN NORMAL.
NO TUMORS. NO INFLAMMATION.

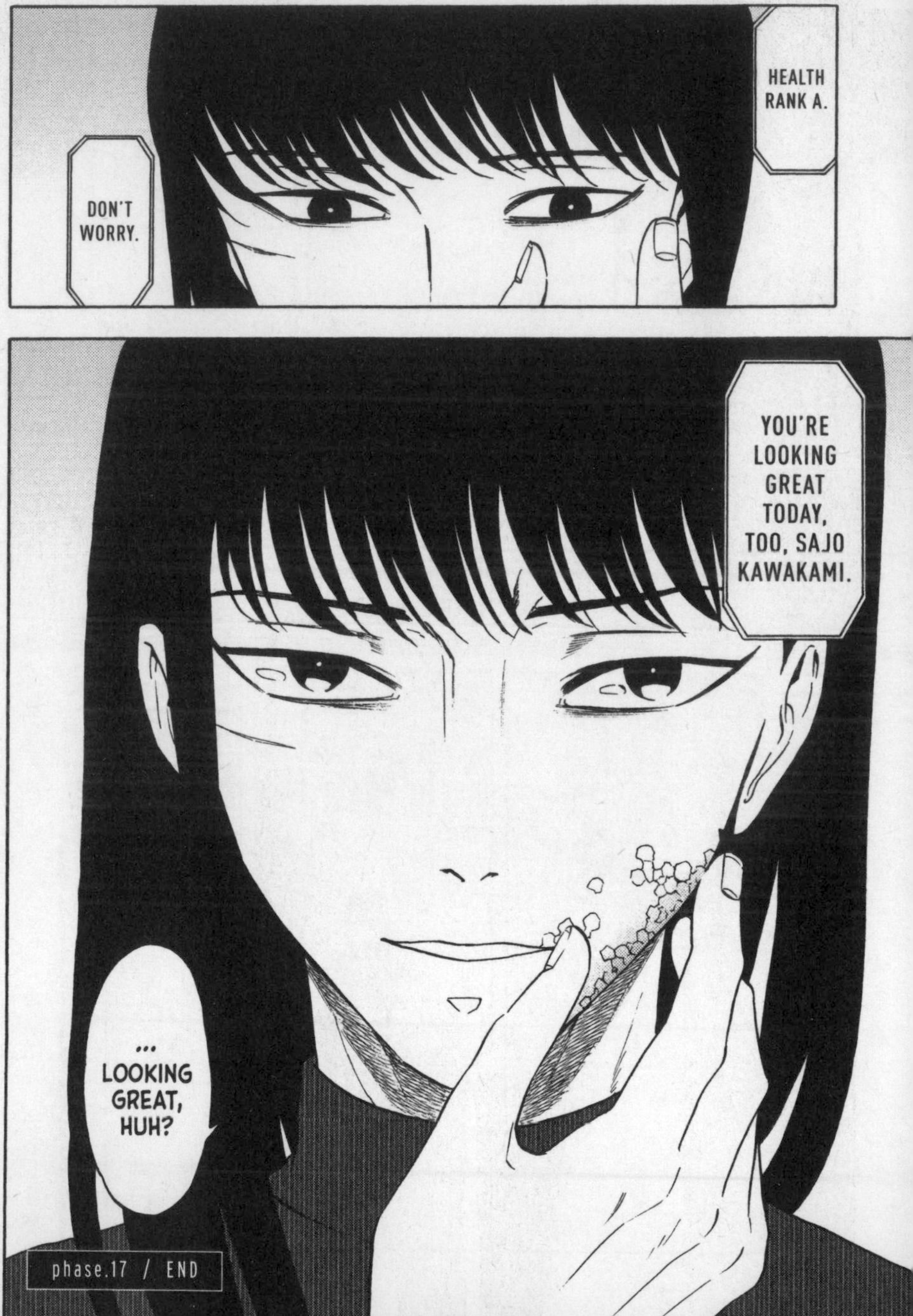
HEALTH RANK A.
DON'T WORRY.
YOU'RE LOOKING GREAT TODAY, TOO, SAJO KAWAKAMI.
... LOOKING GREAT, HUH?
phase.17 / END

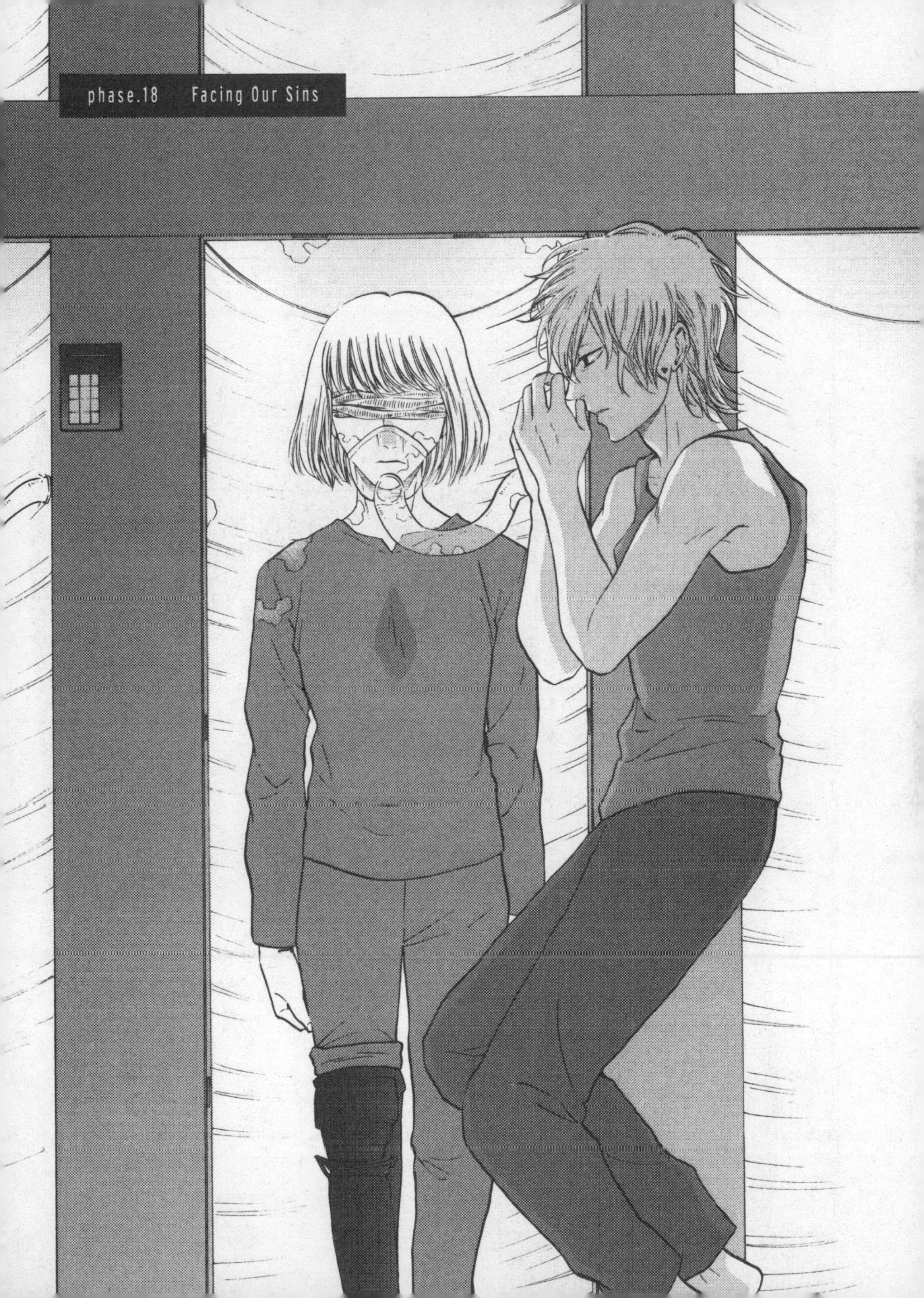
phase.18 Facing Our Sins

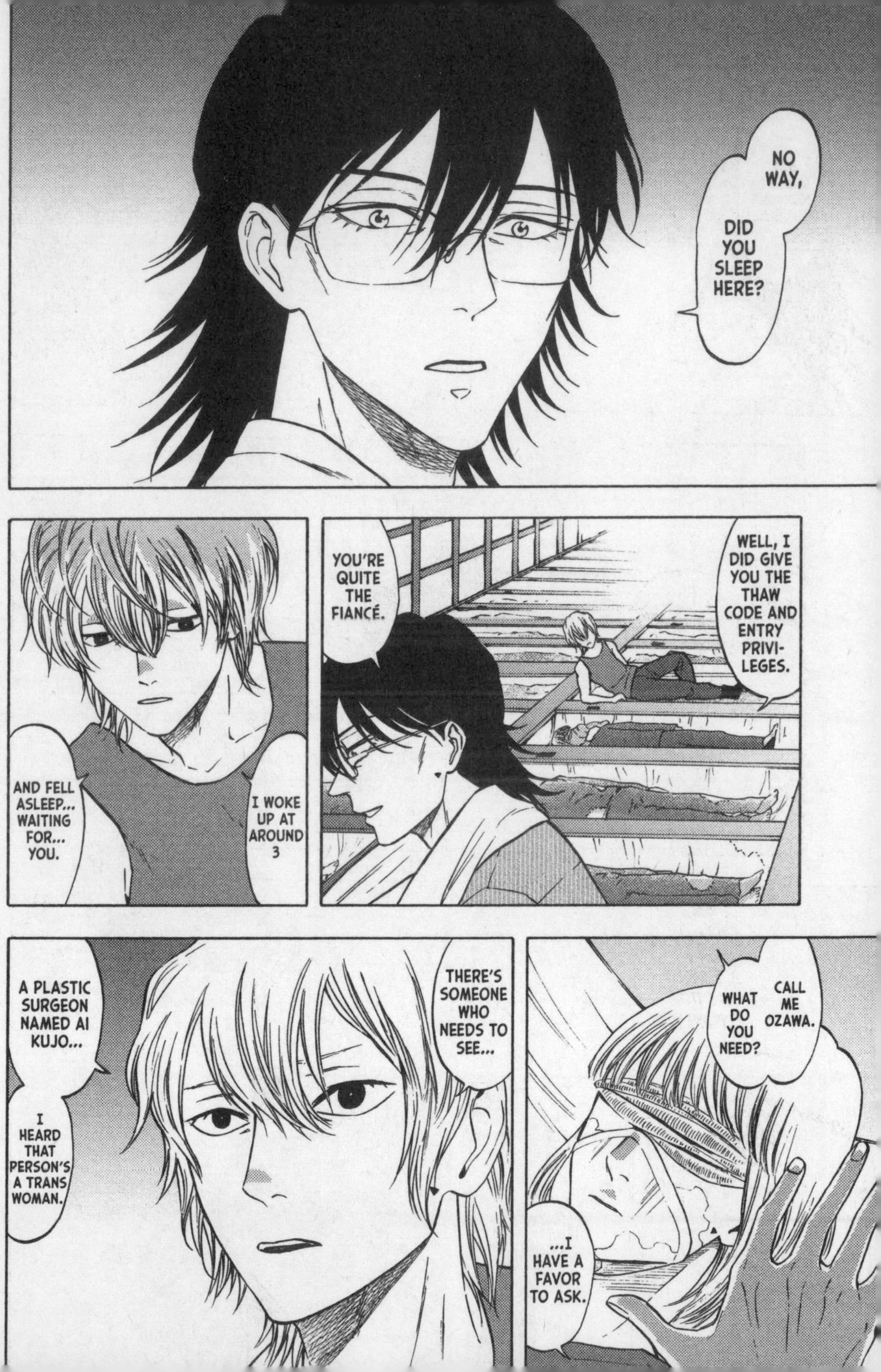
NO WAY,
DID YOU SLEEP HERE?
WELL, I DID GIVE YOU THE THAW CODE AND ENTRY PRIVILEGES.
YOU'RE QUITE THE FIANCÉ.
I WOKE UP AT AROUND 3
AND FELL ASLEEP... WAITING FOR... YOU.
CALL ME OZAWA.
WHAT DO YOU NEED?
...I HAVE A FAVOR TO ASK.
THERE'S SOMEONE WHO NEEDS TO SEE...
A PLASTIC SURGEON NAMED AI KUJO...
I HEARD THAT PERSON'S A TRANS WOMAN.

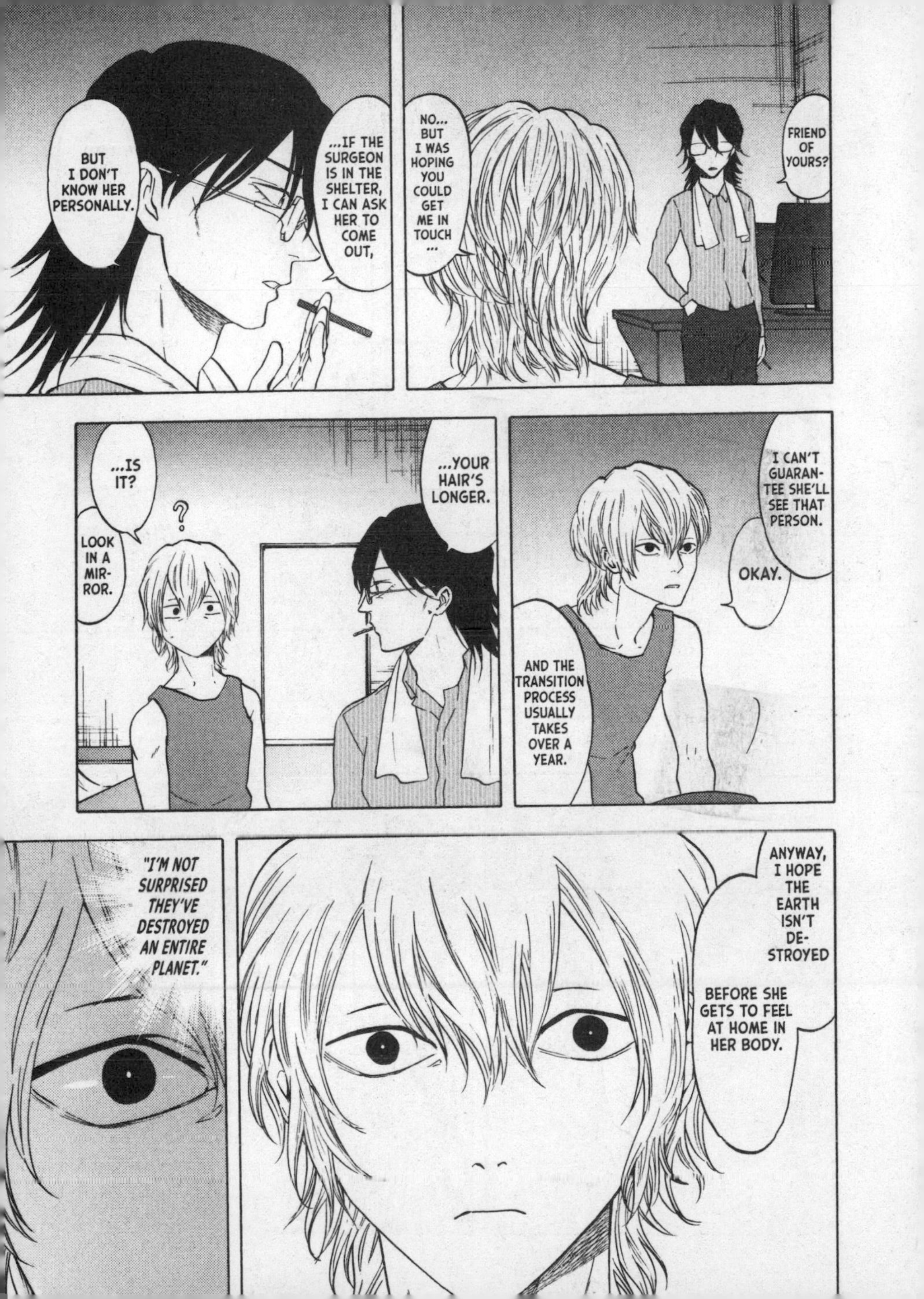
FRIEND OF YOURS?
NO... BUT I WAS HOPING YOU COULD GET ME IN TOUCH ...
...IF THE SURGEON IS IN THE SHELTER, I CAN ASK HER TO COME OUT,
BUT I DON'T KNOW HER PERSONALLY.
I CAN'T GUARAN-TEE SHE'LL SEE THAT PERSON.
OKAY.
AND THE TRANSITION PROCESS USUALLY TAKES OVER A YEAR.
...YOUR HAIR'S LONGER.
...IS IT?
?
LOOK IN A MIR-ROR.
ANYWAY, I HOPE THE EARTH ISN'T DE-STROYED
BEFORE SHE GETS TO FEEL AT HOME IN HER BODY.
"I'M NOT SURPRISED THEY'VE DESTROYED AN ENTIRE PLANET."

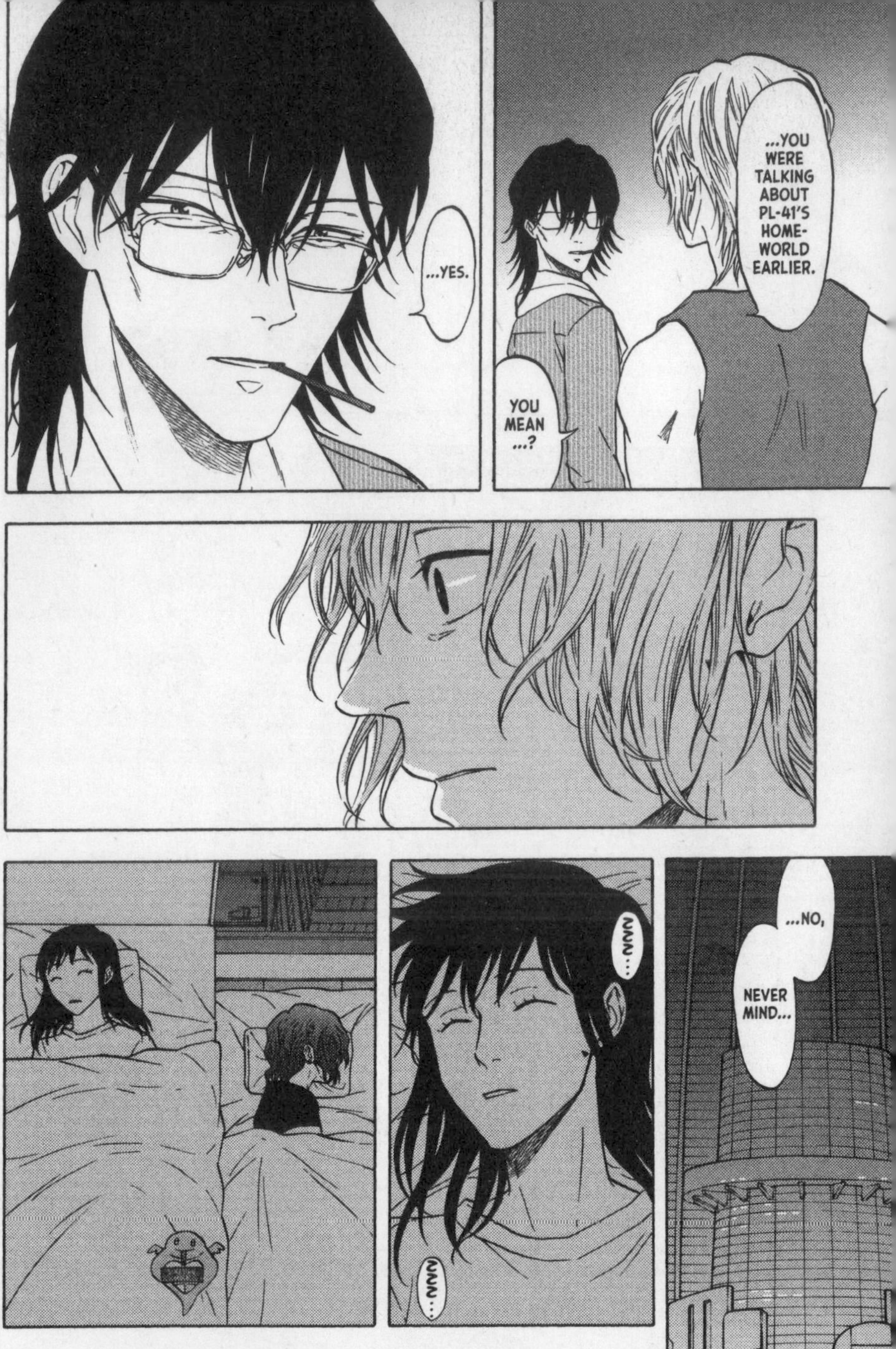
...YOU WERE TALKING ABOUT PL-41'S HOME-WORLD EARLIER.
YOU MEAN ...?
...YES.
...NO,
NEVER MIND...
NNN...
NNN...

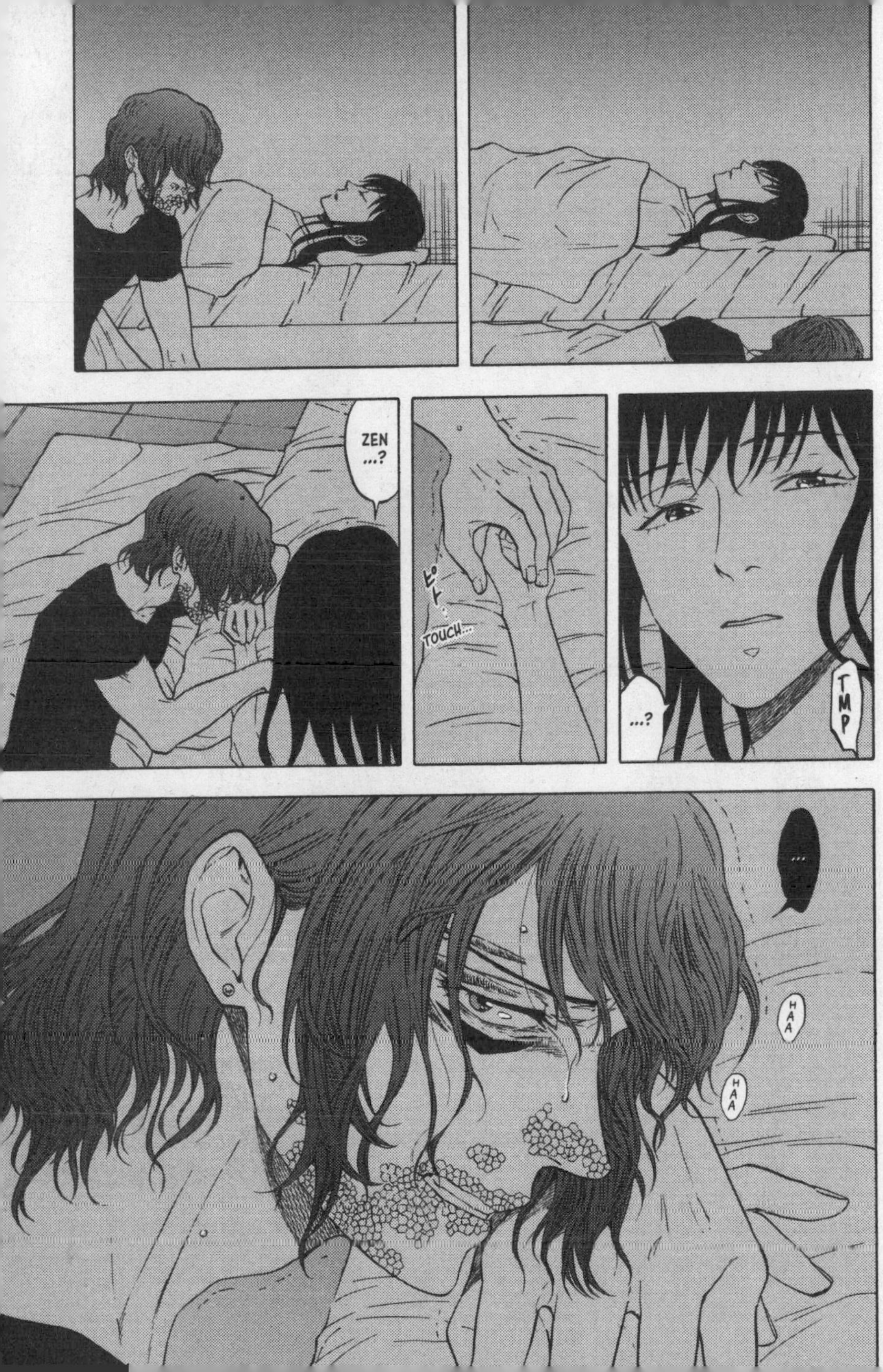
TMP
...?
ピト
TOUCH...
ZEN ...?
...
HAA
HAA

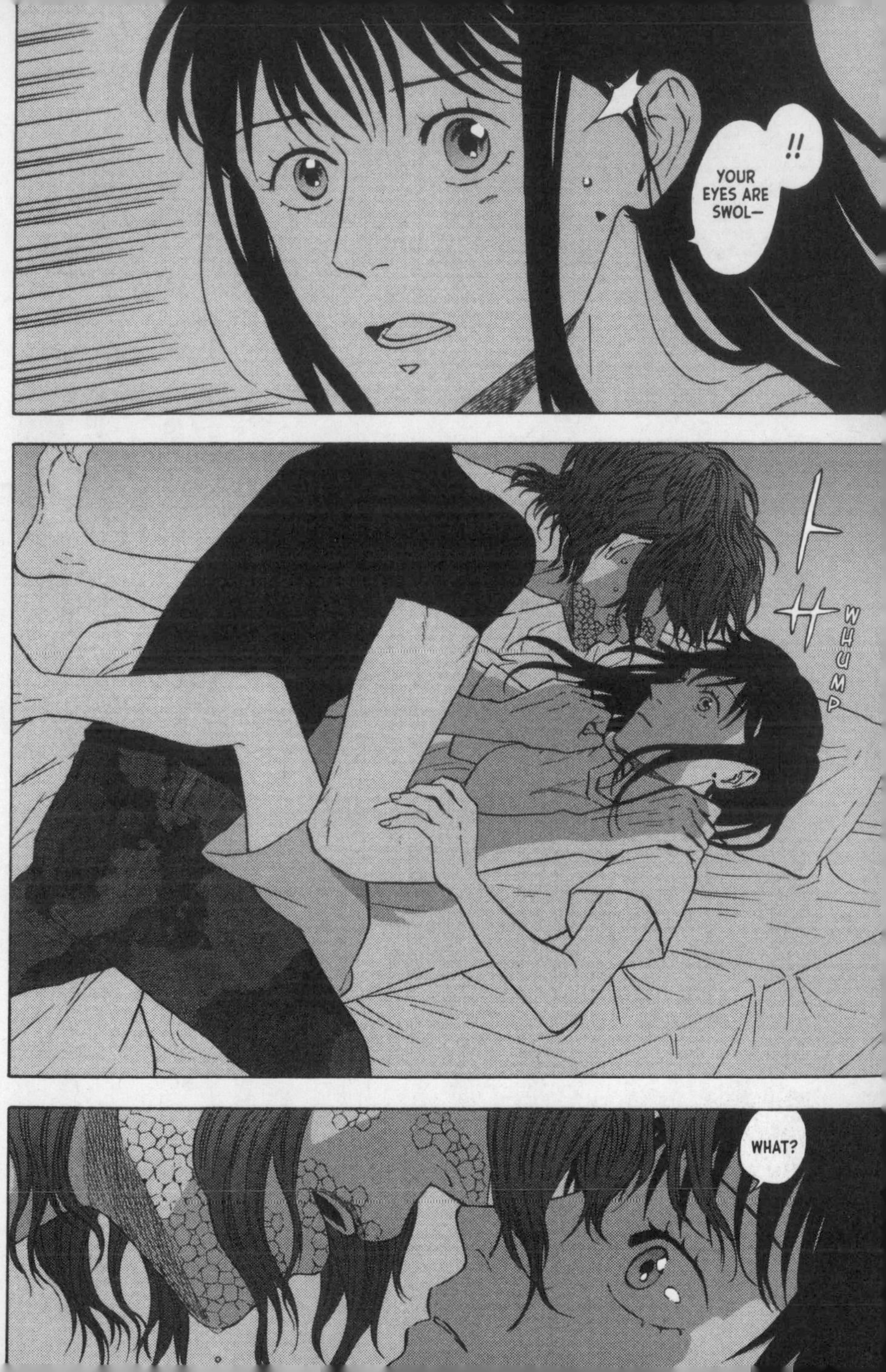
!!
YOUR EYES ARE SWOL—
WHUMP
WHAT?

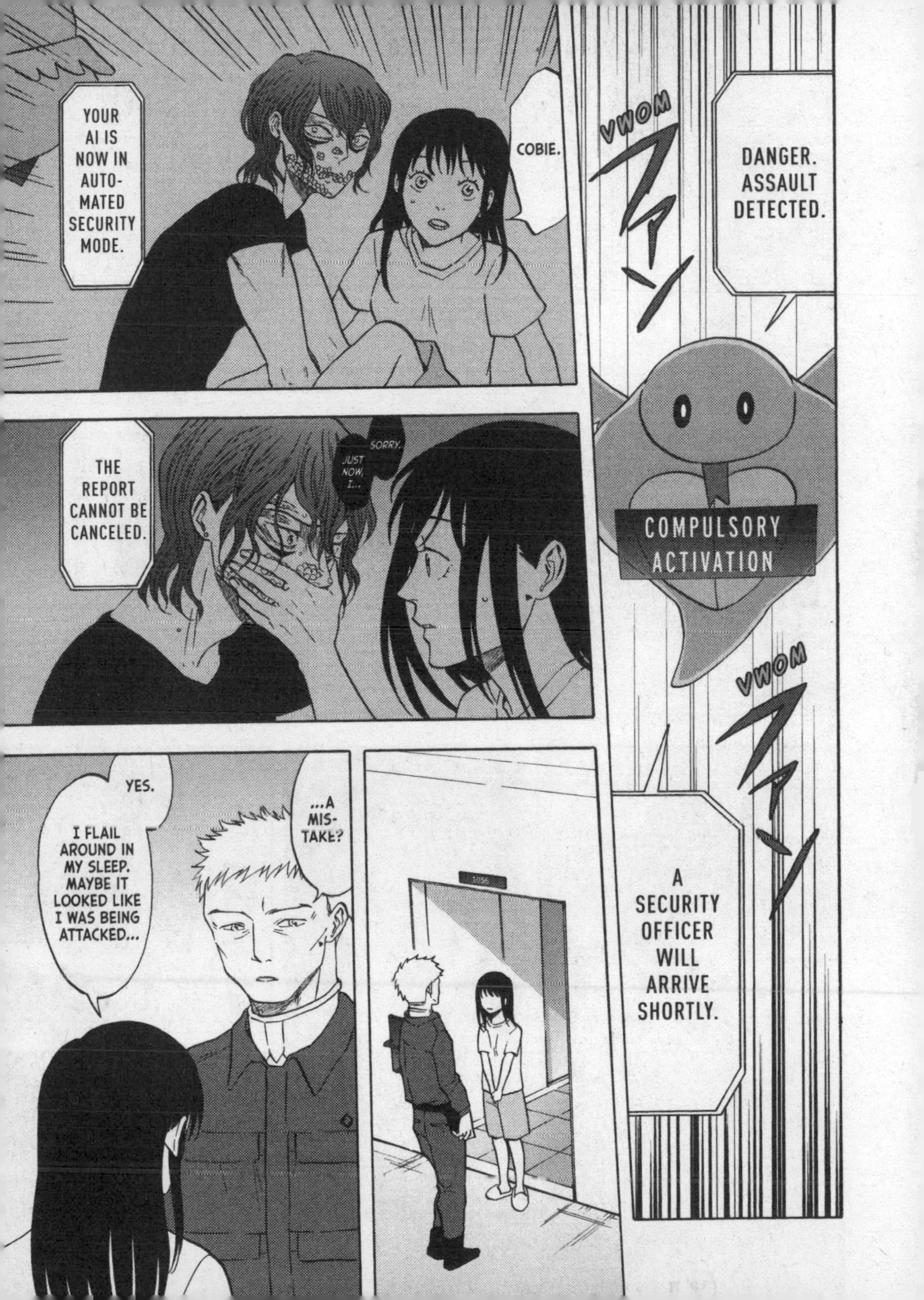
DANGER. ASSAULT DETECTED.
VWOM
COMPULSORY ACTIVATION
VWOM
A SECURITY OFFICER WILL ARRIVE SHORTLY.
COBIE.
YOUR AI IS NOW IN AUTO-MATED SECURITY MODE.
SORRY. JUST NOW, I...
THE REPORT CANNOT BE CANCELED.
...A MIS-TAKE?
YES.
I FLAIL AROUND IN MY SLEEP. MAYBE IT LOOKED LIKE I WAS BEING ATTACKED...

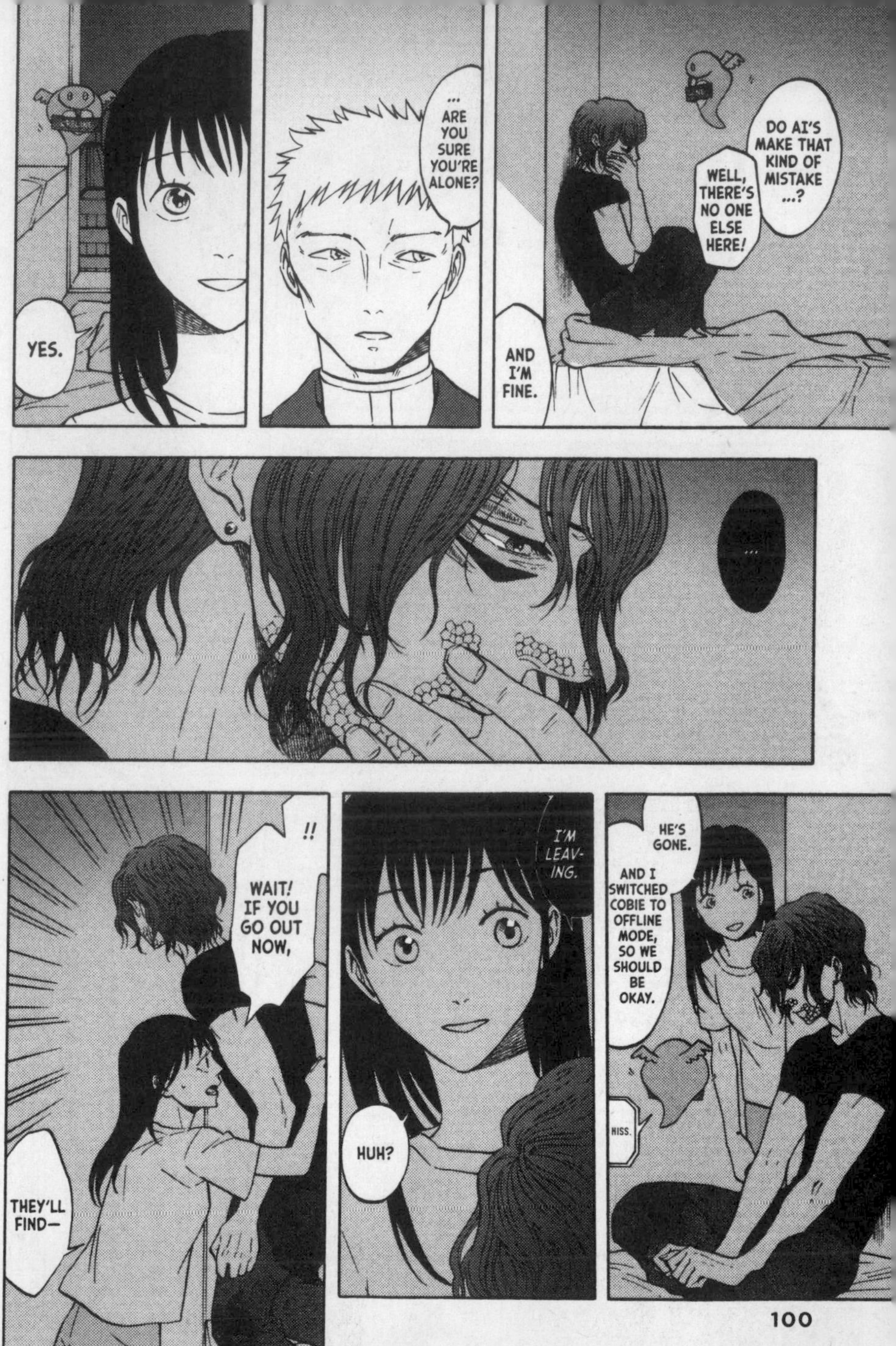
DO AI'S MAKE THAT KIND OF MISTAKE ...?
WELL, THERE'S NO ONE ELSE HERE!
AND I'M FINE.
... ARE YOU SURE YOU'RE ALONE?
YES.
...
HE'S GONE.
AND I SWITCHED COBIE TO OFFLINE MODE, SO WE SHOULD BE OKAY.
HISS.
I'M LEAV-ING.
HUH?
!!
WAIT! IF YOU GO OUT NOW,
THEY'LL FIND—

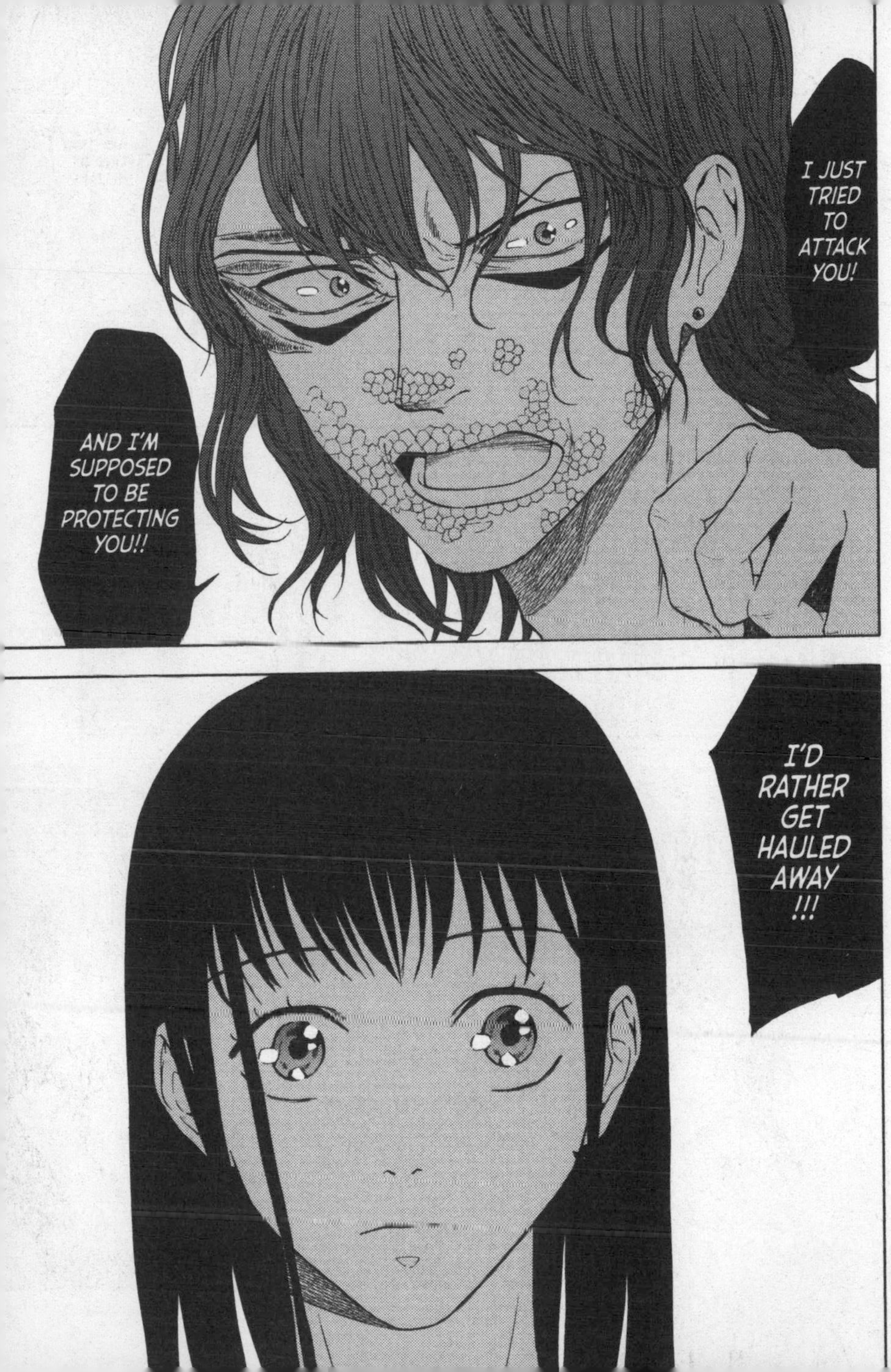
I JUST TRIED TO ATTACK YOU!
AND I'M SUPPOSED TO BE PROTECTING YOU!!
I'D RATHER GET HAULED AWAY!!!

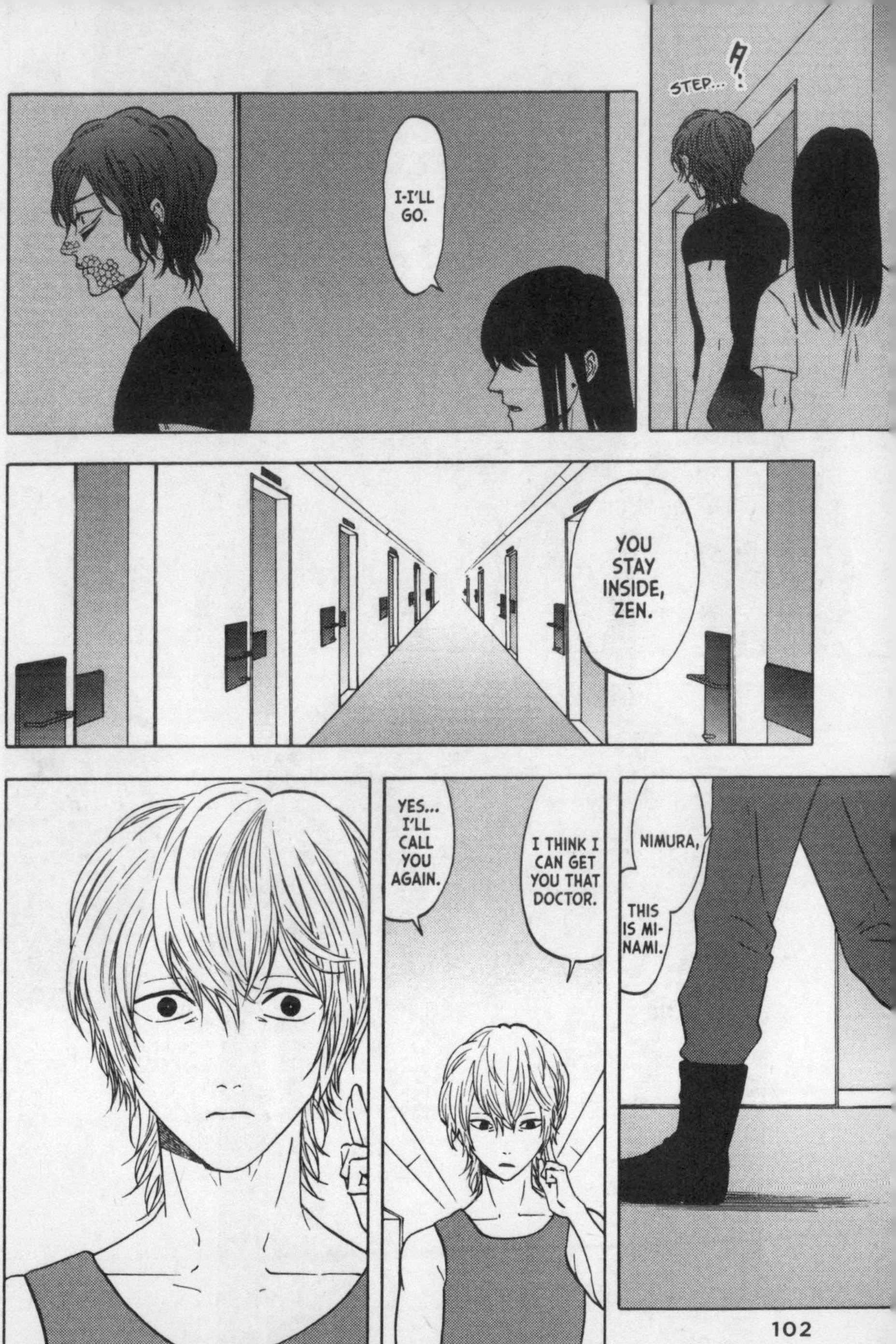
STEP...
I-I'LL GO.
YOU STAY INSIDE, ZEN.
NIMURA,
THIS IS MI-NAMI.
I THINK I CAN GET YOU THAT DOCTOR.
YES... I'LL CALL YOU AGAIN.

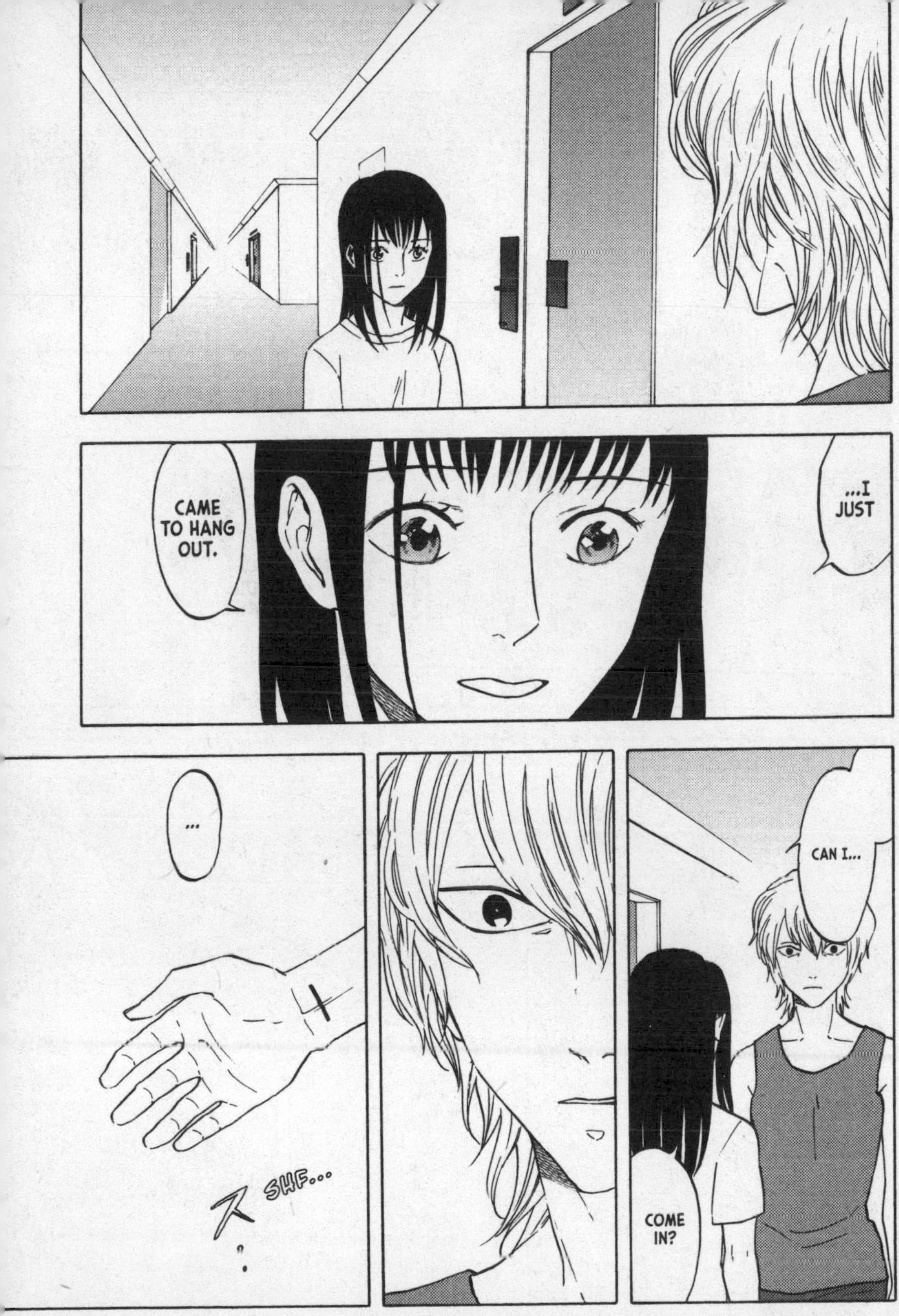
...I JUST
CAME TO HANG OUT.
CAN I...
COME IN?
...
ス SHF...

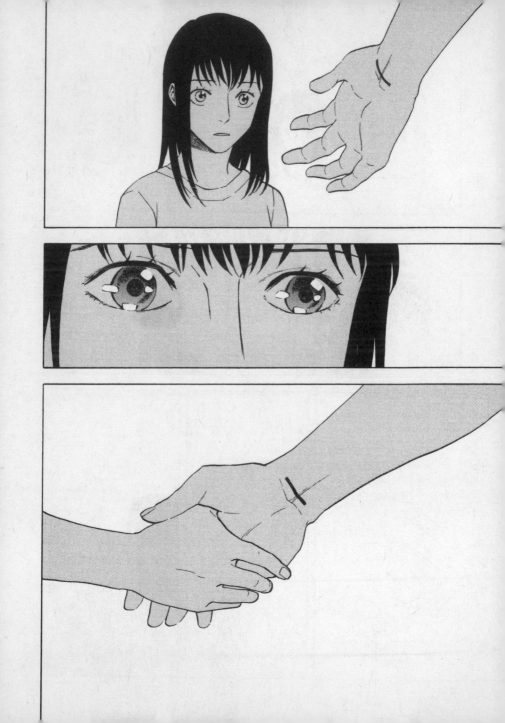

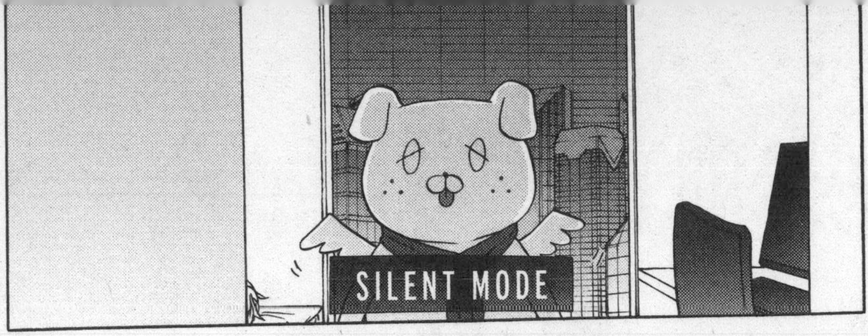
SILENT MODE
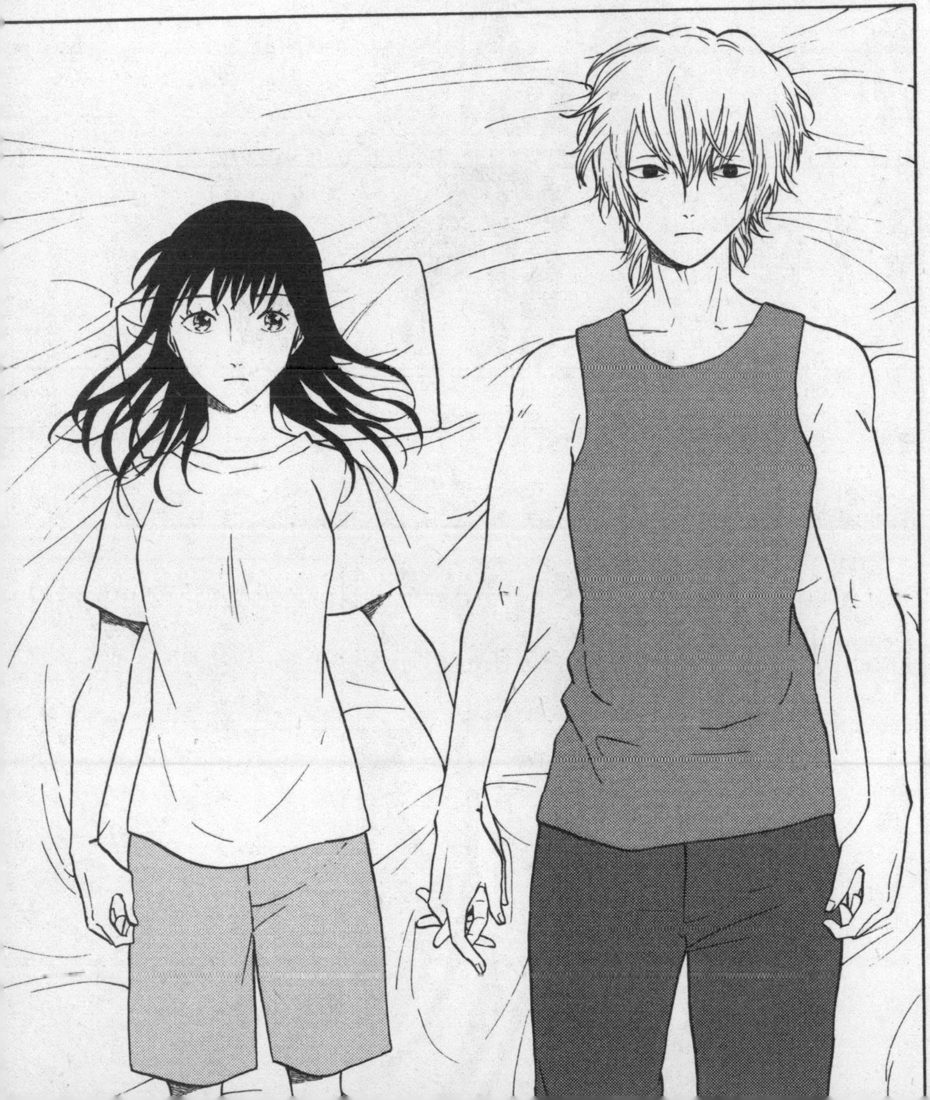

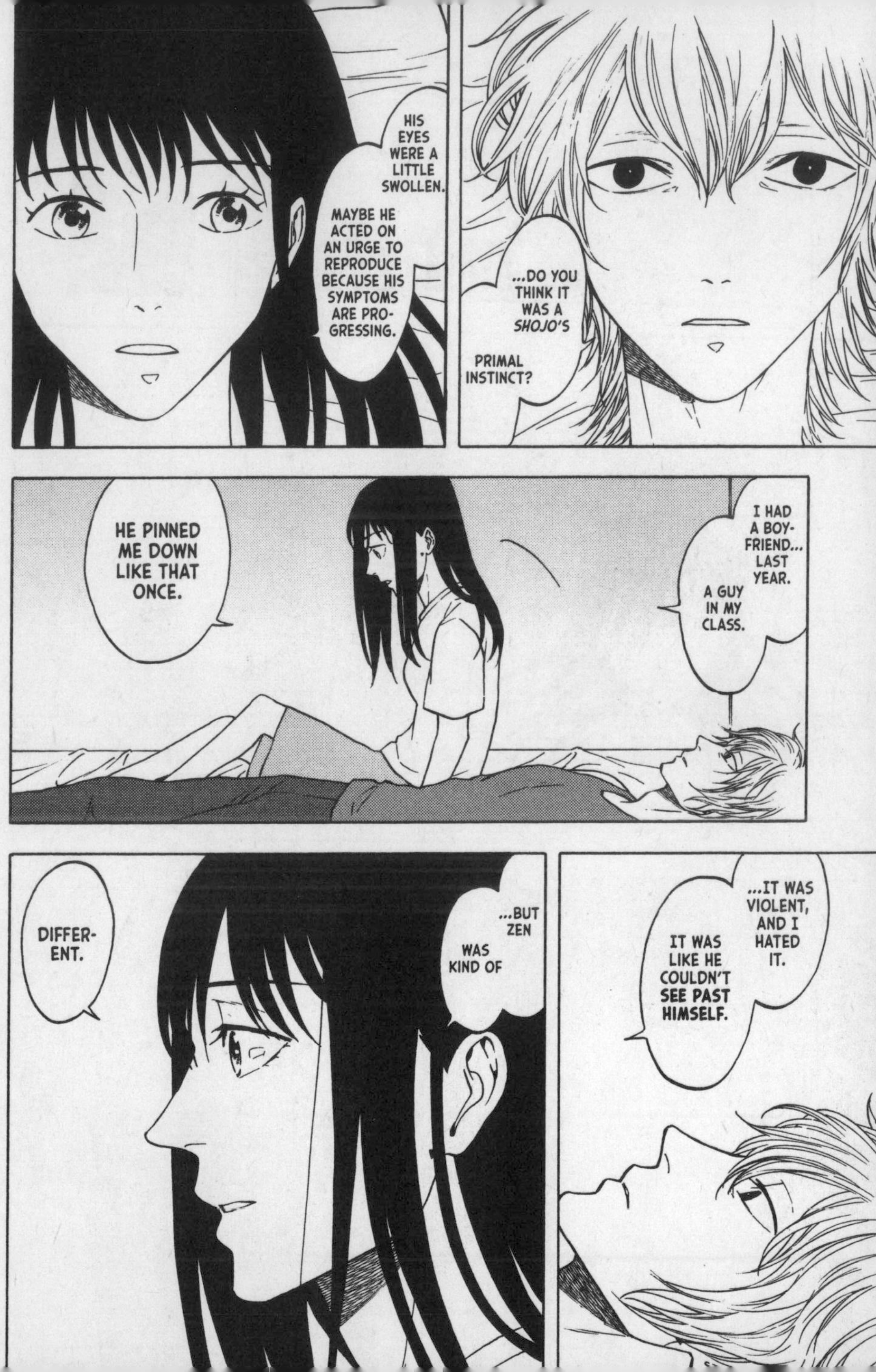
...DO YOU THINK IT WAS A *SHOJO'S* PRIMAL INSTINCT?
HIS EYES WERE A LITTLE SWOLLEN.
MAYBE HE ACTED ON AN URGE TO REPRODUCE BECAUSE HIS SYMPTOMS ARE PRO-GRESSING.
I HAD A BOY-FRIEND... LAST YEAR. A GUY IN MY CLASS.
HE PINNED ME DOWN LIKE THAT ONCE.
...IT WAS VIOLENT, AND I HATED IT.
IT WAS LIKE HE COULDN'T SEE PAST HIMSELF.
...BUT ZEN WAS KIND OF
DIFFER-ENT.

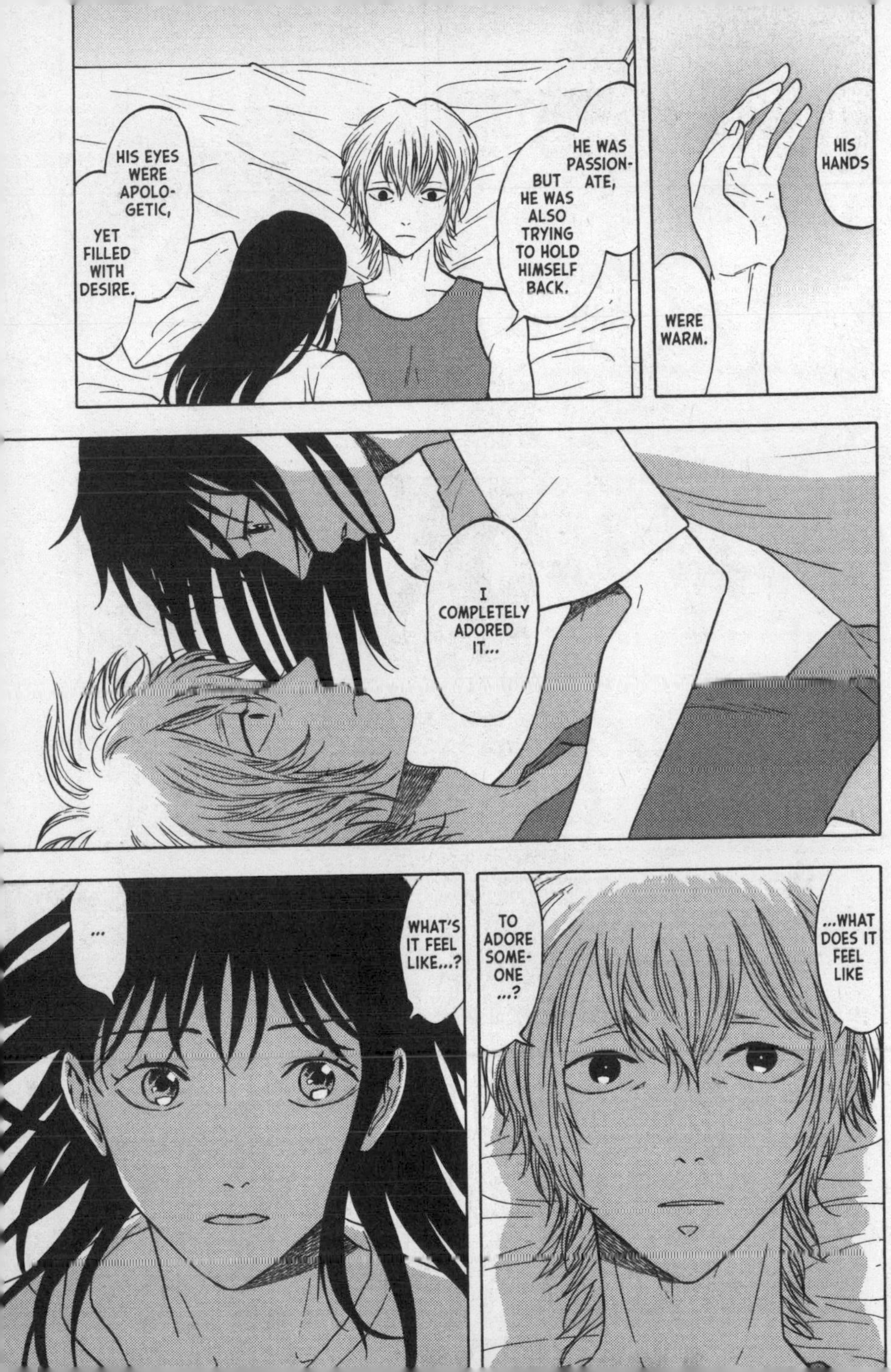
HIS HANDS
WERE WARM.
HE WAS PASSION-ATE,
BUT HE WAS ALSO TRYING TO HOLD HIMSELF BACK.
HIS EYES WERE APOLO-GETIC,
YET FILLED WITH DESIRE.
I COMPLETELY ADORED IT...
...WHAT DOES IT FEEL LIKE
TO ADORE SOME-ONE ...?
WHAT'S IT FEEL LIKE...?
...

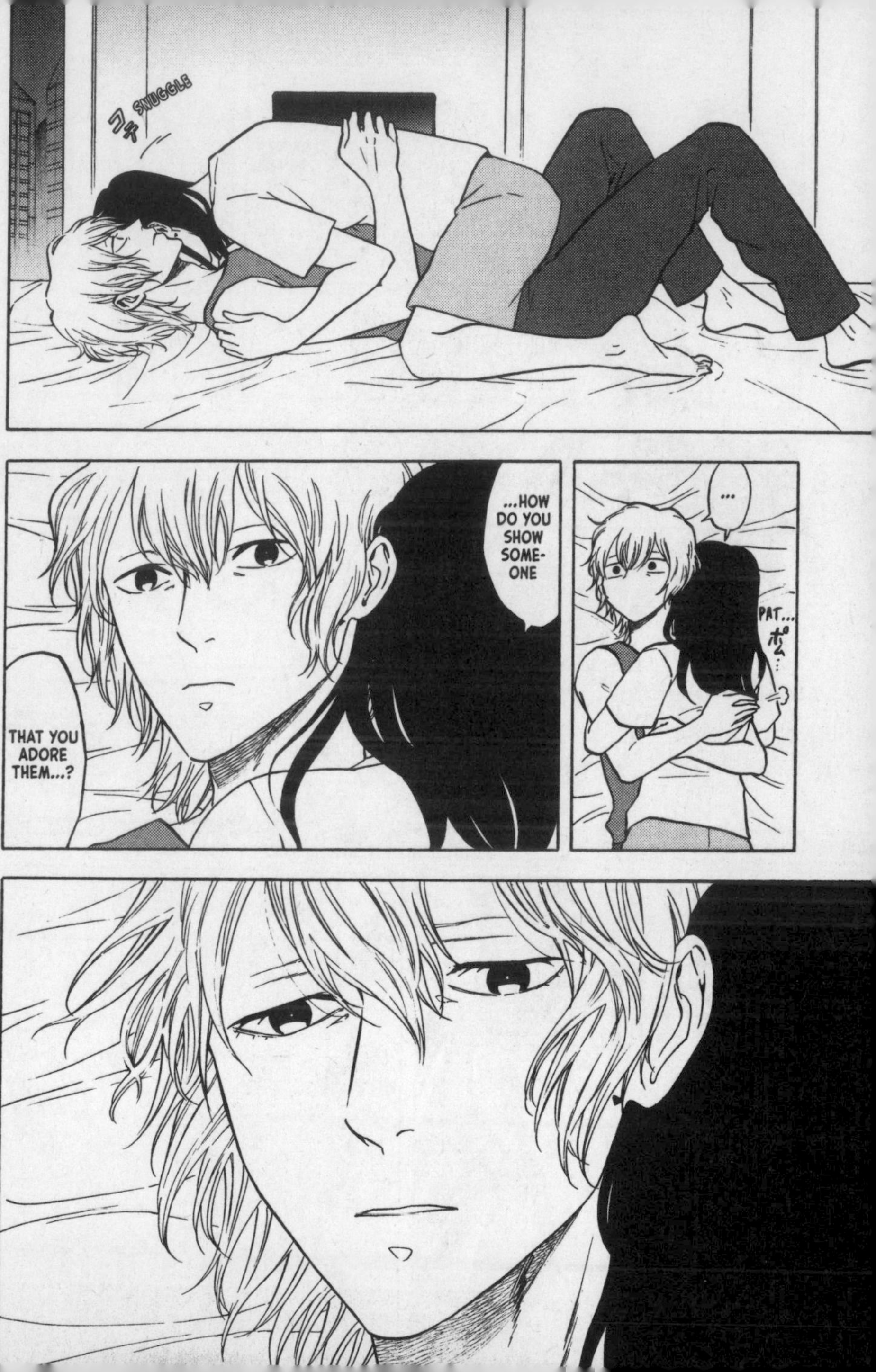
コテ SNUGGLE
...
PAT... ポム...
...HOW DO YOU SHOW SOME-ONE
THAT YOU ADORE THEM...?

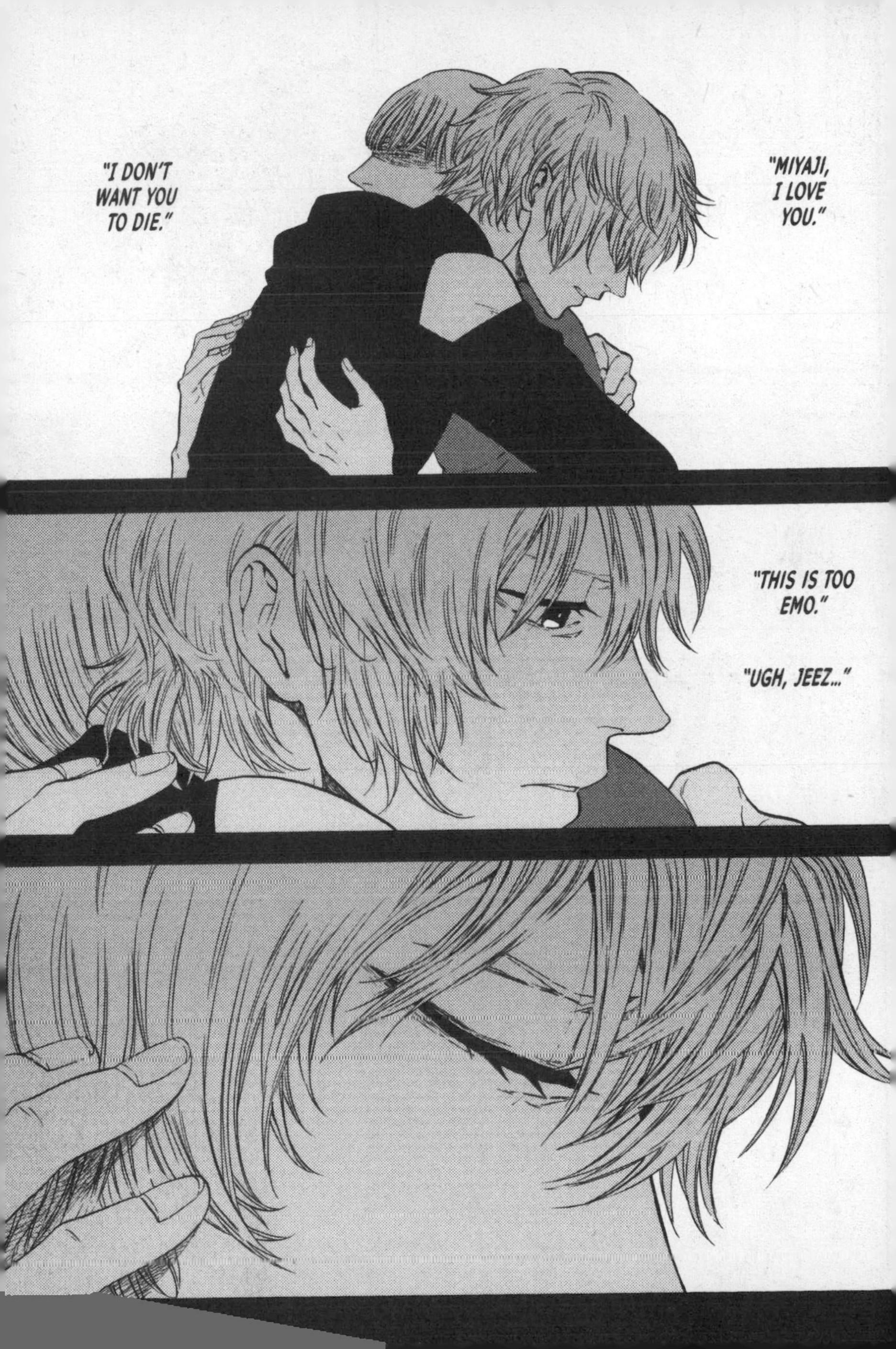
"MIYAJI, I LOVE YOU."
"I DON'T WANT YOU TO DIE."
"THIS IS TOO EMO."
"UGH, JEEZ..."

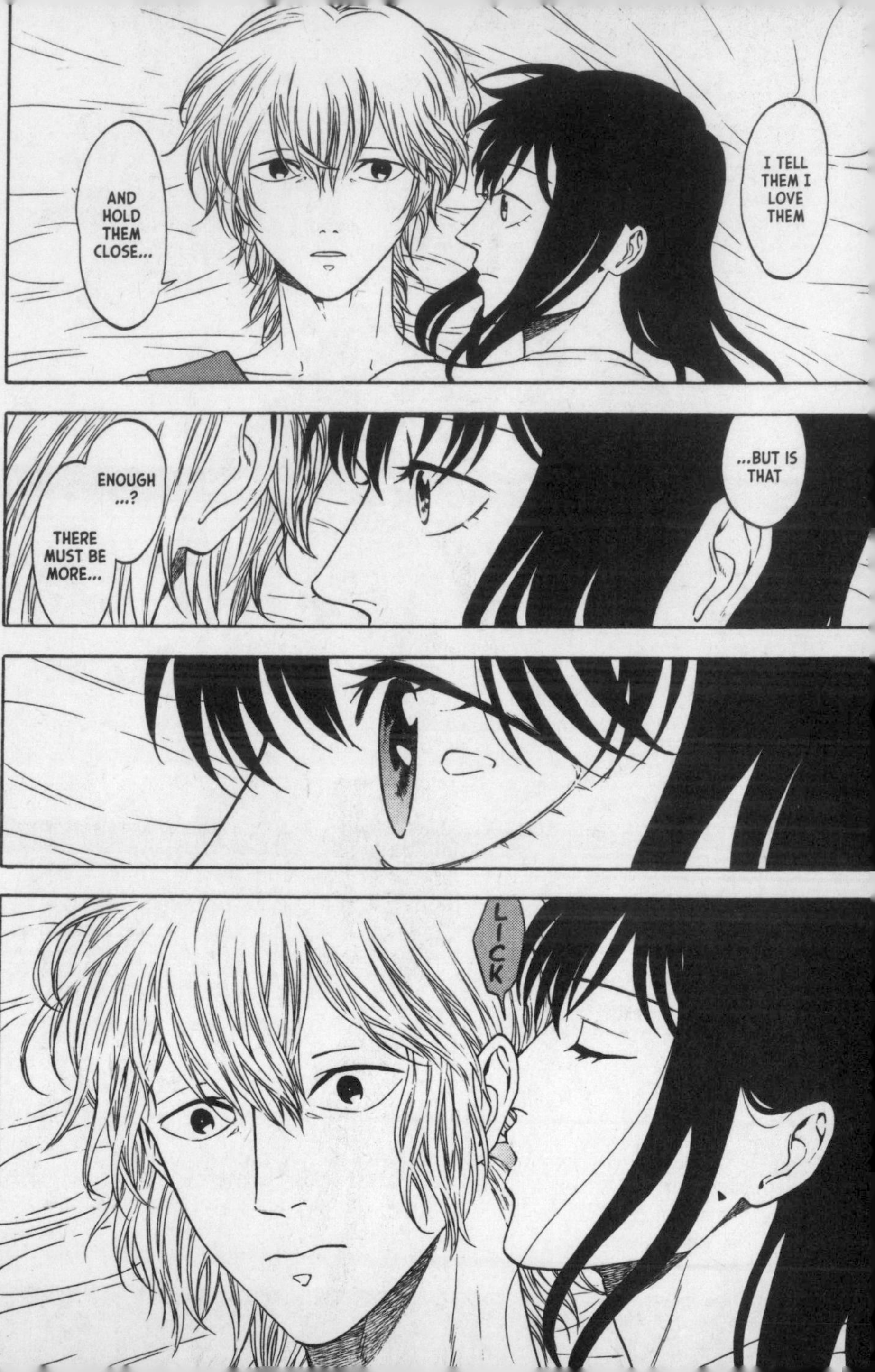
I TELL THEM I LOVE THEM
AND HOLD THEM CLOSE...
...BUT IS THAT
ENOUGH ...?
THERE MUST BE MORE...
LICK

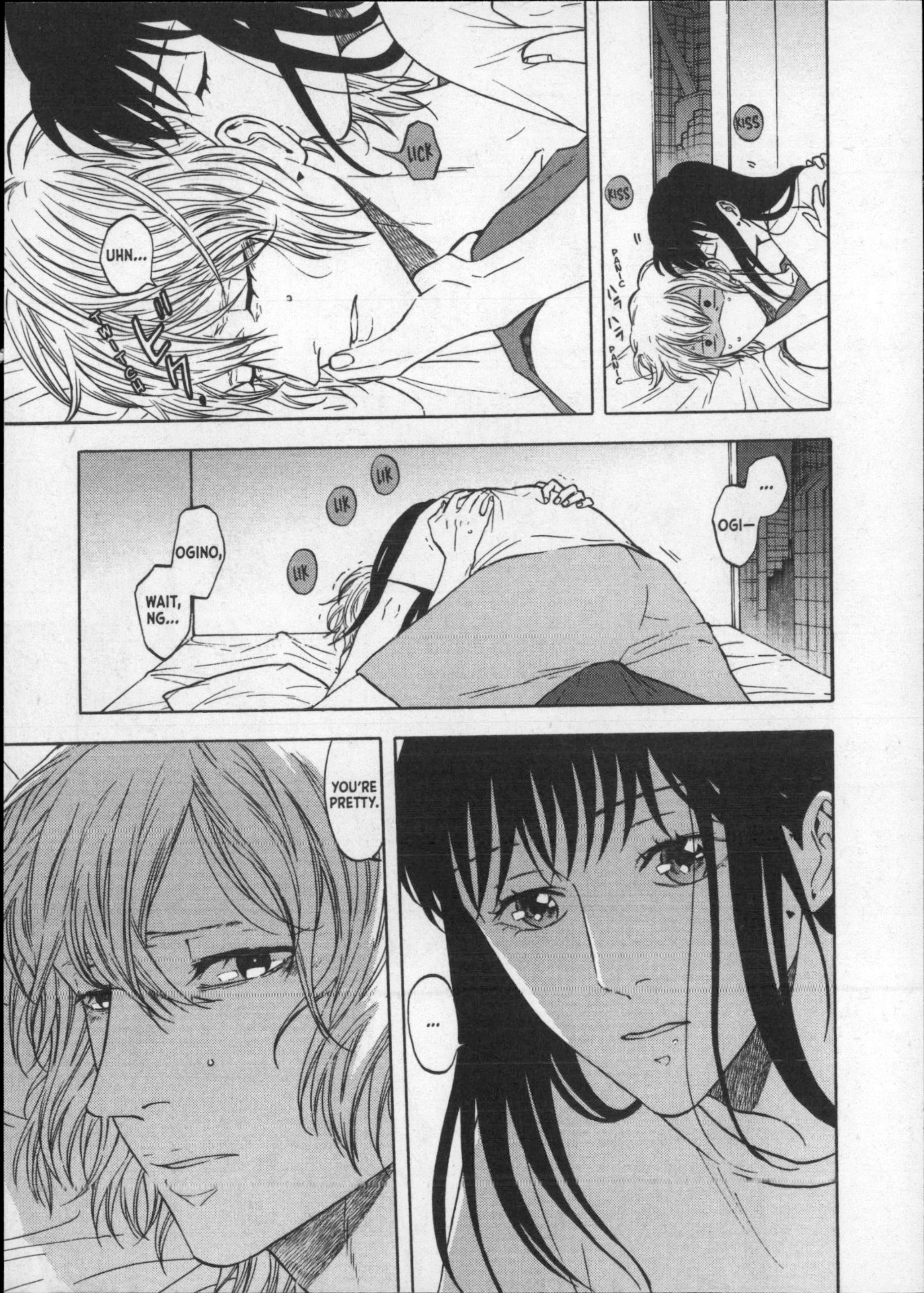
KISS
KISS
PANIC
PANIC
LICK
UHN...
TWITCH
... OGI—
LIK
LIK
LIK
OGINO,
WAIT, NG...
...
YOU'RE PRETTY.

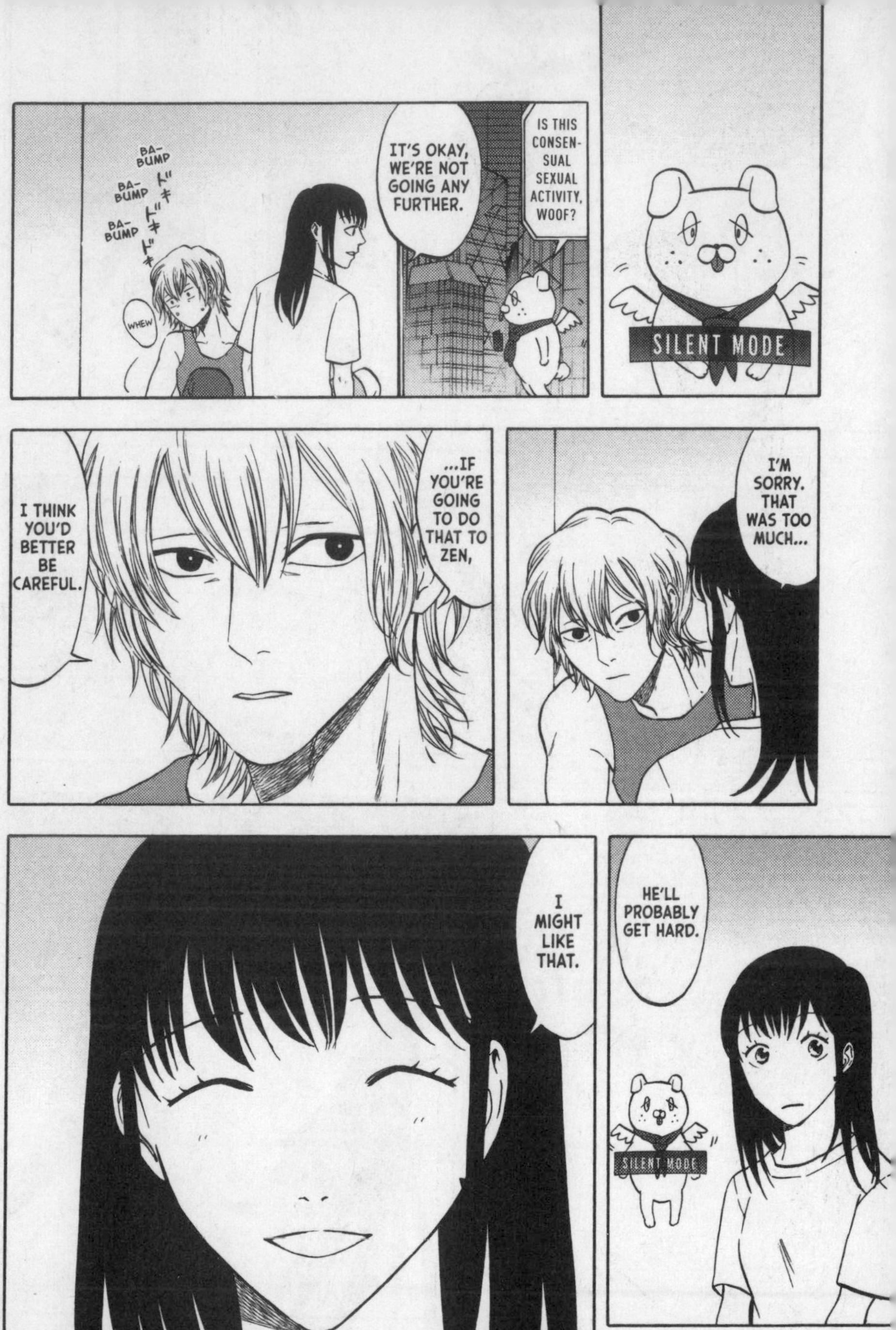
SILENT MODE
IS THIS CONSEN-SUAL SEXUAL ACTIVITY, WOOF?
IT'S OKAY, WE'RE NOT GOING ANY FURTHER.
BA-BUMP BA-BUMP BA-BUMP
ドキドキドキ
WHEW
I'M SORRY. THAT WAS TOO MUCH...
...IF YOU'RE GOING TO DO THAT TO ZEN,
I THINK YOU'D BETTER BE CAREFUL.
HE'LL PROBABLY GET HARD.
SILENT MODE
I MIGHT LIKE THAT.

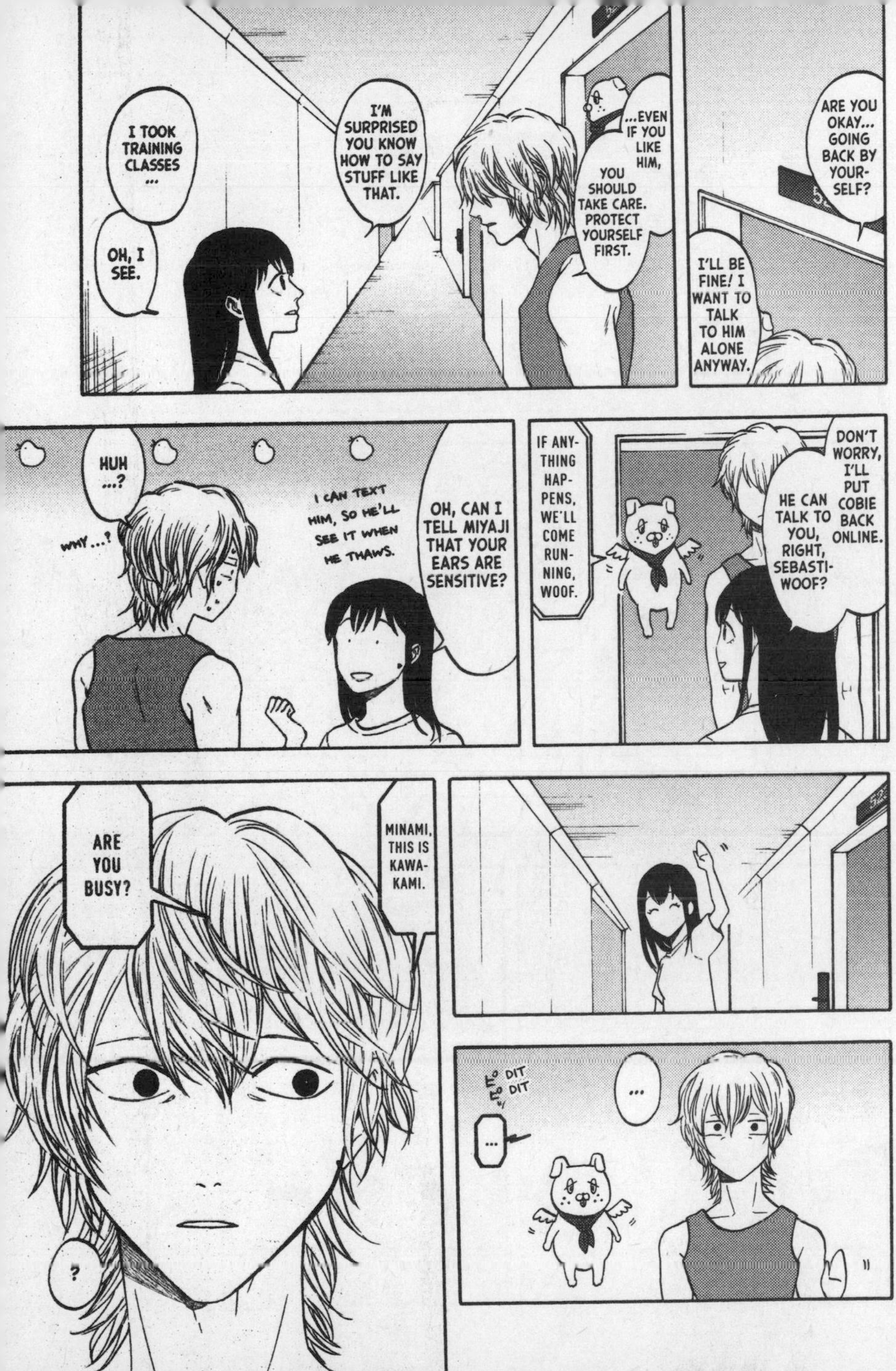
ARE YOU OKAY... GOING BACK BY YOURSELF?
I'LL BE FINE! I WANT TO TALK TO HIM ALONE ANYWAY.
...EVEN IF YOU LIKE HIM, YOU SHOULD TAKE CARE. PROTECT YOURSELF FIRST.
I'M SURPRISED YOU KNOW HOW TO SAY STUFF LIKE THAT.
I TOOK TRAINING CLASSES ...
OH, I SEE.
DON'T WORRY, I'LL PUT COBIE BACK ONLINE.
HE CAN TALK TO YOU, RIGHT, SEBASTI-WOOF?
IF ANYTHING HAPPENS, WE'LL COME RUNNING, WOOF.
OH, CAN I TELL MIYAJI THAT YOUR EARS ARE SENSITIVE?
I CAN TEXT HIM, SO HE'LL SEE IT WHEN HE THAWS.
HUH ...?
WHY ...?
DIT DIT
...
...
MINAMI, THIS IS KAWAKAMI.
ARE YOU BUSY?
?

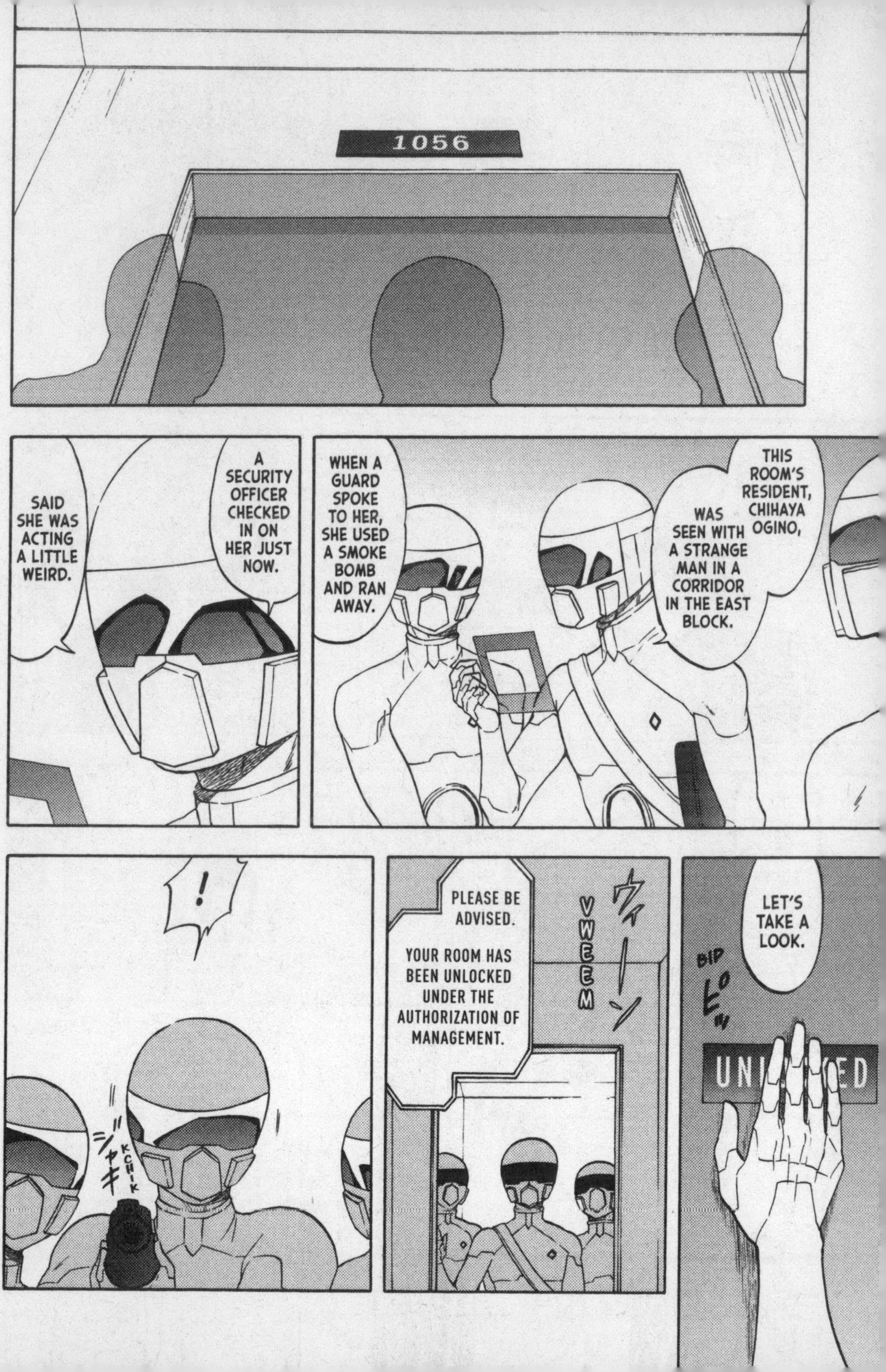
1056
THIS ROOM'S RESIDENT, CHIHAYA OGINO,
WAS SEEN WITH A STRANGE MAN IN A CORRIDOR IN THE EAST BLOCK.
WHEN A GUARD SPOKE TO HER, SHE USED A SMOKE BOMB AND RAN AWAY.
A SECURITY OFFICER CHECKED IN ON HER JUST NOW.
SAID SHE WAS ACTING A LITTLE WEIRD.
LET'S TAKE A LOOK.
ピ
BIP
ヴィーン
VWEEM
PLEASE BE ADVISED.
YOUR ROOM HAS BEEN UNLOCKED UNDER THE AUTHORIZATION OF MANAGEMENT.
!
ジャキ
KCHIK

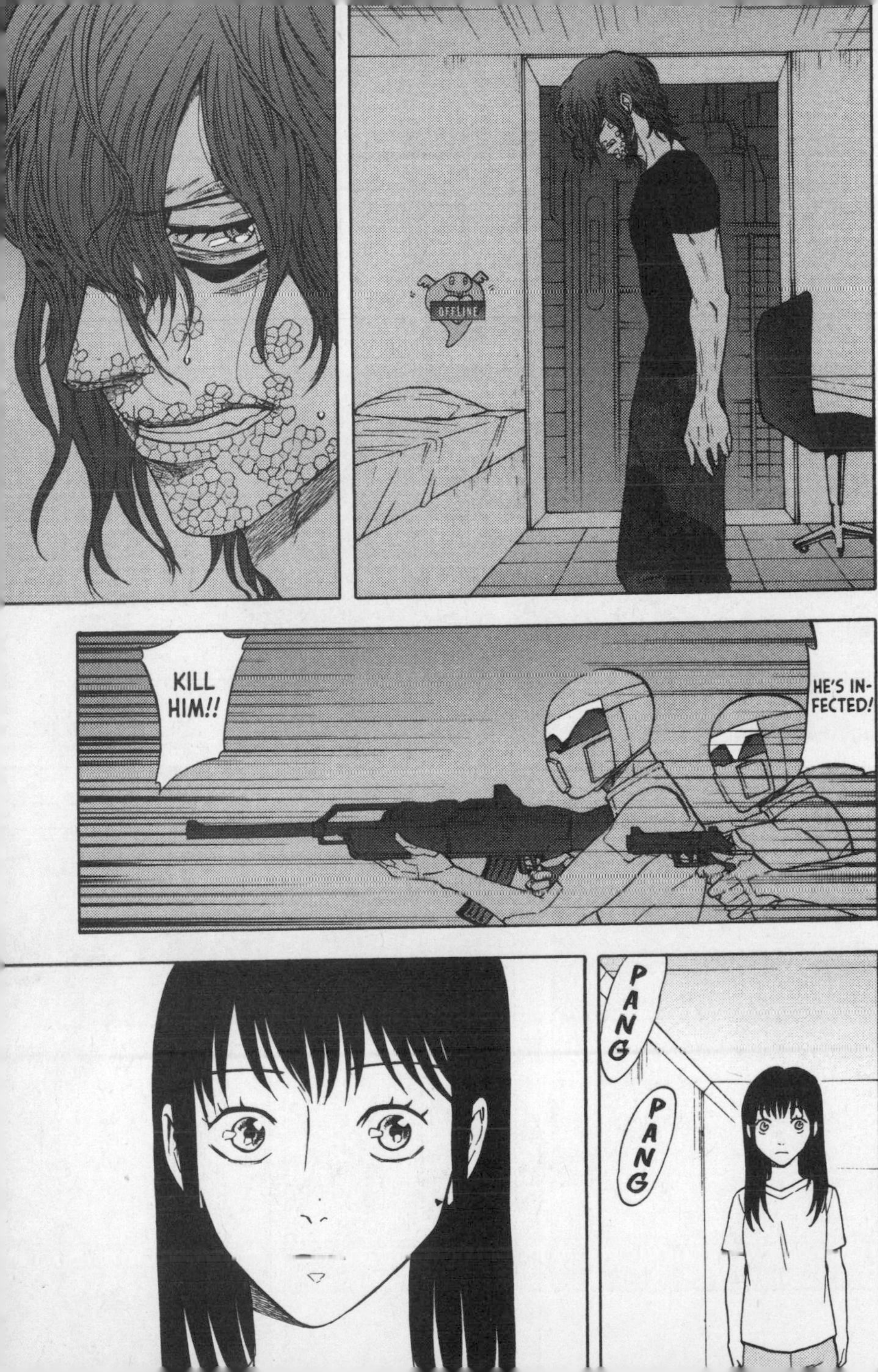
OFFLINE
HE'S IN-FECTED!
KILL HIM!!
PANG
PANG
PANG

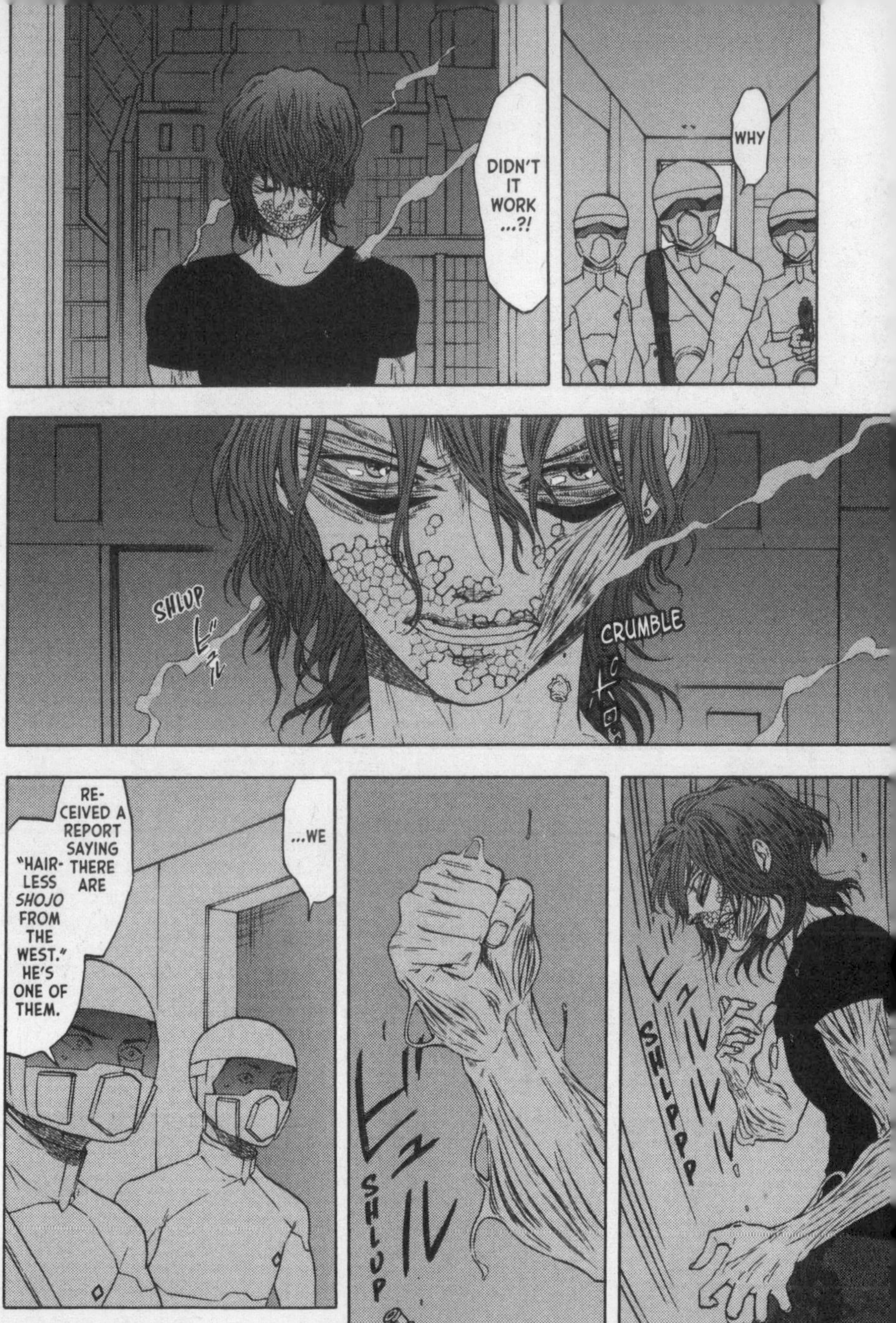
WHY
DIDN'T IT WORK ...?!
CRUMBLE
SHLUP
SHLUPPP
SHLUP
...WE
RECEIVED A REPORT SAYING THERE ARE "HAIRLESS *SHOJO* FROM THE WEST." HE'S ONE OF THEM.

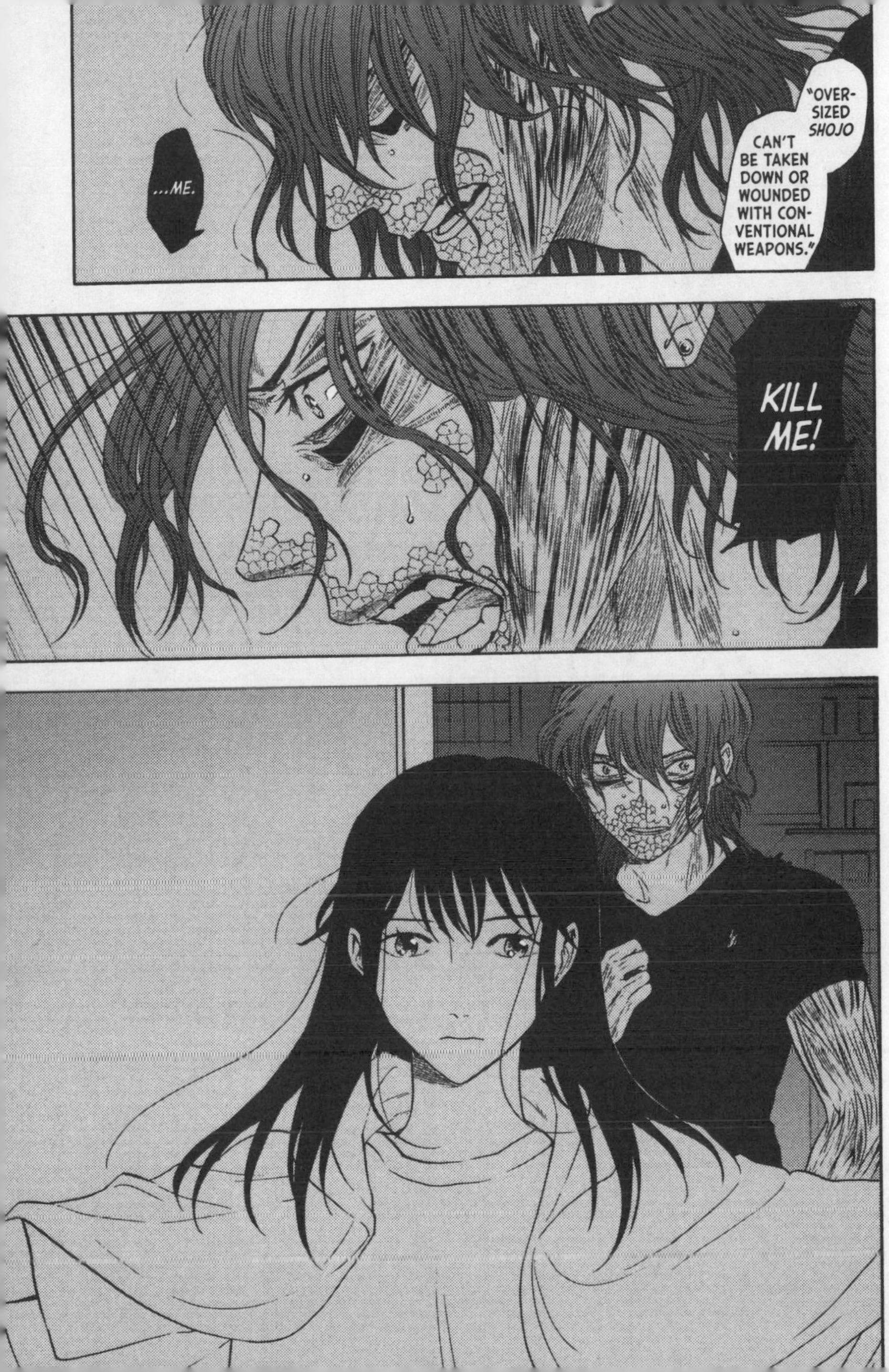
"OVER-SIZED SHOJO CAN'T BE TAKEN DOWN OR WOUNDED WITH CONVENTIONAL WEAPONS."
...ME.
KILL ME!

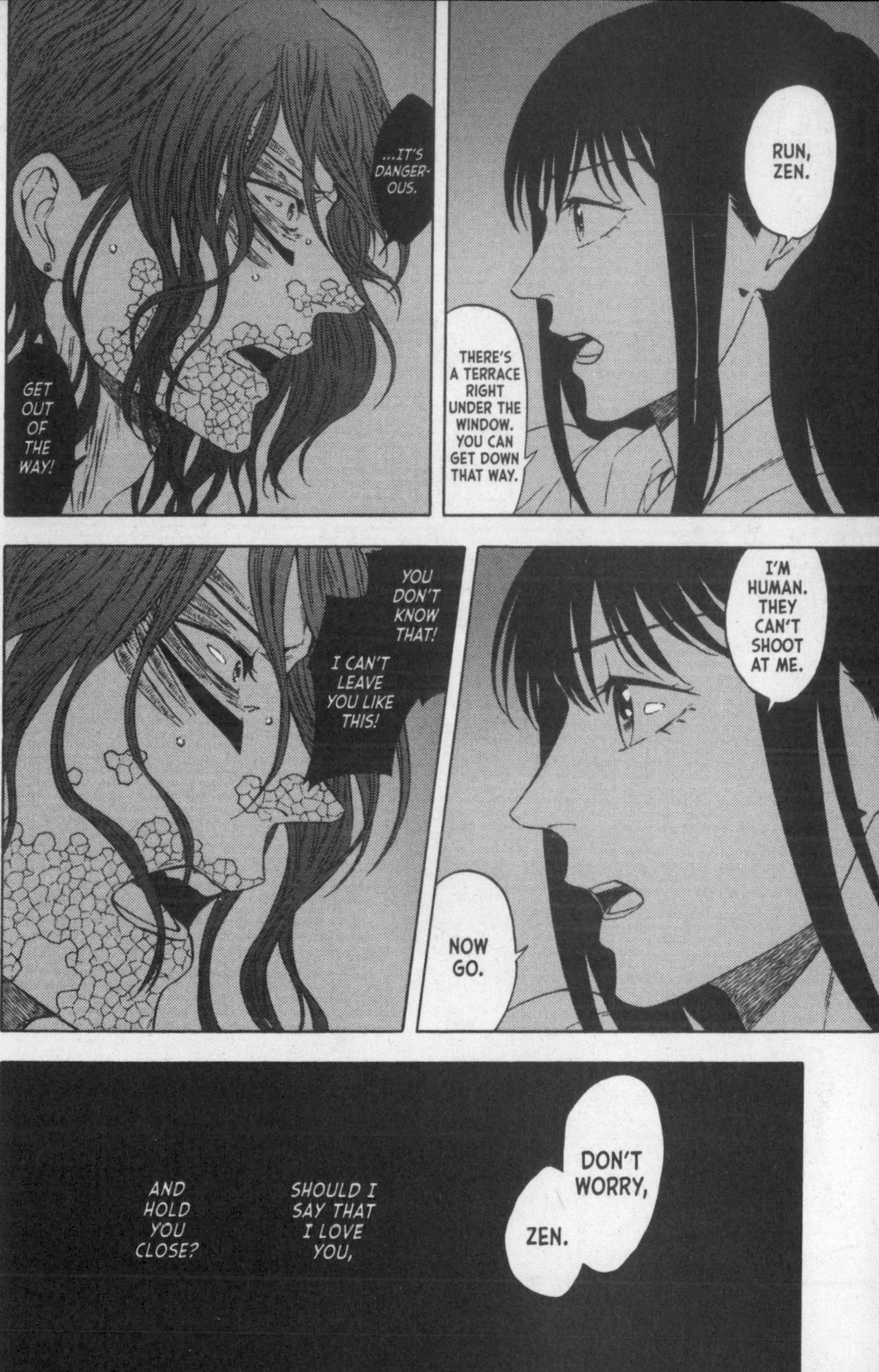
RUN, ZEN.
THERE'S A TERRACE RIGHT UNDER THE WINDOW. YOU CAN GET DOWN THAT WAY.
...IT'S DANGER-OUS.
GET OUT OF THE WAY!
I'M HUMAN. THEY CAN'T SHOOT AT ME.
NOW GO.
YOU DON'T KNOW THAT!
I CAN'T LEAVE YOU LIKE THIS!
DON'T WORRY,
ZEN.
SHOULD I SAY THAT I LOVE YOU,
AND HOLD YOU CLOSE?

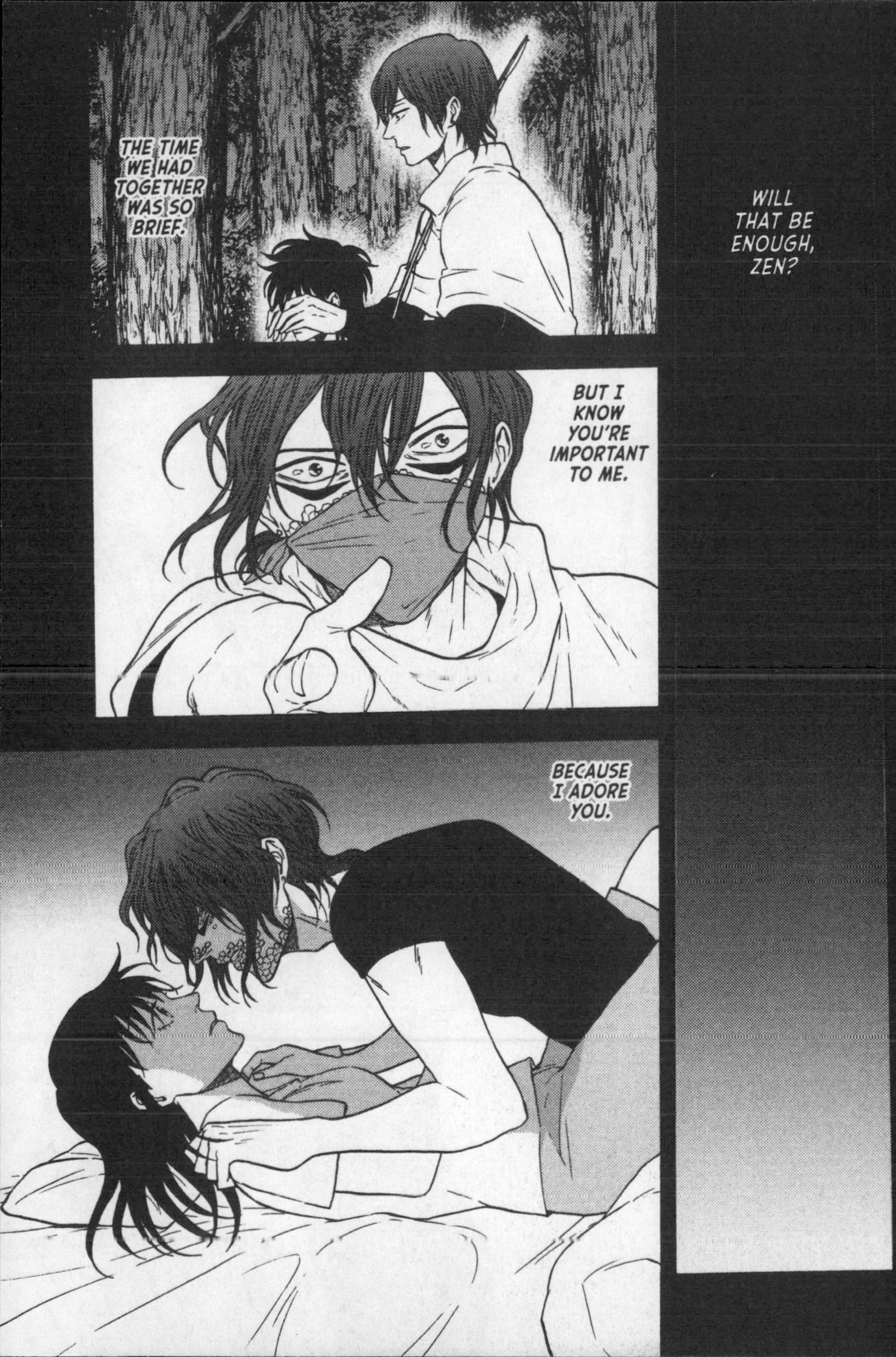
WILL THAT BE ENOUGH, ZEN?
THE TIME WE HAD TOGETHER WAS SO BRIEF.
BUT I KNOW YOU'RE IMPORTANT TO ME.
BECAUSE I ADORE YOU.

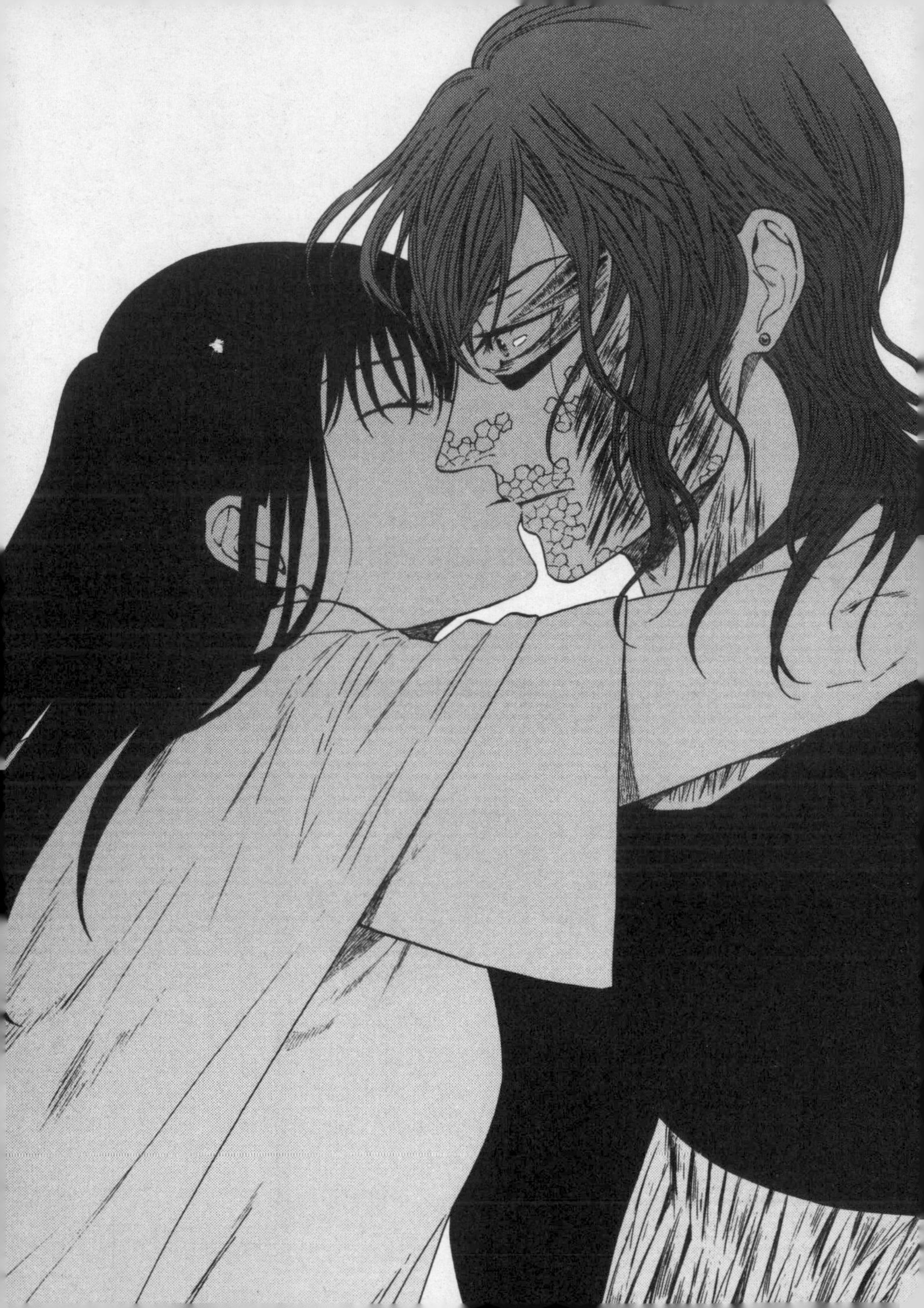

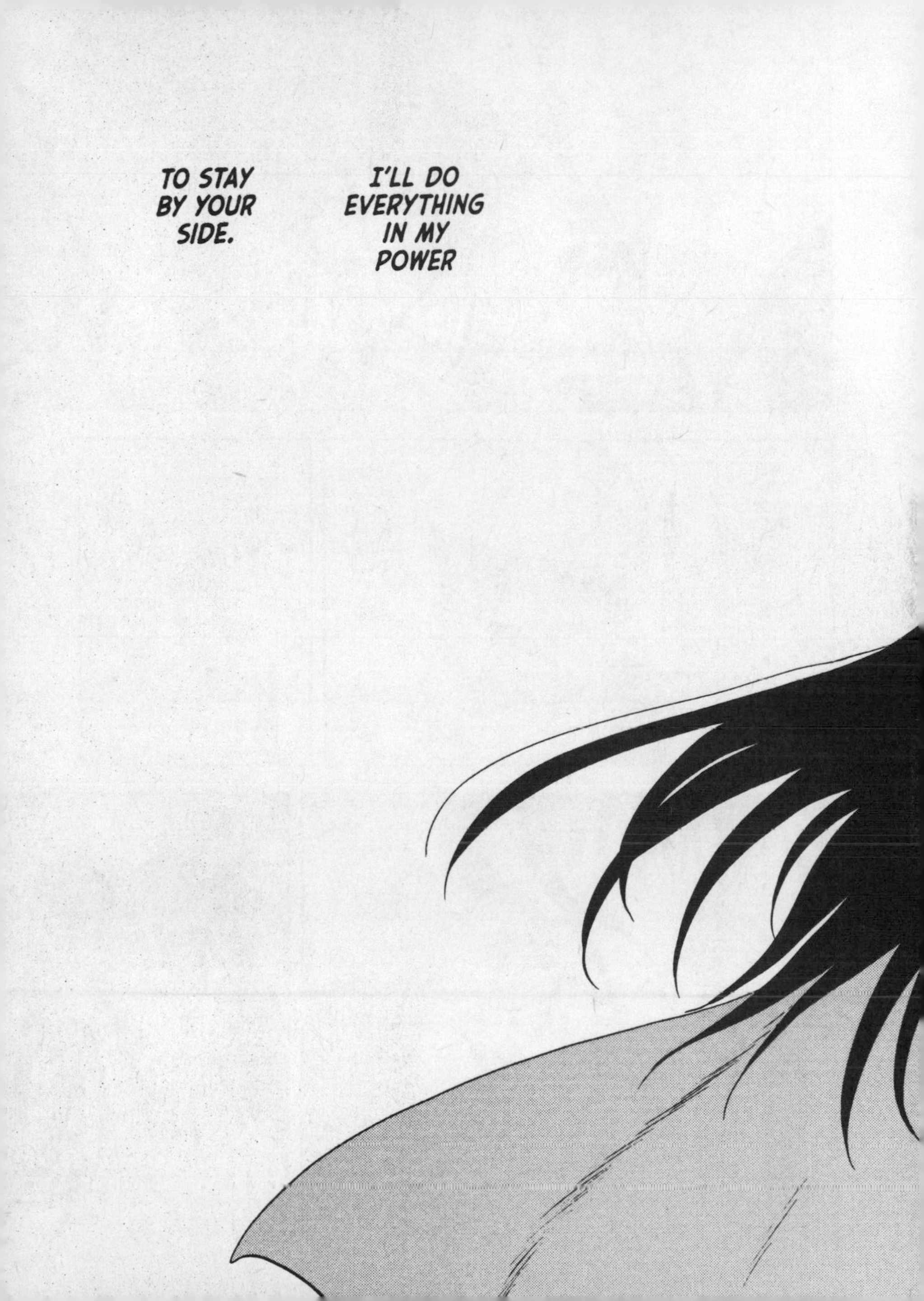
I'LL DO EVERYTHING IN MY POWER
TO STAY BY YOUR SIDE.

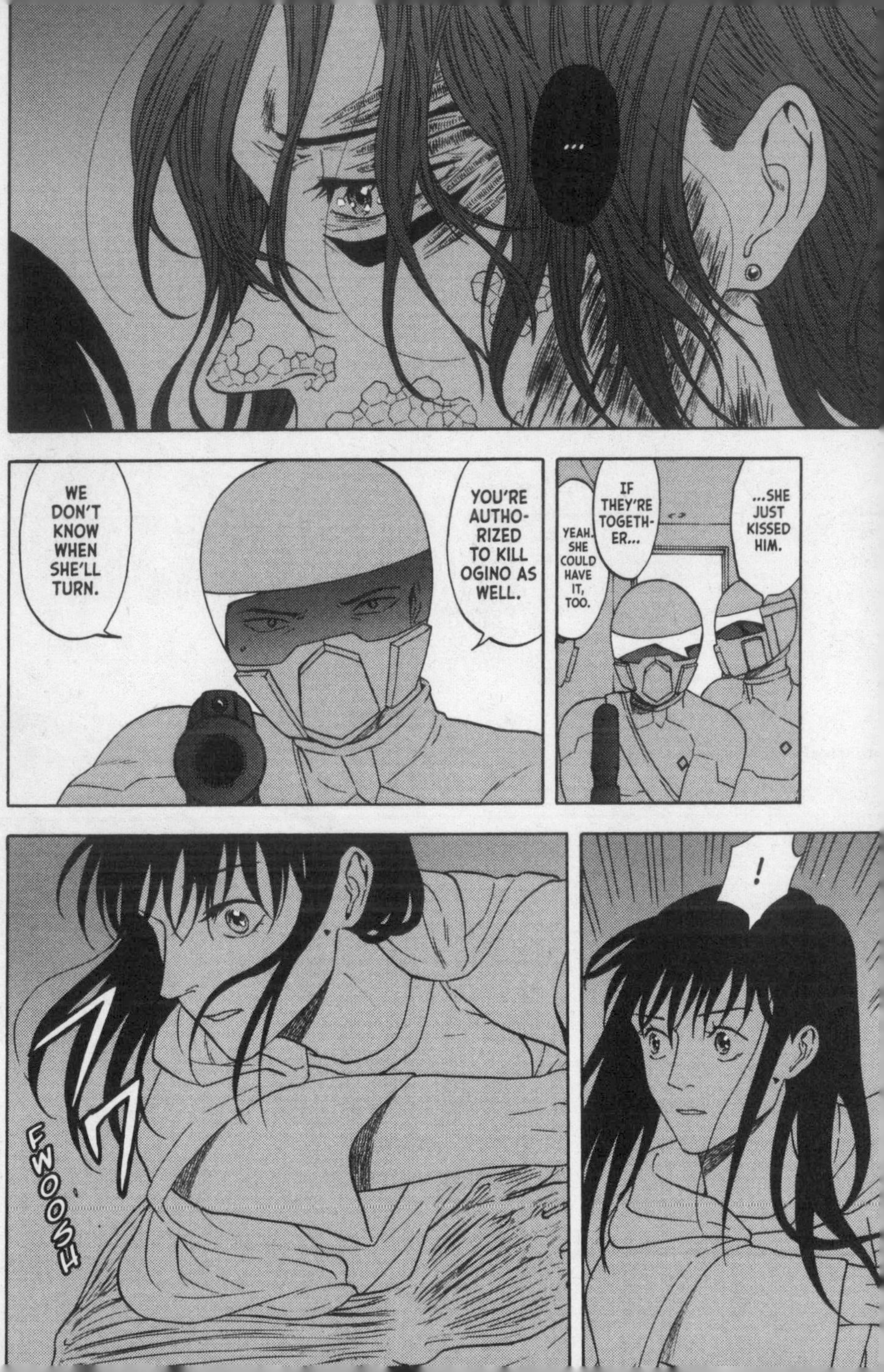
...
...SHE JUST KISSED HIM.
IF THEY'RE TOGETHER...
YEAH. SHE COULD HAVE IT, TOO.
YOU'RE AUTHORIZED TO KILL OGINO AS WELL.
WE DON'T KNOW WHEN SHE'LL TURN.
!
FWOOSH

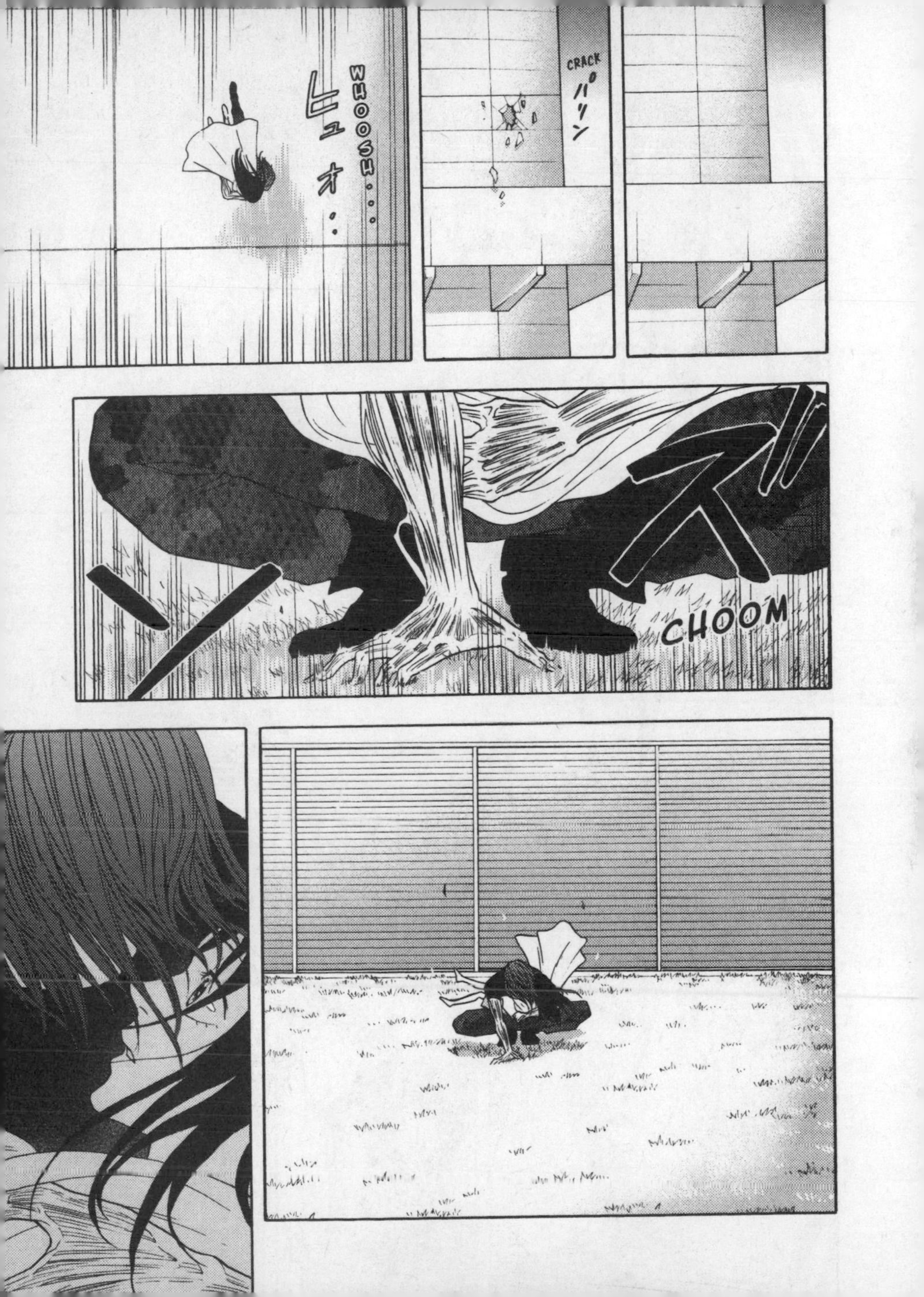
CRACK
パッン
WHOOSH...
ヒュオ..
CHOOM
ズン

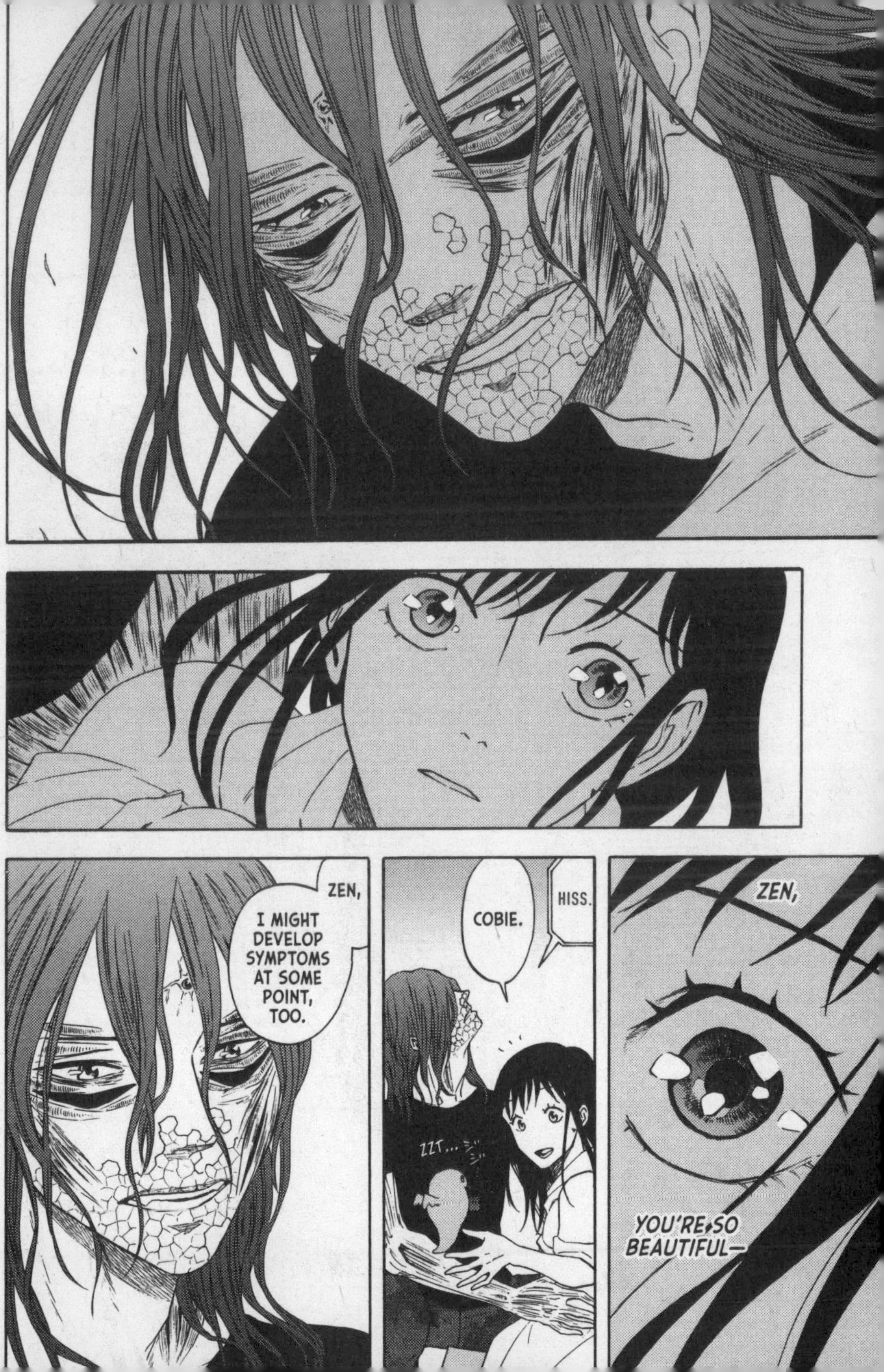
ZEN,
YOU'RE SO BEAUTIFUL—
HISS.
COBIE.
ZZT...
ZEN,
I MIGHT DEVELOP SYMPTOMS AT SOME POINT, TOO.

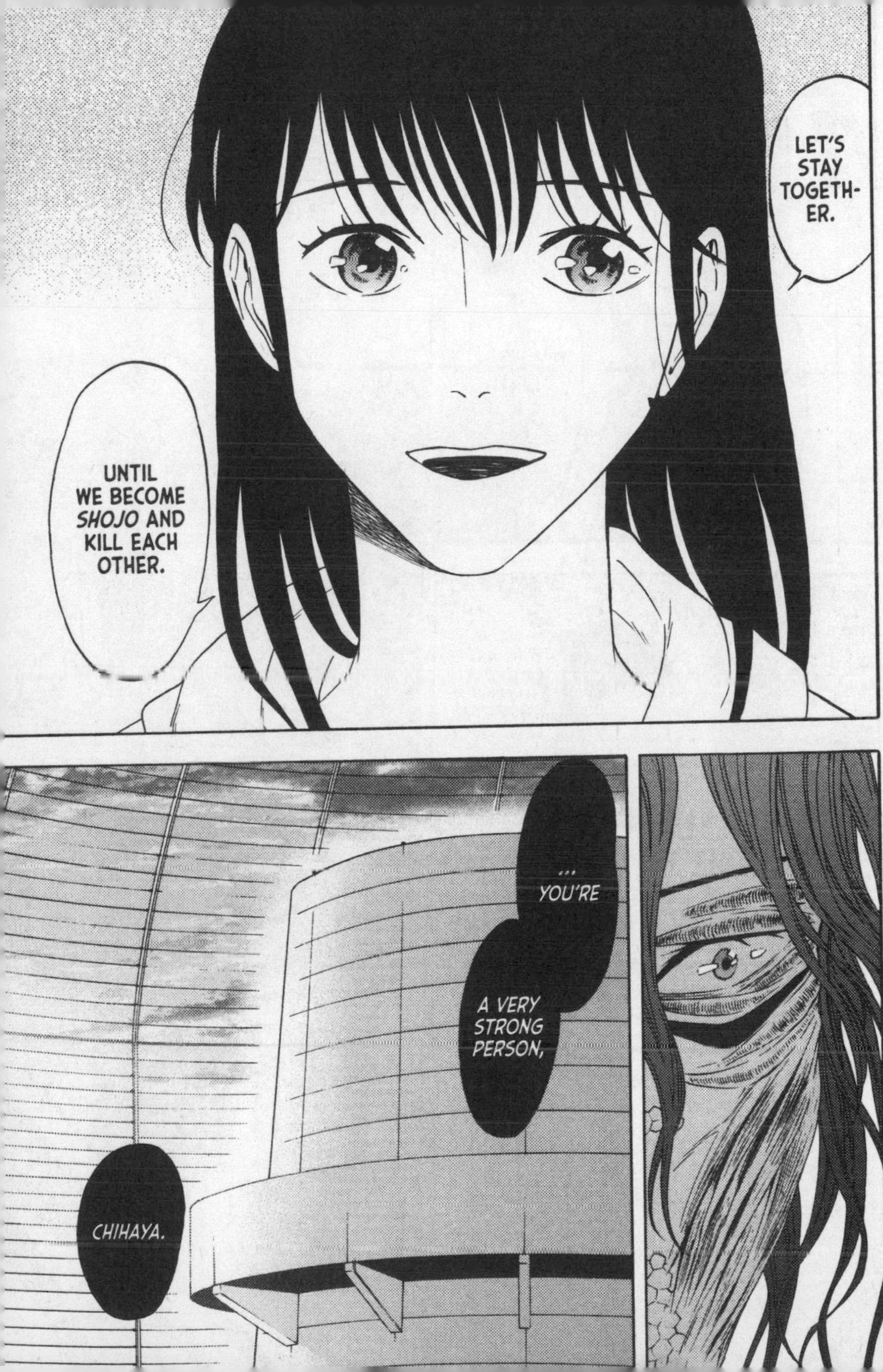
LET'S STAY TOGETH-ER.
UNTIL WE BECOME *SHOJO* AND KILL EACH OTHER.
... YOU'RE
A VERY STRONG PERSON,
CHIHAYA.

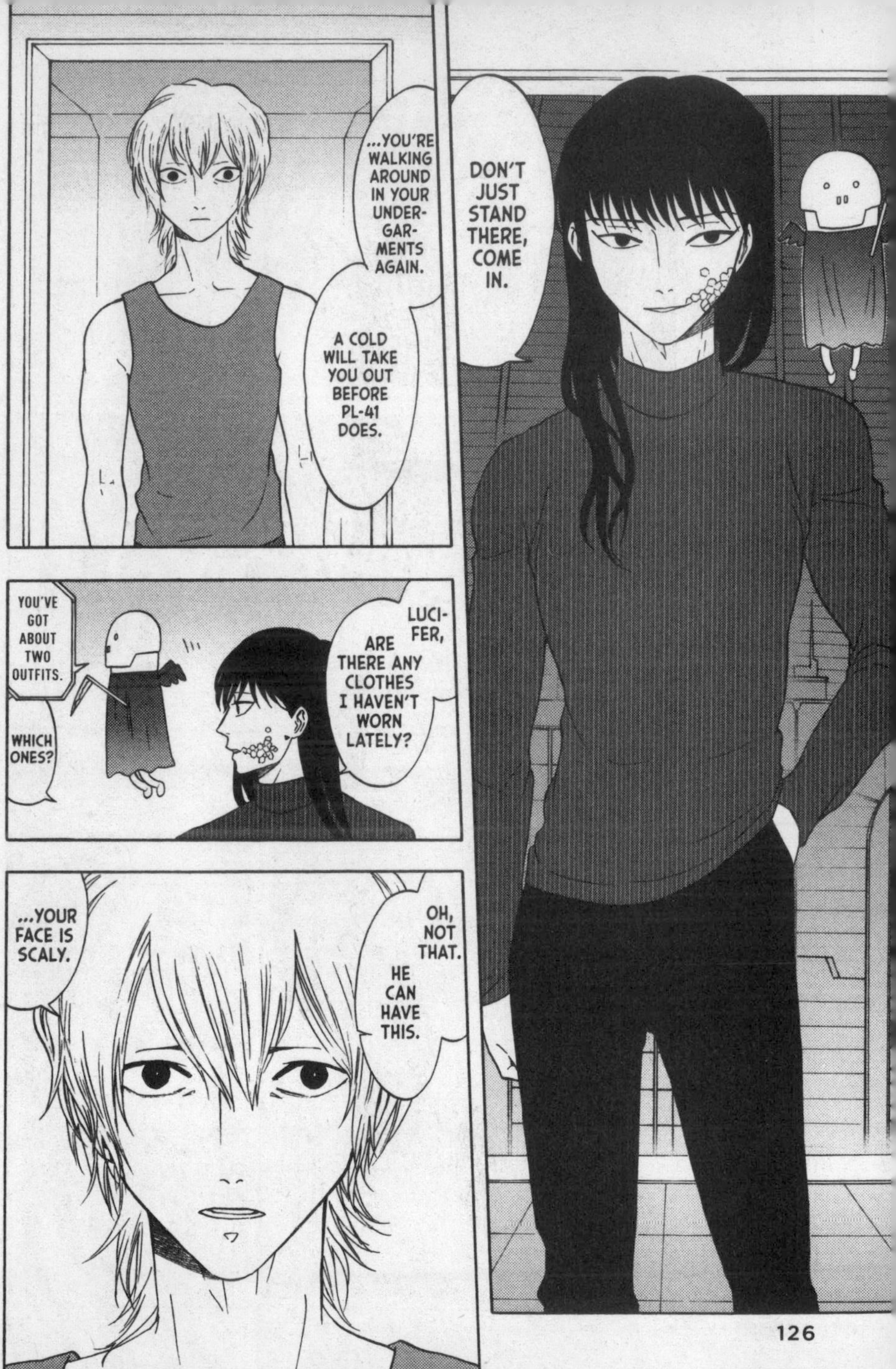
DON'T JUST STAND THERE, COME IN.
...YOU'RE WALKING AROUND IN YOUR UNDER-GAR-MENTS AGAIN.
A COLD WILL TAKE YOU OUT BEFORE PL-41 DOES.
LUCI-FER, ARE THERE ANY CLOTHES I HAVEN'T WORN LATELY?
YOU'VE GOT ABOUT TWO OUTFITS.
WHICH ONES?
OH, NOT THAT. HE CAN HAVE THIS.
...YOUR FACE IS SCALY.

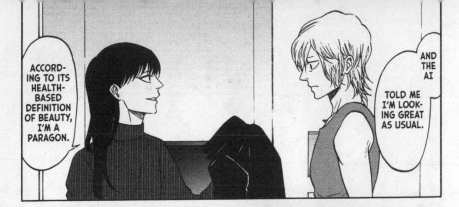

AND THE AI TOLD ME I'M LOOKING GREAT AS USUAL.
ACCORDING TO ITS HEALTH-BASED DEFINITION OF BEAUTY, I'M A PARAGON.
AI'S DON'T HAVE SOULS.
BUT THAT'S WHY THEY'RE SO PRACTICAL.
THEY DON'T GET SWAYED BY BOTHERSOME EMOTIONS.
YOU USED TO BE LIKE THAT, TOO.
...PLEASE SIT DOWN. I WANT TO TALK TO YOU.
BIP
CAPTAIN TAKUMI OZAWA HAS PERMISSION TO ENTER.
STEP
HOW DOES IT LOOK, LAB MANAGER AI?

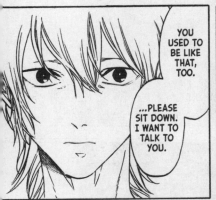

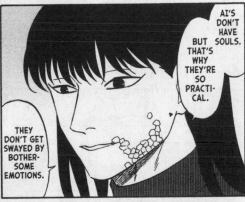

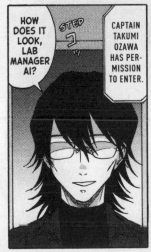

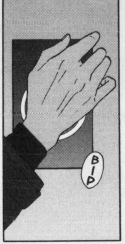

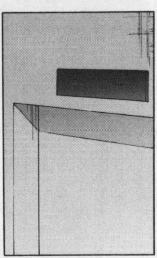

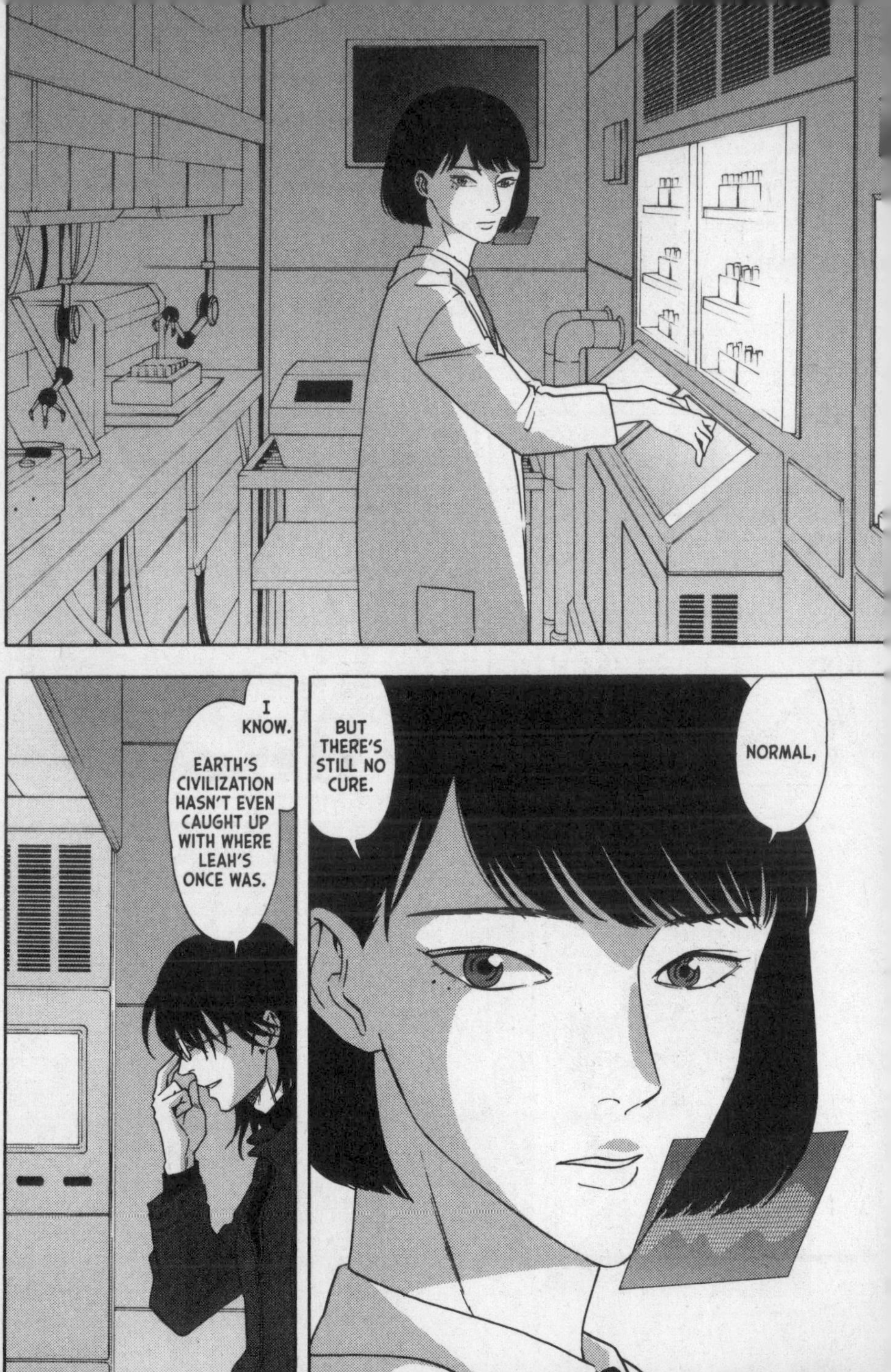
NORMAL,
BUT THERE'S STILL NO CURE.
I KNOW.
EARTH'S CIVILIZATION HASN'T EVEN CAUGHT UP WITH WHERE LEAH'S ONCE WAS.

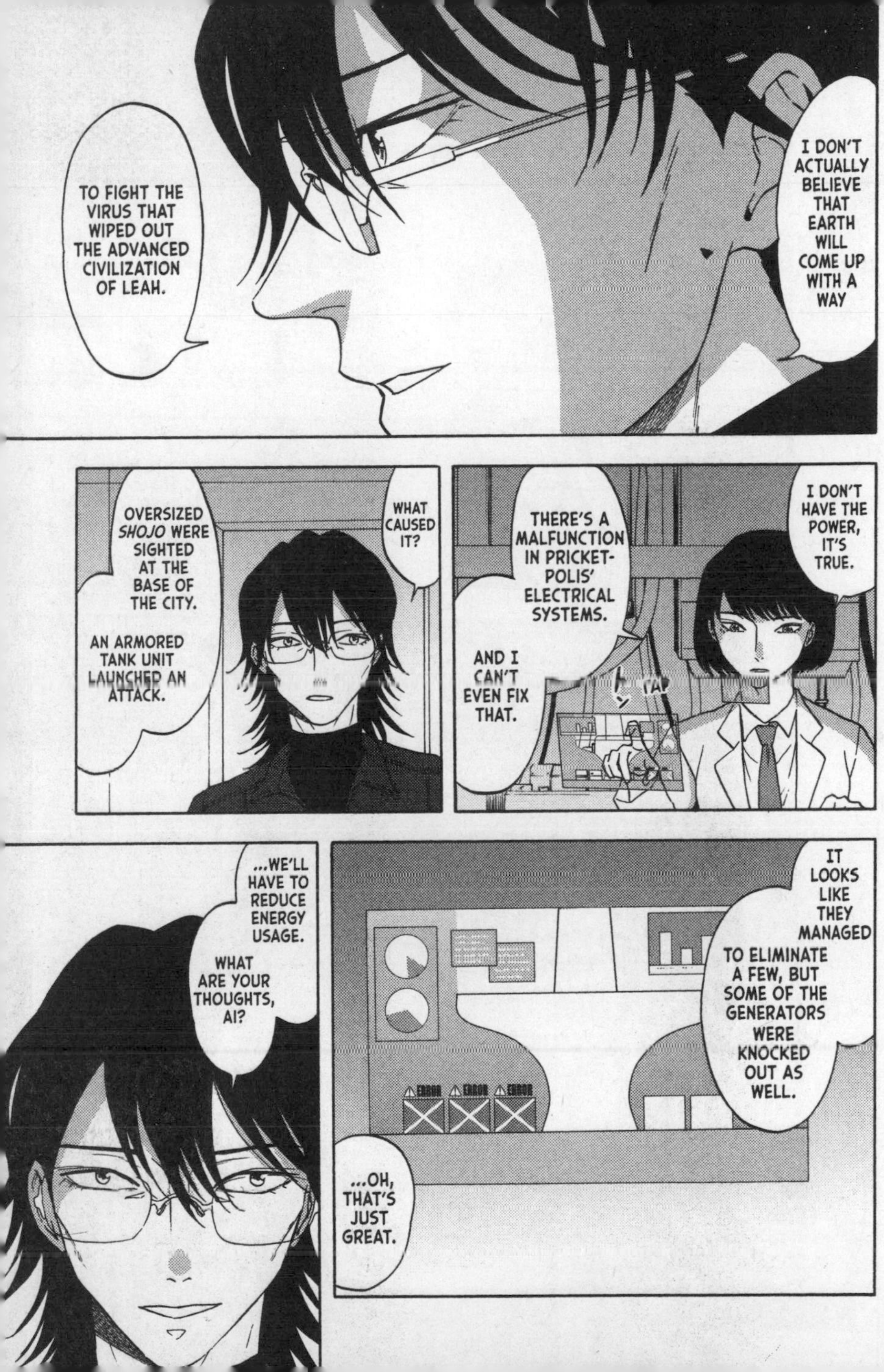
I DON'T ACTUALLY BELIEVE THAT EARTH WILL COME UP WITH A WAY
TO FIGHT THE VIRUS THAT WIPED OUT THE ADVANCED CIVILIZATION OF LEAH.
I DON'T HAVE THE POWER, IT'S TRUE.
THERE'S A MALFUNCTION IN PRICKET-POLIS' ELECTRICAL SYSTEMS.
AND I CAN'T EVEN FIX THAT.
WHAT CAUSED IT?
OVERSIZED *SHOJO* WERE SIGHTED AT THE BASE OF THE CITY.
AN ARMORED TANK UNIT LAUNCHED AN ATTACK.
IT LOOKS LIKE THEY MANAGED TO ELIMINATE A FEW, BUT SOME OF THE GENERATORS WERE KNOCKED OUT AS WELL.
ERROR
ERROR
ERROR
...OH, THAT'S JUST GREAT.
...WE'LL HAVE TO REDUCE ENERGY USAGE.
WHAT ARE YOUR THOUGHTS, AI?

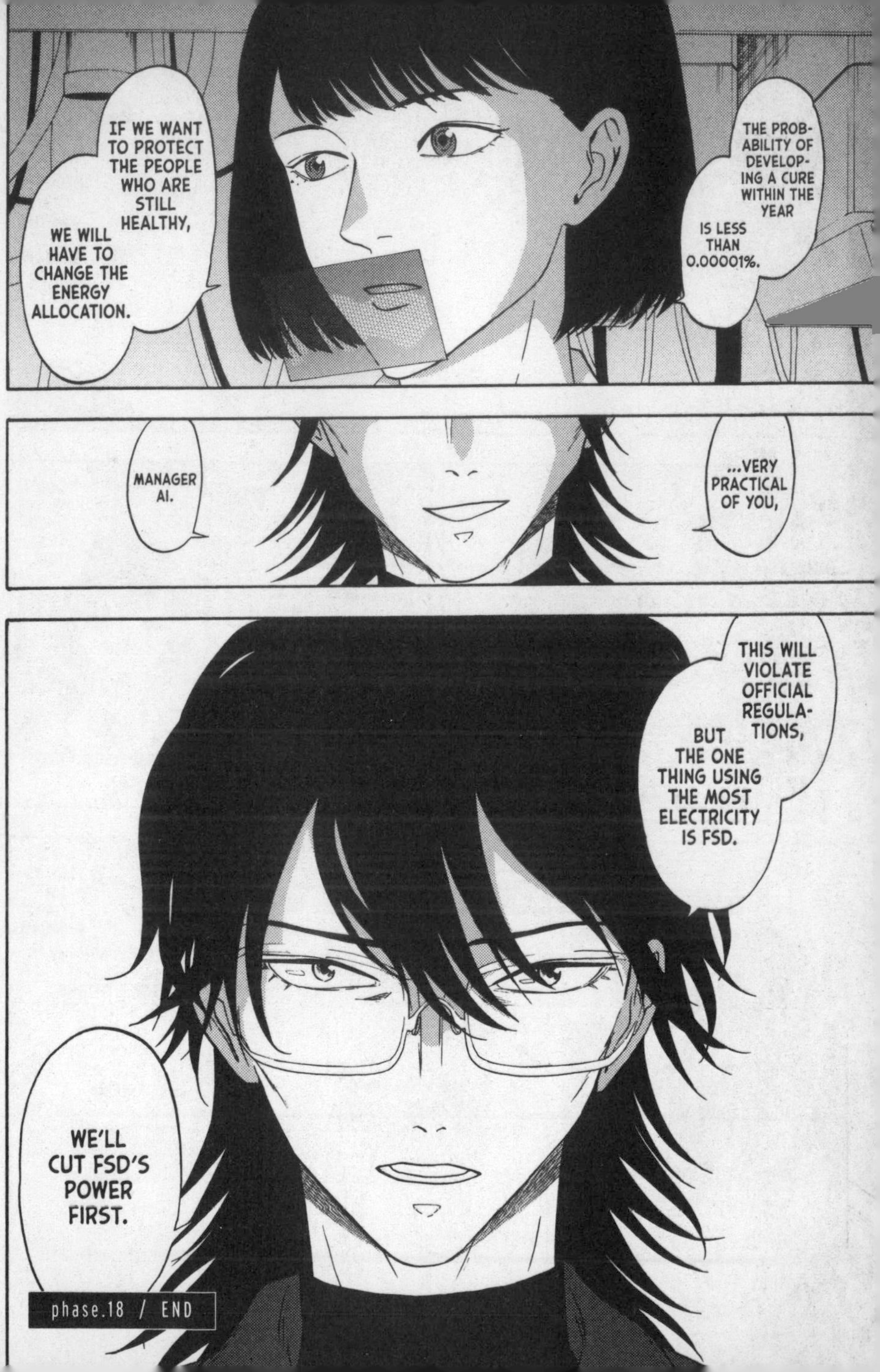
THE PROBABILITY OF DEVELOPING A CURE WITHIN THE YEAR
IS LESS THAN 0.00001%.
IF WE WANT TO PROTECT THE PEOPLE WHO ARE STILL HEALTHY,
WE WILL HAVE TO CHANGE THE ENERGY ALLOCATION.
...VERY PRACTICAL OF YOU,
MANAGER AI.
THIS WILL VIOLATE OFFICIAL REGULATIONS,
BUT THE ONE THING USING THE MOST ELECTRICITY IS FSD.
WE'LL CUT FSD'S POWER FIRST.
phase.18 / END

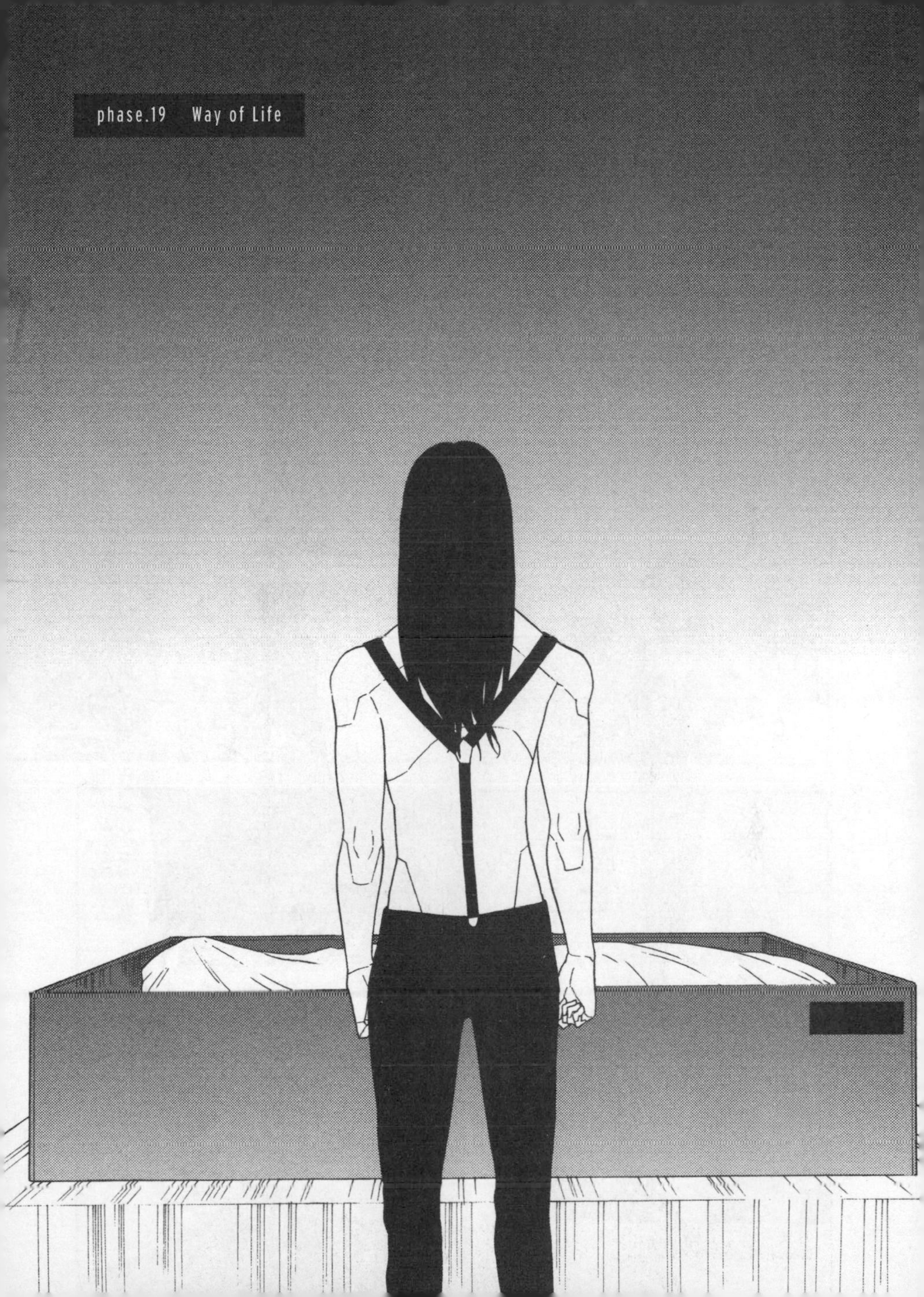
phase.19 Way of Life

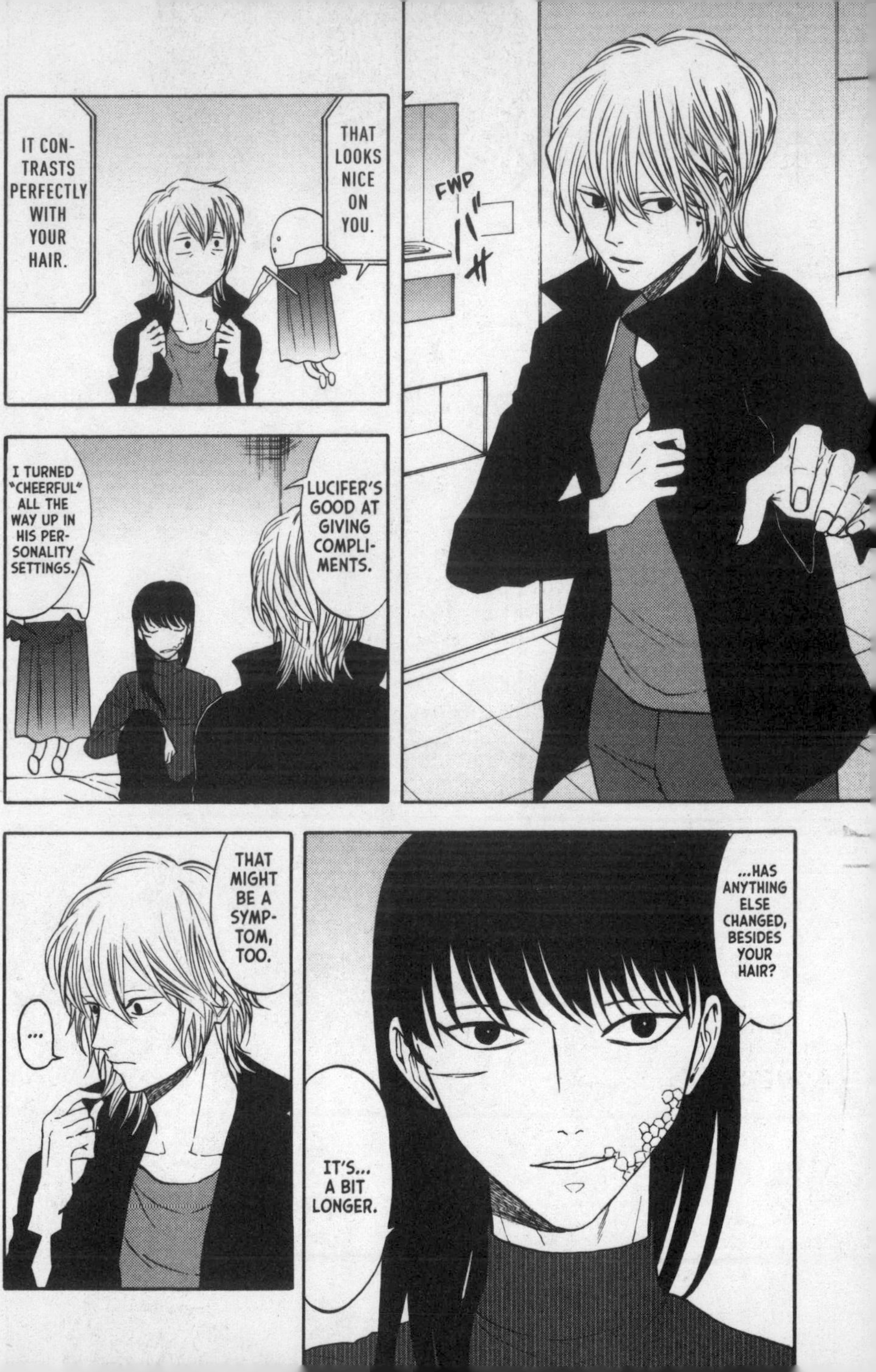
FWP
THAT LOOKS NICE ON YOU.
IT CONTRASTS PERFECTLY WITH YOUR HAIR.
LUCIFER'S GOOD AT GIVING COMPLIMENTS.
I TURNED "CHEERFUL" ALL THE WAY UP IN HIS PERSONALITY SETTINGS.
...HAS ANYTHING ELSE CHANGED, BESIDES YOUR HAIR?
IT'S... A BIT LONGER.
THAT MIGHT BE A SYMPTOM, TOO.
...

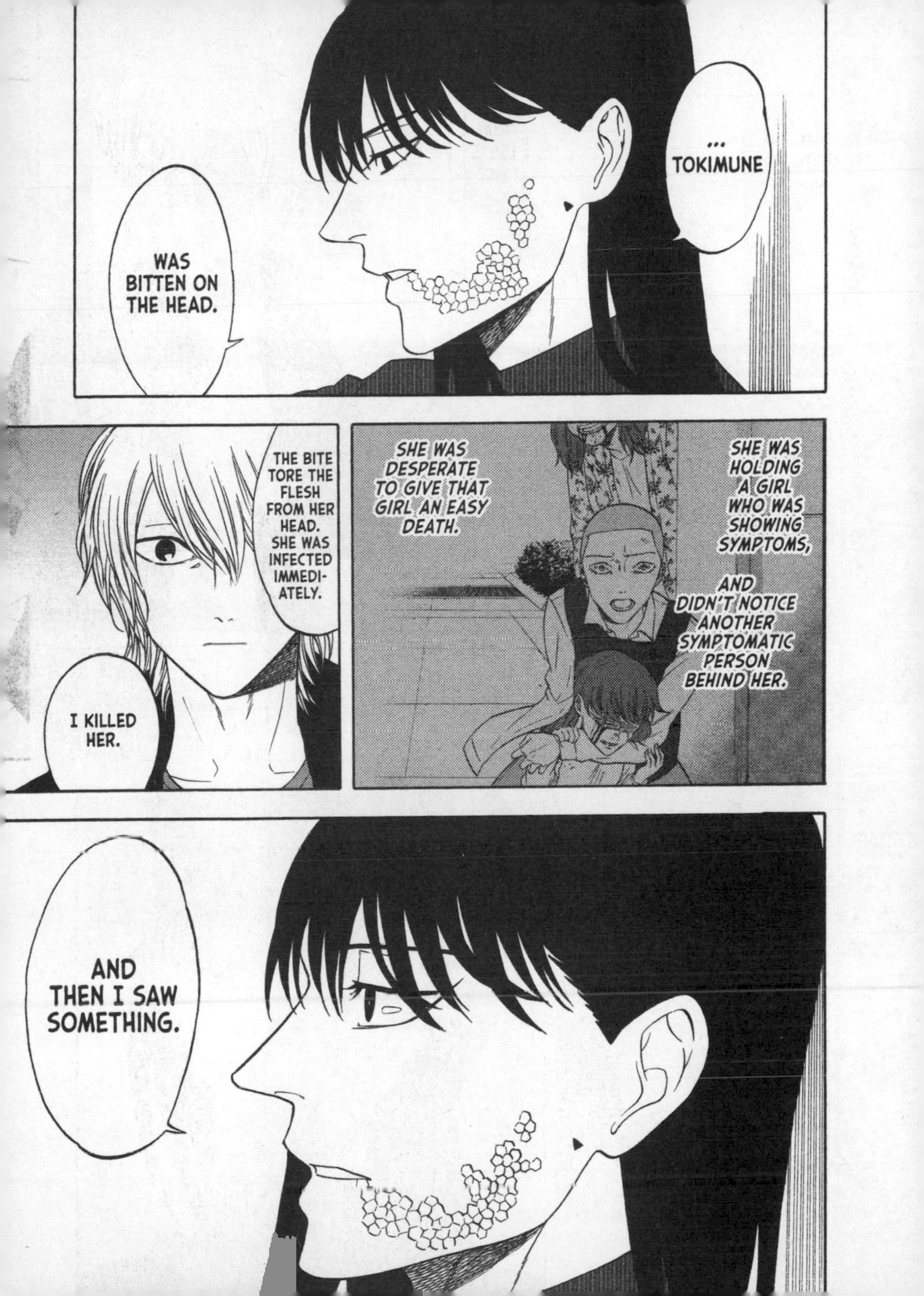
...TOKIMUNE
WAS BITTEN ON THE HEAD.
SHE WAS HOLDING A GIRL WHO WAS SHOWING SYMPTOMS,
SHE WAS DESPERATE TO GIVE THAT GIRL AN EASY DEATH.
AND DIDN'T NOTICE ANOTHER SYMPTOMATIC PERSON BEHIND HER.
THE BITE TORE THE FLESH FROM HER HEAD. SHE WAS INFECTED IMMEDI-ATELY.
I KILLED HER.
AND THEN I SAW SOMETHING.

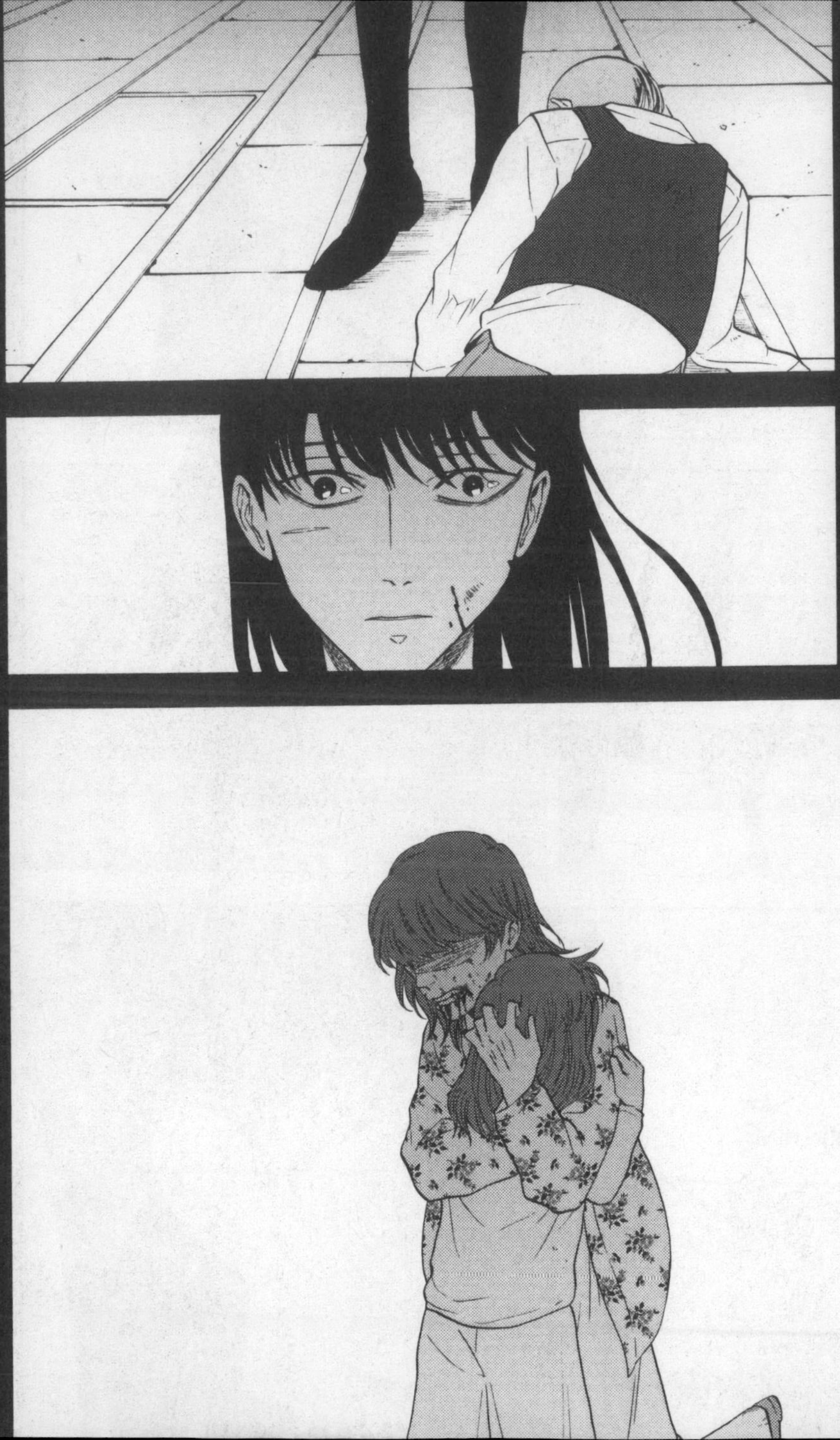

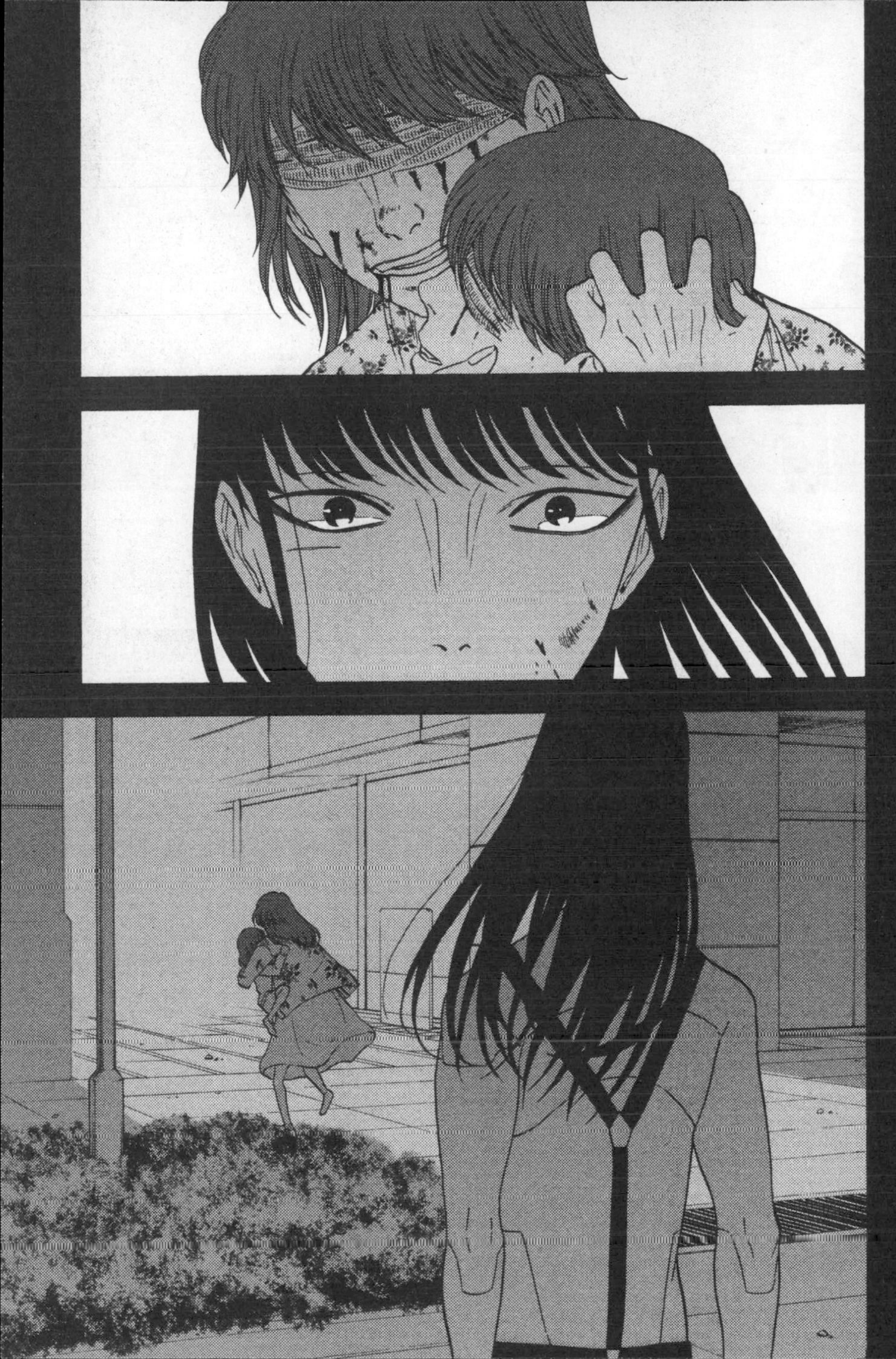

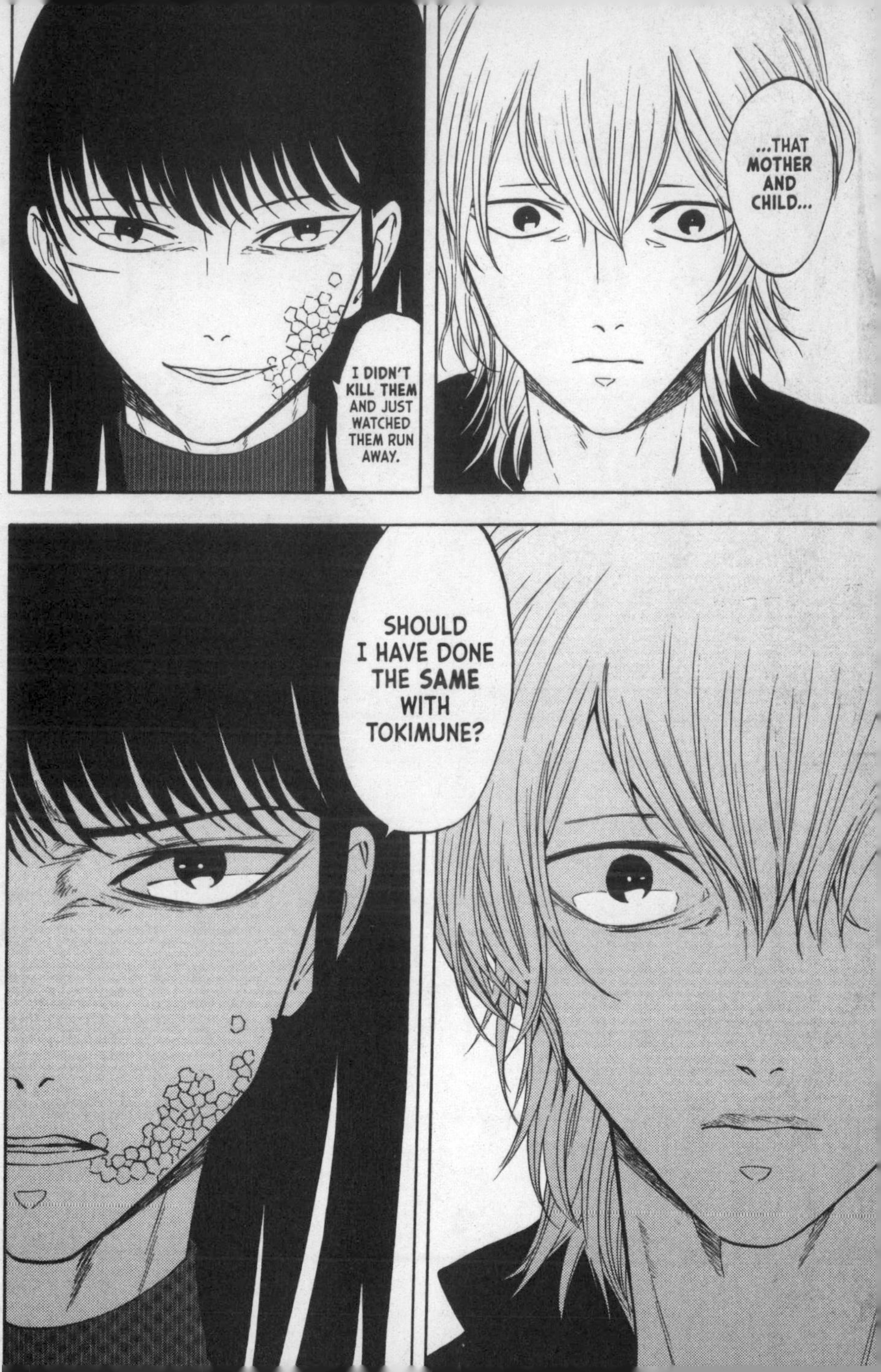
...THAT MOTHER AND CHILD...
I DIDN'T KILL THEM AND JUST WATCHED THEM RUN AWAY.
SHOULD I HAVE DONE THE SAME WITH TOKIMUNE?

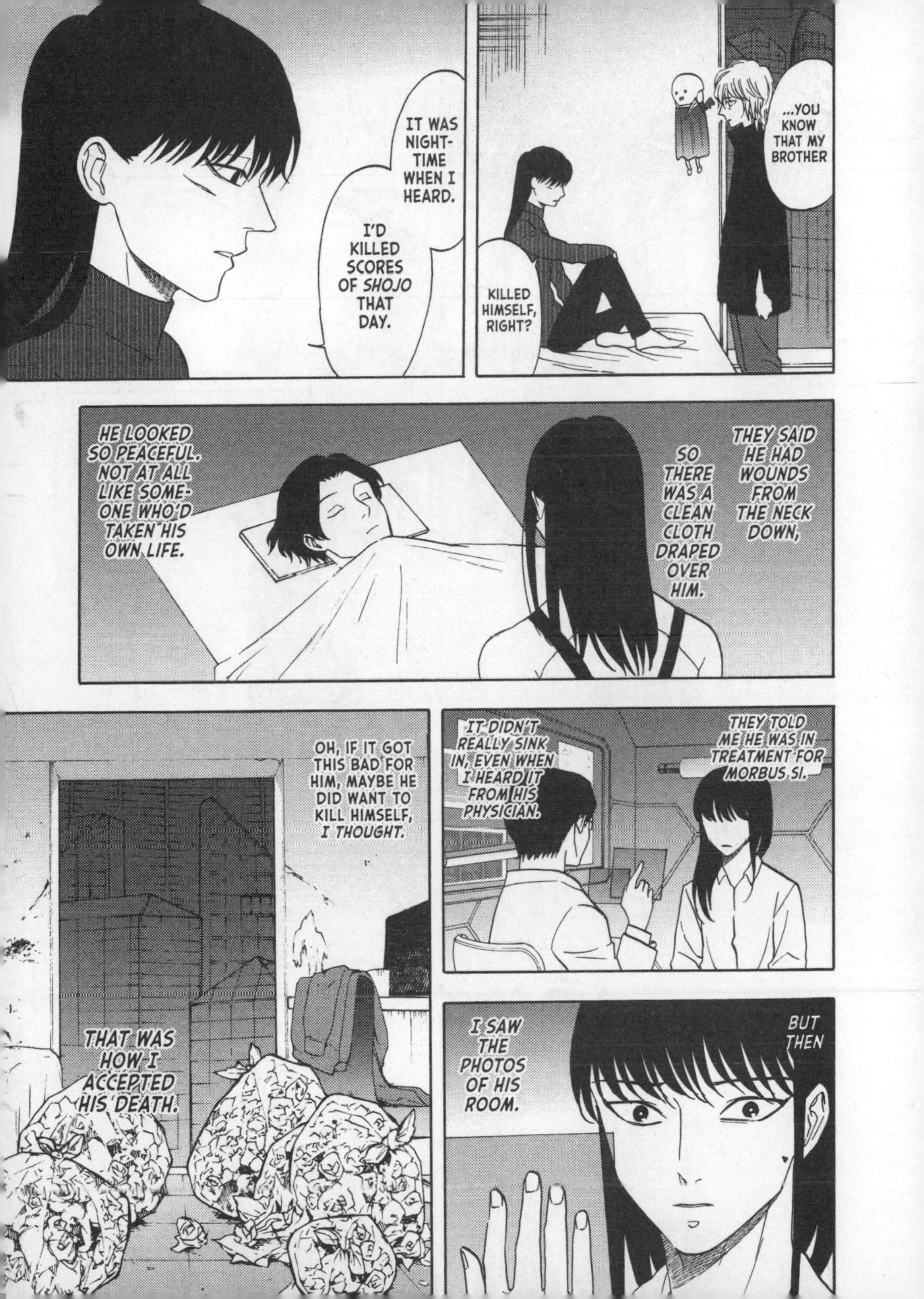
...YOU KNOW THAT MY BROTHER
KILLED HIMSELF, RIGHT?
IT WAS NIGHT-TIME WHEN I HEARD.
I'D KILLED SCORES OF *SHOJO* THAT DAY.
THEY SAID HE HAD WOUNDS FROM THE NECK DOWN,
SO THERE WAS A CLEAN CLOTH DRAPED OVER HIM.
HE LOOKED SO PEACEFUL. NOT AT ALL LIKE SOME-ONE WHO'D TAKEN HIS OWN LIFE.
THEY TOLD ME HE WAS IN TREATMENT FOR MORBUS SI.
IT DIDN'T REALLY SINK IN, EVEN WHEN I HEARD IT FROM HIS PHYSICIAN.
BUT THEN
I SAW THE PHOTOS OF HIS ROOM.
OH, IF IT GOT THIS BAD FOR HIM, MAYBE HE DID WANT TO KILL HIMSELF, *I THOUGHT.*
THAT WAS HOW I ACCEPTED HIS DEATH.

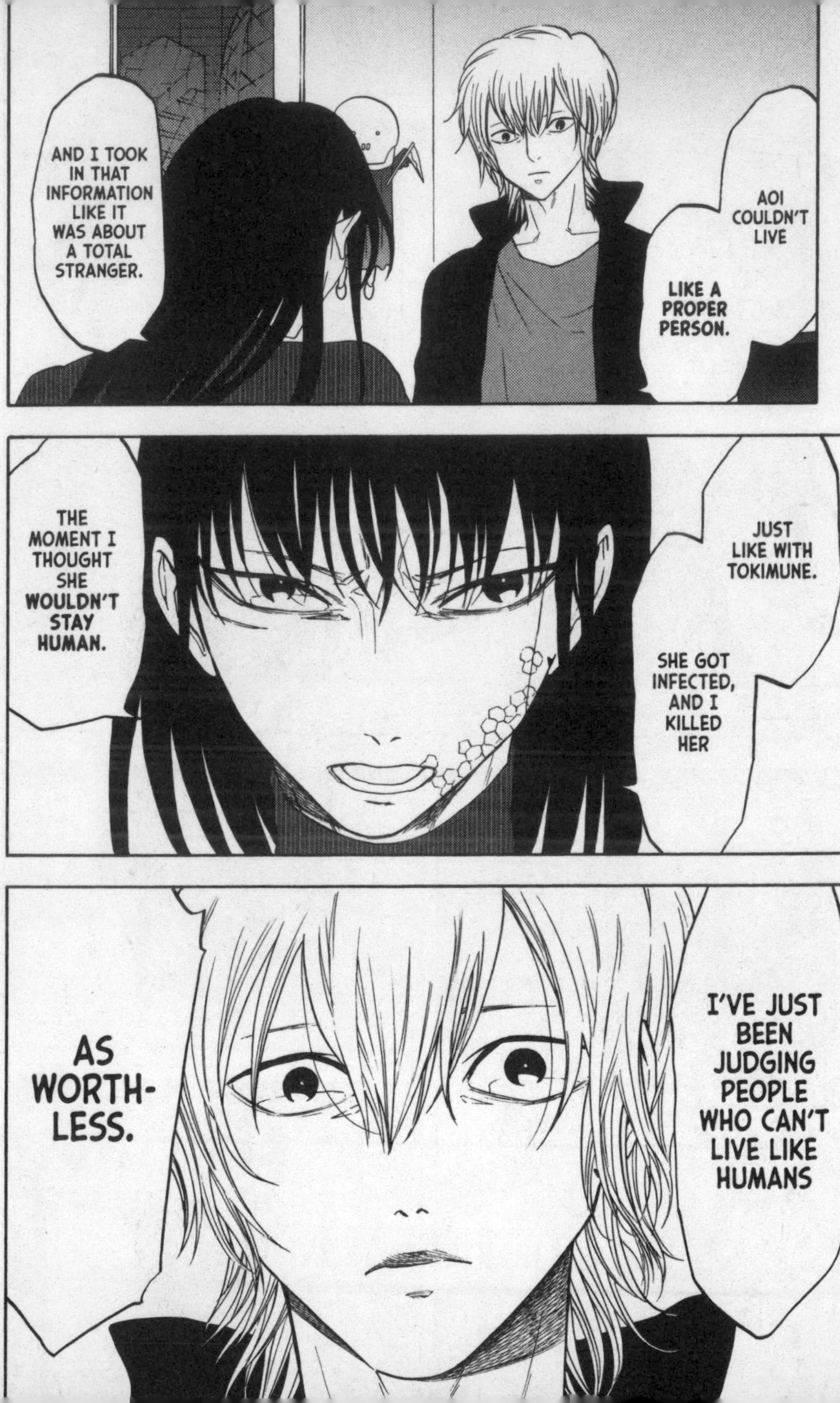
AOI COULDN'T LIVE
LIKE A PROPER PERSON.
AND I TOOK IN THAT INFORMATION LIKE IT WAS ABOUT A TOTAL STRANGER.
JUST LIKE WITH TOKIMUNE.
SHE GOT INFECTED, AND I KILLED HER
THE MOMENT I THOUGHT SHE WOULDN'T STAY HUMAN.
I'VE JUST BEEN JUDGING PEOPLE WHO CAN'T LIVE LIKE HUMANS
AS WORTH-LESS.

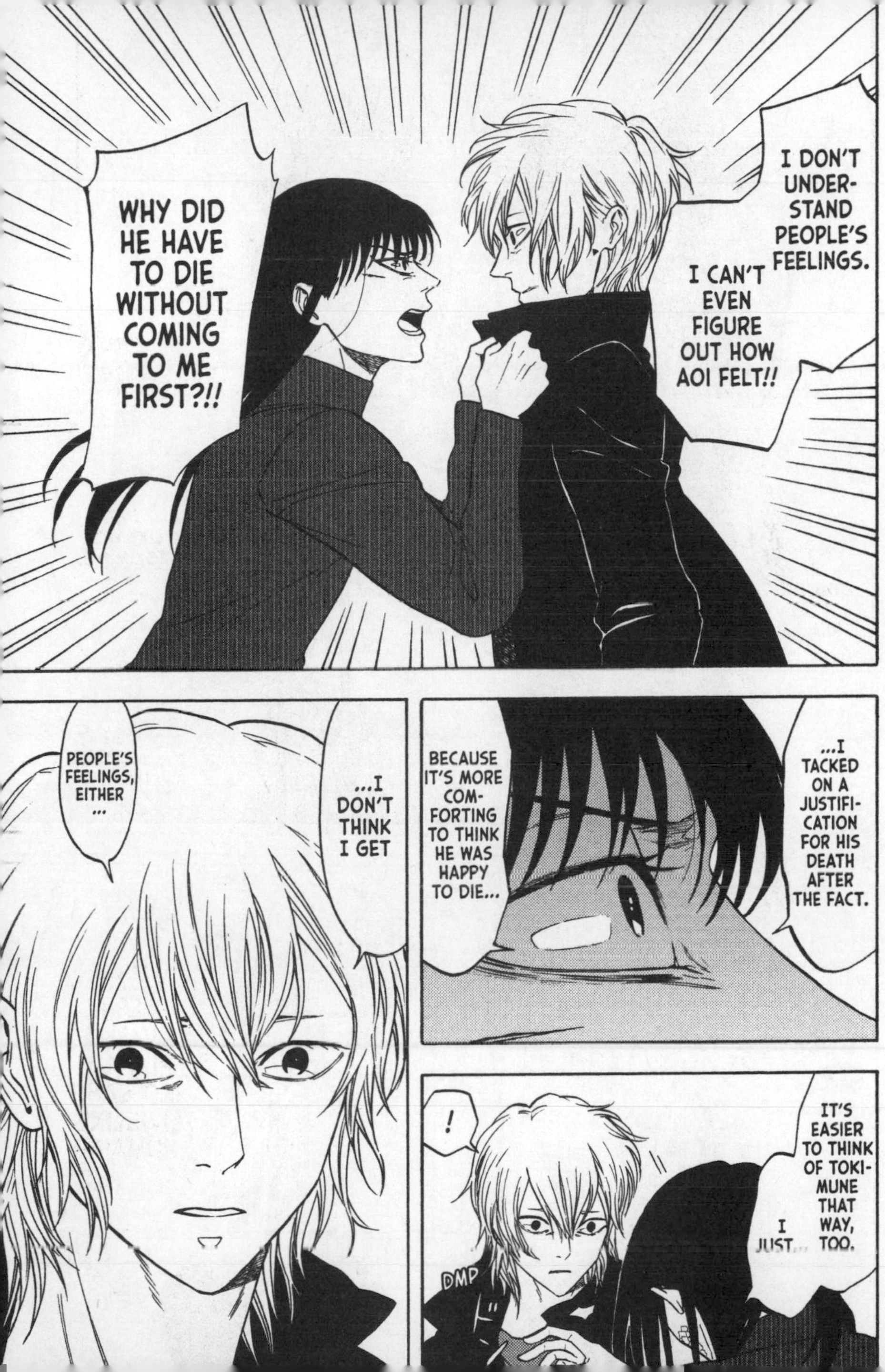
I DON'T UNDER-STAND PEOPLE'S FEELINGS.
I CAN'T EVEN FIGURE OUT HOW AOI FELT!!
WHY DID HE HAVE TO DIE WITHOUT COMING TO ME FIRST?!!
...I TACKED ON A JUSTIFI-CATION FOR HIS DEATH AFTER THE FACT.
BECAUSE IT'S MORE COM-FORTING TO THINK HE WAS HAPPY TO DIE...
IT'S EASIER TO THINK OF TOKI-MUNE THAT WAY, TOO.
I JUST...
!
DMP
...I DON'T THINK I GET
PEOPLE'S FEELINGS, EITHER ...

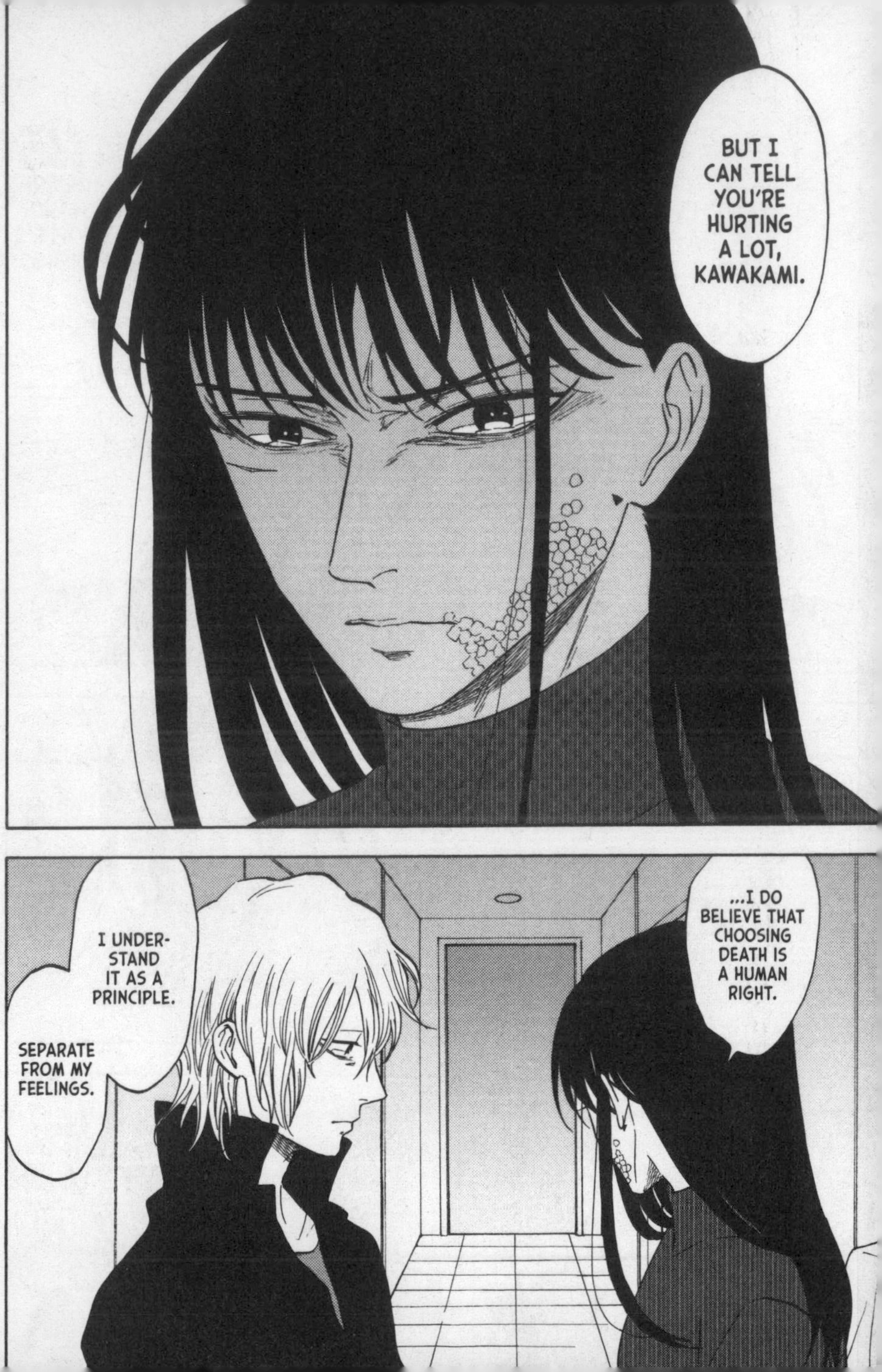
BUT I CAN TELL YOU'RE HURTING A LOT, KAWAKAMI.
...I DO BELIEVE THAT CHOOSING DEATH IS A HUMAN RIGHT.
I UNDER-STAND IT AS A PRINCIPLE.
SEPARATE FROM MY FEELINGS.

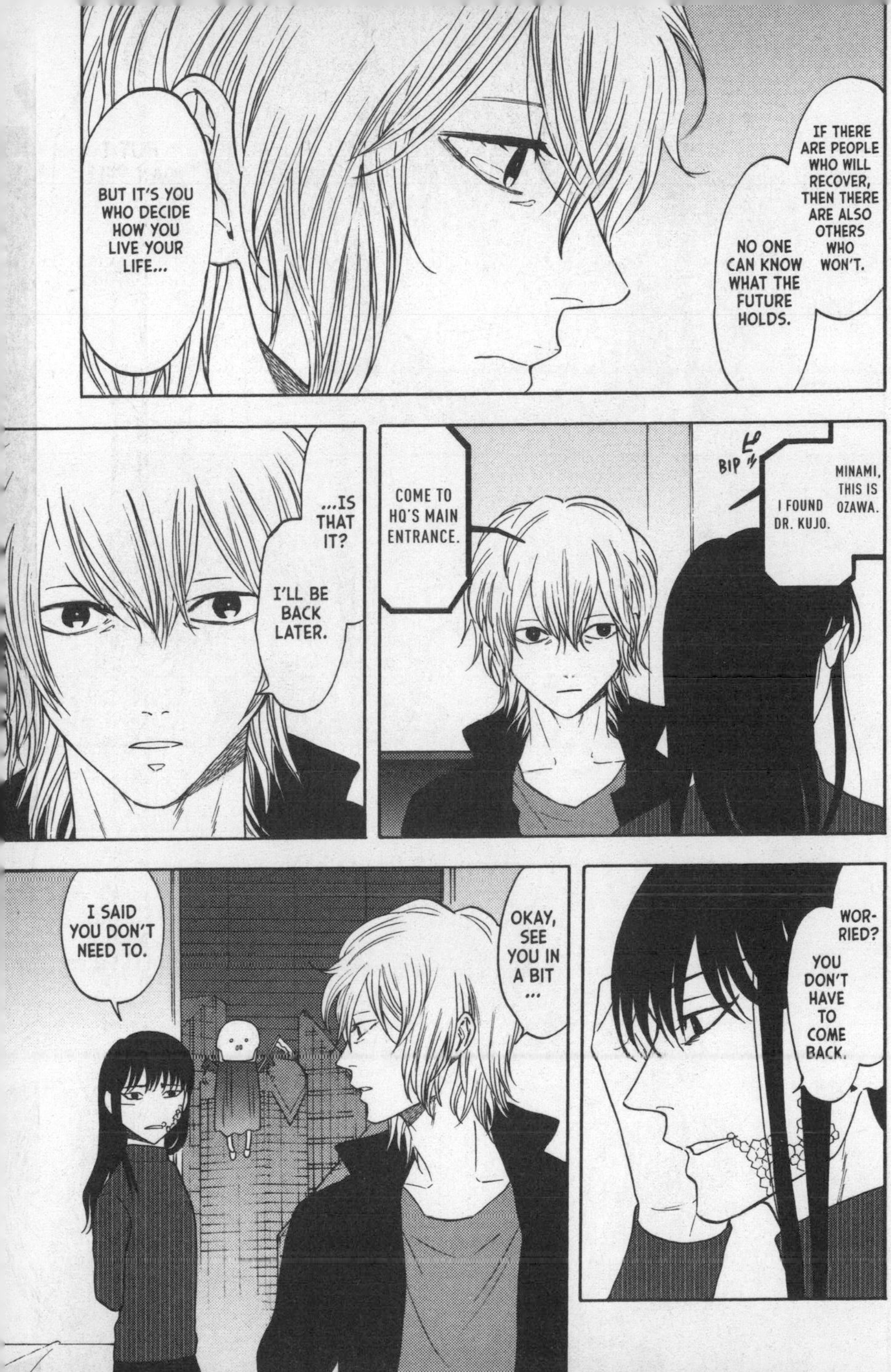
IF THERE ARE PEOPLE WHO WILL RECOVER, THEN THERE ARE ALSO OTHERS WHO WON'T.
NO ONE CAN KNOW WHAT THE FUTURE HOLDS.
BUT IT'S YOU WHO DECIDE HOW YOU LIVE YOUR LIFE...
BIP
MINAMI, THIS IS OZAWA.
I FOUND DR. KUJO.
COME TO HQ'S MAIN ENTRANCE.
...IS THAT IT?
I'LL BE BACK LATER.
WOR-RIED?
YOU DON'T HAVE TO COME BACK.
OKAY, SEE YOU IN A BIT...
I SAID YOU DON'T NEED TO.

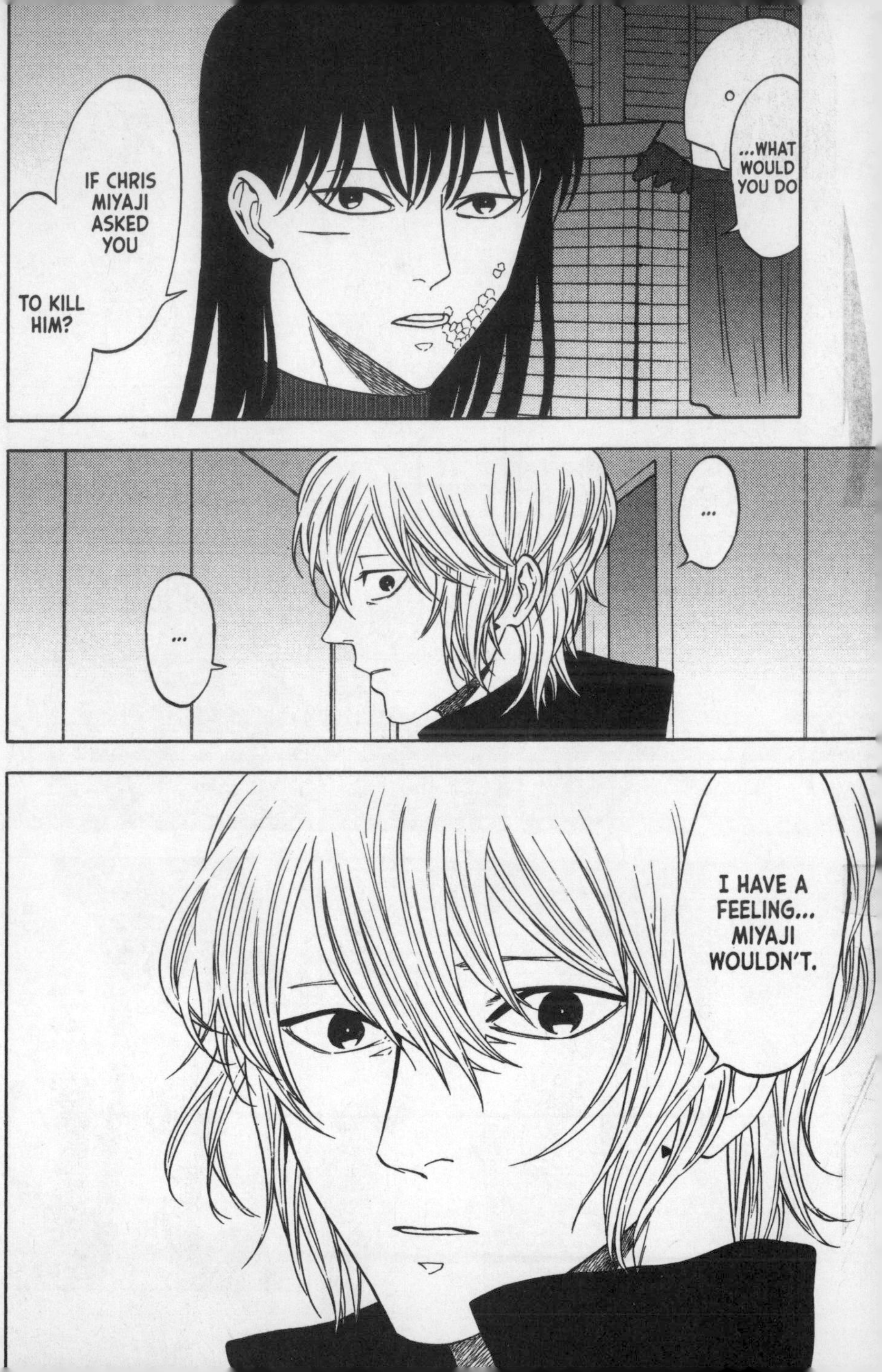
...WHAT WOULD YOU DO
IF CHRIS MIYAJI ASKED YOU
TO KILL HIM?
...
...
I HAVE A FEELING... MIYAJI WOULDN'T.

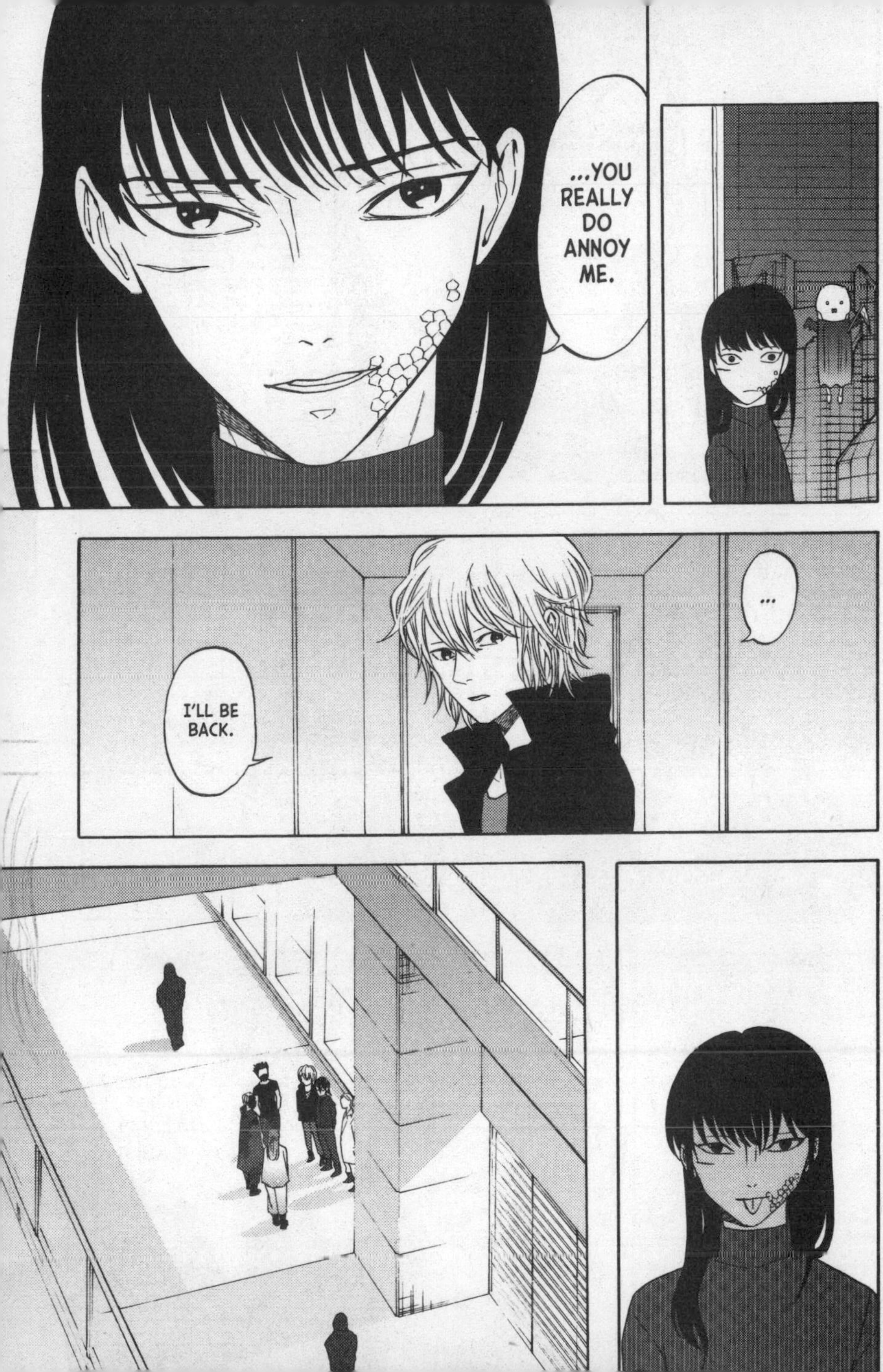
...YOU REALLY DO ANNOY ME.
...
I'LL BE BACK.

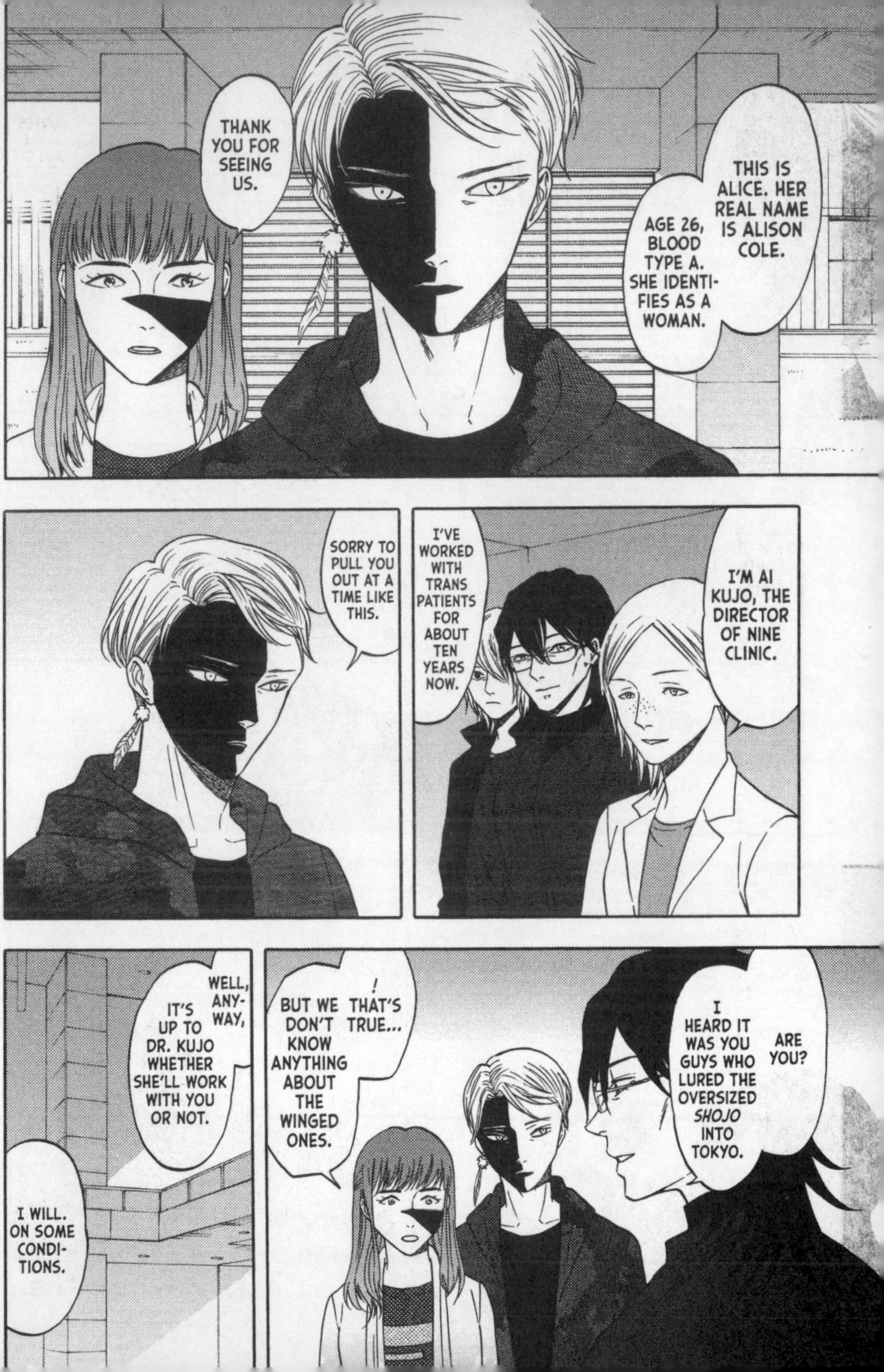
THIS IS ALICE. HER REAL NAME IS ALISON COLE.
AGE 26, BLOOD TYPE A. SHE IDENTIFIES AS A WOMAN.
THANK YOU FOR SEEING US.
I'M AI KUJO, THE DIRECTOR OF NINE CLINIC.
I'VE WORKED WITH TRANS PATIENTS FOR ABOUT TEN YEARS NOW.
SORRY TO PULL YOU OUT AT A TIME LIKE THIS.
ARE YOU?
I HEARD IT WAS YOU GUYS WHO LURED THE OVERSIZED *SHOJO* INTO TOKYO.
! THAT'S TRUE...
BUT WE DON'T KNOW ANYTHING ABOUT THE WINGED ONES.
WELL, ANYWAY,
IT'S UP TO DR. KUJO WHETHER SHE'LL WORK WITH YOU OR NOT.
I WILL. ON SOME CONDITIONS.

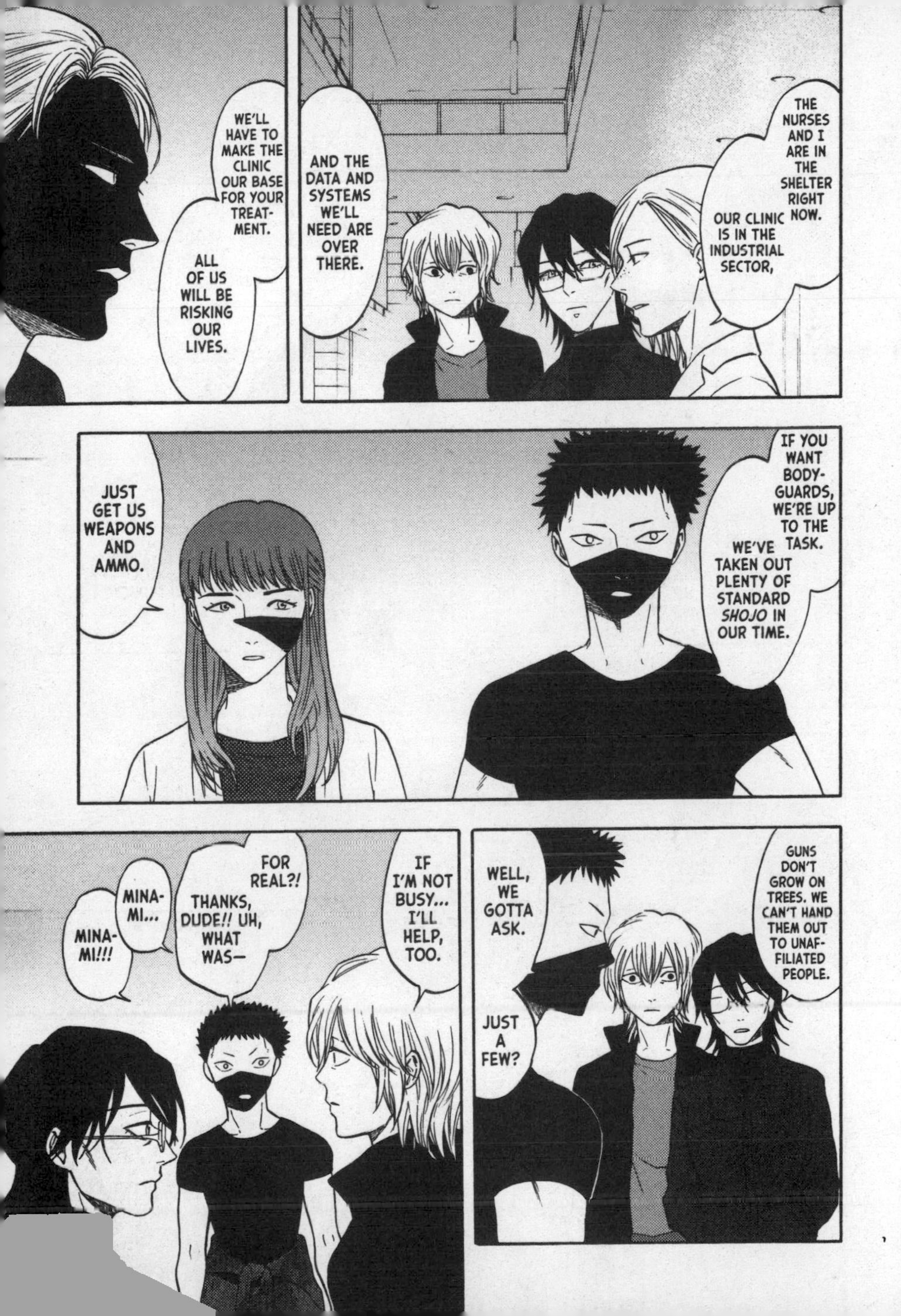
THE NURSES AND I ARE IN THE SHELTER RIGHT NOW.
OUR CLINIC IS IN THE INDUSTRIAL SECTOR,
AND THE DATA AND SYSTEMS WE'LL NEED ARE OVER THERE.
WE'LL HAVE TO MAKE THE CLINIC OUR BASE FOR YOUR TREAT-MENT.
ALL OF US WILL BE RISKING OUR LIVES.
IF YOU WANT BODY-GUARDS, WE'RE UP TO THE TASK.
WE'VE TAKEN OUT PLENTY OF STANDARD *SHOJO* IN OUR TIME.
JUST GET US WEAPONS AND AMMO.
GUNS DON'T GROW ON TREES. WE CAN'T HAND THEM OUT TO UNAF-FILIATED PEOPLE.
WELL, WE GOTTA ASK.
JUST A FEW?
IF I'M NOT BUSY... I'LL HELP, TOO.
FOR REAL?! THANKS, DUDE!! UH, WHAT WAS—
MINA-MI...
MINA-MI!!!

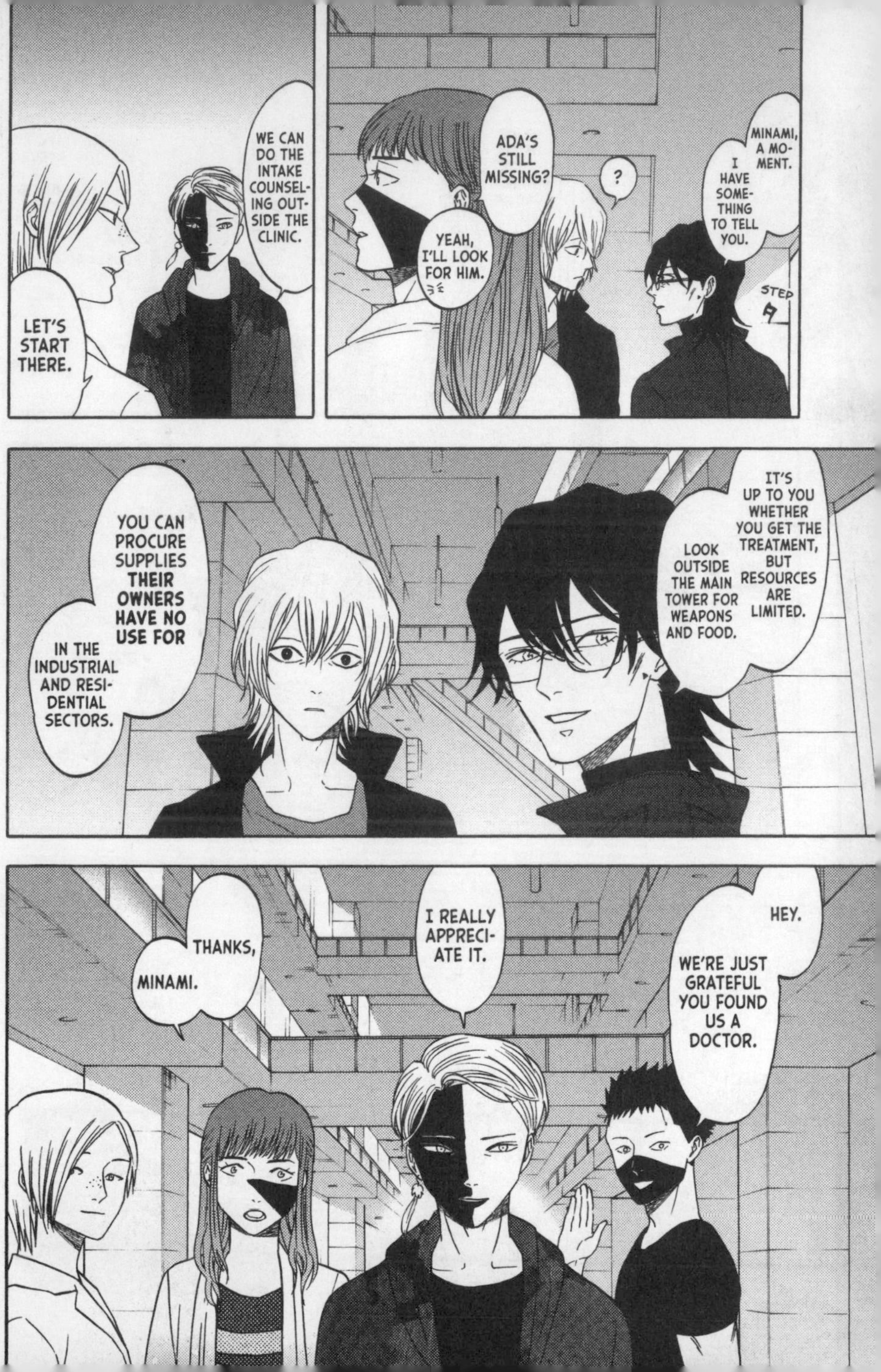
MINAMI, A MOMENT.
I HAVE SOMETHING TO TELL YOU.
?
ADA'S STILL MISSING?
YEAH, I'LL LOOK FOR HIM.
STEP
WE CAN DO THE INTAKE COUNSELING OUTSIDE THE CLINIC.
LET'S START THERE.
IT'S UP TO YOU WHETHER YOU GET THE TREATMENT, BUT RESOURCES ARE LIMITED.
LOOK OUTSIDE THE MAIN TOWER FOR WEAPONS AND FOOD.
YOU CAN PROCURE SUPPLIES **THEIR OWNERS HAVE NO USE FOR**
IN THE INDUSTRIAL AND RESIDENTIAL SECTORS.
HEY.
WE'RE JUST GRATEFUL YOU FOUND US A DOCTOR.
I REALLY APPRECIATE IT.
THANKS,
MINAMI.

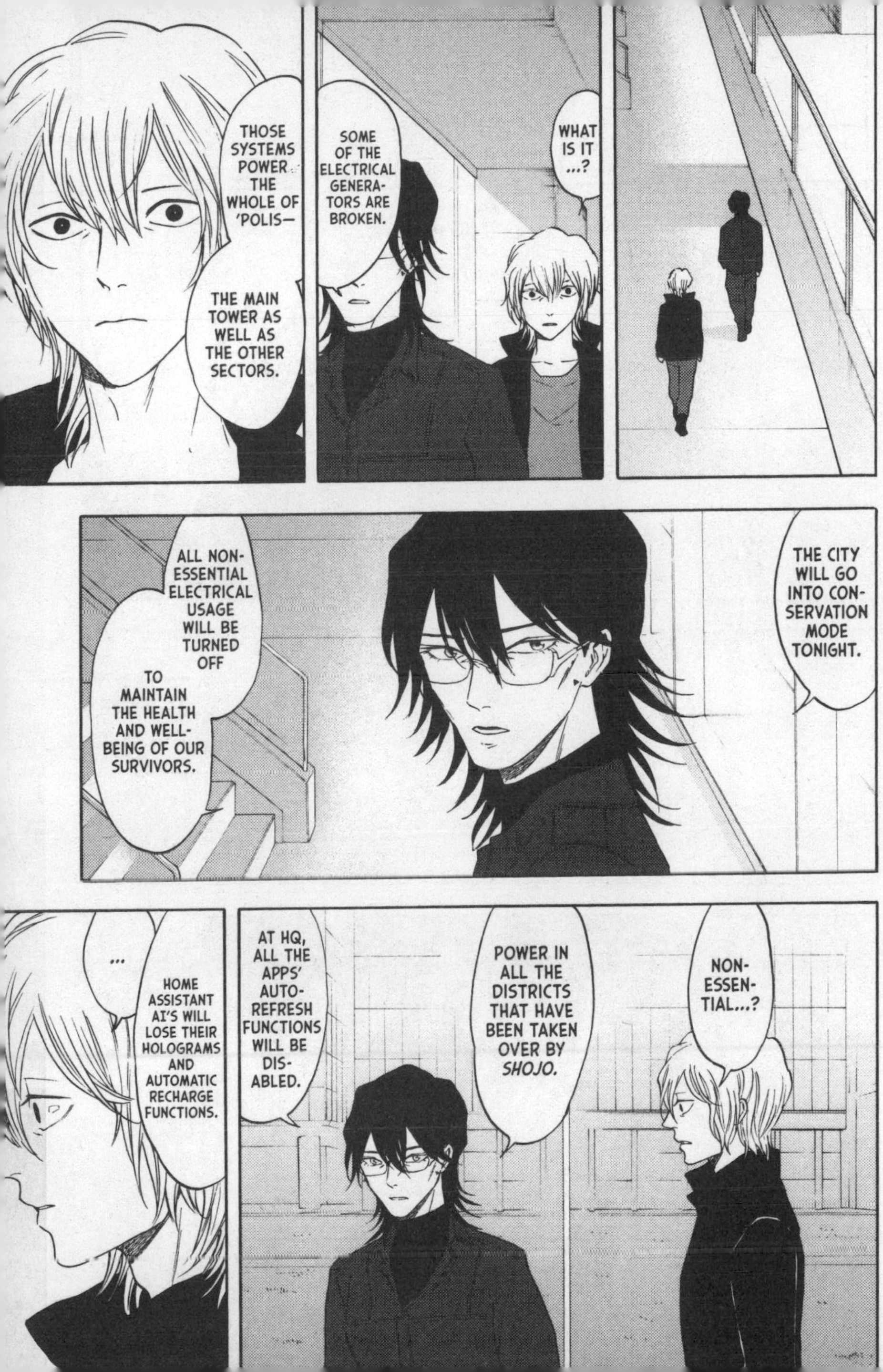
WHAT IS IT ...?
SOME OF THE ELECTRICAL GENERATORS ARE BROKEN.
THOSE SYSTEMS POWER THE WHOLE OF 'POLIS—
THE MAIN TOWER AS WELL AS THE OTHER SECTORS.
THE CITY WILL GO INTO CONSERVATION MODE TONIGHT.
ALL NON-ESSENTIAL ELECTRICAL USAGE WILL BE TURNED OFF
TO MAINTAIN THE HEALTH AND WELL-BEING OF OUR SURVIVORS.
NON-ESSENTIAL...?
POWER IN ALL THE DISTRICTS THAT HAVE BEEN TAKEN OVER BY *SHOJO.*
AT HQ, ALL THE APPS' AUTO-REFRESH FUNCTIONS WILL BE DISABLED.
...
HOME ASSISTANT AI'S WILL LOSE THEIR HOLOGRAMS AND AUTOMATIC RECHARGE FUNCTIONS.

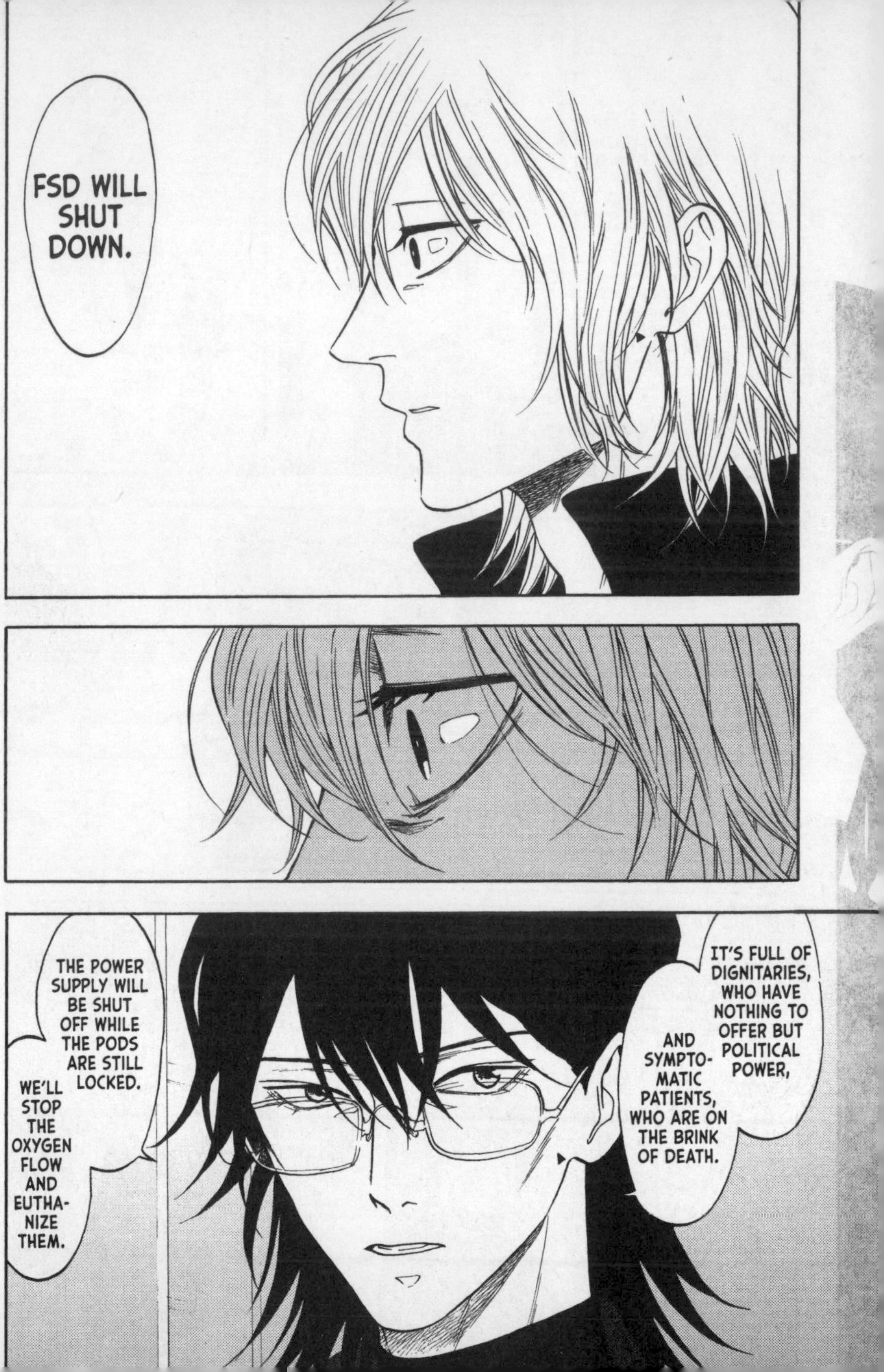
FSD WILL SHUT DOWN.
IT'S FULL OF DIGNITARIES, WHO HAVE NOTHING TO OFFER BUT POLITICAL POWER,
AND SYMPTO-MATIC PATIENTS, WHO ARE ON THE BRINK OF DEATH.
THE POWER SUPPLY WILL BE SHUT OFF WHILE THE PODS ARE STILL LOCKED.
WE'LL STOP THE OXYGEN FLOW AND EUTHA-NIZE THEM.

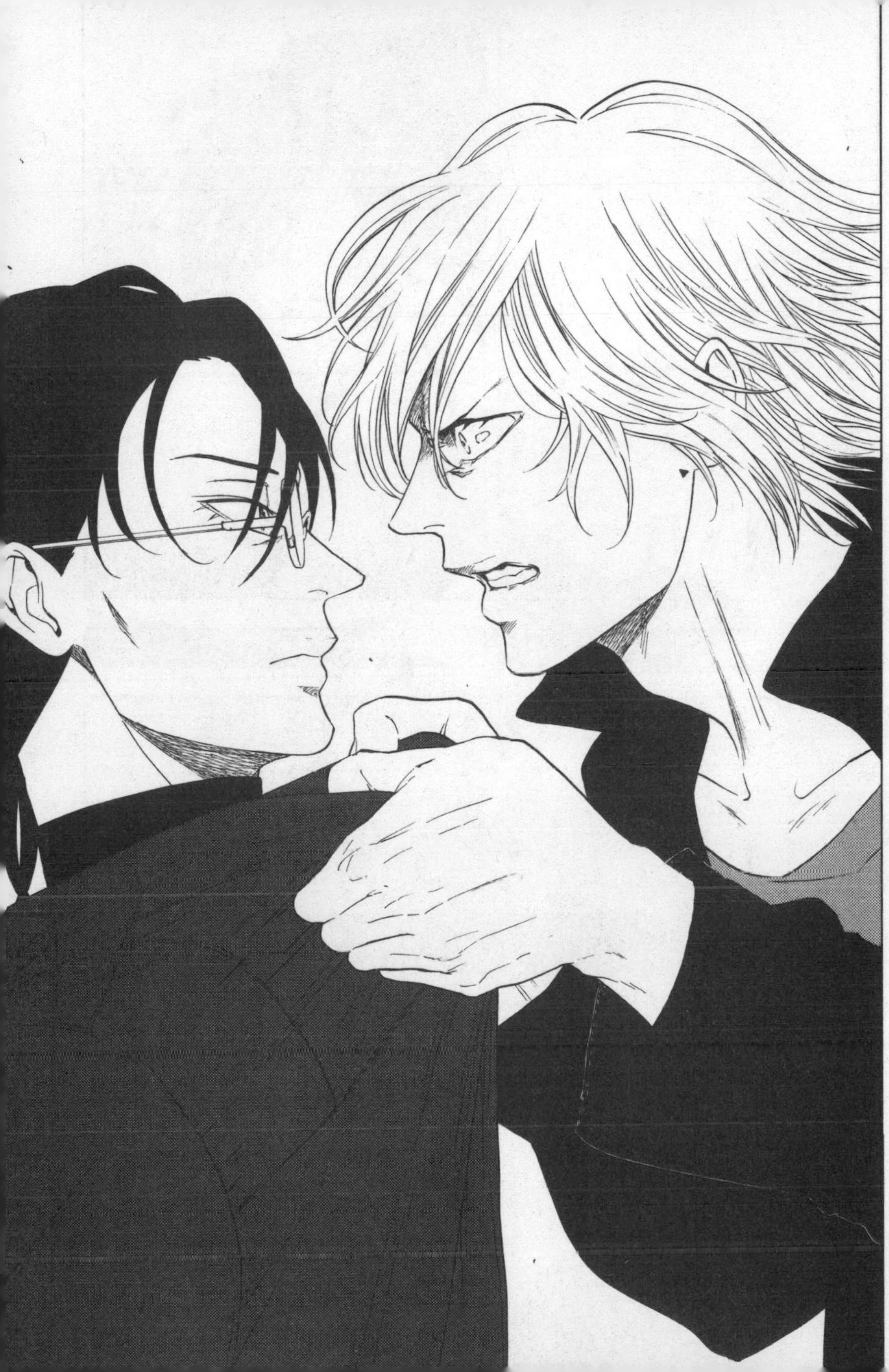

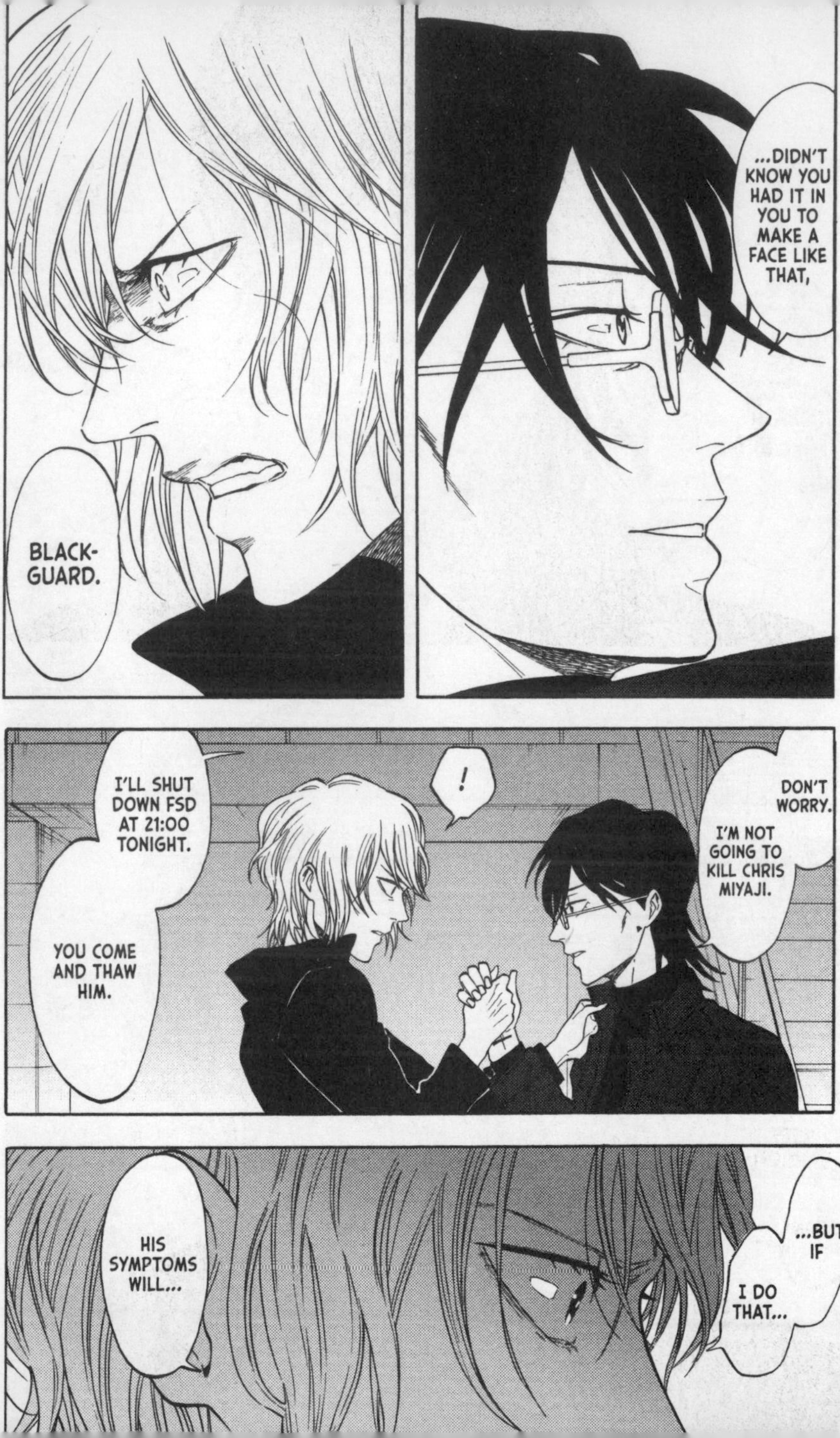
...DIDN'T KNOW YOU HAD IT IN YOU TO MAKE A FACE LIKE THAT,
BLACK-GUARD.
DON'T WORRY.
I'M NOT GOING TO KILL CHRIS MIYAJI.
!
I'LL SHUT DOWN FSD AT 21:00 TONIGHT.
YOU COME AND THAW HIM.
...BUT IF
I DO THAT...
HIS SYMPTOMS WILL...

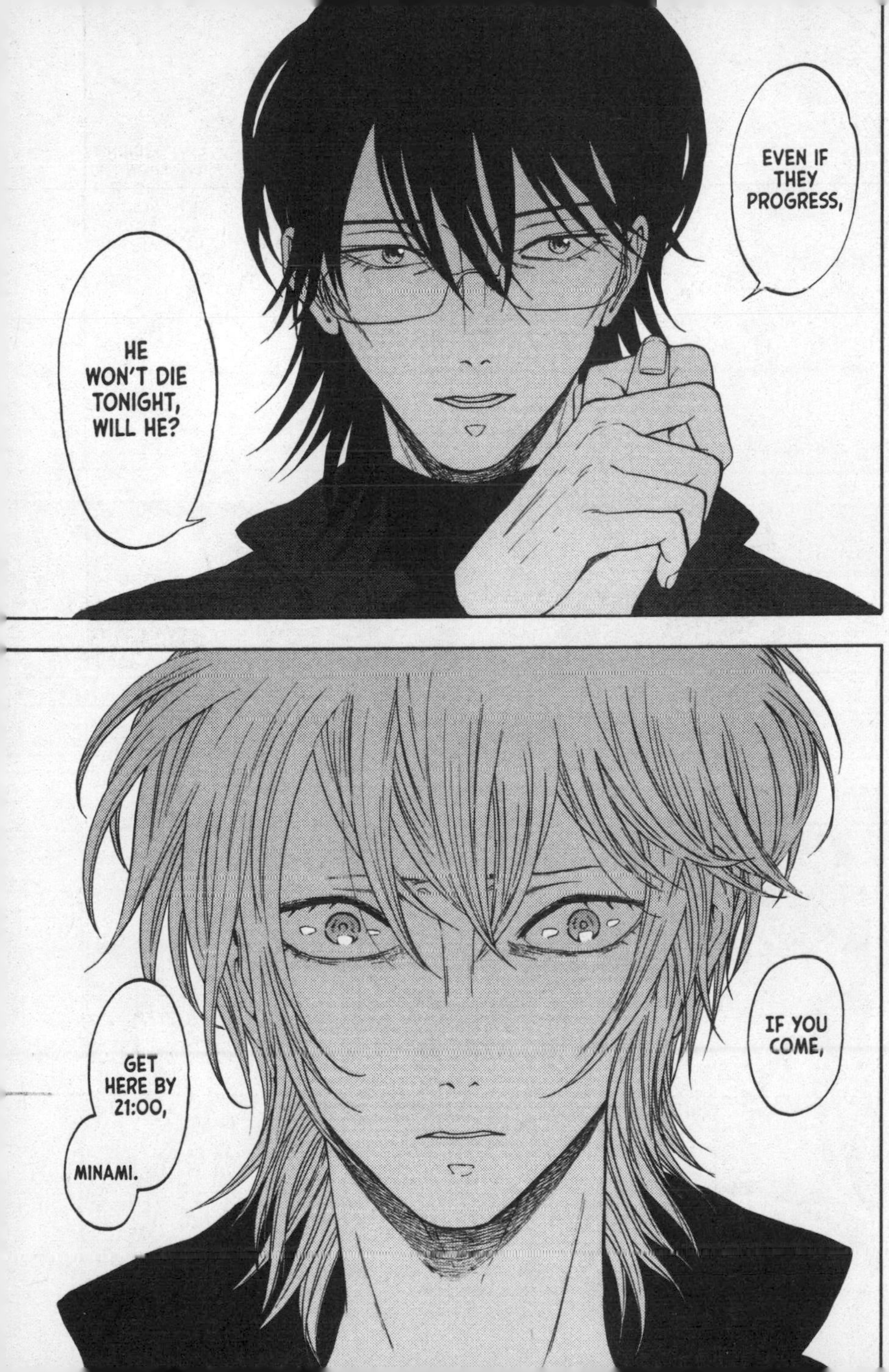
EVEN IF THEY PROGRESS,
HE WON'T DIE TONIGHT, WILL HE?
IF YOU COME,
GET HERE BY 21:00,
MINAMI.

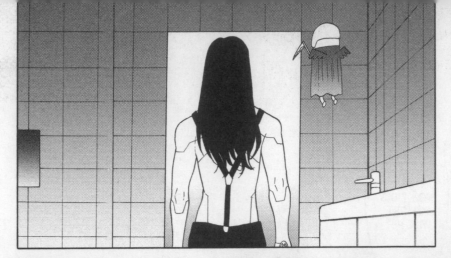

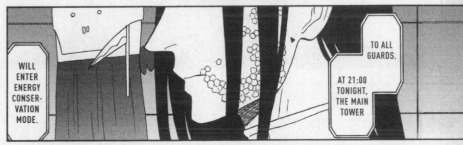

TO ALL GUARDS.
AT 21:00 TONIGHT, THE MAIN TOWER
WILL ENTER ENERGY CONSERVATION MODE.
ILLUMINATION WILL BE EMERGENCY LIGHTING ONLY.
EACH DORM WILL BE ALLOCATED 200 LITERS OF WATER PER DAY, WITH A TEMPERATURE CAP OF 43 DEGREES.
THE HOLOGRAM FUNCTION FOR HOME ASSISTANT AI'S WILL BE DISABLED,
AND AUTOMATIC CHARGING WILL TURN OFF.

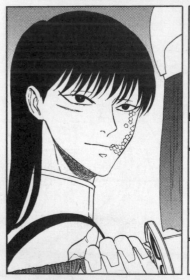

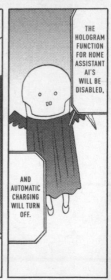

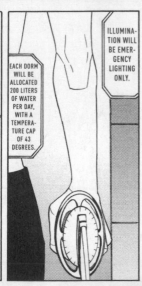

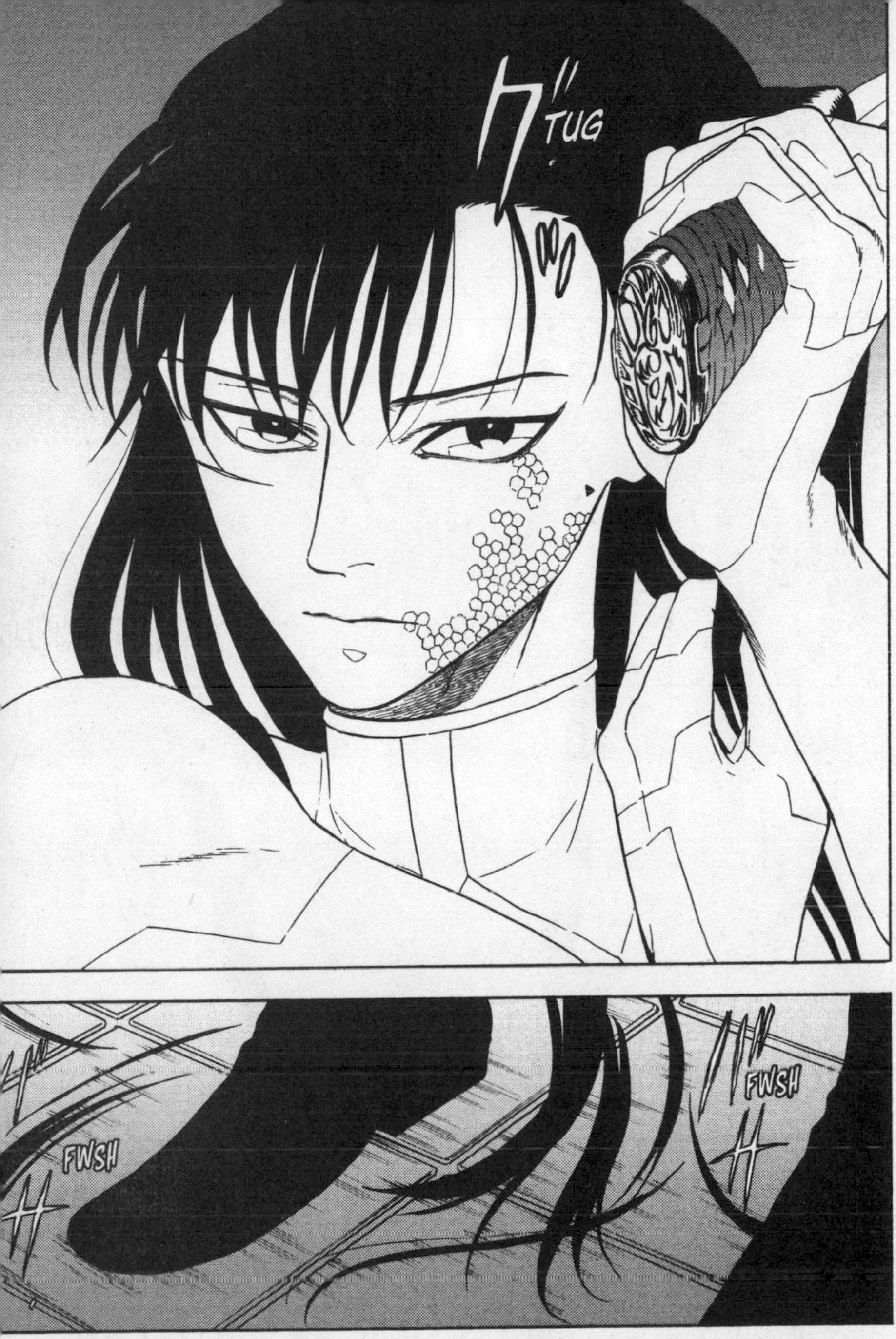
TUG
FWSH
FWSH

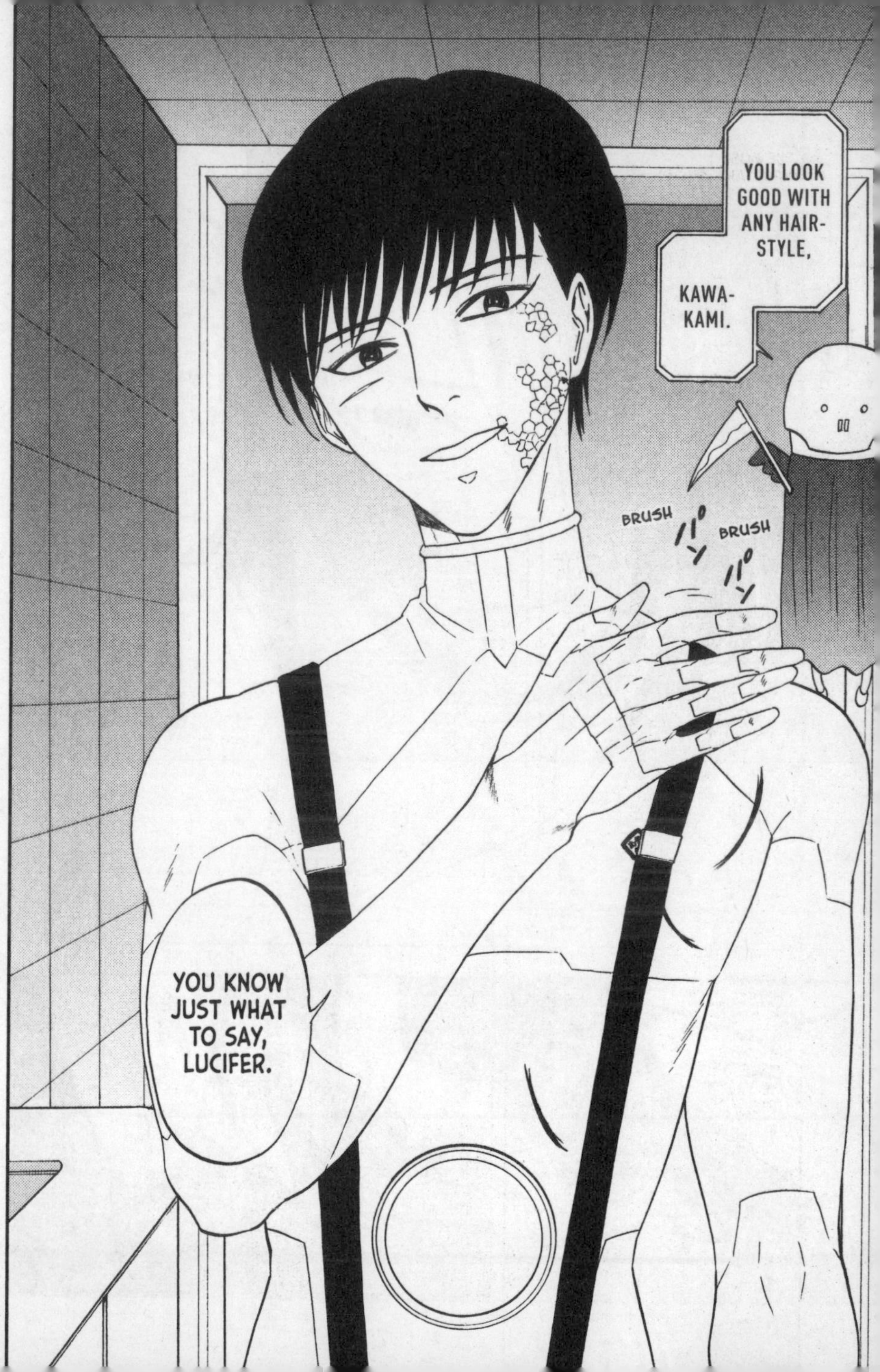
YOU LOOK GOOD WITH ANY HAIR-STYLE,
KAWA-KAMI.
BRUSH
BRUSH
YOU KNOW JUST WHAT TO SAY, LUCIFER.

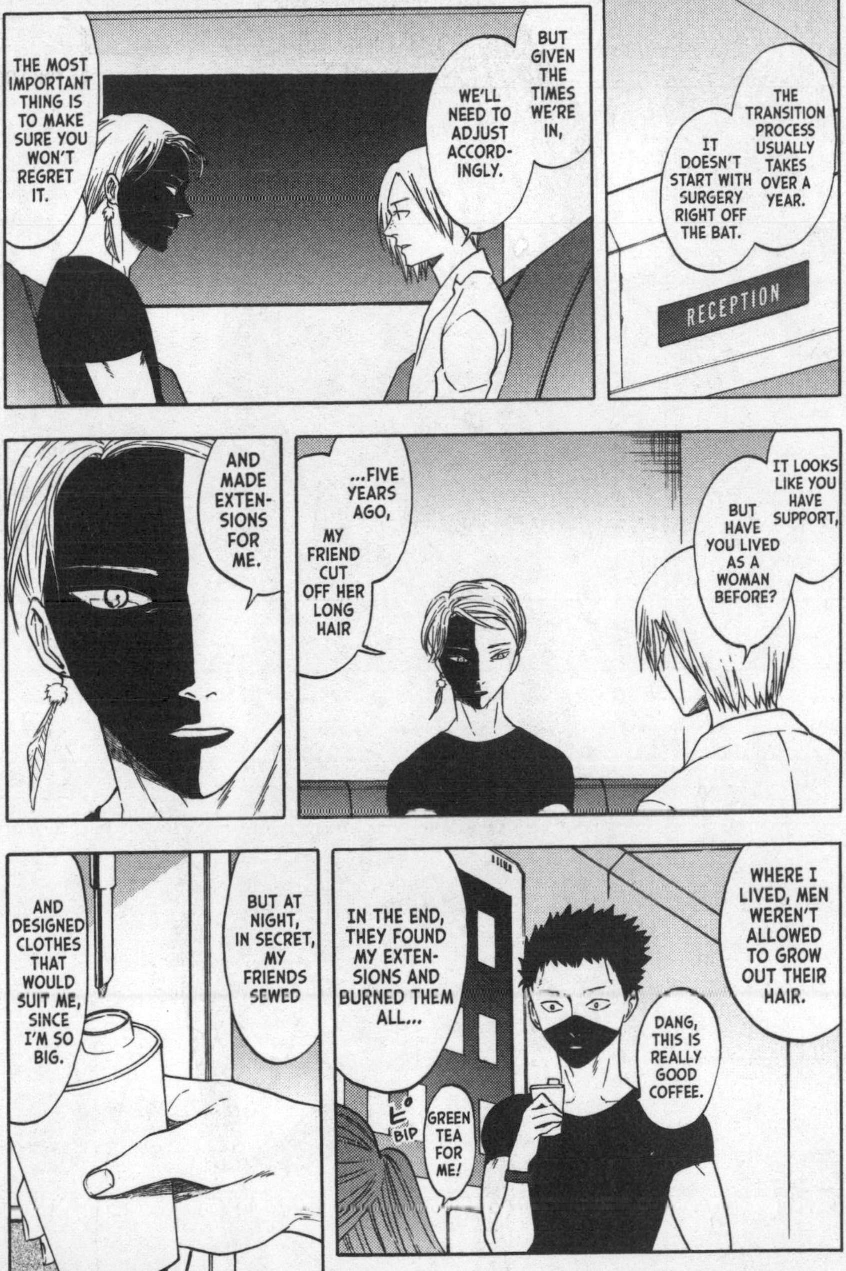
THE TRANSITION PROCESS USUALLY TAKES OVER A YEAR.
IT DOESN'T START WITH SURGERY RIGHT OFF THE BAT.
RECEPTION
BUT GIVEN THE TIMES WE'RE IN,
WE'LL NEED TO ADJUST ACCORDINGLY.
THE MOST IMPORTANT THING IS TO MAKE SURE YOU WON'T REGRET IT.
IT LOOKS LIKE YOU HAVE SUPPORT,
BUT HAVE YOU LIVED AS A WOMAN BEFORE?
...FIVE YEARS AGO,
MY FRIEND CUT OFF HER LONG HAIR
AND MADE EXTENSIONS FOR ME.
WHERE I LIVED, MEN WEREN'T ALLOWED TO GROW OUT THEIR HAIR.
DANG, THIS IS REALLY GOOD COFFEE.
GREEN TEA FOR ME!
BIP
IN THE END, THEY FOUND MY EXTENSIONS AND BURNED THEM ALL...
BUT AT NIGHT, IN SECRET, MY FRIENDS SEWED
AND DESIGNED CLOTHES THAT WOULD SUIT ME, SINCE I'M SO BIG.

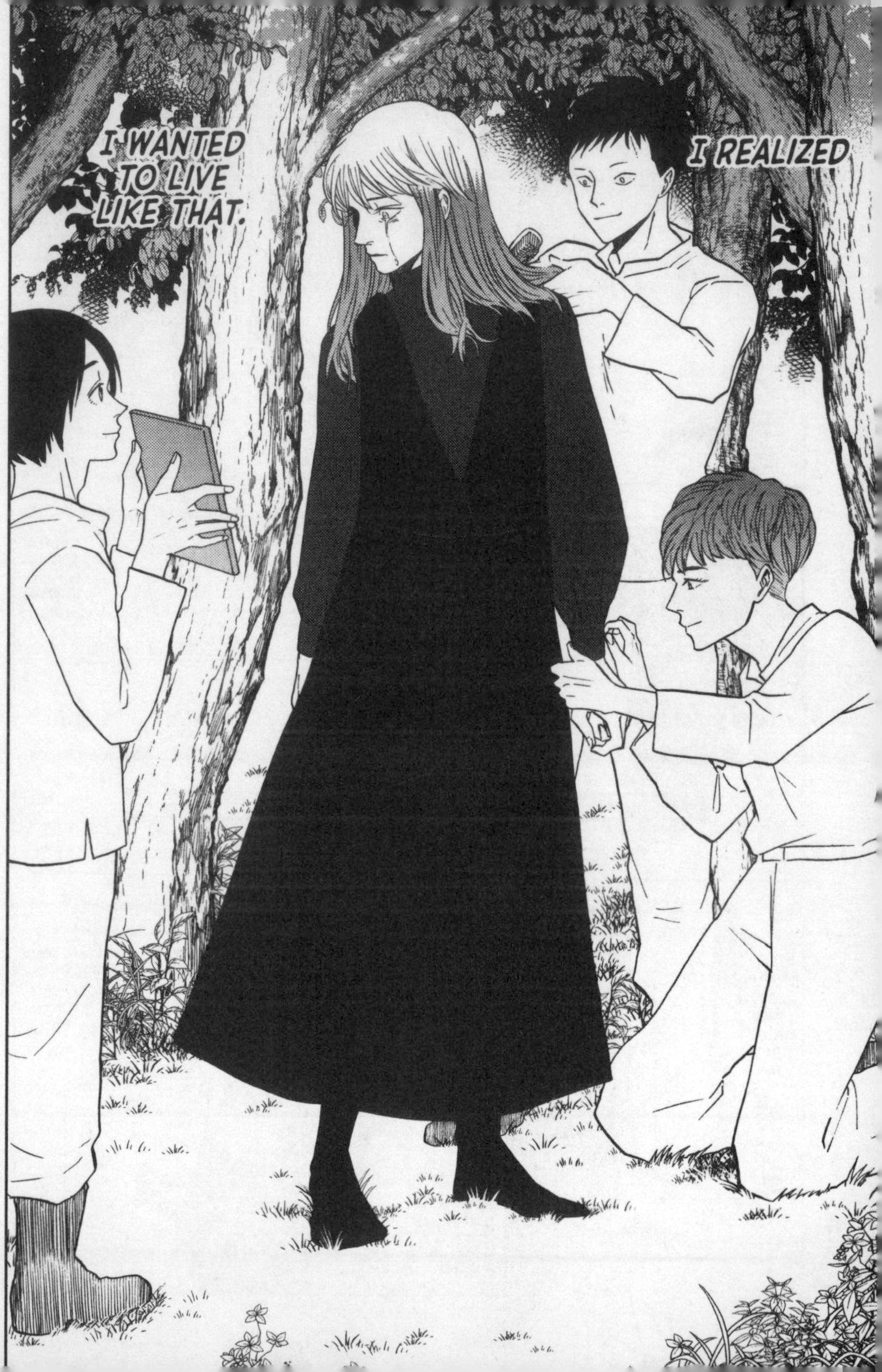
I REALIZED
I WANTED TO LIVE LIKE THAT.

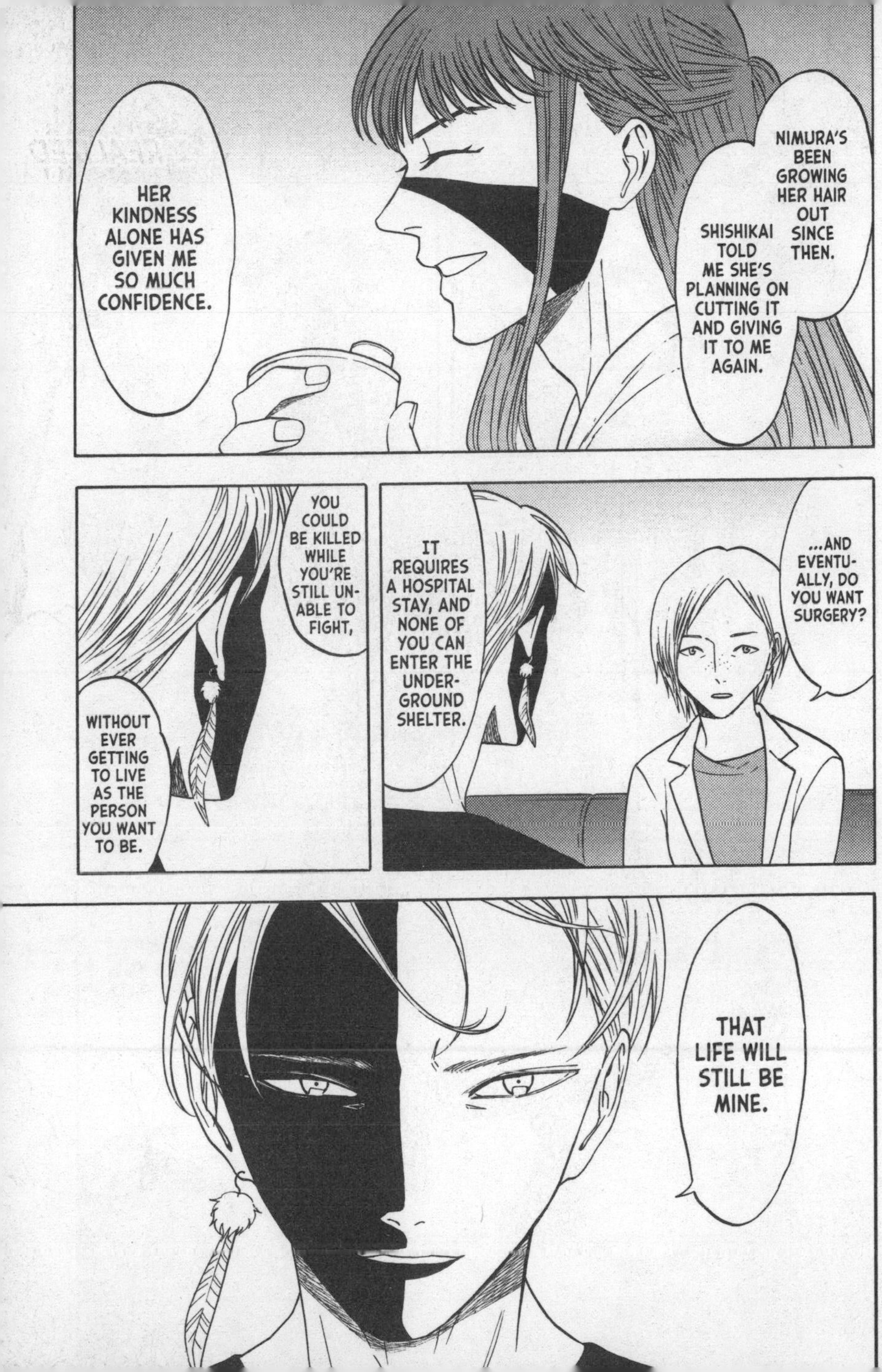
NIMURA'S BEEN GROWING HER HAIR OUT SINCE THEN.
SHISHIKAI TOLD ME SHE'S PLANNING ON CUTTING IT AND GIVING IT TO ME AGAIN.
HER KINDNESS ALONE HAS GIVEN ME SO MUCH CONFIDENCE.
...AND EVENTUALLY, DO YOU WANT SURGERY?
IT REQUIRES A HOSPITAL STAY, AND NONE OF YOU CAN ENTER THE UNDERGROUND SHELTER.
YOU COULD BE KILLED WHILE YOU'RE STILL UNABLE TO FIGHT,
WITHOUT EVER GETTING TO LIVE AS THE PERSON YOU WANT TO BE.
THAT LIFE WILL STILL BE MINE.

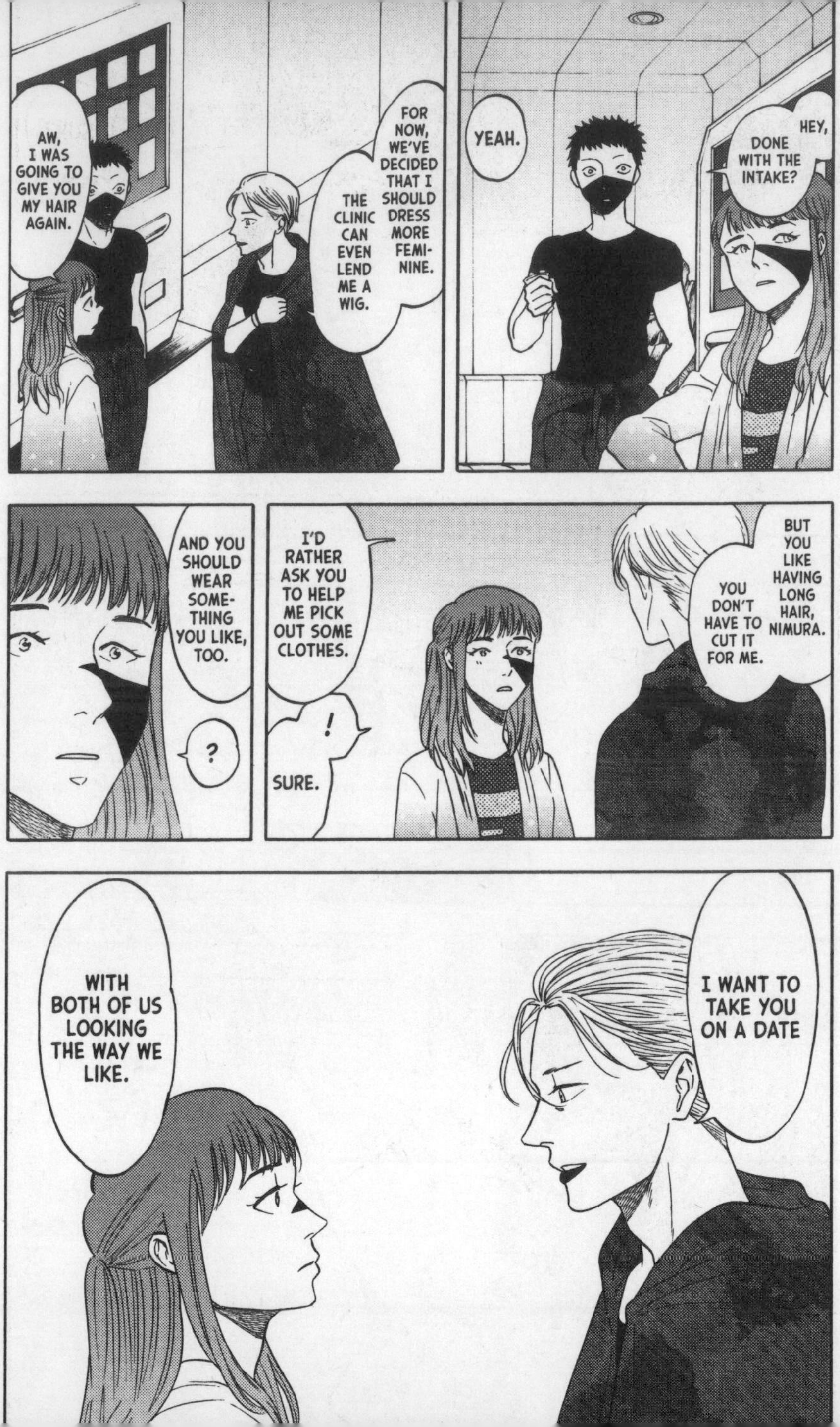
HEY, DONE WITH THE INTAKE?
YEAH.
FOR NOW, WE'VE DECIDED THAT I SHOULD DRESS MORE FEMI-NINE.
THE CLINIC CAN EVEN LEND ME A WIG.
AW, I WAS GOING TO GIVE YOU MY HAIR AGAIN.
BUT YOU LIKE HAVING LONG HAIR, NIMURA.
YOU DON'T HAVE TO CUT IT FOR ME.
I'D RATHER ASK YOU TO HELP ME PICK OUT SOME CLOTHES.
!
SURE.
AND YOU SHOULD WEAR SOME-THING YOU LIKE, TOO.
?
I WANT TO TAKE YOU ON A DATE
WITH BOTH OF US LOOKING THE WAY WE LIKE.

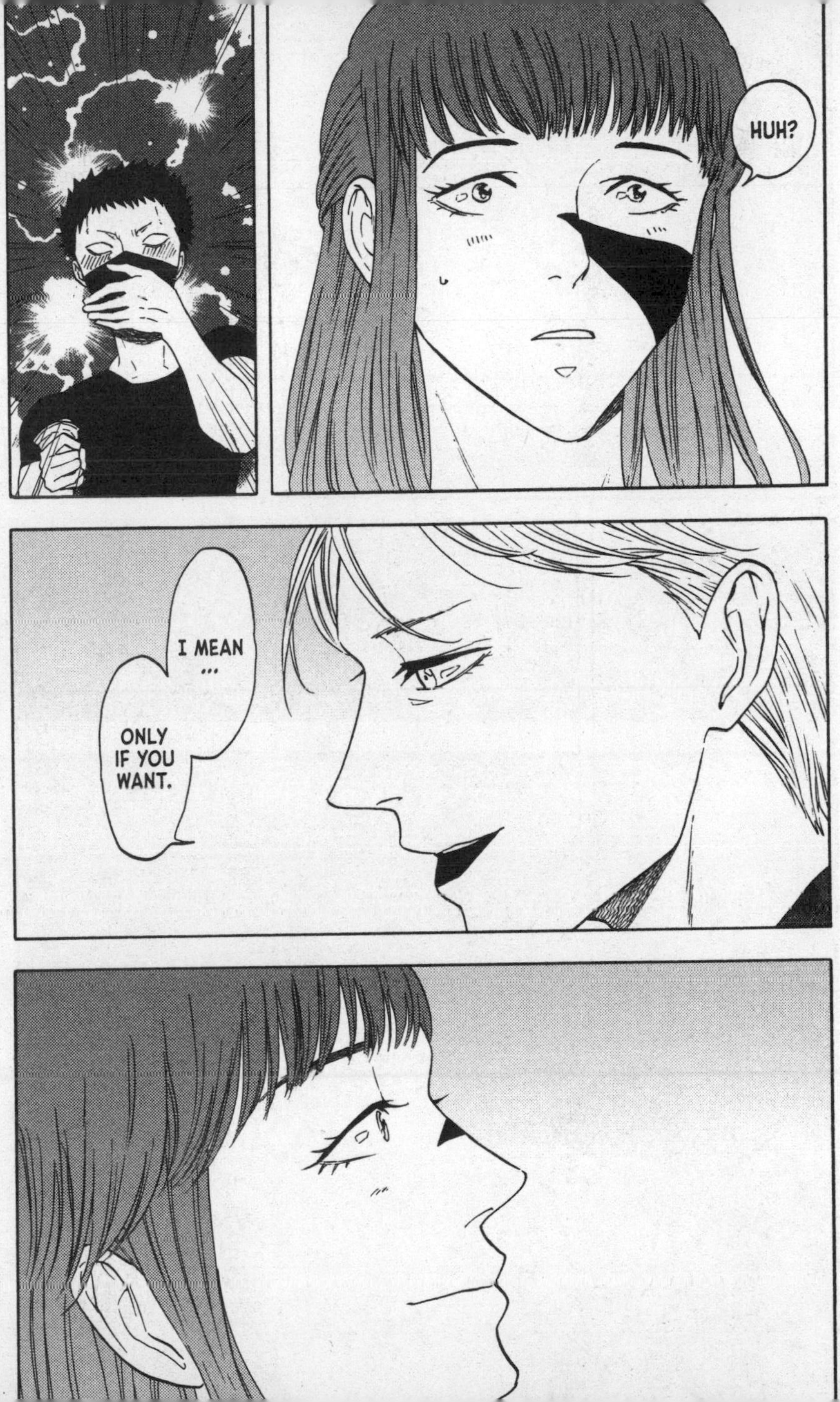
HUH?
I MEAN ...
ONLY IF YOU WANT.

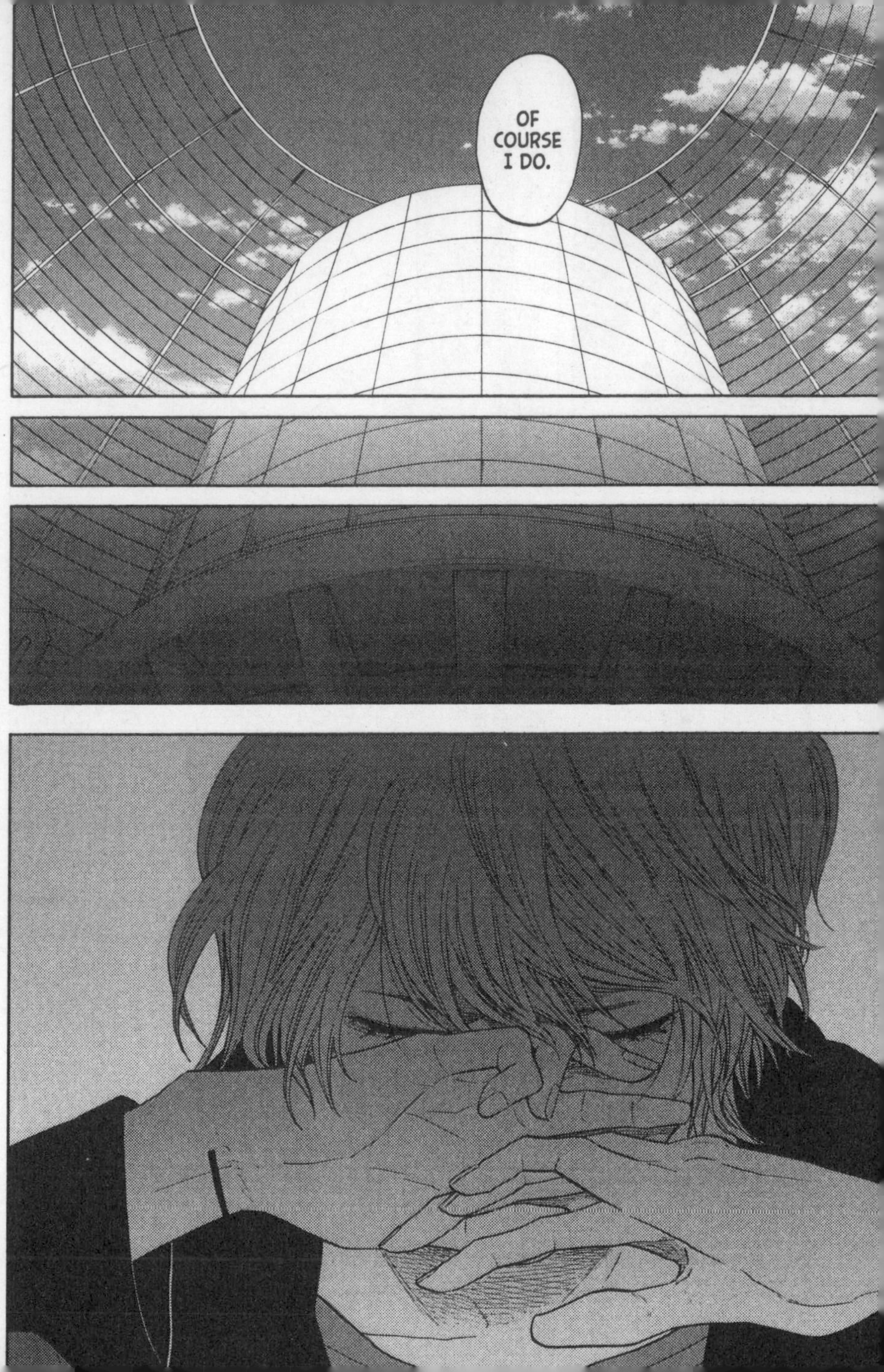
OF COURSE I DO.

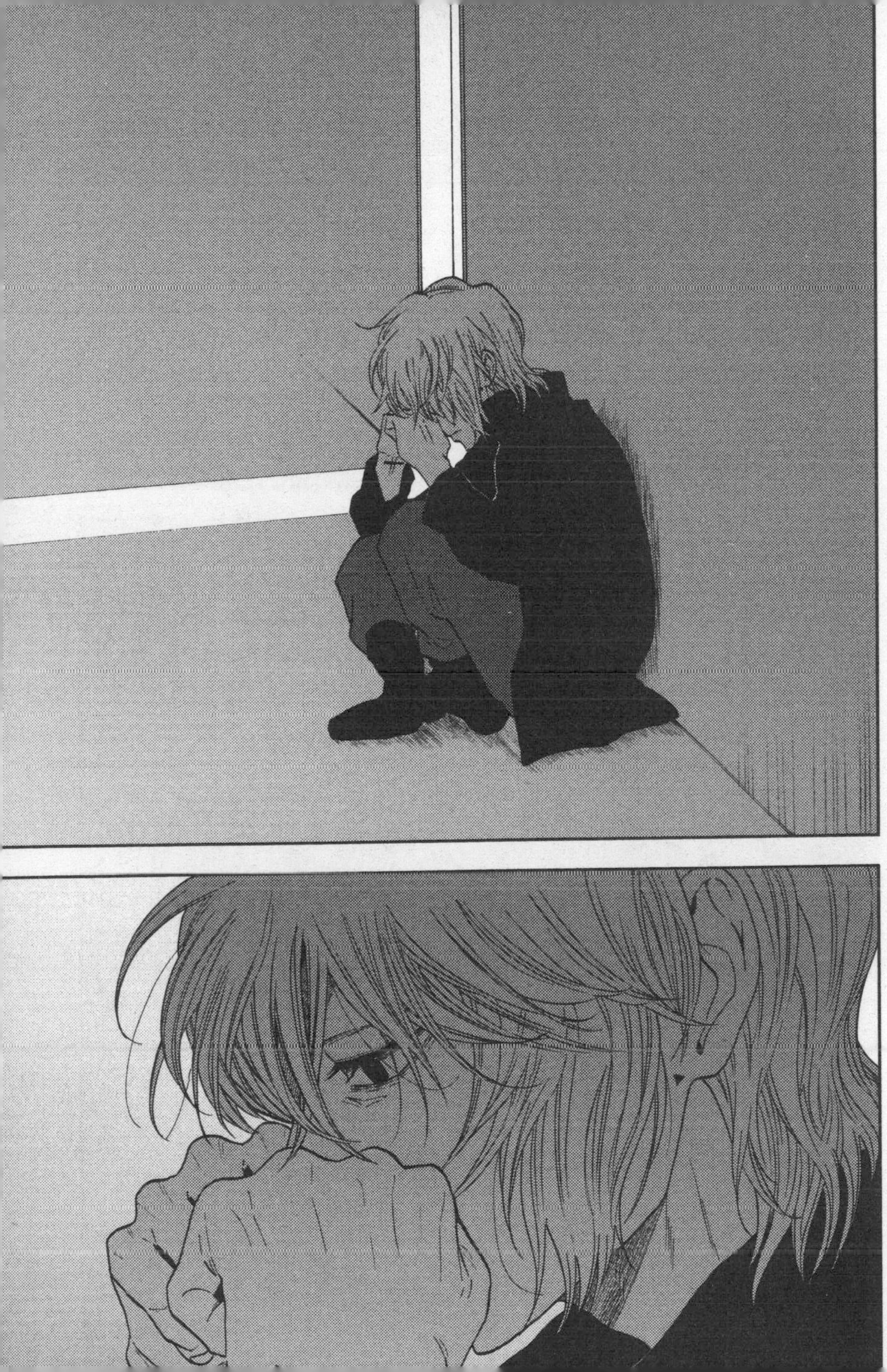

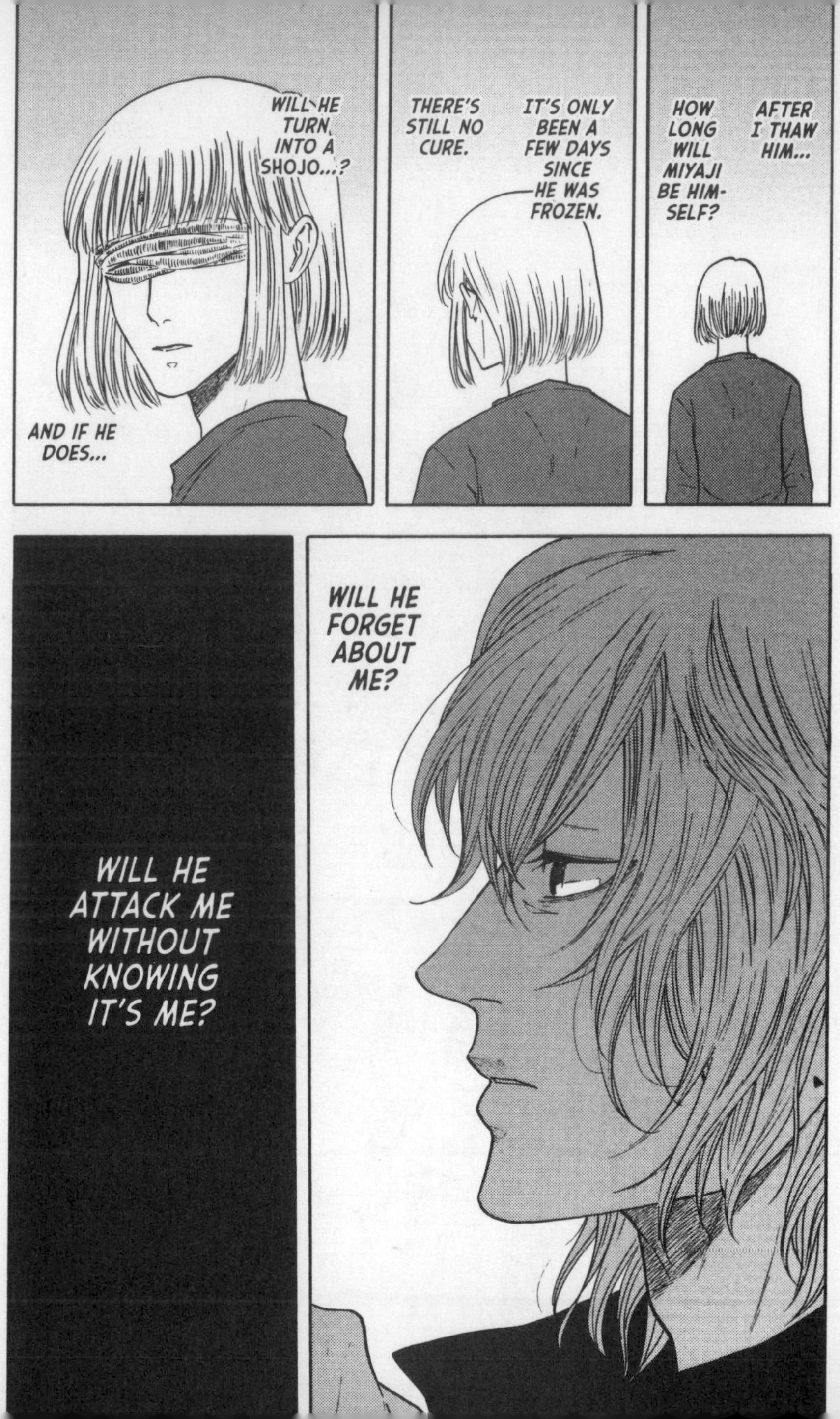
AFTER I THAW HIM...
HOW LONG WILL MIYAJI BE HIMSELF?
IT'S ONLY BEEN A FEW DAYS SINCE HE WAS FROZEN.
THERE'S STILL NO CURE.
WILL HE TURN INTO A SHOJO...?
AND IF HE DOES...
WILL HE FORGET ABOUT ME?
WILL HE ATTACK ME WITHOUT KNOWING IT'S ME?

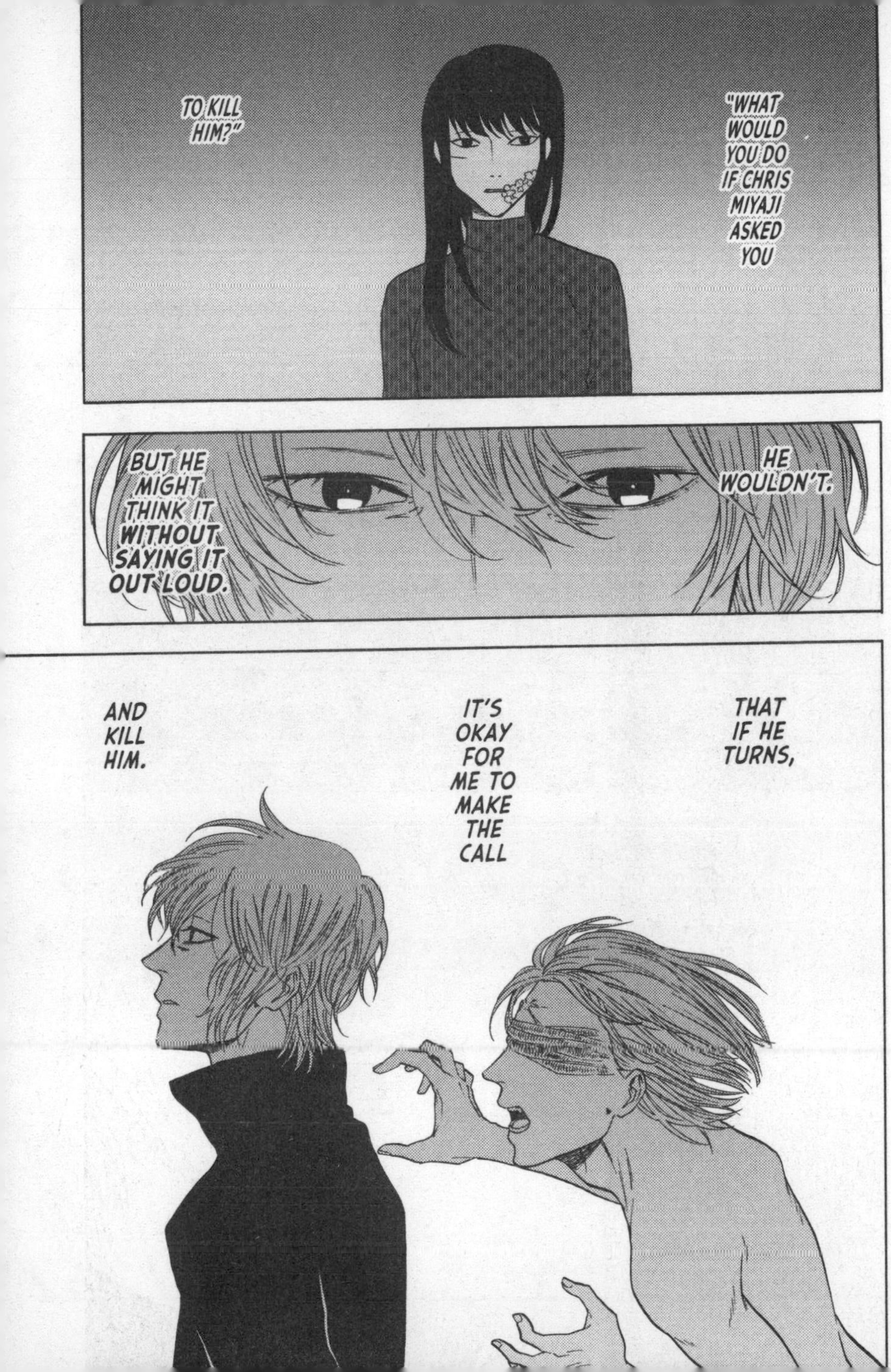
"WHAT WOULD YOU DO IF CHRIS MIYAJI ASKED YOU
TO KILL HIM?"
HE WOULDN'T.
BUT HE MIGHT THINK IT WITHOUT SAYING IT OUT LOUD.
THAT IF HE TURNS,
IT'S OKAY FOR ME TO MAKE THE CALL
AND KILL HIM.

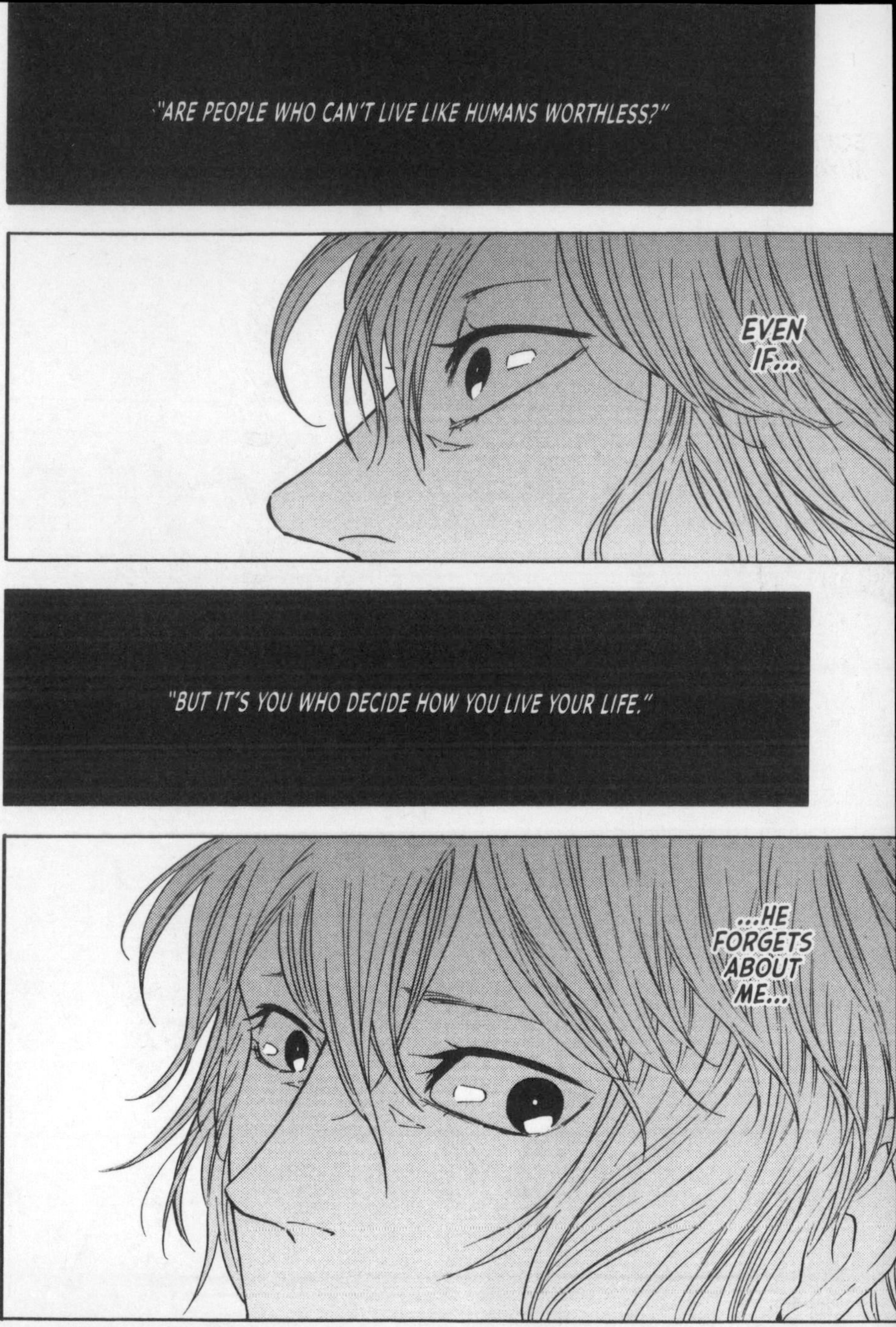
"ARE PEOPLE WHO CAN'T LIVE LIKE HUMANS WORTHLESS?"
EVEN IF...
"BUT IT'S YOU WHO DECIDE HOW YOU LIVE YOUR LIFE."
...HE FORGETS ABOUT ME...

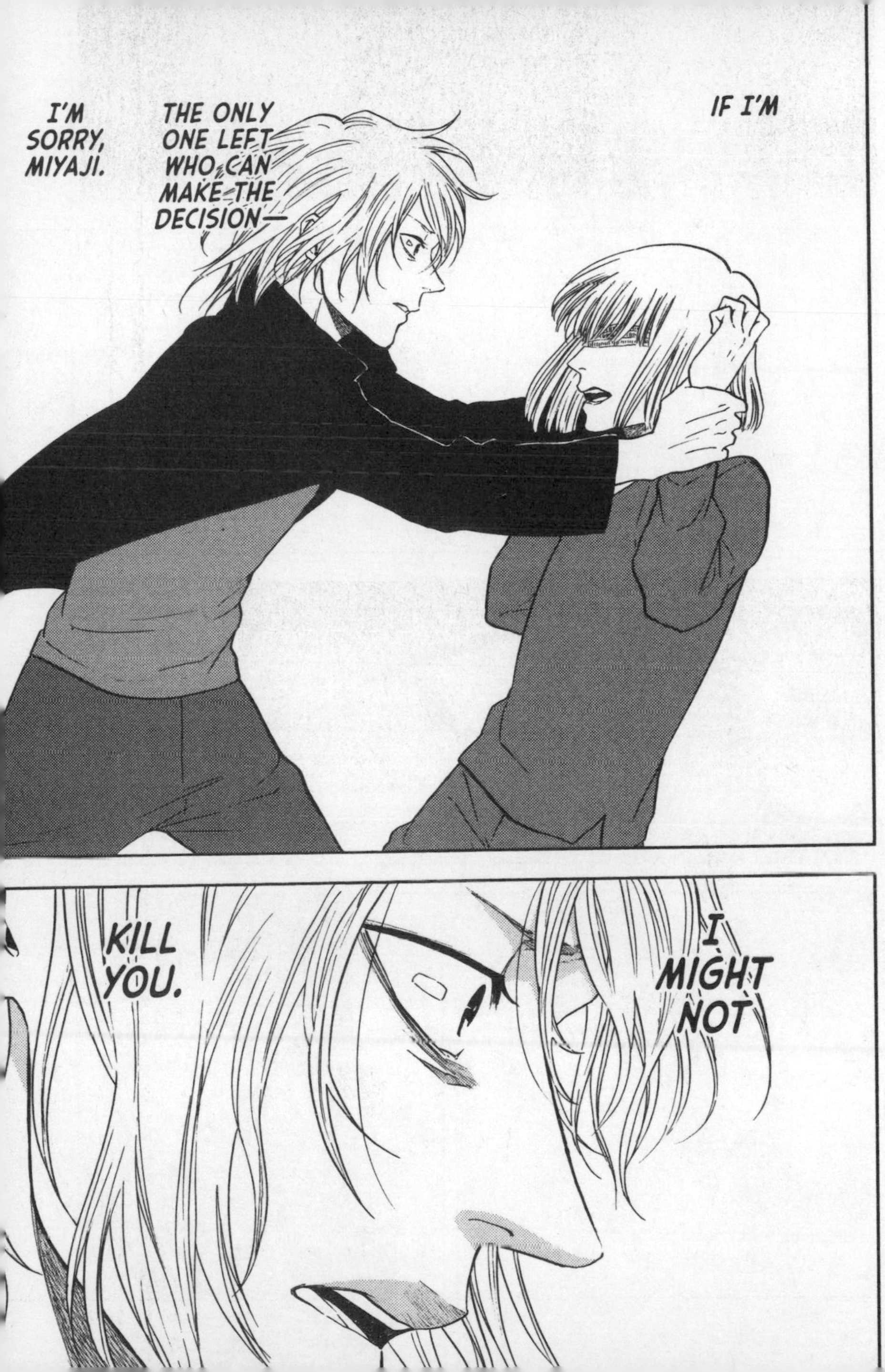
IF I'M
THE ONLY ONE LEFT WHO CAN MAKE THE DECISION—
I'M SORRY, MIYAJI.
I MIGHT NOT
KILL YOU.

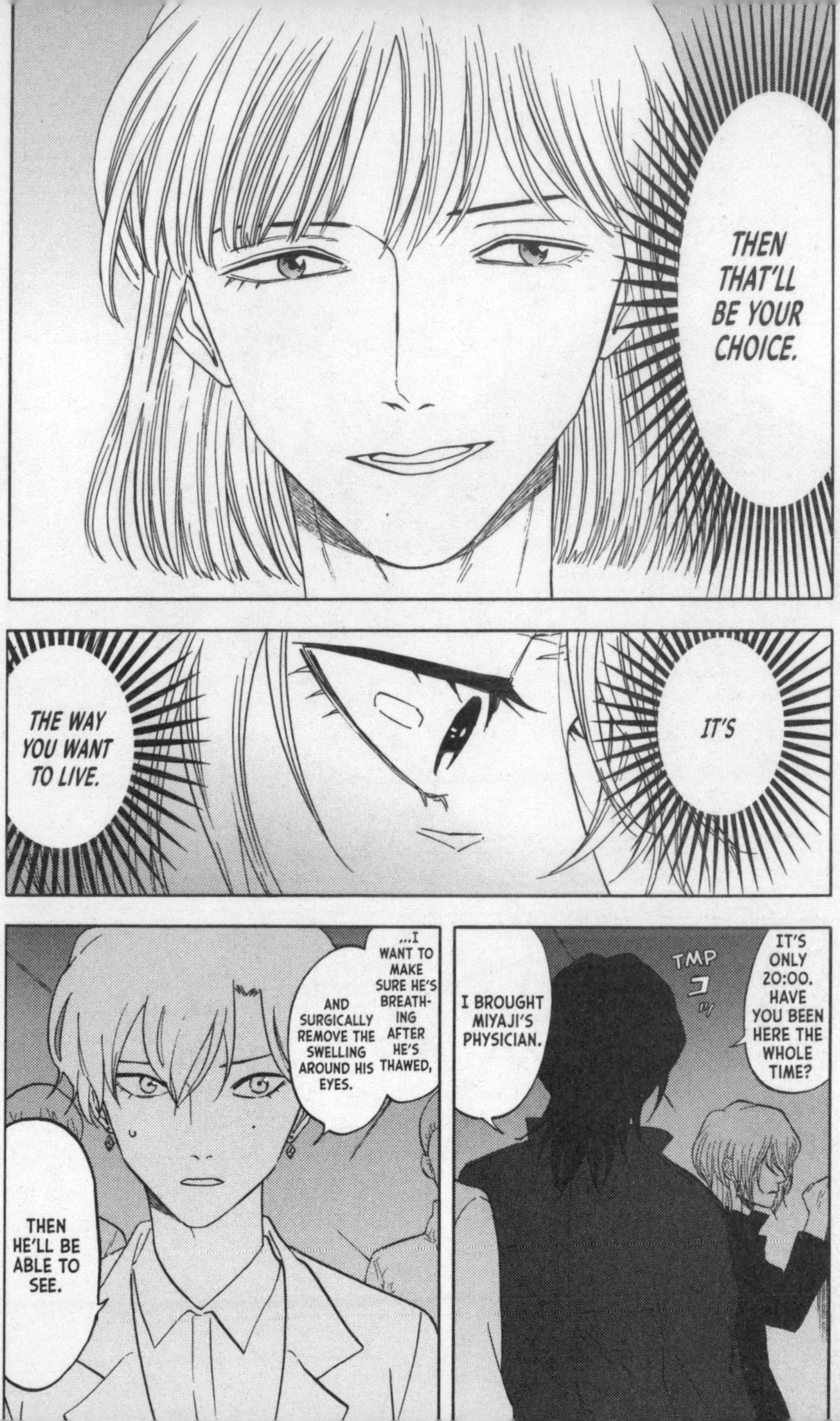
THEN THAT'LL BE YOUR CHOICE.
IT'S
THE WAY YOU WANT TO LIVE.
IT'S ONLY 20:00. HAVE YOU BEEN HERE THE WHOLE TIME?
TMP
I BROUGHT MIYAJI'S PHYSICIAN.
...I WANT TO MAKE SURE HE'S BREATHING AFTER HE'S THAWED,
AND SURGICALLY REMOVE THE SWELLING AROUND HIS EYES.
THEN HE'LL BE ABLE TO SEE.

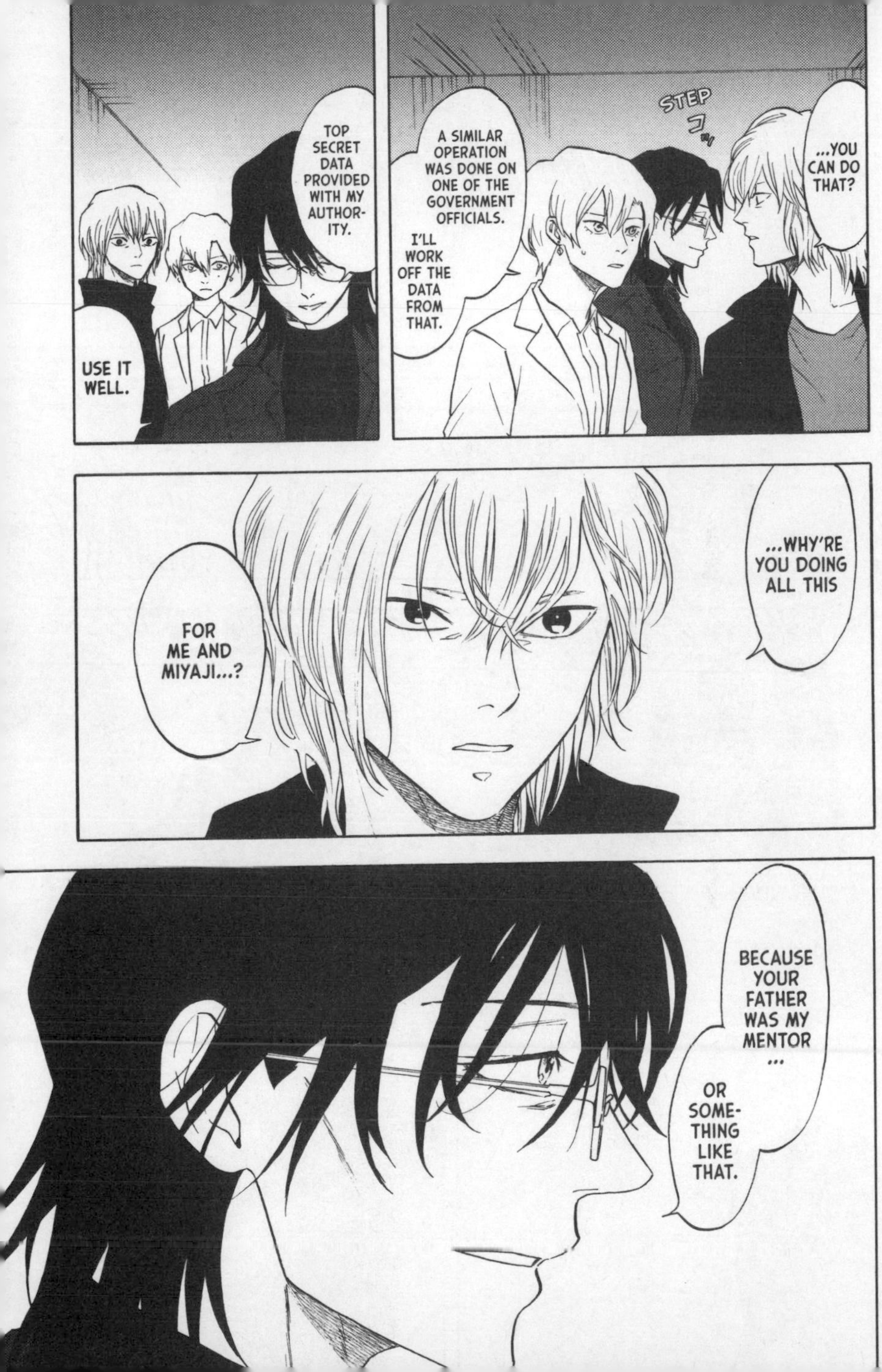
...YOU CAN DO THAT?
STEP
A SIMILAR OPERATION WAS DONE ON ONE OF THE GOVERNMENT OFFICIALS.
I'LL WORK OFF THE DATA FROM THAT.
TOP SECRET DATA PROVIDED WITH MY AUTHOR-ITY.
USE IT WELL.
...WHY'RE YOU DOING ALL THIS
FOR ME AND MIYAJI...?
BECAUSE YOUR FATHER WAS MY MENTOR ...
OR SOME-THING LIKE THAT.

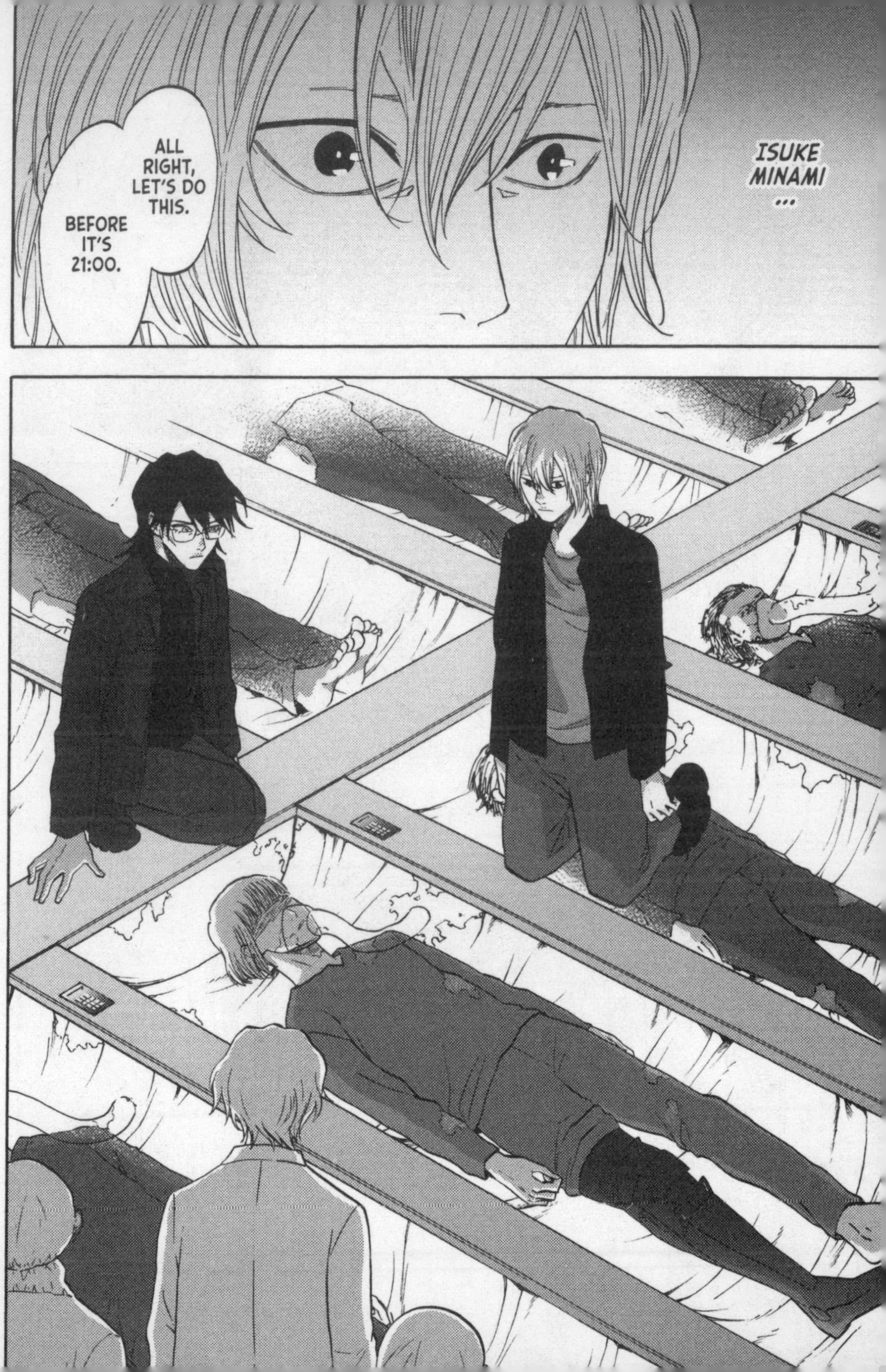
ISUKE MINAMI ...
ALL RIGHT, LET'S DO THIS. BEFORE IT'S 21:00.

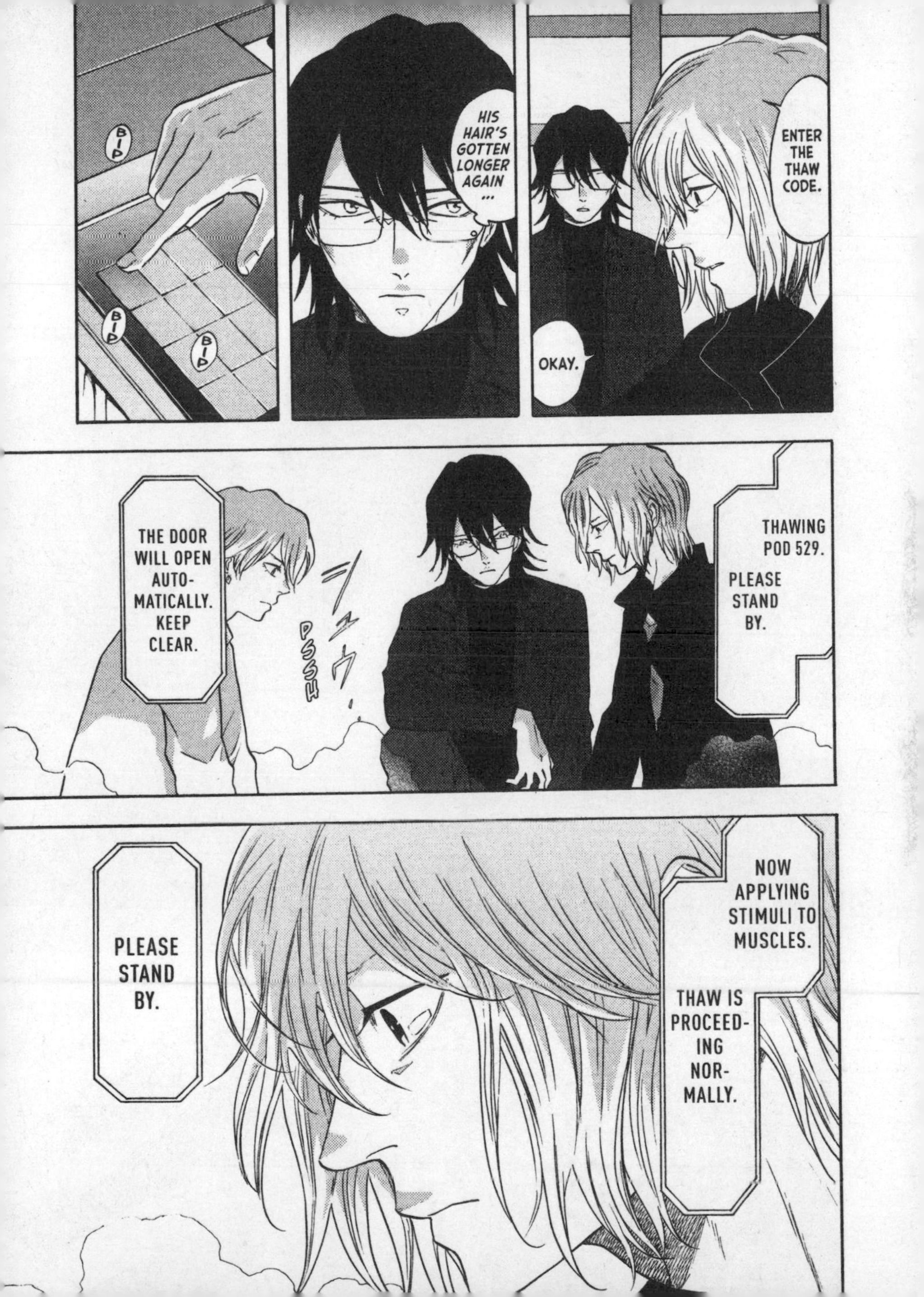
ENTER THE THAW CODE.
OKAY.
HIS HAIR'S GOTTEN LONGER AGAIN ...
BIP
BIP
BIP
THAWING POD 529.
PLEASE STAND BY.
PSSH
THE DOOR WILL OPEN AUTO-MATICALLY. KEEP CLEAR.
NOW APPLYING STIMULI TO MUSCLES.
THAW IS PROCEED-ING NOR-MALLY.
PLEASE STAND BY.

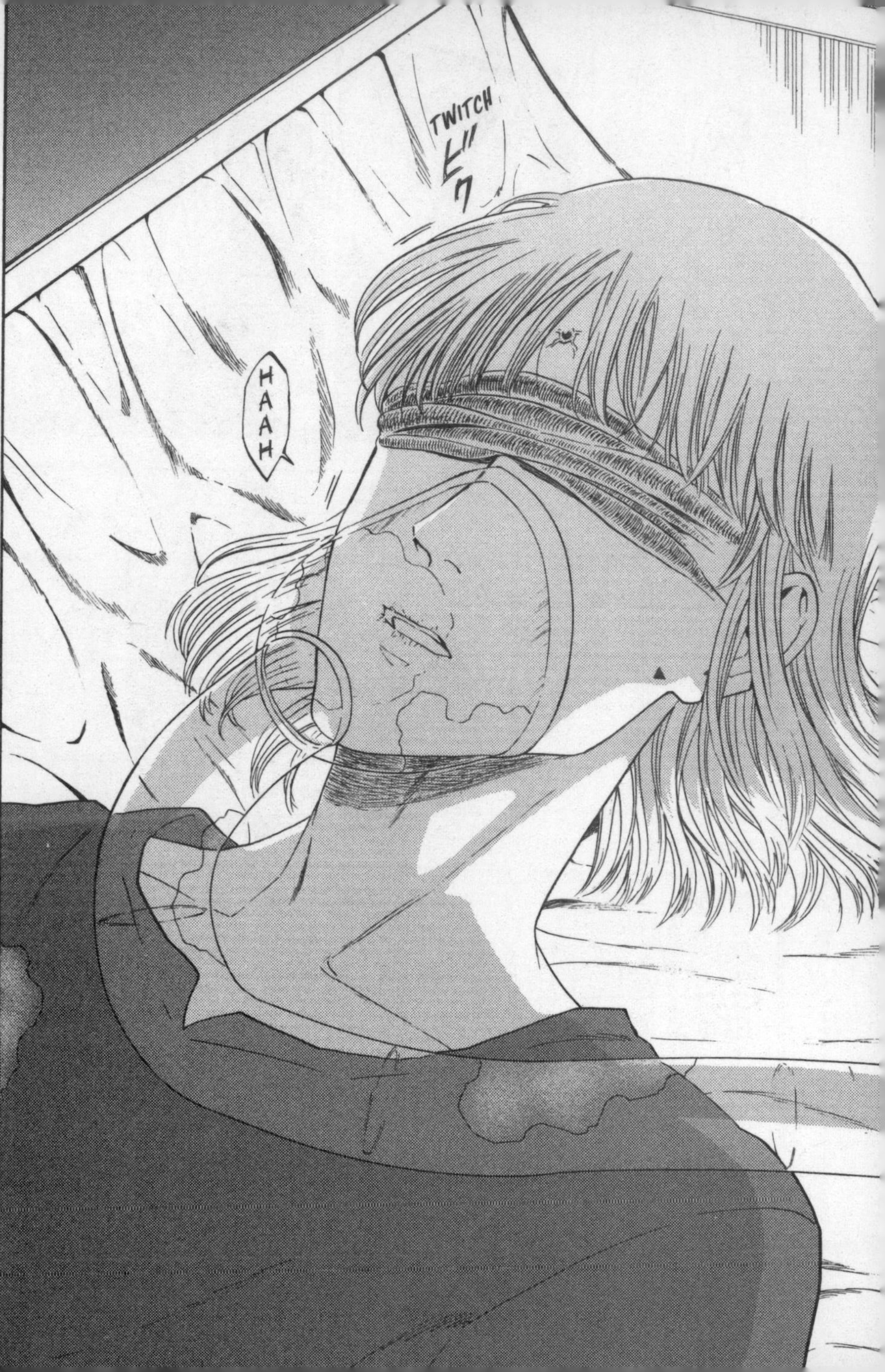
TWITCH
ビク
HAAAH

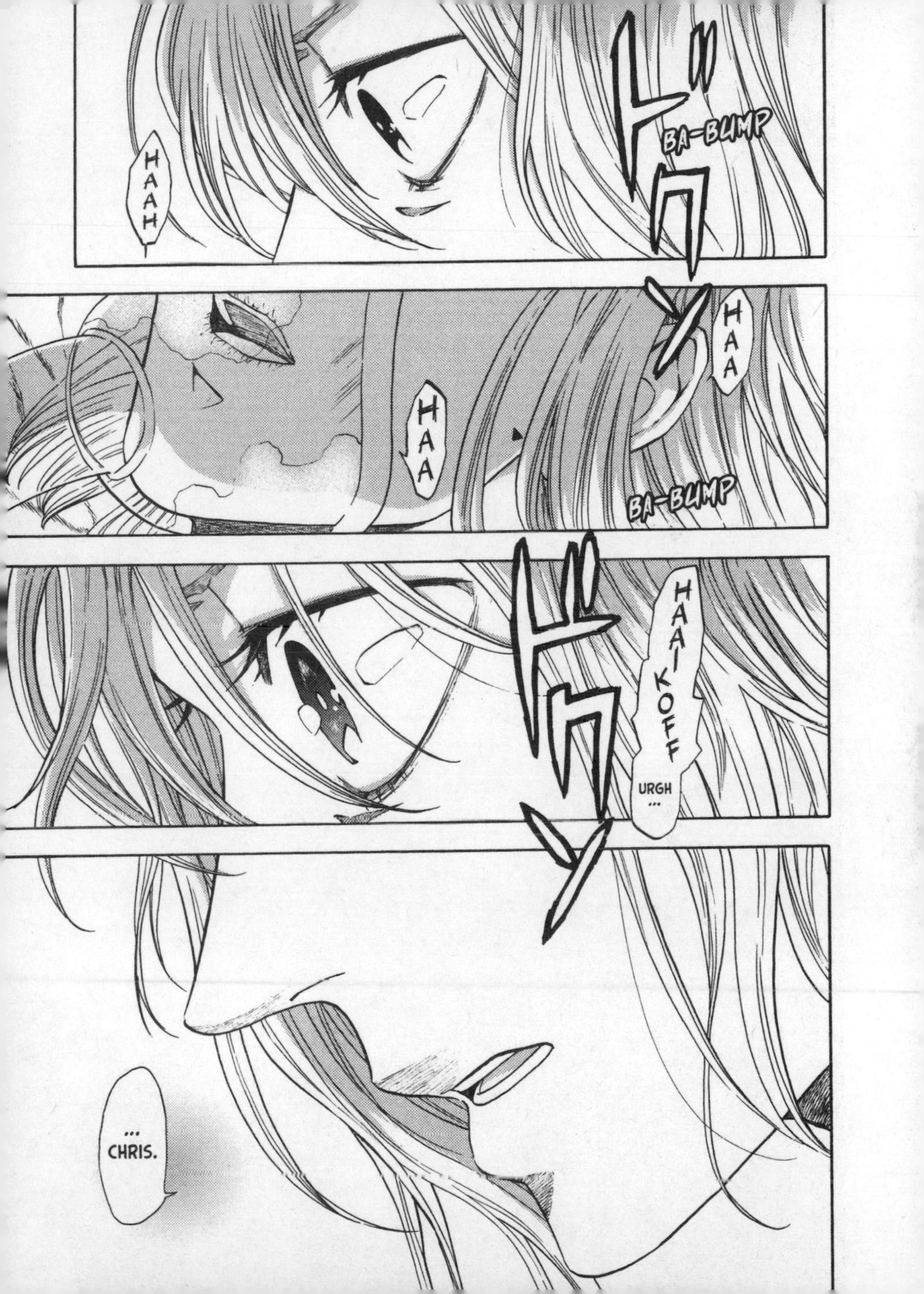

ドクン
BA-BUMP
HAAAH
HAA
HAA
BA-BUMP
ドクン
HAA! KOFF
URGH...
... CHRIS.

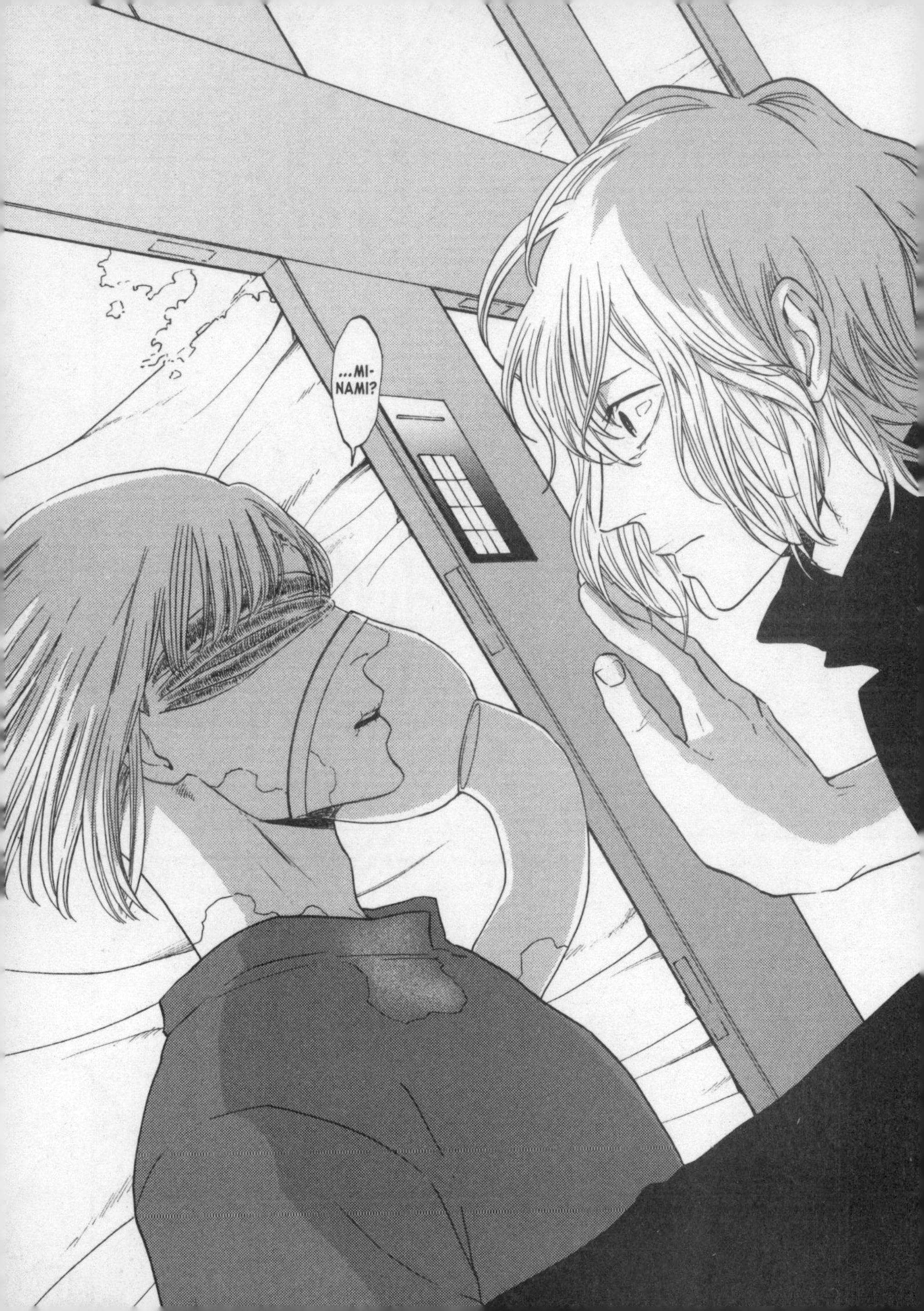
...MI-
NAMI?

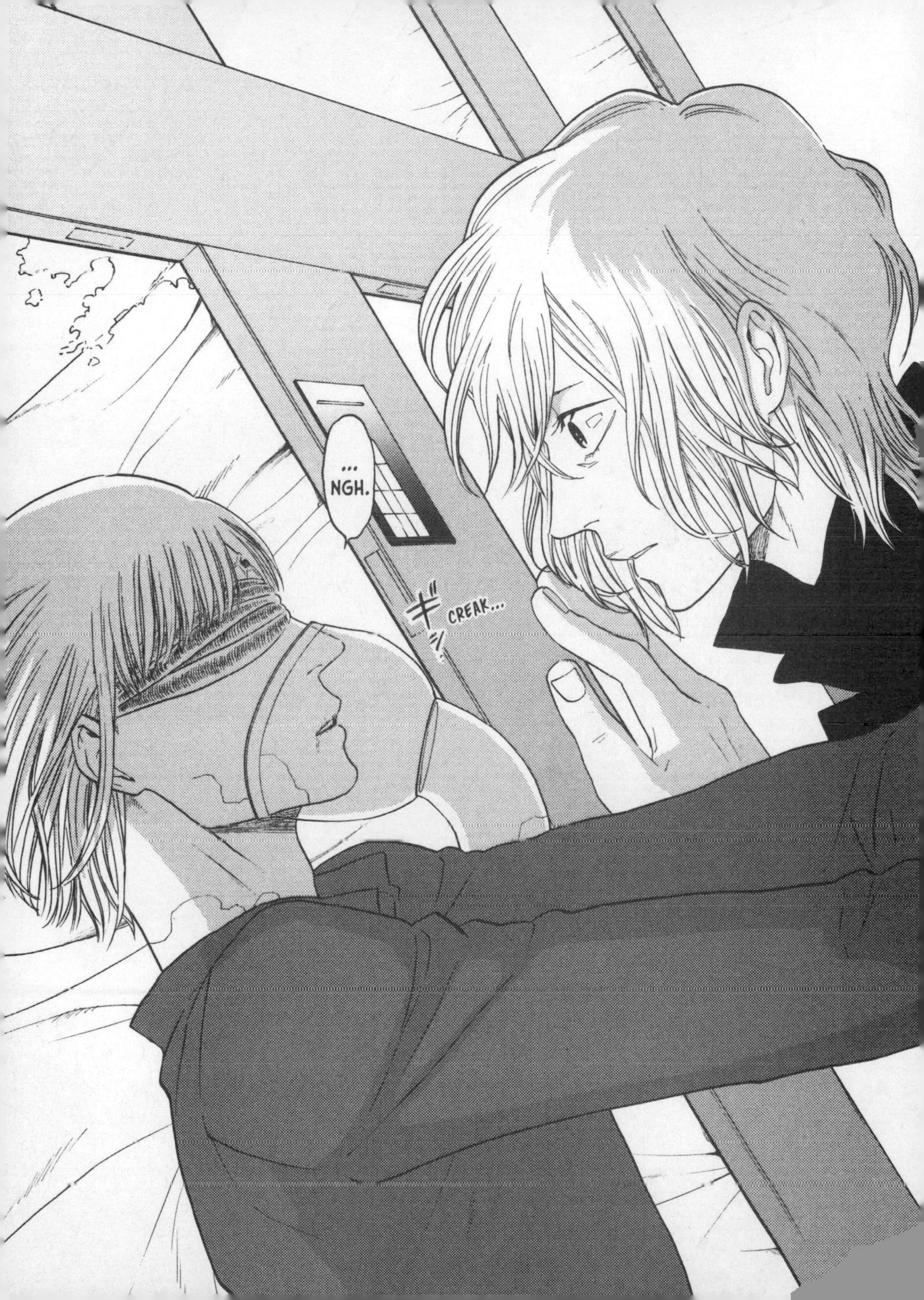
...NGH.
ギシ
CREAK...

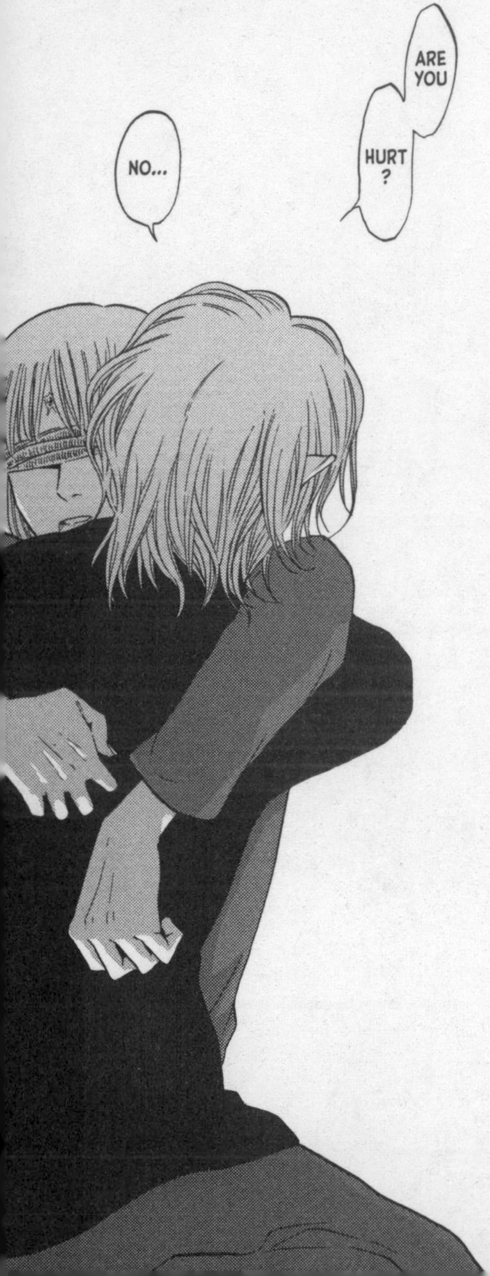
ARE YOU
HURT?
NO...

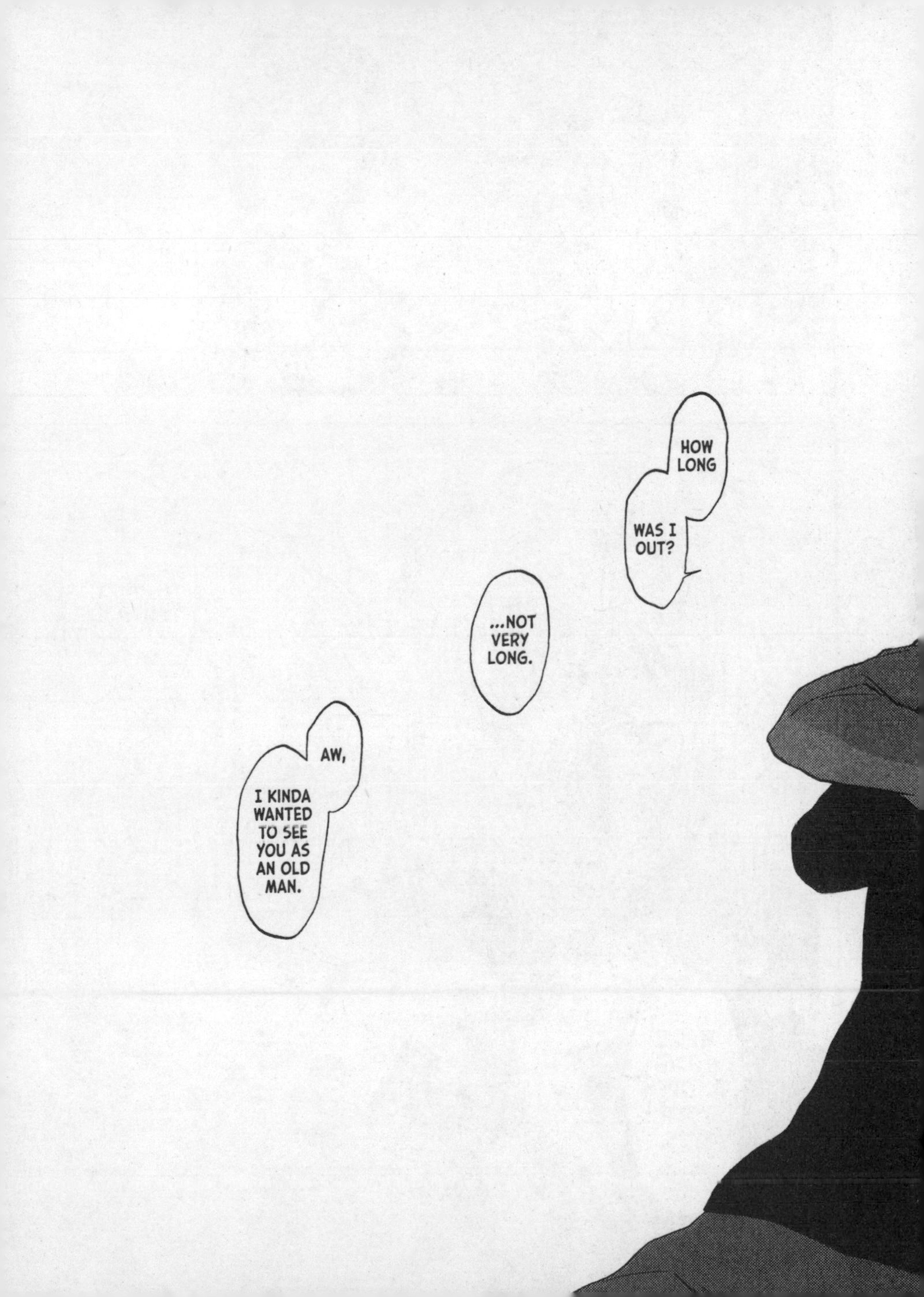
HOW LONG
WAS I OUT?
...NOT VERY LONG.
AW,
I KINDA WANTED TO SEE YOU AS AN OLD MAN.

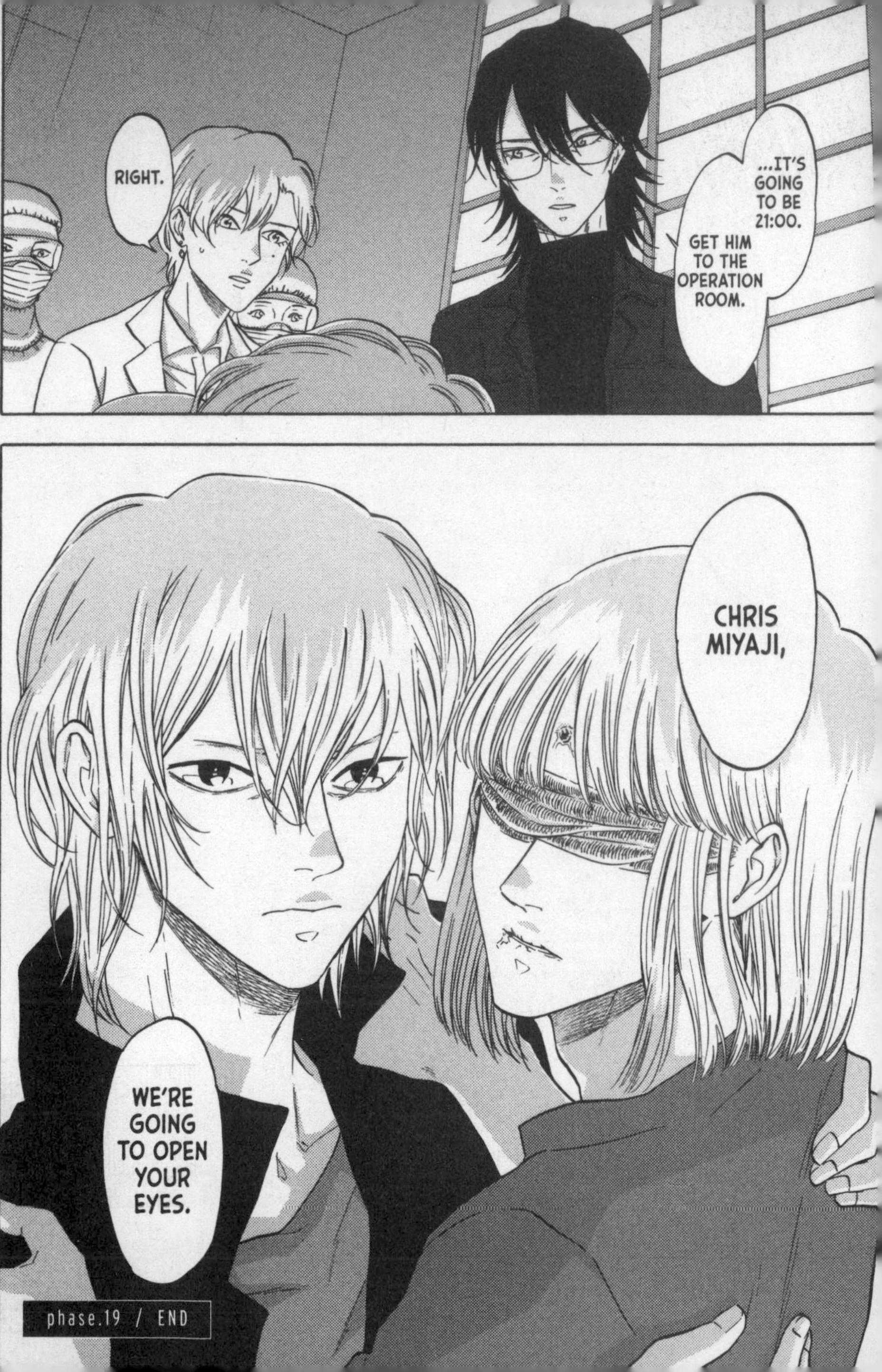
...IT'S GOING TO BE 21:00.
GET HIM TO THE OPERATION ROOM.
RIGHT.
CHRIS MIYAJI,
WE'RE GOING TO OPEN YOUR EYES.
phase.19 / END

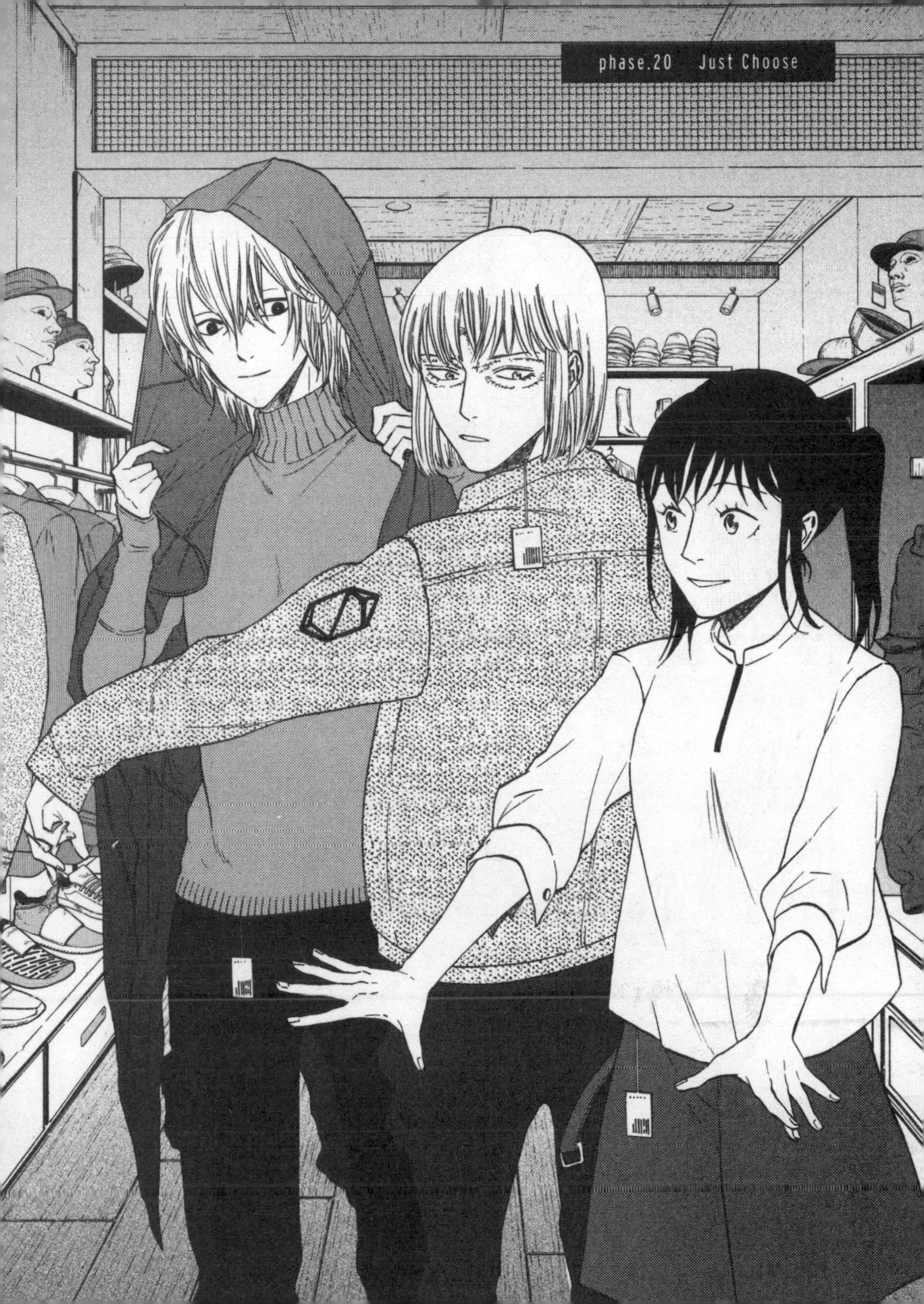
phase.20 Just Choose

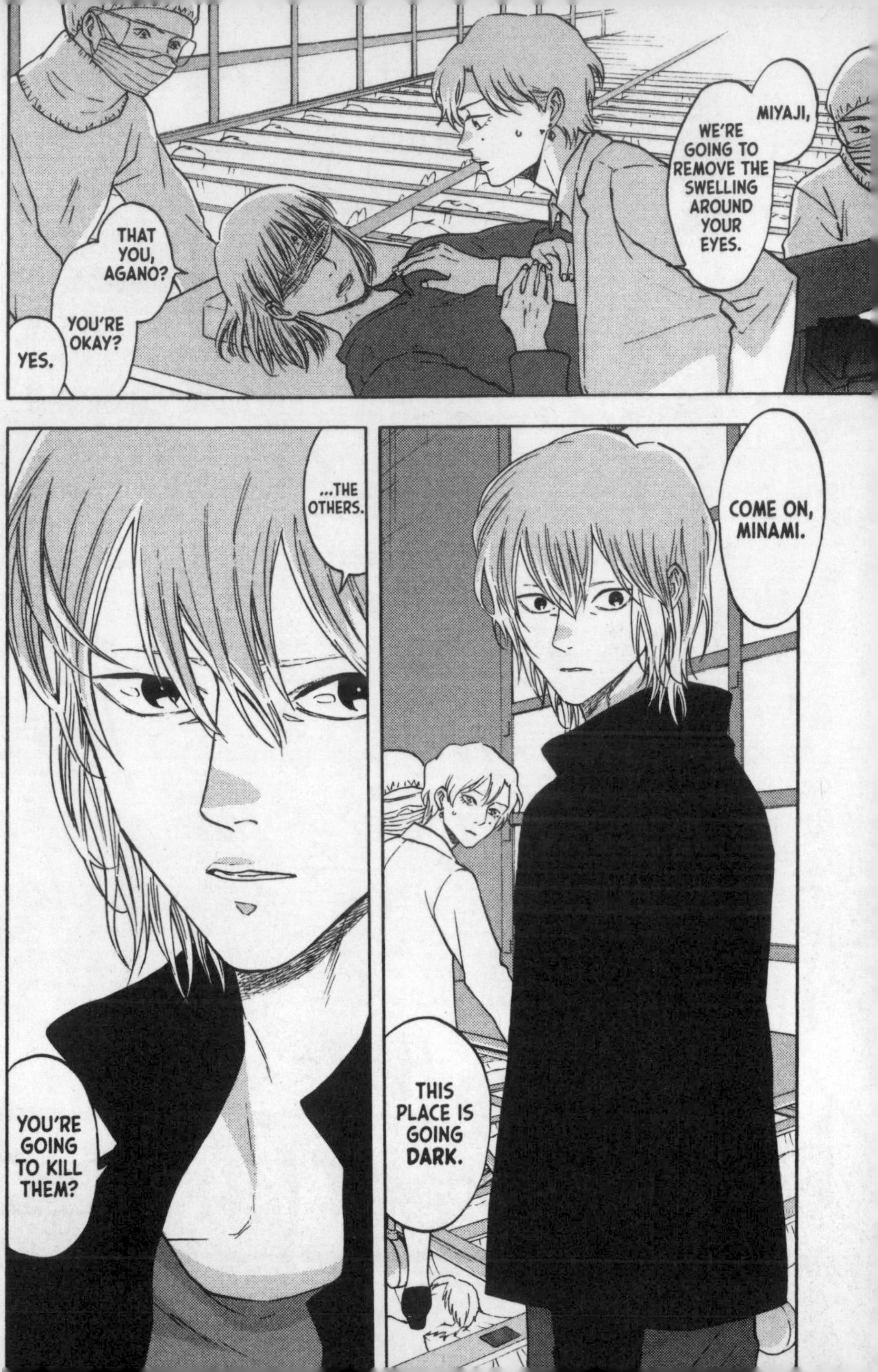
MIYAJI, WE'RE GOING TO REMOVE THE SWELLING AROUND YOUR EYES.
THAT YOU, AGANO?
YOU'RE OKAY?
YES.
COME ON, MINAMI.
THIS PLACE IS GOING DARK.
...THE OTHERS.
YOU'RE GOING TO KILL THEM?

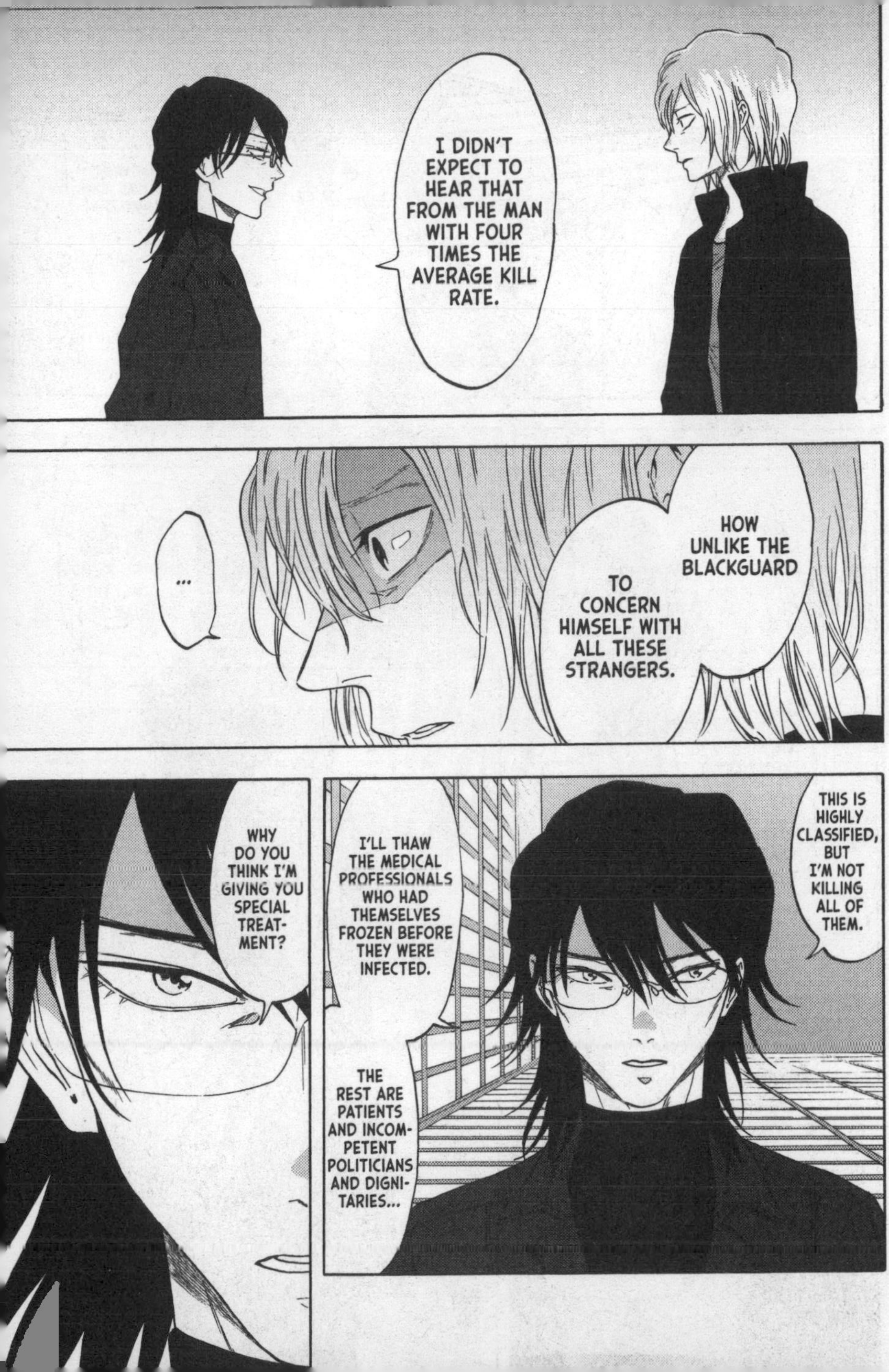
I DIDN'T EXPECT TO HEAR THAT FROM THE MAN WITH FOUR TIMES THE AVERAGE KILL RATE.
HOW UNLIKE THE BLACKGUARD
TO CONCERN HIMSELF WITH ALL THESE STRANGERS.
...
THIS IS HIGHLY CLASSIFIED, BUT I'M NOT KILLING ALL OF THEM.
I'LL THAW THE MEDICAL PROFESSIONALS WHO HAD THEMSELVES FROZEN BEFORE THEY WERE INFECTED.
THE REST ARE PATIENTS AND INCOM-PETENT POLITICIANS AND DIGNI-TARIES...
WHY DO YOU THINK I'M GIVING YOU SPECIAL TREATMENT?

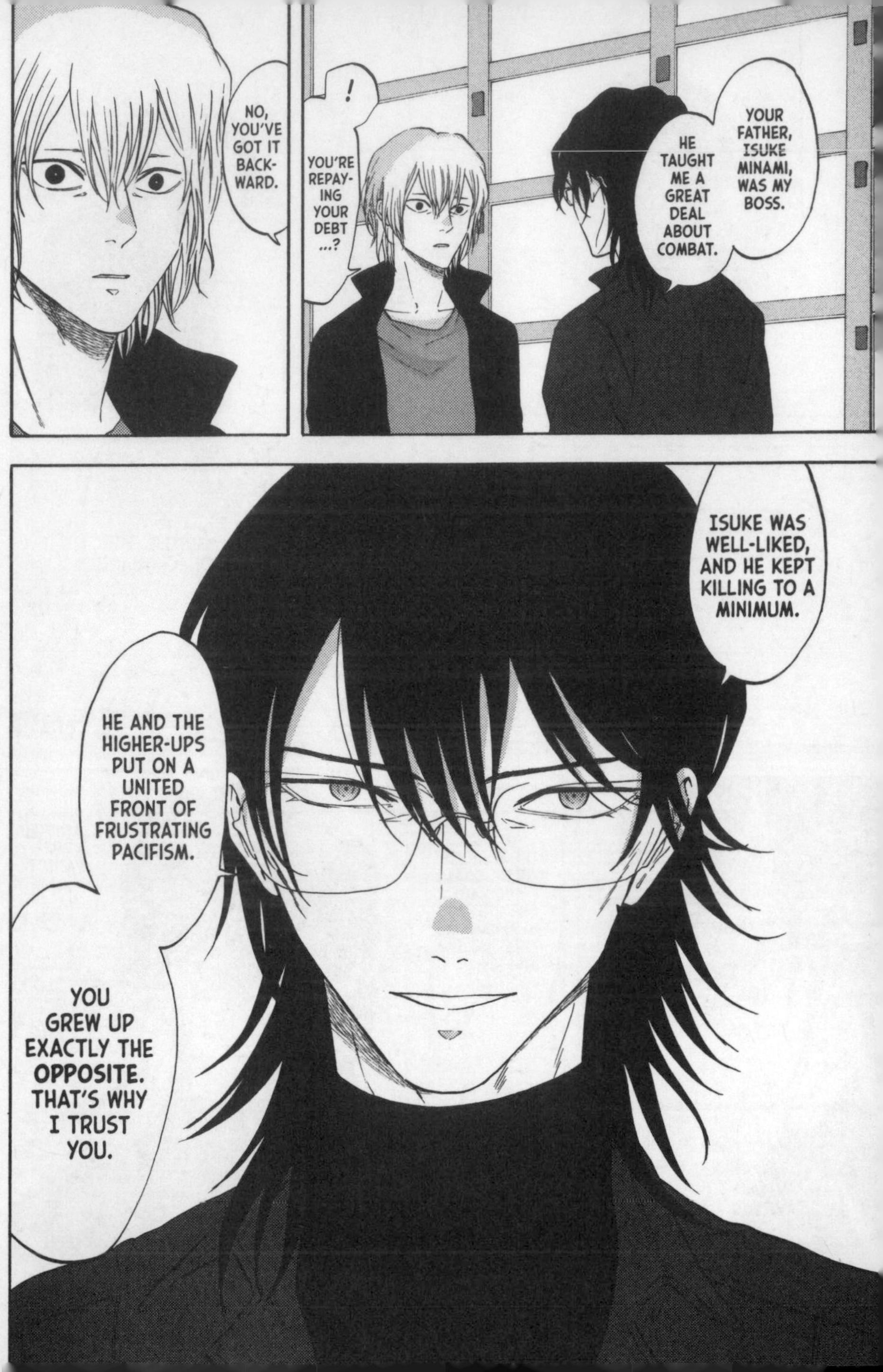
YOUR FATHER, ISUKE MINAMI, WAS MY BOSS.
HE TAUGHT ME A GREAT DEAL ABOUT COMBAT.
!
YOU'RE REPAYING YOUR DEBT ...?
NO, YOU'VE GOT IT BACKWARD.
ISUKE WAS WELL-LIKED, AND HE KEPT KILLING TO A MINIMUM.
HE AND THE HIGHER-UPS PUT ON A UNITED FRONT OF FRUSTRATING PACIFISM.
YOU GREW UP EXACTLY THE **OPPOSITE**. THAT'S WHY I TRUST YOU.

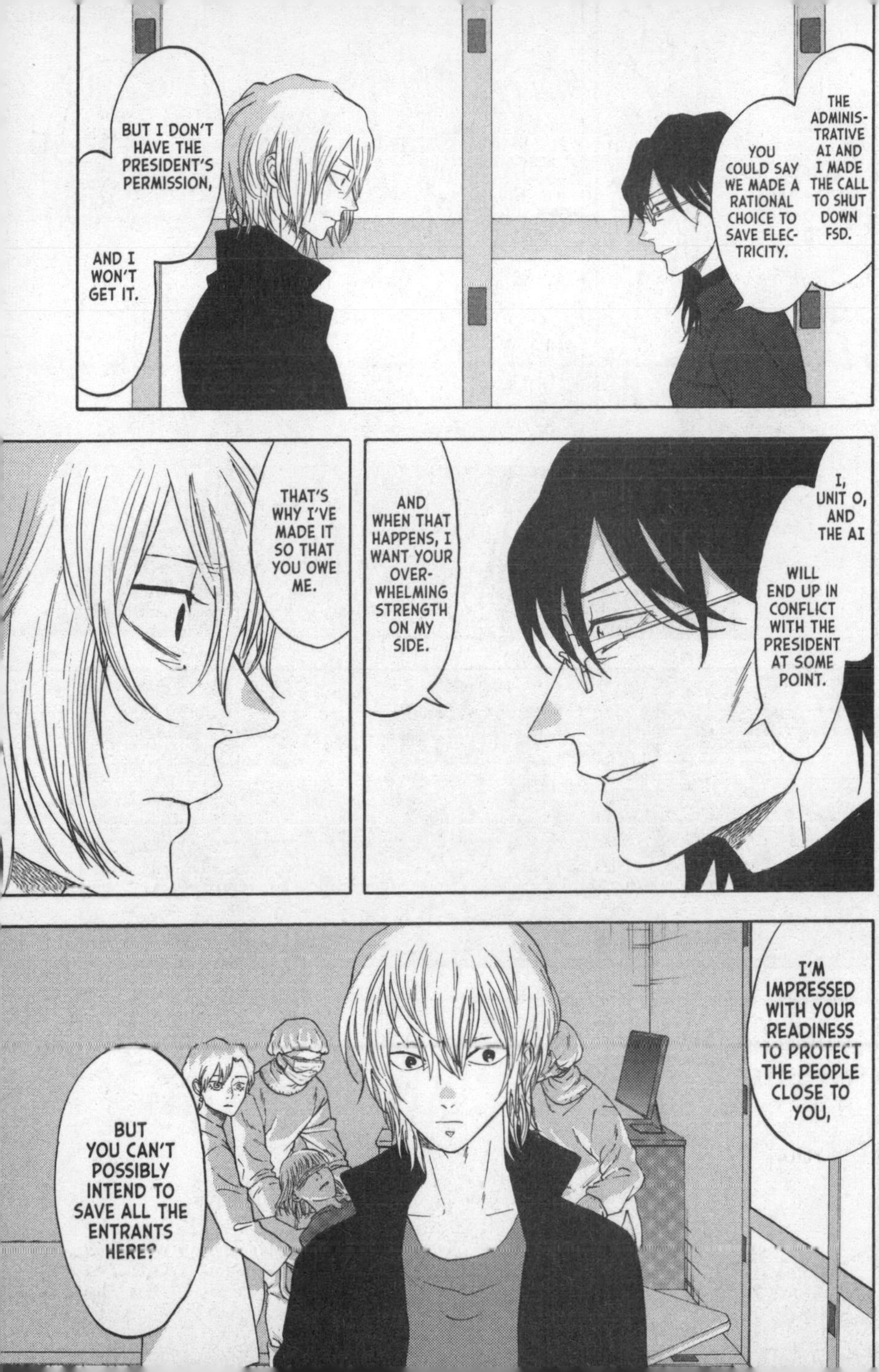

THE ADMINISTRATIVE AI AND I MADE THE CALL TO SHUT DOWN FSD.
YOU COULD SAY WE MADE A RATIONAL CHOICE TO SAVE ELECTRICITY.
BUT I DON'T HAVE THE PRESIDENT'S PERMISSION,
AND I WON'T GET IT.
I, UNIT 0, AND THE AI
WILL END UP IN CONFLICT WITH THE PRESIDENT AT SOME POINT.
AND WHEN THAT HAPPENS, I WANT YOUR OVERWHELMING STRENGTH ON MY SIDE.
THAT'S WHY I'VE MADE IT SO THAT YOU OWE ME.
I'M IMPRESSED WITH YOUR READINESS TO PROTECT THE PEOPLE CLOSE TO YOU,
BUT YOU CAN'T POSSIBLY INTEND TO SAVE ALL THE ENTRANTS HERE?

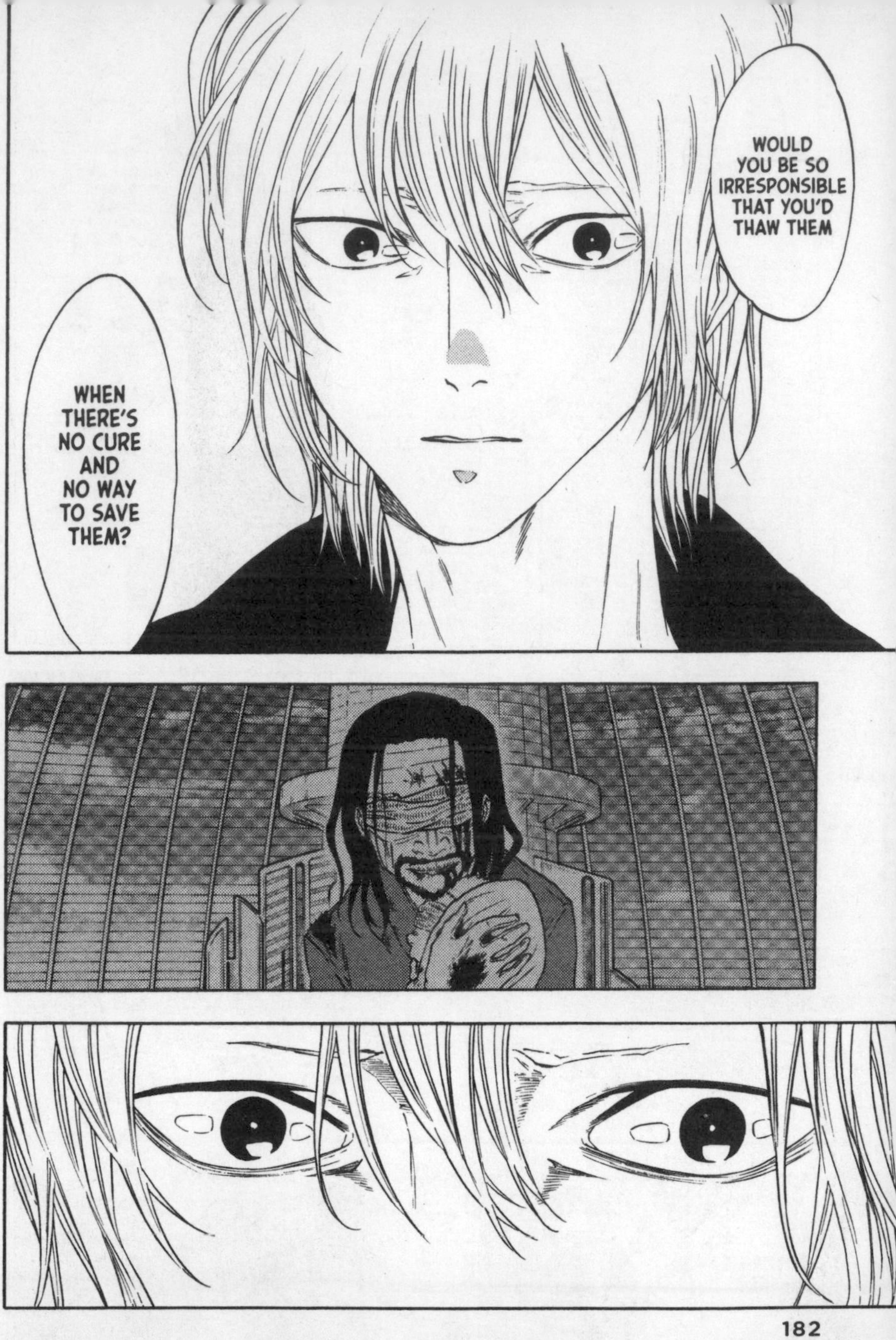
WOULD YOU BE SO IRRESPONSIBLE THAT YOU'D THAW THEM
WHEN THERE'S NO CURE AND NO WAY TO SAVE THEM?

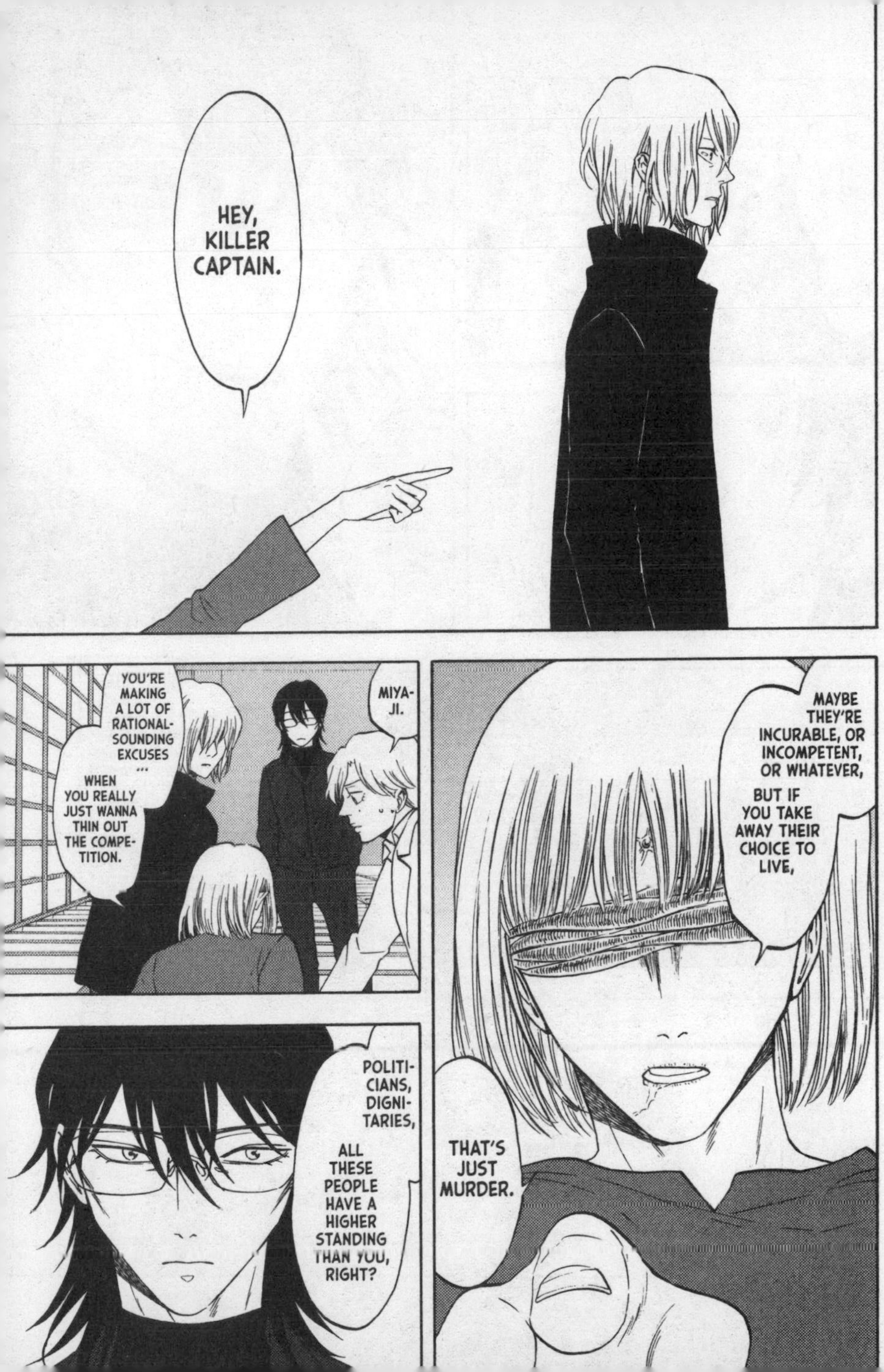
HEY, KILLER CAPTAIN.
MAYBE THEY'RE INCURABLE, OR INCOMPETENT, OR WHATEVER,
BUT IF YOU TAKE AWAY THEIR CHOICE TO LIVE,
THAT'S JUST MURDER.
MIYA-JI.
YOU'RE MAKING A LOT OF RATIONAL-SOUNDING EXCUSES...
WHEN YOU REALLY JUST WANNA THIN OUT THE COMPE-TITION.
POLITI-CIANS, DIGNI-TARIES,
ALL THESE PEOPLE HAVE A HIGHER STANDING THAN YOU, RIGHT?

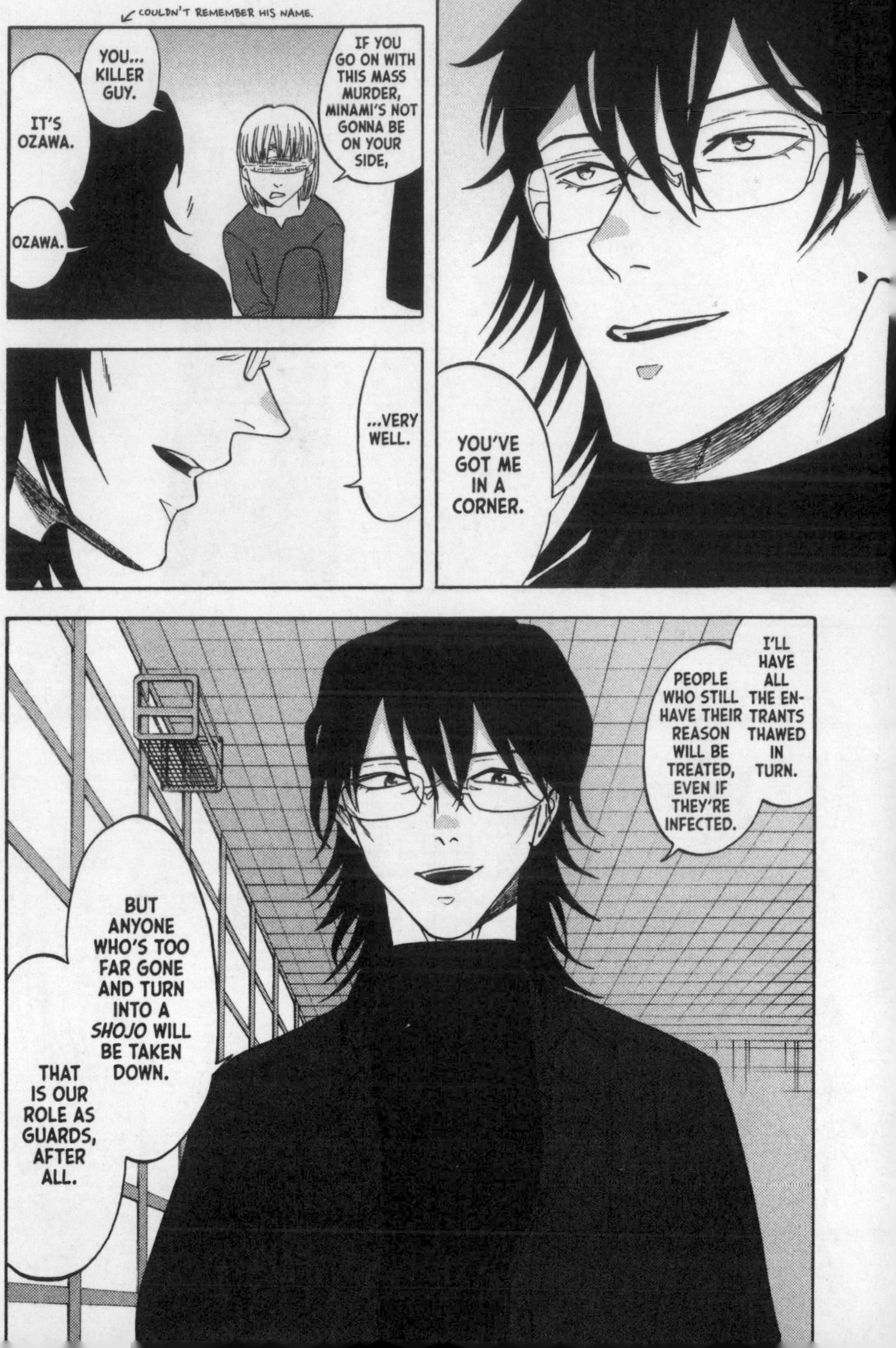
YOU'VE GOT ME IN A CORNER.
COULDN'T REMEMBER HIS NAME.
IF YOU GO ON WITH THIS MASS MURDER, MINAMI'S NOT GONNA BE ON YOUR SIDE,
YOU... KILLER GUY.
IT'S OZAWA.
OZAWA.
...VERY WELL.
I'LL HAVE ALL THE EN-TRANTS THAWED IN TURN.
PEOPLE WHO STILL HAVE THEIR REASON WILL BE TREATED, EVEN IF THEY'RE INFECTED.
BUT ANYONE WHO'S TOO FAR GONE AND TURN INTO A *SHOJO* WILL BE TAKEN DOWN.
THAT IS OUR ROLE AS GUARDS, AFTER ALL.

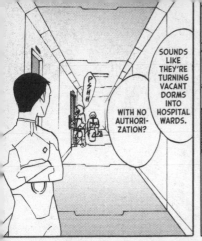

PLIP
Area A
FULL
0
PLIP
Area B
FULL
0
PLIP
Area C
FULL
0
PLIP
Area D
FULL
0
Area E
FULL
0
NOTICE TO MEDICAL STAFF.
DUE TO THE CURRENT PERSONNEL SHORTAGE—
SOUNDS LIKE THEY'RE TURNING VACANT DORMS INTO HOSPITAL WARDS.
PSHH
WITH NO AUTHORIZATION?
OPERATION IN PROGRESS
ENERGY CONSERVATION PLANS HAVE BEEN UPDATED AS FOLLOWS.
TO EXPAND HOSPITAL CAPACITY, ALL FLOORS WILL EXPERIENCE
A TEMPORARY POWER OUTAGE STARTING AT 21:00.
FOR NUTRITIONAL SUPPLIES, PLEASE USE THE EMERGENCY LEVER
TO MANUALLY RELEASE—

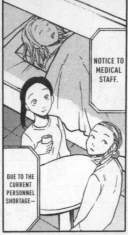

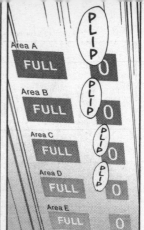

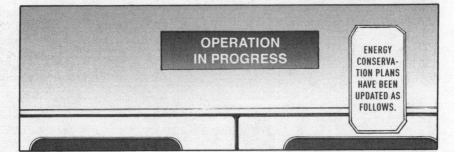

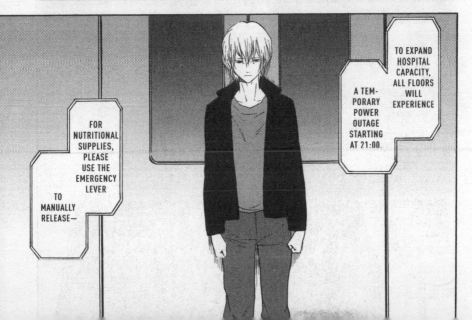

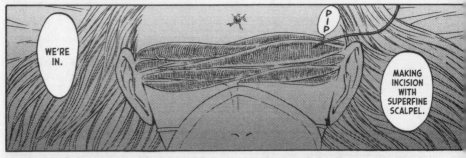

WE'RE IN.

PIP

MAKING INCISION WITH SUPERFINE SCALPEL.

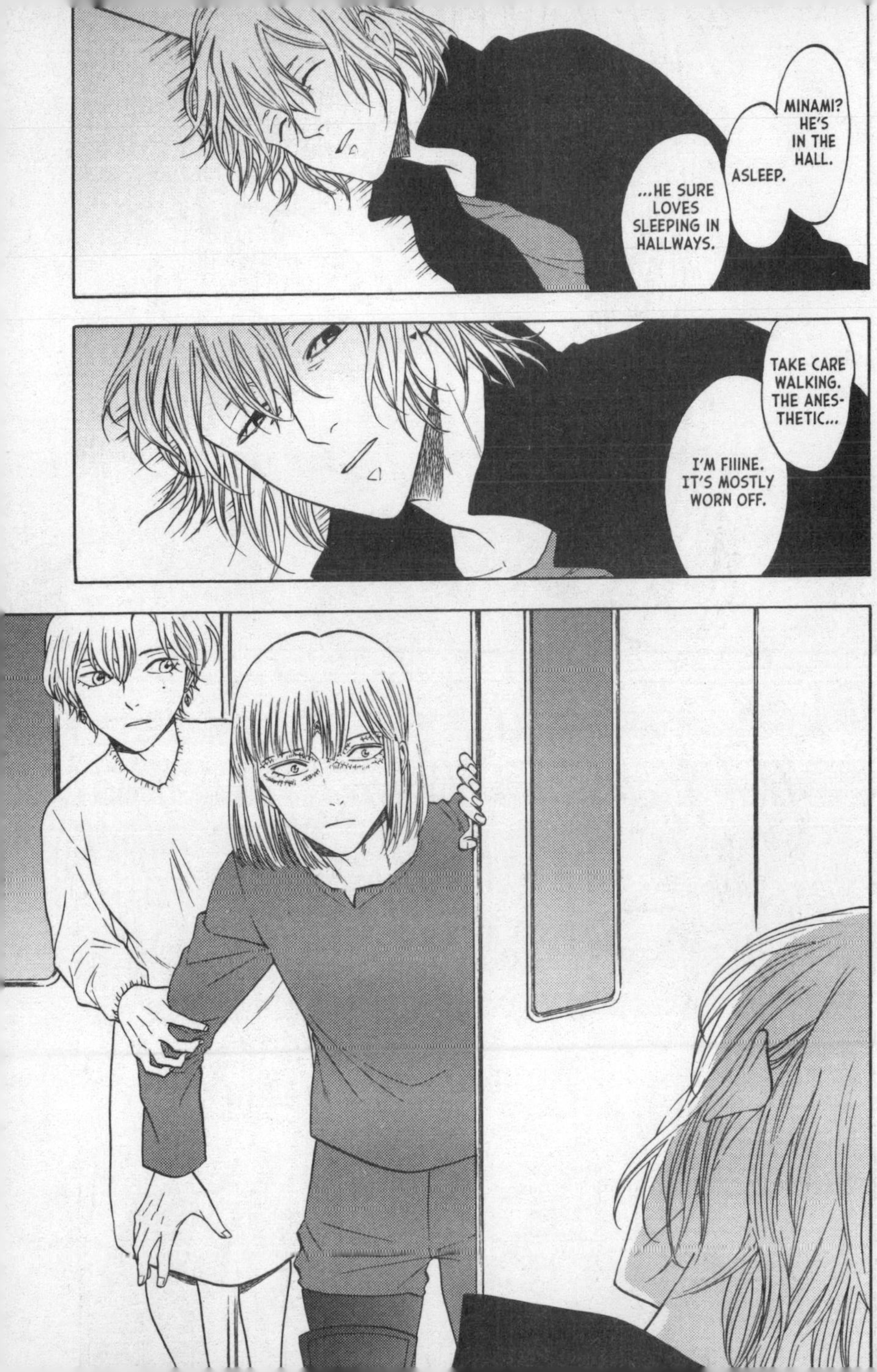
MINAMI? HE'S IN THE HALL.
ASLEEP.
...HE SURE LOVES SLEEPING IN HALLWAYS.
TAKE CARE WALKING. THE ANES-THETIC...
I'M FIIINE. IT'S MOSTLY WORN OFF.

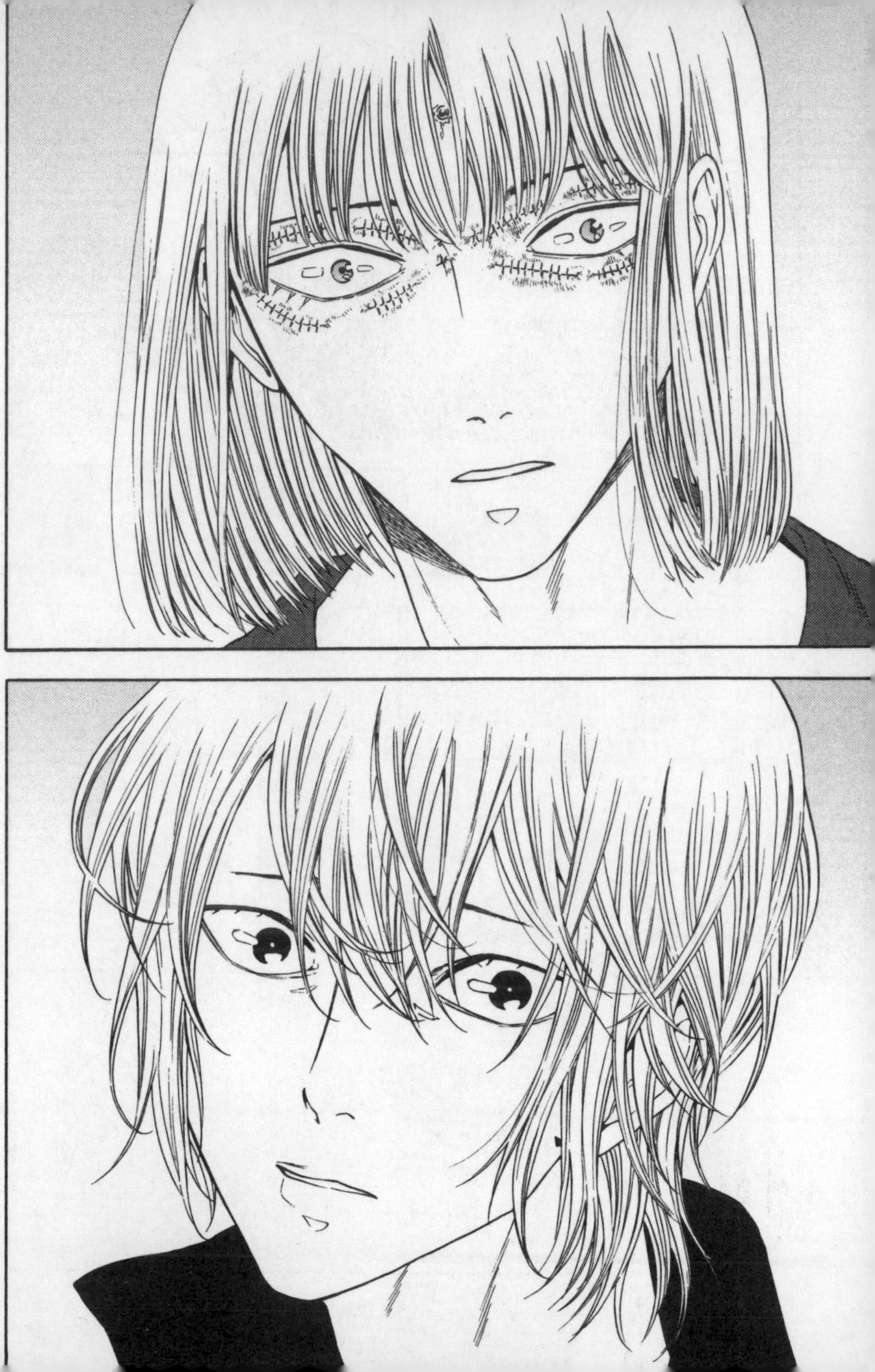

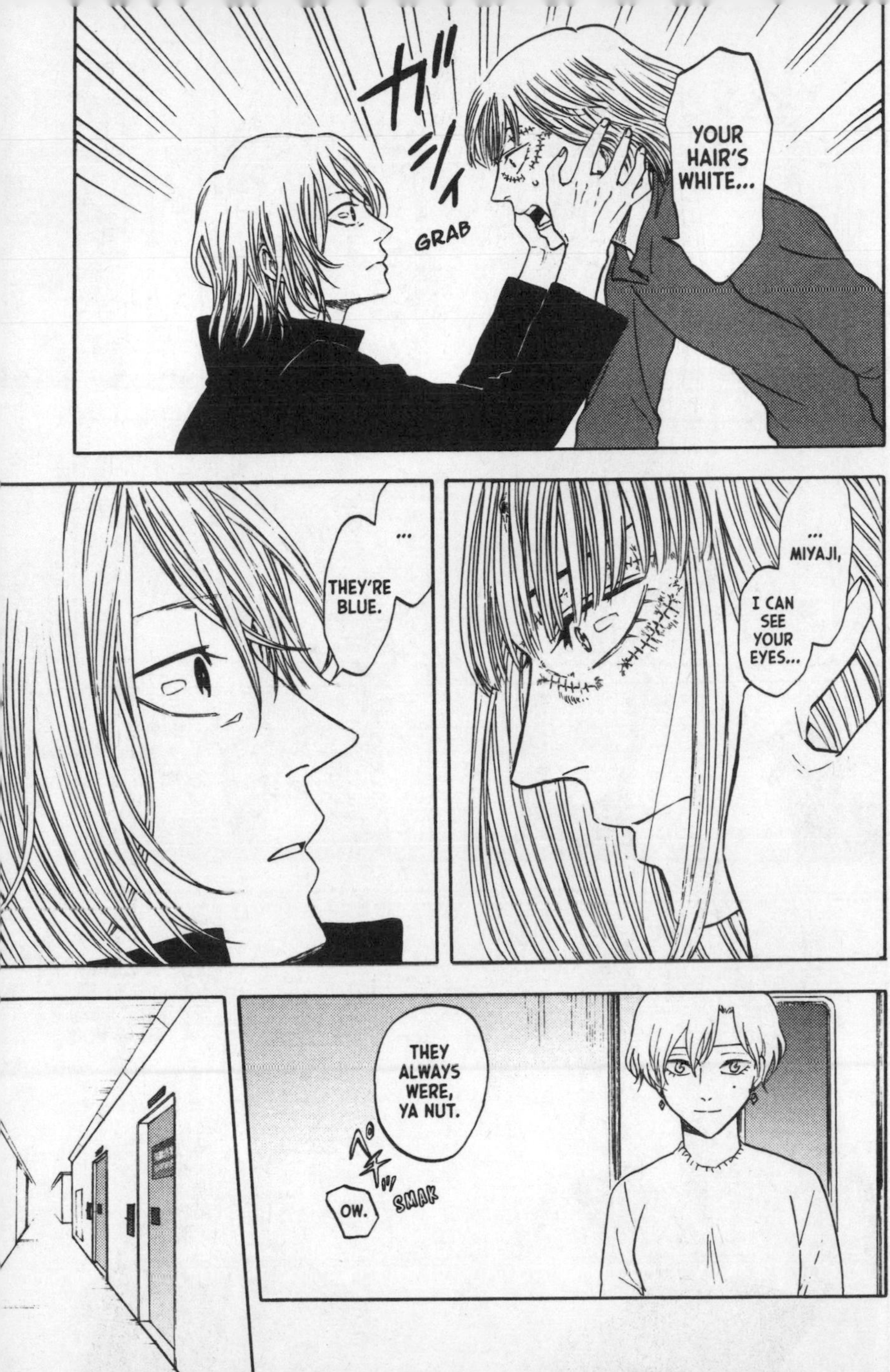
YOUR HAIR'S WHITE...
ガシィ
GRAB
... MIYAJI, I CAN SEE YOUR EYES...
... THEY'RE BLUE.
THEY ALWAYS WERE, YA NUT.
SMAK
OW.

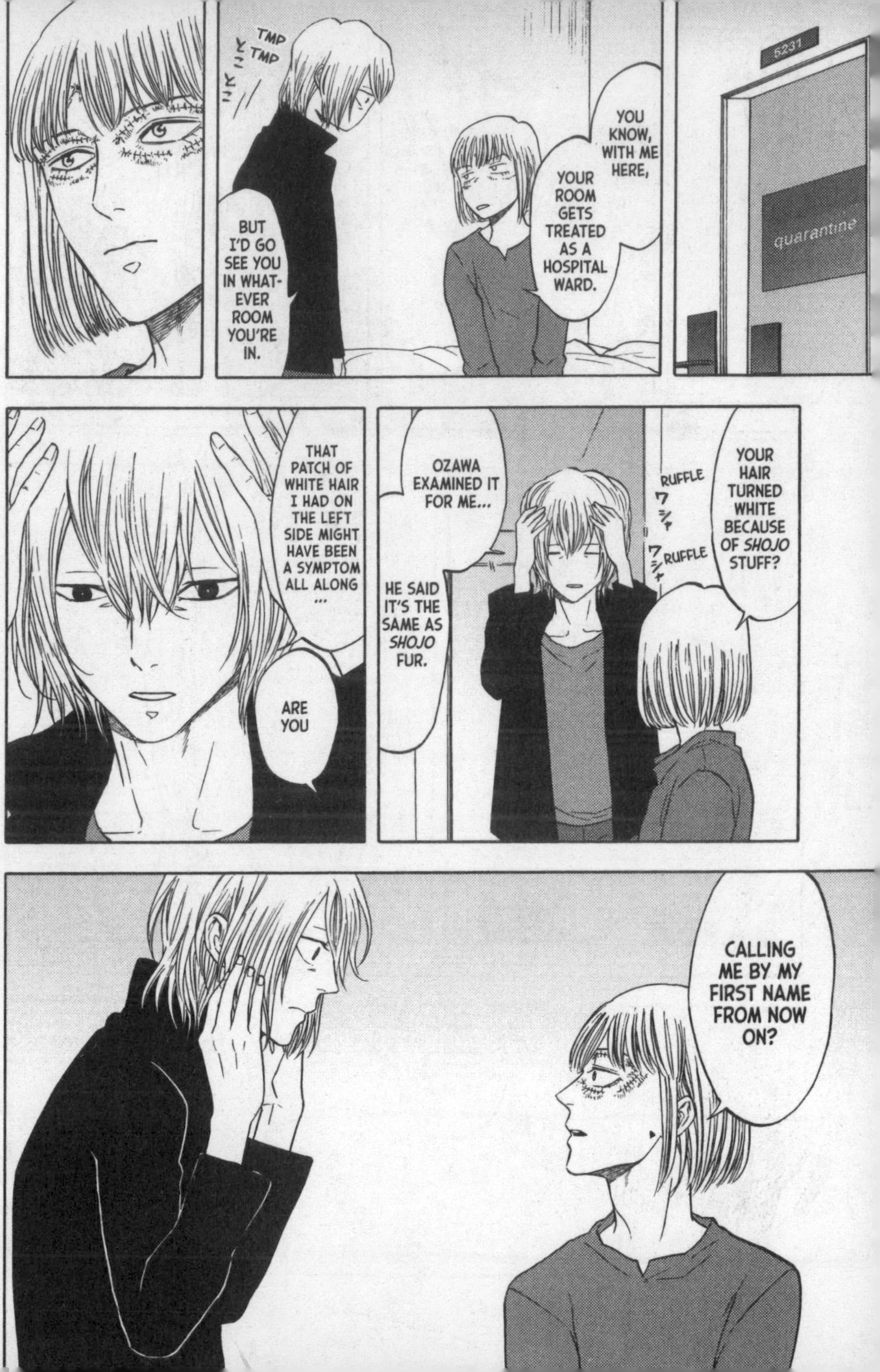
5231
quarantine
YOU KNOW, WITH ME HERE,
YOUR ROOM GETS TREATED AS A HOSPITAL WARD.
TMP TMP
BUT I'D GO SEE YOU IN WHAT-EVER ROOM YOU'RE IN.
YOUR HAIR TURNED WHITE BECAUSE OF *SHOJO* STUFF?
RUFFLE
ワシャ
RUFFLE
ワシャ
OZAWA EXAMINED IT FOR ME...
HE SAID IT'S THE SAME AS *SHOJO* FUR.
THAT PATCH OF WHITE HAIR I HAD ON THE LEFT SIDE MIGHT HAVE BEEN A SYMPTOM ALL ALONG ...
ARE YOU
CALLING ME BY MY FIRST NAME FROM NOW ON?

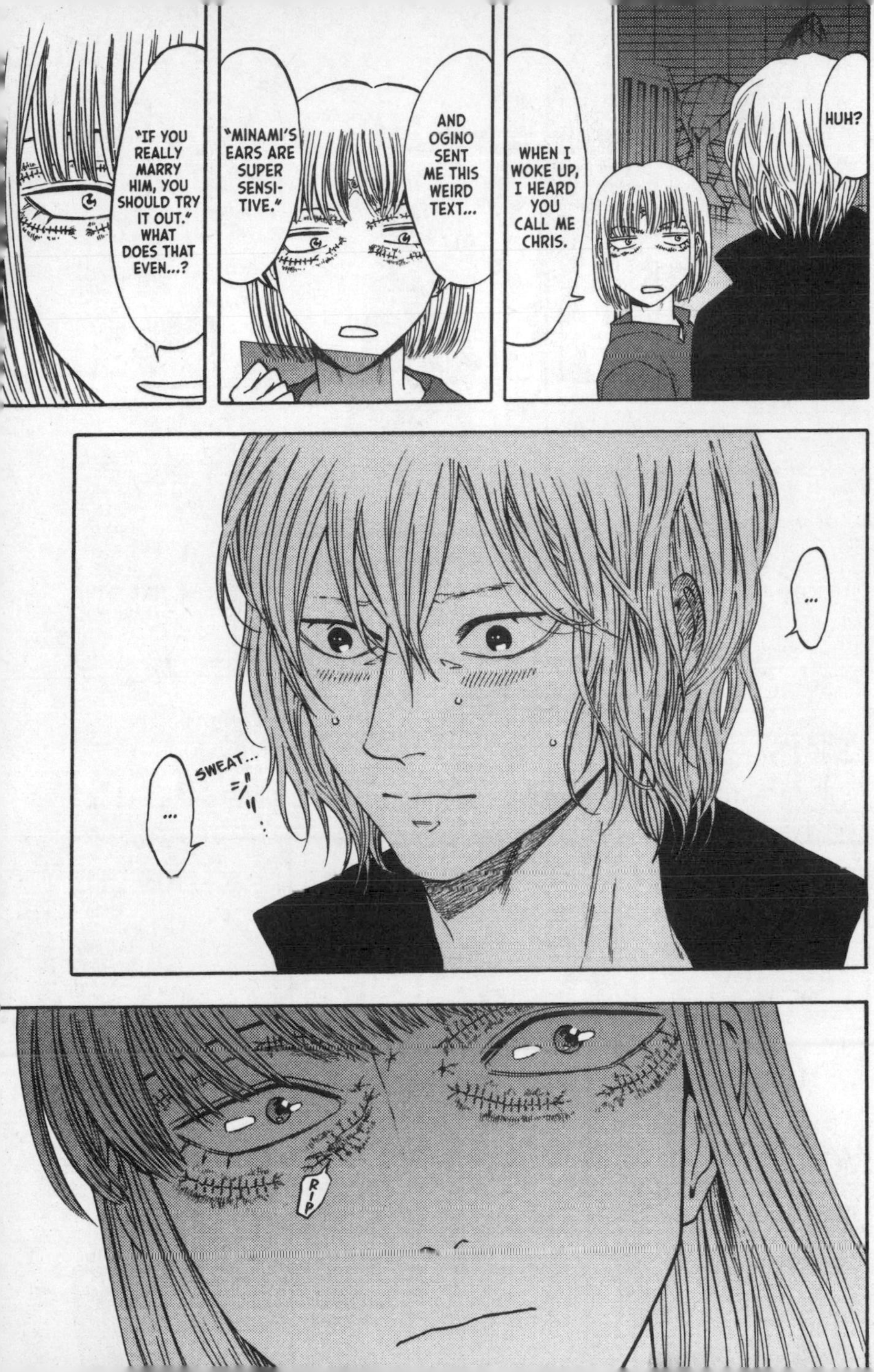
HUH?
WHEN I WOKE UP, I HEARD YOU CALL ME CHRIS.
AND OGINO SENT ME THIS WEIRD TEXT...
"MINAMI'S EARS ARE SUPER SENSITIVE."
"IF YOU REALLY MARRY HIM, YOU SHOULD TRY IT OUT." WHAT DOES THAT EVEN...?
...
SWEAT...
...
RIP

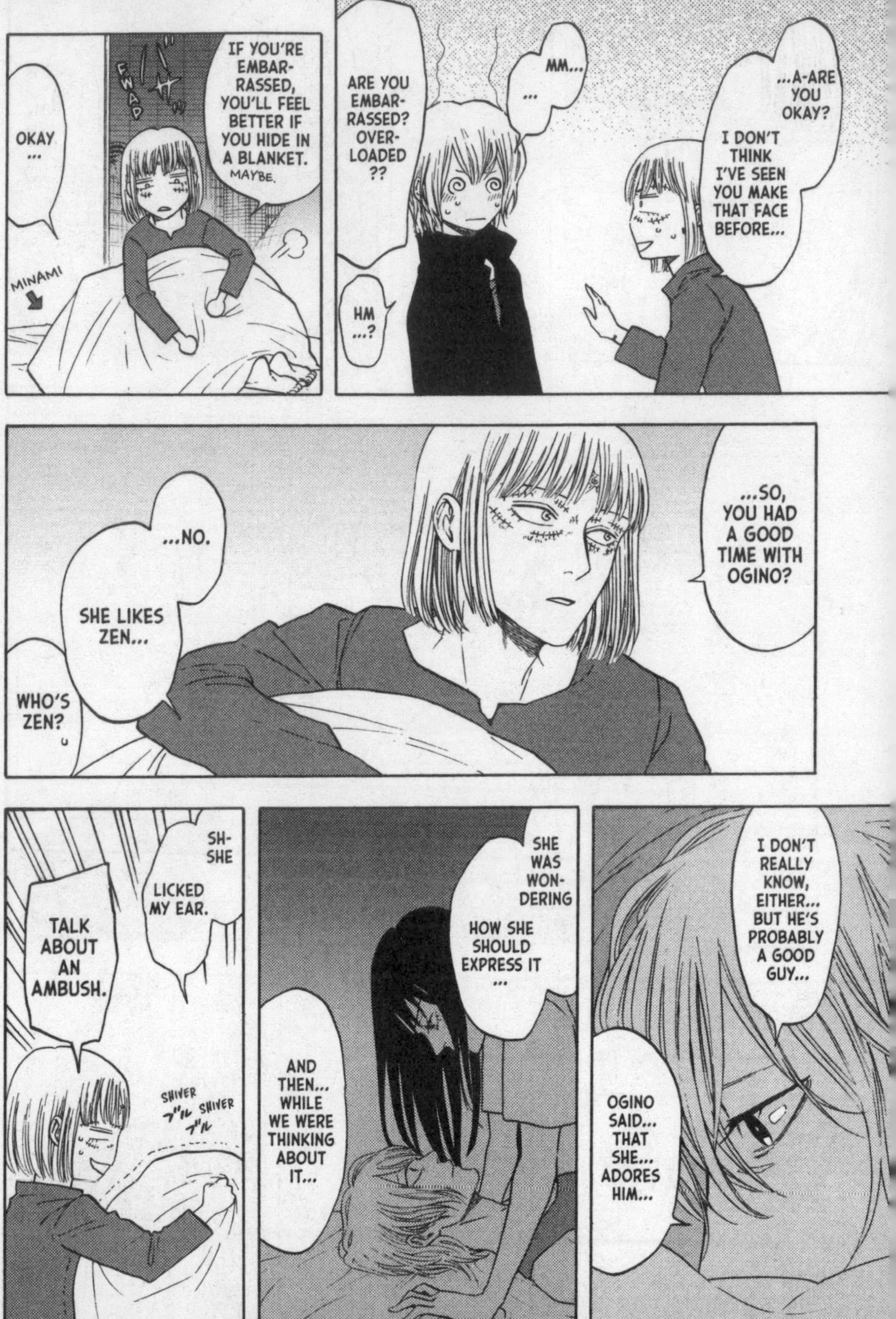
...A-ARE YOU OKAY?
I DON'T THINK I'VE SEEN YOU MAKE THAT FACE BEFORE...
MM... ...
ARE YOU EMBARRASSED? OVERLOADED??
HM ...?
IF YOU'RE EMBARRASSED, YOU'LL FEEL BETTER IF YOU HIDE IN A BLANKET. MAYBE.
FWAP
OKAY ...
MINAMI
...SO, YOU HAD A GOOD TIME WITH OGINO?
...NO.
SHE LIKES ZEN...
WHO'S ZEN?
I DON'T REALLY KNOW, EITHER... BUT HE'S PROBABLY A GOOD GUY...
OGINO SAID... THAT SHE... ADORES HIM...
SHE WAS WONDERING
HOW SHE SHOULD EXPRESS IT ...
AND THEN... WHILE WE WERE THINKING ABOUT IT...
SH-SHE
LICKED MY EAR.
TALK ABOUT AN AMBUSH.
SHIVER ブル SHIVER ブル

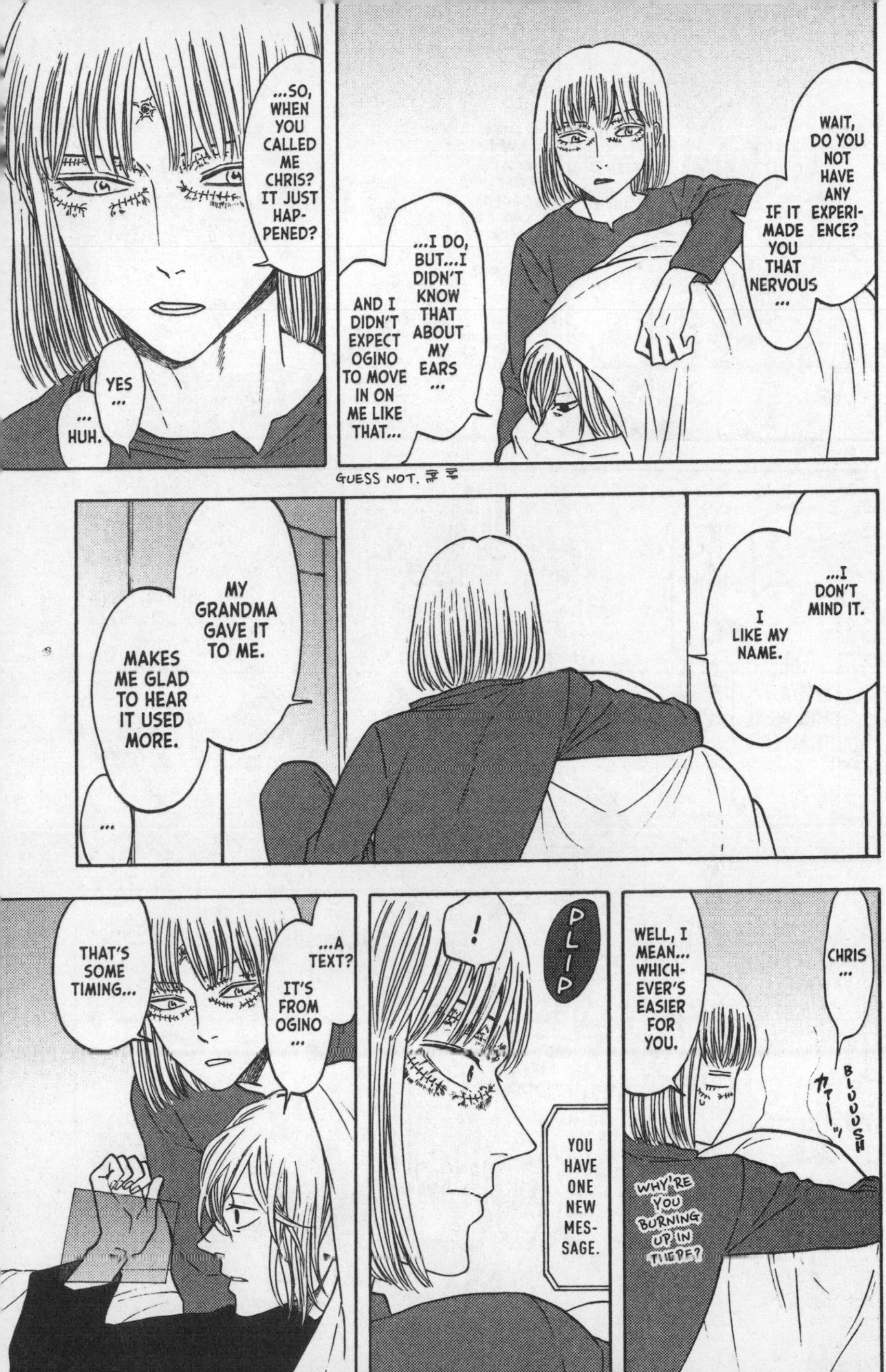
WAIT, DO YOU NOT HAVE ANY EXPERIENCE?
IF IT MADE YOU THAT NERVOUS...
...I DO, BUT...I DIDN'T KNOW THAT ABOUT MY EARS...
AND I DIDN'T EXPECT OGINO TO MOVE IN ON ME LIKE THAT...
GUESS NOT.
...SO, WHEN YOU CALLED ME CHRIS? IT JUST HAPPENED?
YES...
...HUH.
...I DON'T MIND IT.
I LIKE MY NAME.
MY GRANDMA GAVE IT TO ME.
MAKES ME GLAD TO HEAR IT USED MORE.
...
CHRIS...
WELL, I MEAN... WHICHEVER'S EASIER FOR YOU.
BLUUUSH
WHY'RE YOU BURNING UP IN THERE?
PLIP
!
YOU HAVE ONE NEW MESSAGE.
...A TEXT?
IT'S FROM OGINO...
THAT'S SOME TIMING...

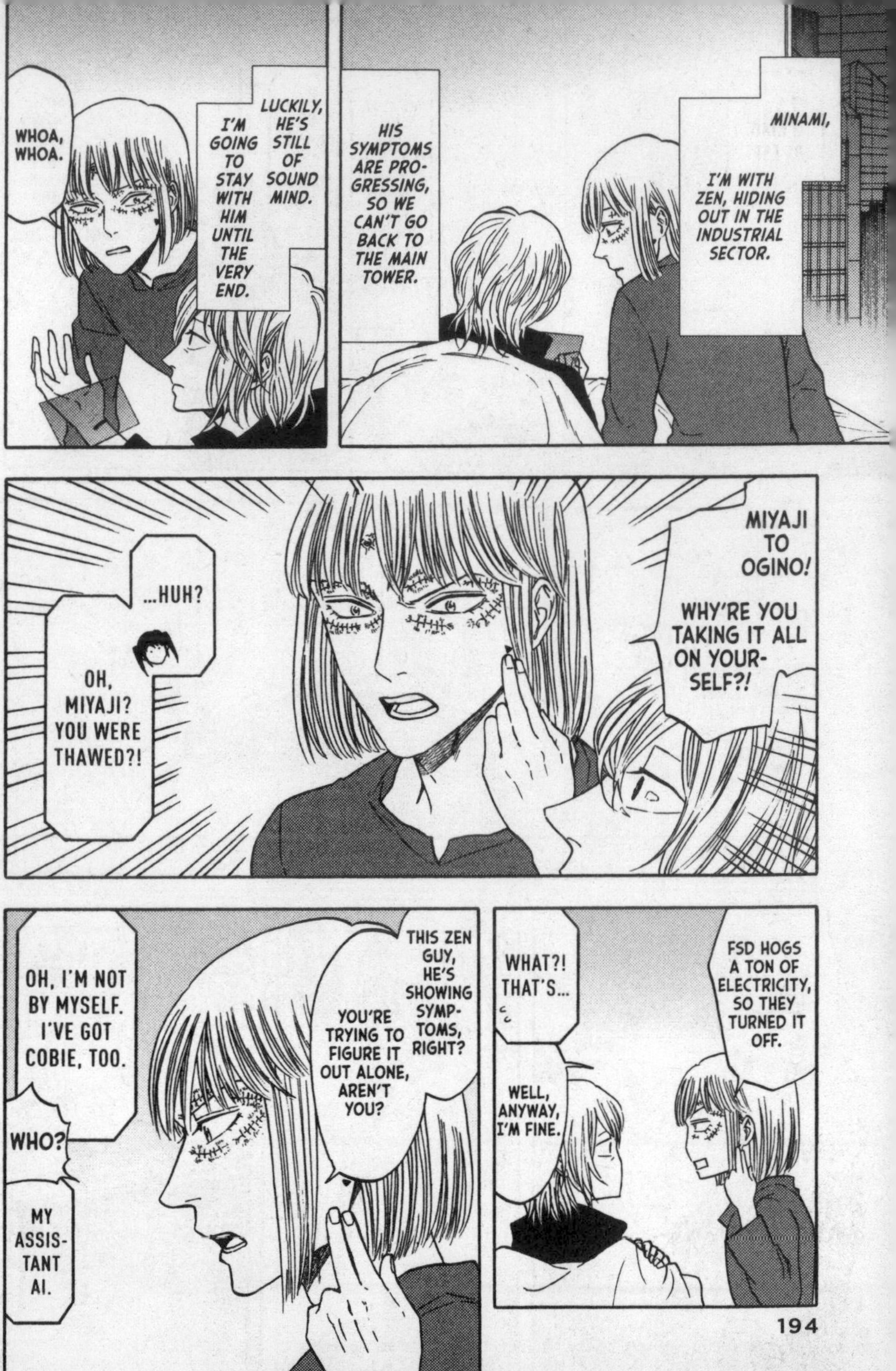
MINAMI,
I'M WITH ZEN, HIDING OUT IN THE INDUSTRIAL SECTOR.
HIS SYMPTOMS ARE PROGRESSING, SO WE CAN'T GO BACK TO THE MAIN TOWER.
LUCKILY, HE'S STILL OF SOUND MIND.
I'M GOING TO STAY WITH HIM UNTIL THE VERY END.
WHOA, WHOA.
MIYAJI TO OGINO!
WHY'RE YOU TAKING IT ALL ON YOURSELF?!
...HUH?
OH, MIYAJI? YOU WERE THAWED?!
FSD HOGS A TON OF ELECTRICITY, SO THEY TURNED IT OFF.
WHAT?! THAT'S...
WELL, ANYWAY, I'M FINE.
THIS ZEN GUY, HE'S SHOWING SYMPTOMS, RIGHT?
YOU'RE TRYING TO FIGURE IT OUT ALONE, AREN'T YOU?
OH, I'M NOT BY MYSELF. I'VE GOT COBIE, TOO.
WHO?
MY ASSISTANT AI.

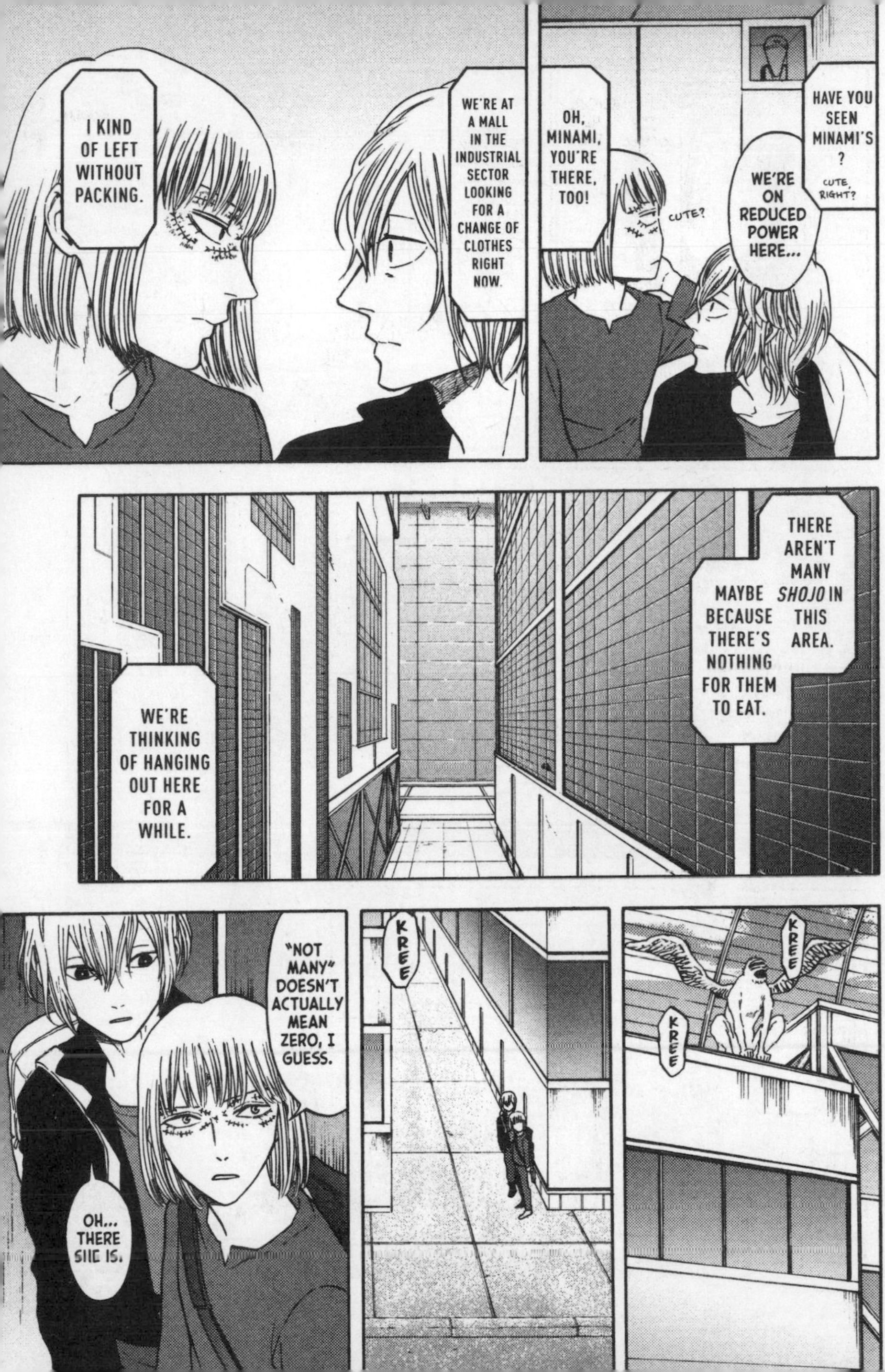
HAVE YOU SEEN MINAMI'S ?
CUTE, RIGHT?
WE'RE ON REDUCED POWER HERE...
OH, MINAMI, YOU'RE THERE, TOO!
CUTE?
WE'RE AT A MALL IN THE INDUSTRIAL SECTOR LOOKING FOR A CHANGE OF CLOTHES RIGHT NOW.
I KIND OF LEFT WITHOUT PACKING.
THERE AREN'T MANY *SHOJO* IN THIS AREA.
MAYBE BECAUSE THERE'S NOTHING FOR THEM TO EAT.
WE'RE THINKING OF HANGING OUT HERE FOR A WHILE.
KREE
KREE
KREE
"NOT MANY" DOESN'T ACTUALLY MEAN ZERO, I GUESS.
OH... THERE SHE IS.

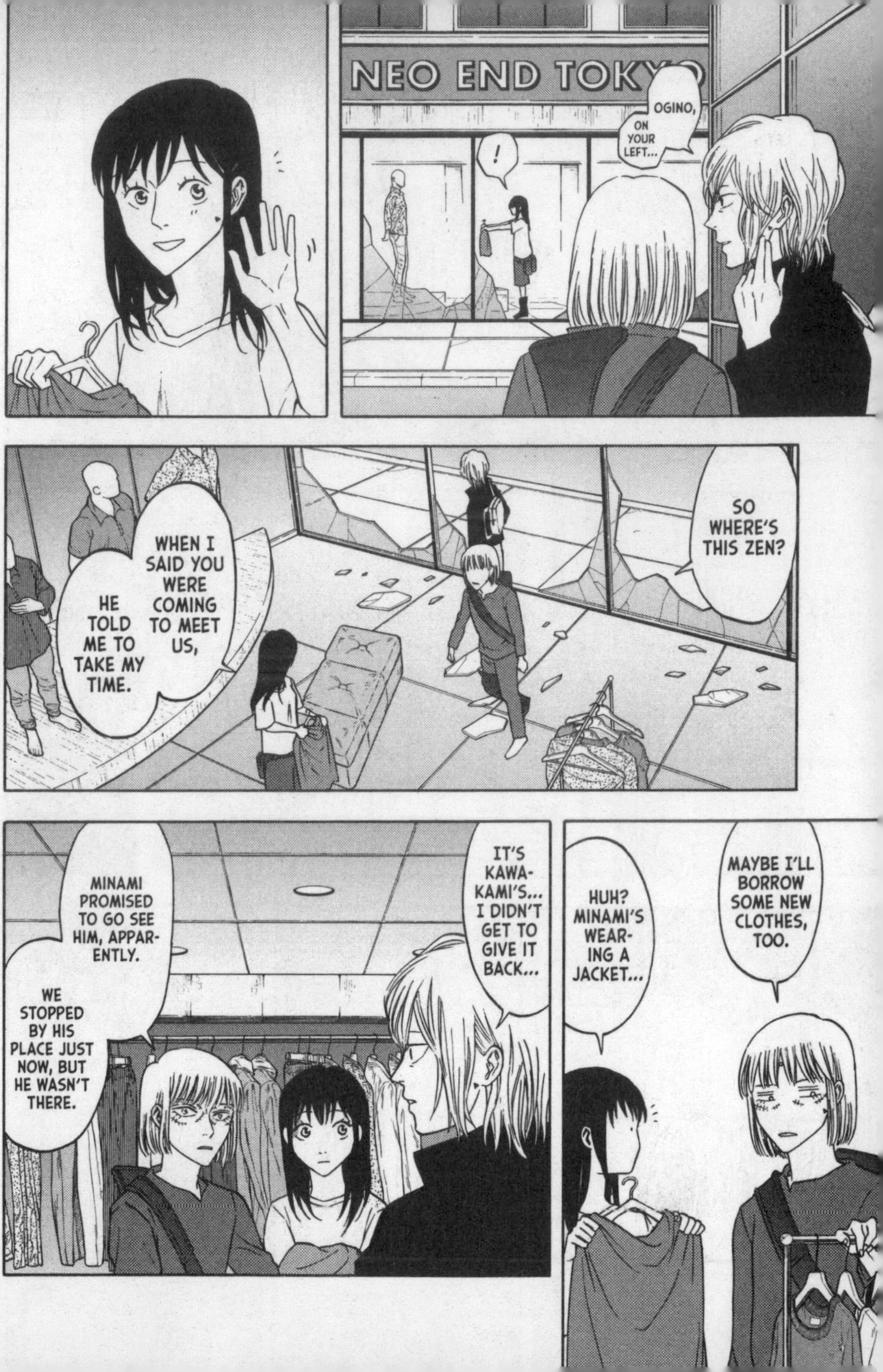
NEO END TOKYO
OGINO, ON YOUR LEFT...
!
SO WHERE'S THIS ZEN?
WHEN I SAID YOU WERE COMING TO MEET US, HE TOLD ME TO TAKE MY TIME.
MAYBE I'LL BORROW SOME NEW CLOTHES, TOO.
HUH? MINAMI'S WEARING A JACKET...
IT'S KAWAKAMI'S... I DIDN'T GET TO GIVE IT BACK...
MINAMI PROMISED TO GO SEE HIM, APPARENTLY.
WE STOPPED BY HIS PLACE JUST NOW, BUT HE WASN'T THERE.

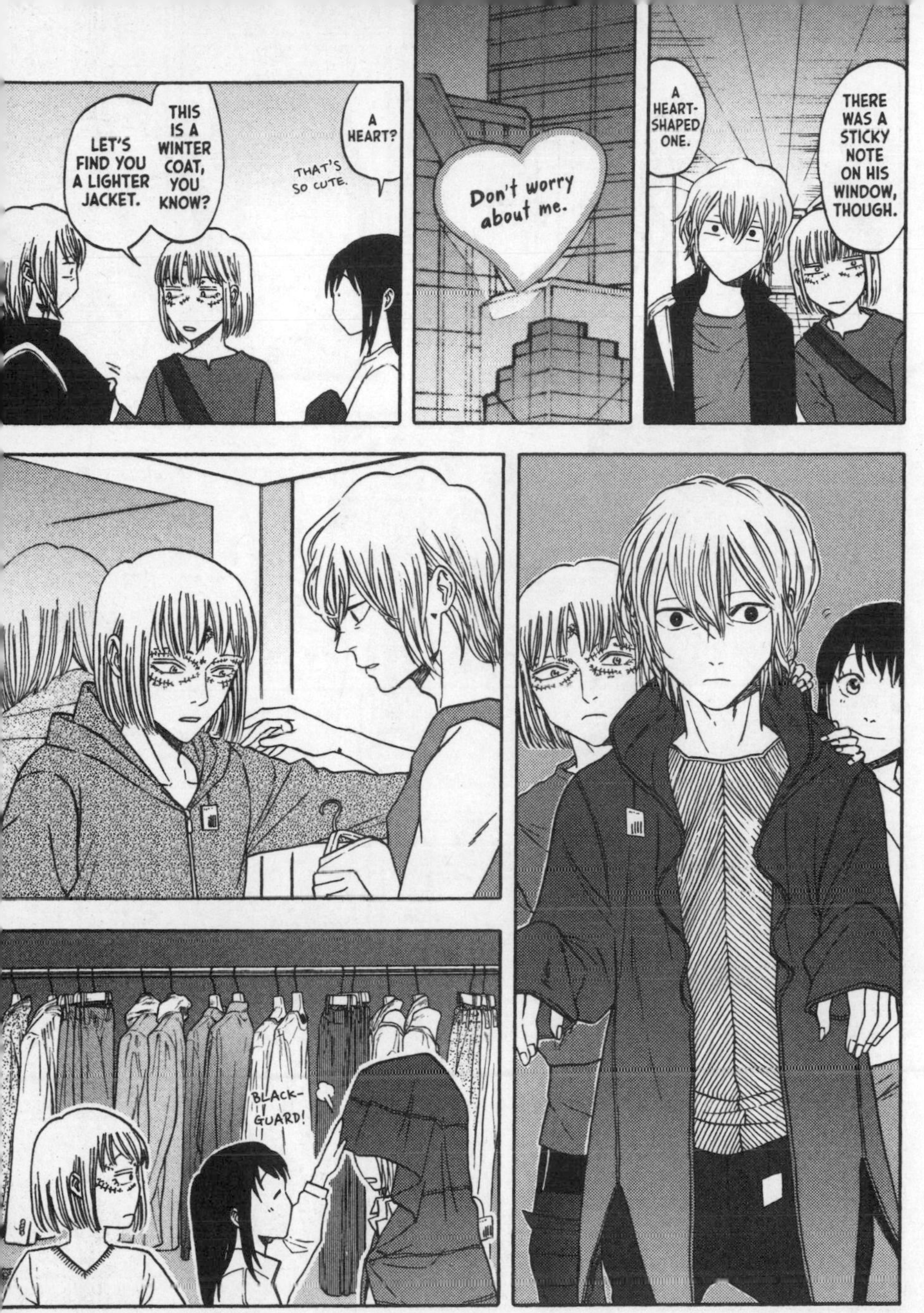
THERE WAS A STICKY NOTE ON HIS WINDOW, THOUGH.
A HEART-SHAPED ONE.
Don't worry about me.
A HEART?
THAT'S SO CUTE.
THIS IS A WINTER COAT, YOU KNOW?
LET'S FIND YOU A LIGHTER JACKET.
BLACK-GUARD!

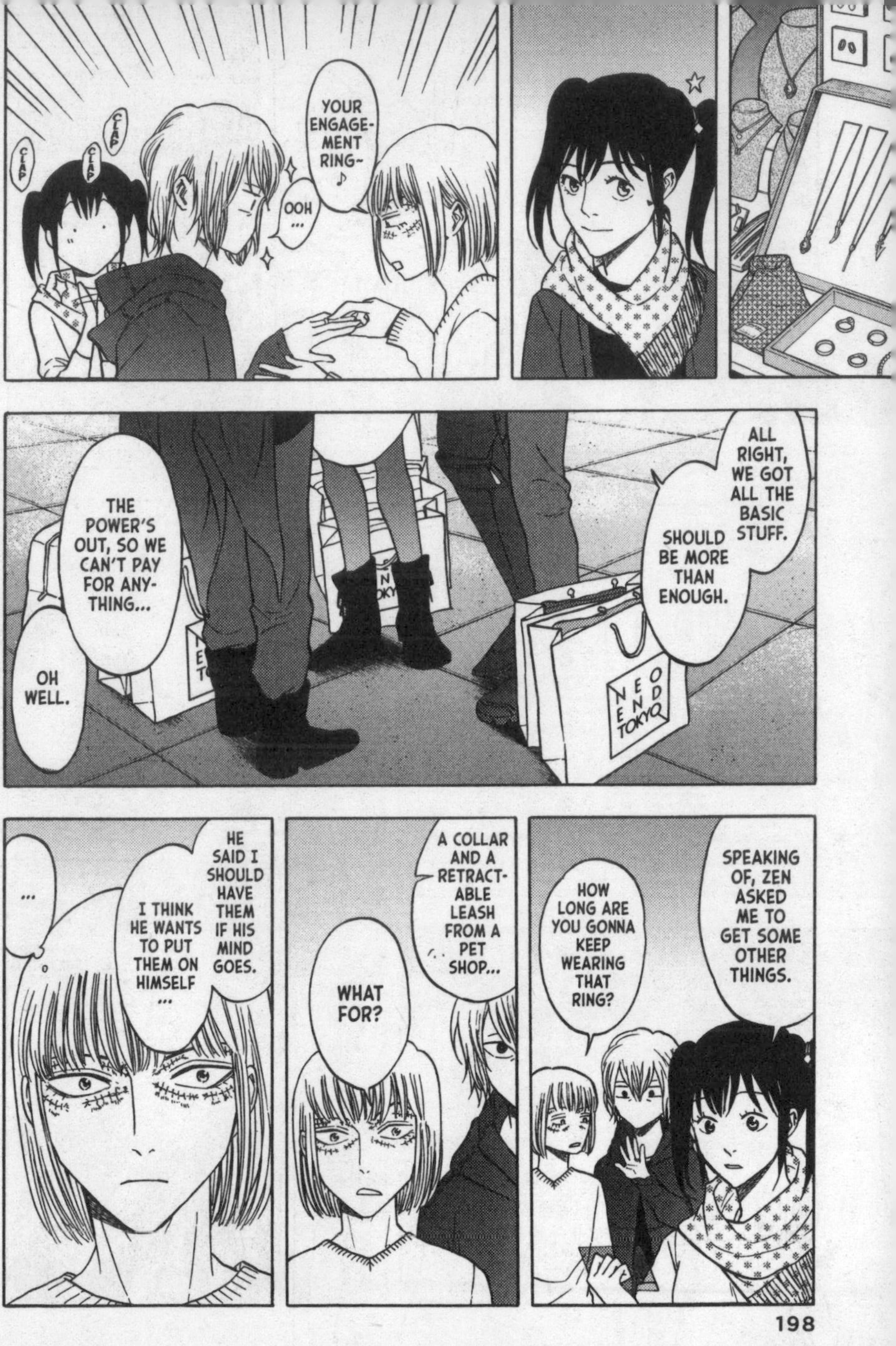
YOUR ENGAGE-MENT RING~ ♪
OOH...
CLAP
CLAP
CLAP
ALL RIGHT, WE GOT ALL THE BASIC STUFF.
SHOULD BE MORE THAN ENOUGH.
THE POWER'S OUT, SO WE CAN'T PAY FOR ANY-THING...
OH WELL.
NEO END TOKYO
SPEAKING OF, ZEN ASKED ME TO GET SOME OTHER THINGS.
HOW LONG ARE YOU GONNA KEEP WEARING THAT RING?
A COLLAR AND A RETRACT-ABLE LEASH FROM A PET SHOP...
WHAT FOR?
HE SAID I SHOULD HAVE THEM IF HIS MIND GOES.
I THINK HE WANTS TO PUT THEM ON HIMSELF...
...

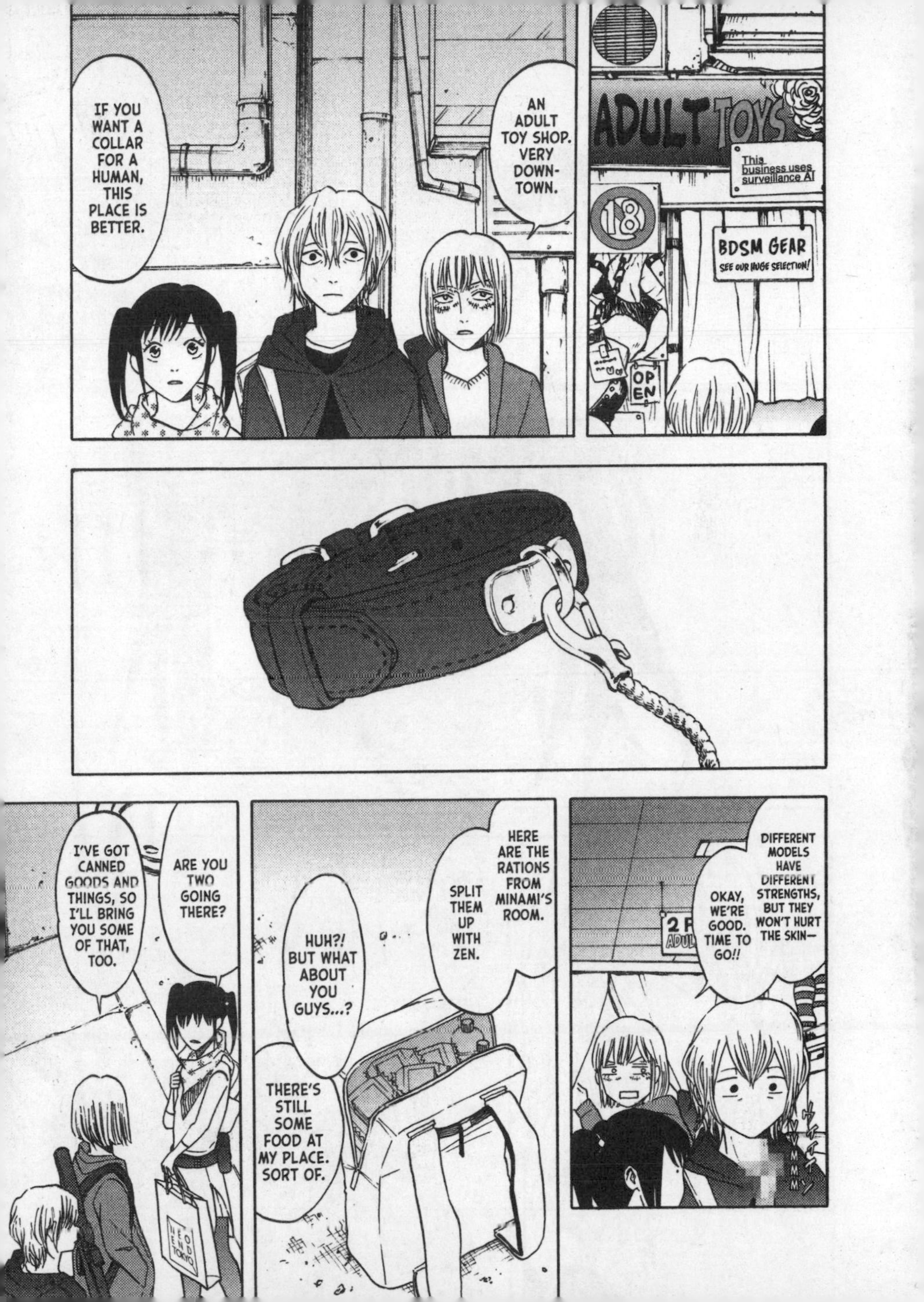
ADULT TOYS
This business uses surveillance AI
18
BDSM GEAR
SEE OUR HUGE SELECTION!
OPEN
AN ADULT TOY SHOP. VERY DOWN-TOWN.
IF YOU WANT A COLLAR FOR A HUMAN, THIS PLACE IS BETTER.
DIFFERENT MODELS HAVE DIFFERENT STRENGTHS, BUT THEY WON'T HURT THE SKIN—
OKAY, WE'RE GOOD. TIME TO GO!!
HERE ARE THE RATIONS FROM MINAMI'S ROOM.
SPLIT THEM UP WITH ZEN.
HUH?! BUT WHAT ABOUT YOU GUYS...?
THERE'S STILL SOME FOOD AT MY PLACE. SORT OF.
ARE YOU TWO GOING THERE?
I'VE GOT CANNED GOODS AND THINGS, SO I'LL BRING YOU SOME OF THAT, TOO.
NEO END TOKYO

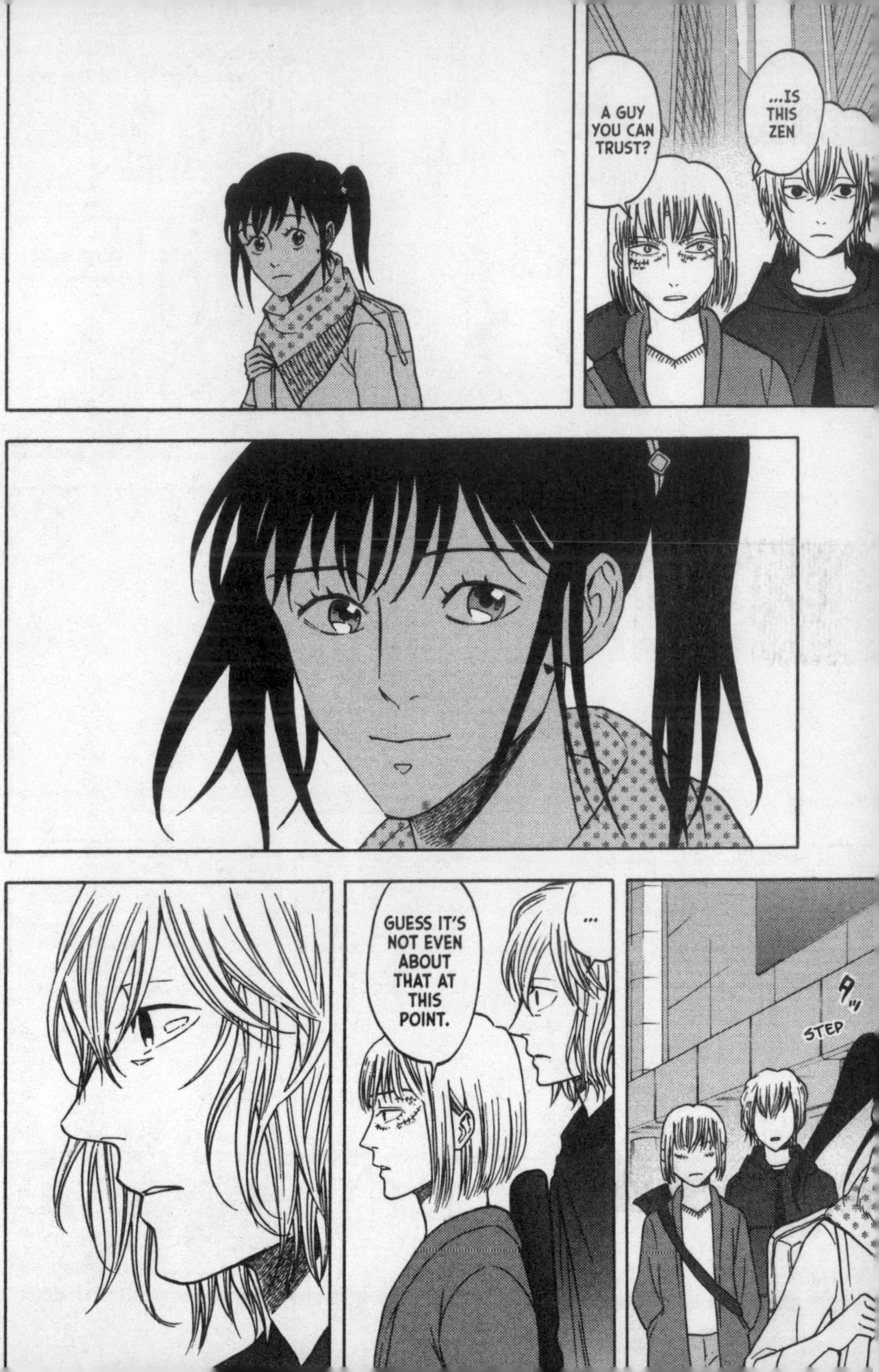

...IS THIS ZEN
A GUY YOU CAN TRUST?
STEP
...
GUESS IT'S NOT EVEN ABOUT THAT AT THIS POINT.

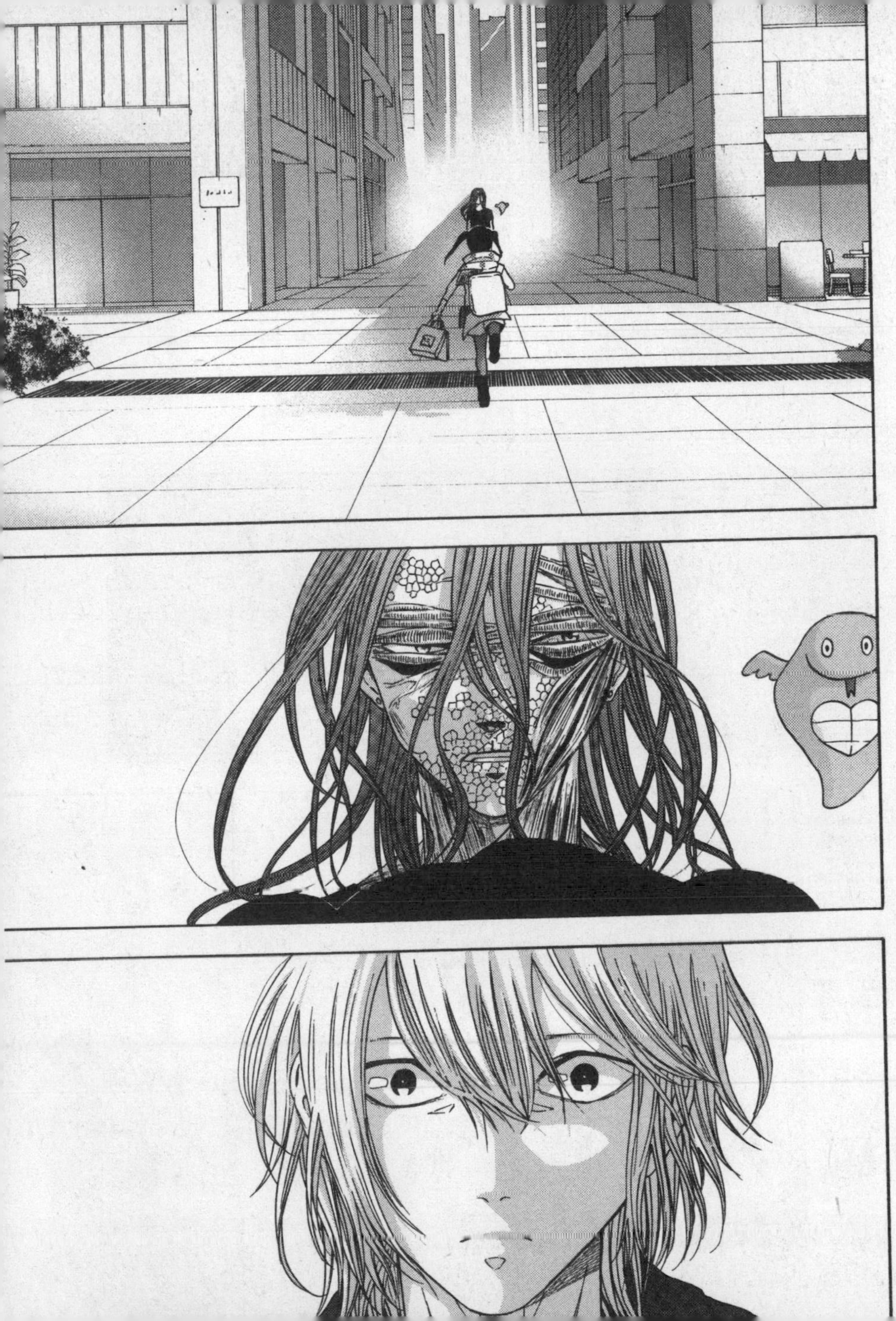

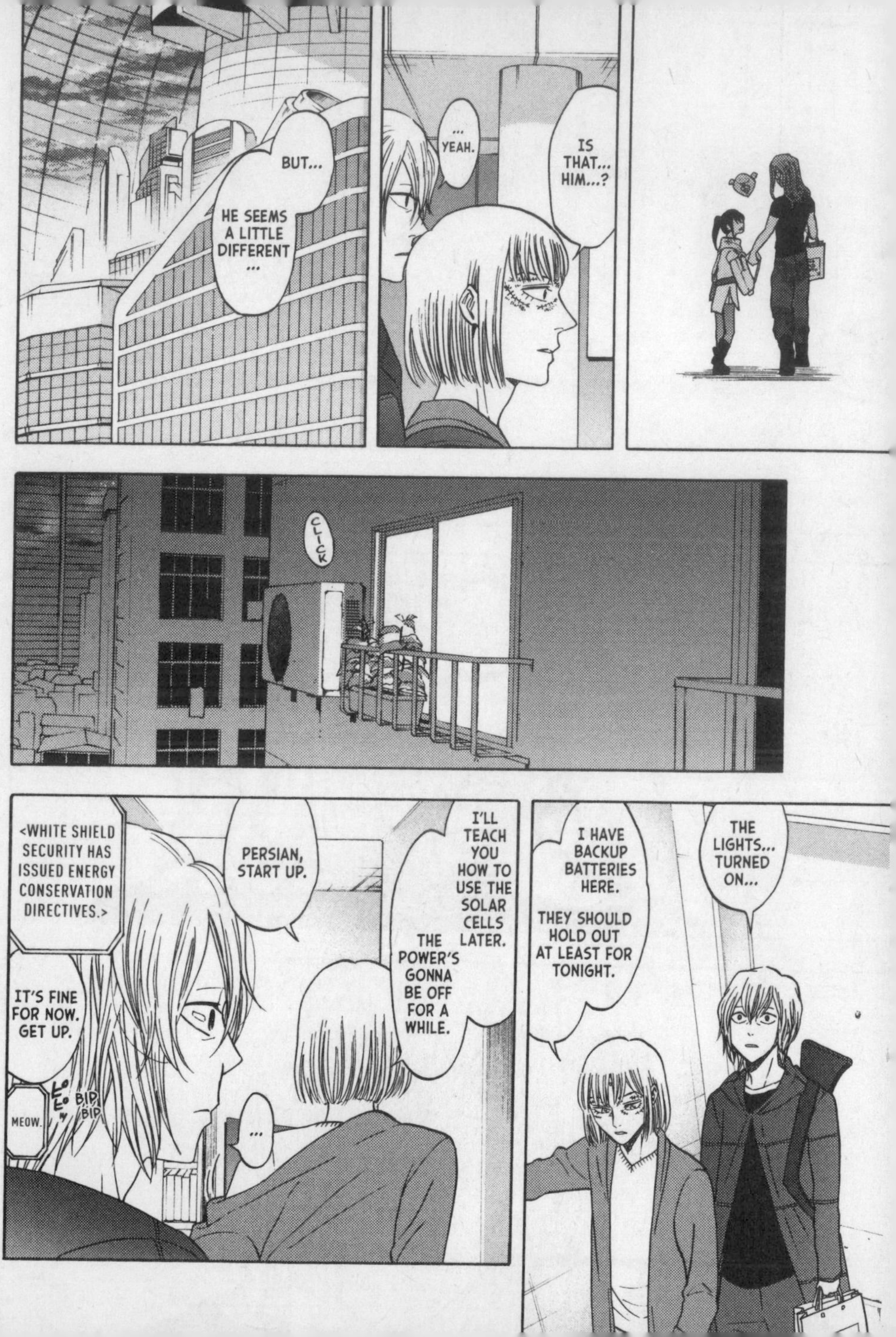
IS THAT... HIM...?
... YEAH.
BUT...
HE SEEMS A LITTLE DIFFERENT ...
CLICK
THE LIGHTS... TURNED ON...
I HAVE BACKUP BATTERIES HERE.
THEY SHOULD HOLD OUT AT LEAST FOR TONIGHT.
I'LL TEACH YOU HOW TO USE THE SOLAR CELLS LATER.
THE POWER'S GONNA BE OFF FOR A WHILE.
PERSIAN, START UP.
<WHITE SHIELD SECURITY HAS ISSUED ENERGY CONSERVATION DIRECTIVES.>
IT'S FINE FOR NOW. GET UP.
...
BIP BIP
MEOW.

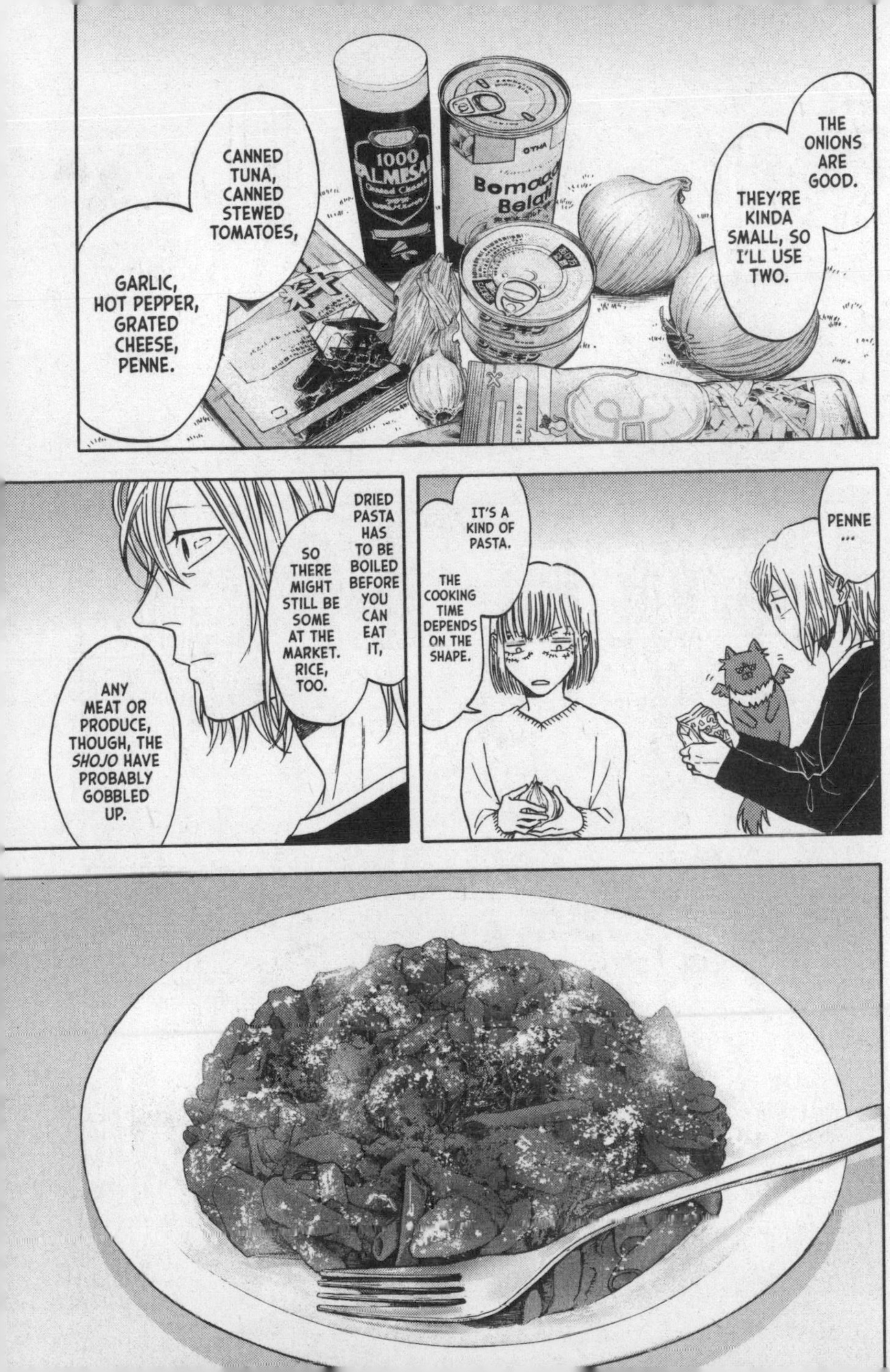
THE ONIONS ARE GOOD.
THEY'RE KINDA SMALL, SO I'LL USE TWO.
CANNED TUNA, CANNED STEWED TOMATOES,
GARLIC, HOT PEPPER, GRATED CHEESE, PENNE.
PENNE ...
IT'S A KIND OF PASTA.
THE COOKING TIME DEPENDS ON THE SHAPE.
DRIED PASTA HAS TO BE BOILED BEFORE YOU CAN EAT IT,
SO THERE MIGHT STILL BE SOME AT THE MARKET. RICE, TOO.
ANY MEAT OR PRODUCE, THOUGH, THE *SHOJO* HAVE PROBABLY GOBBLED UP.

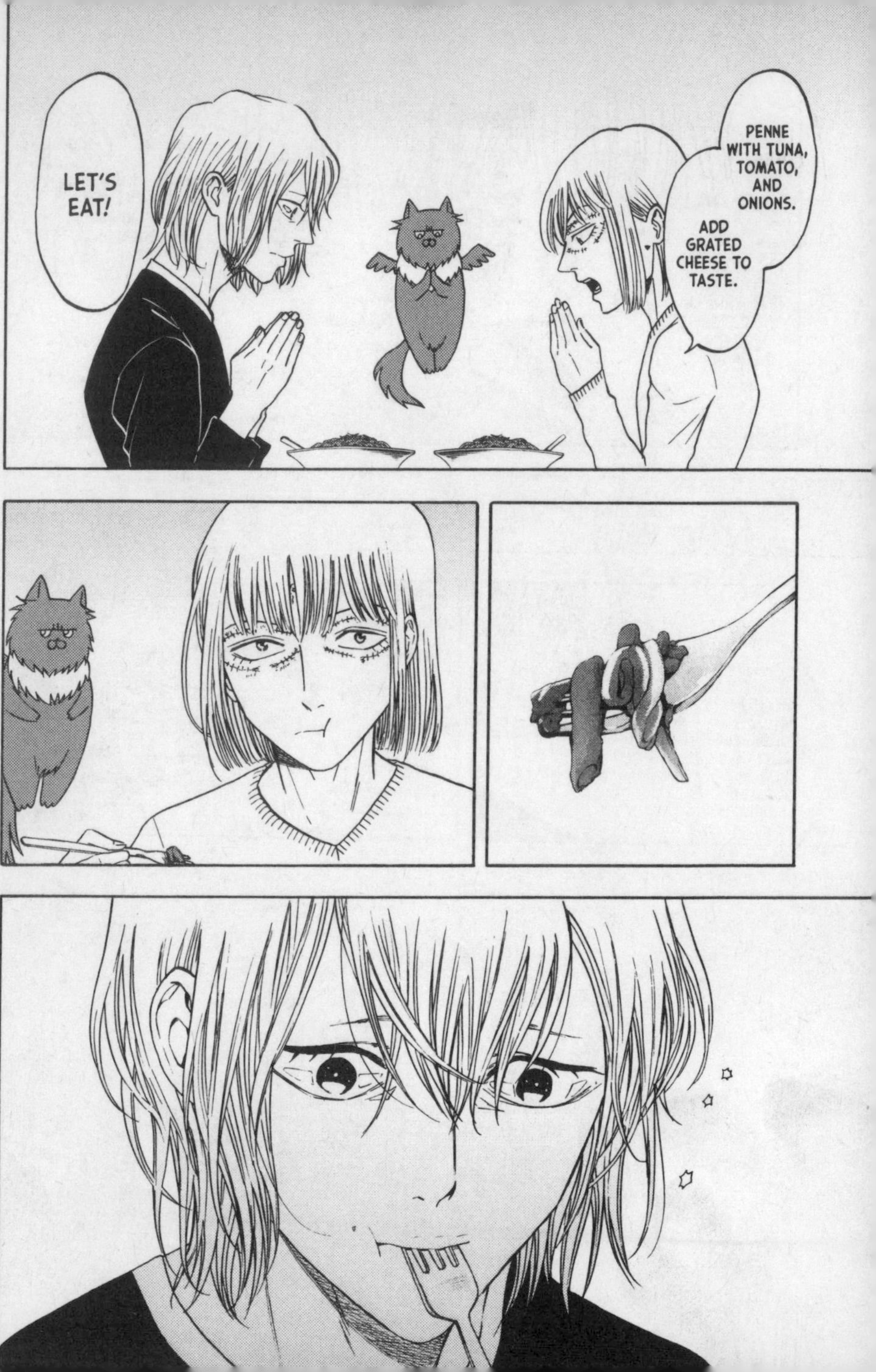
PENNE WITH TUNA, TOMATO, AND ONIONS.
ADD GRATED CHEESE TO TASTE.
LET'S EAT!

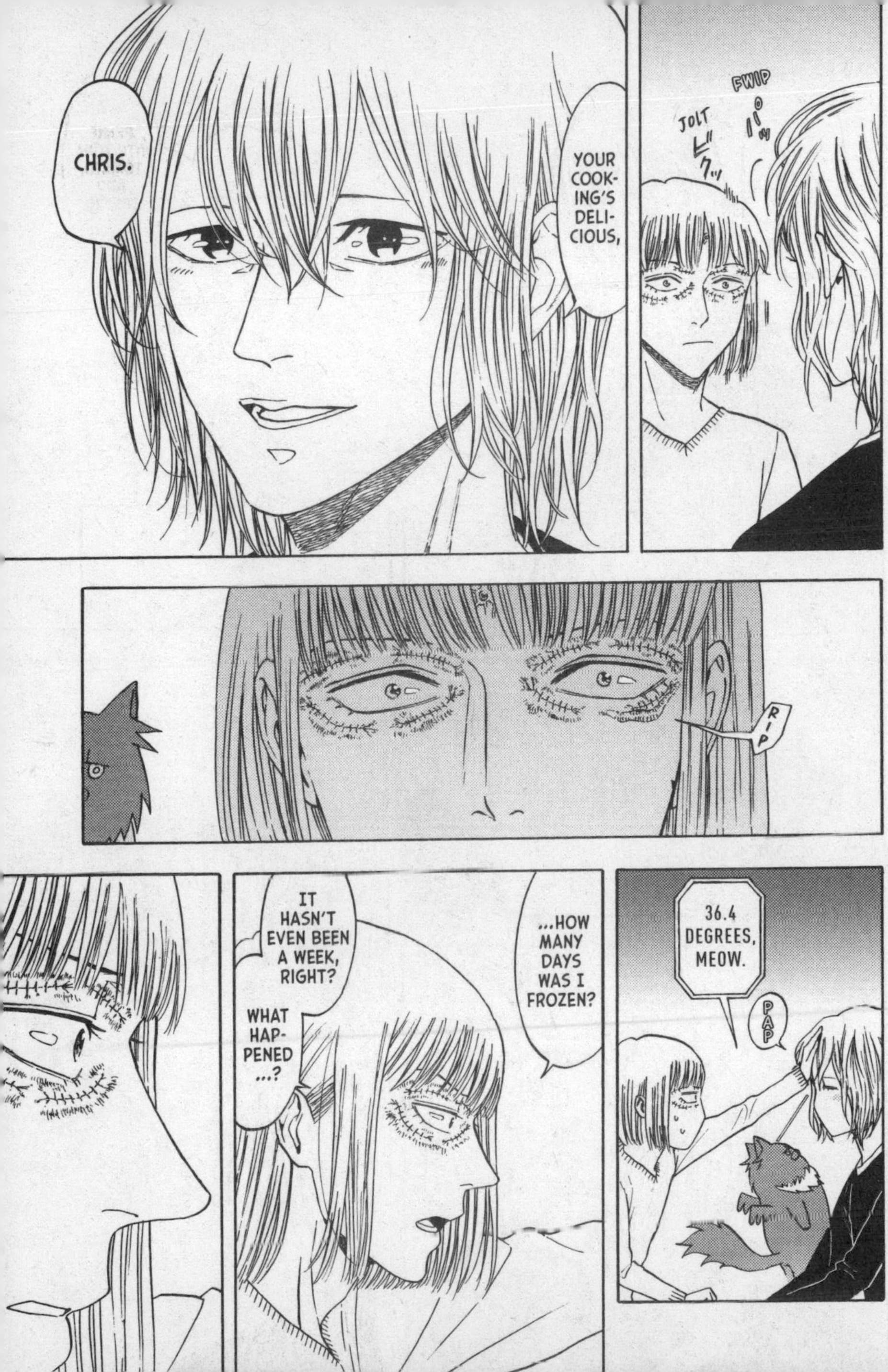
FWIP
JOLT
YOUR COOKING'S DELICIOUS,
CHRIS.
RIP
36.4 DEGREES, MEOW.
PAP PAP
...HOW MANY DAYS WAS I FROZEN?
IT HASN'T EVEN BEEN A WEEK, RIGHT?
WHAT HAPPENED ...?

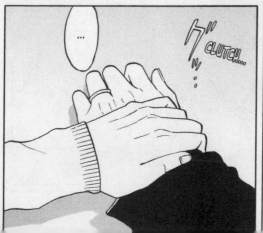

...

ケ゛゛CLUTCH...

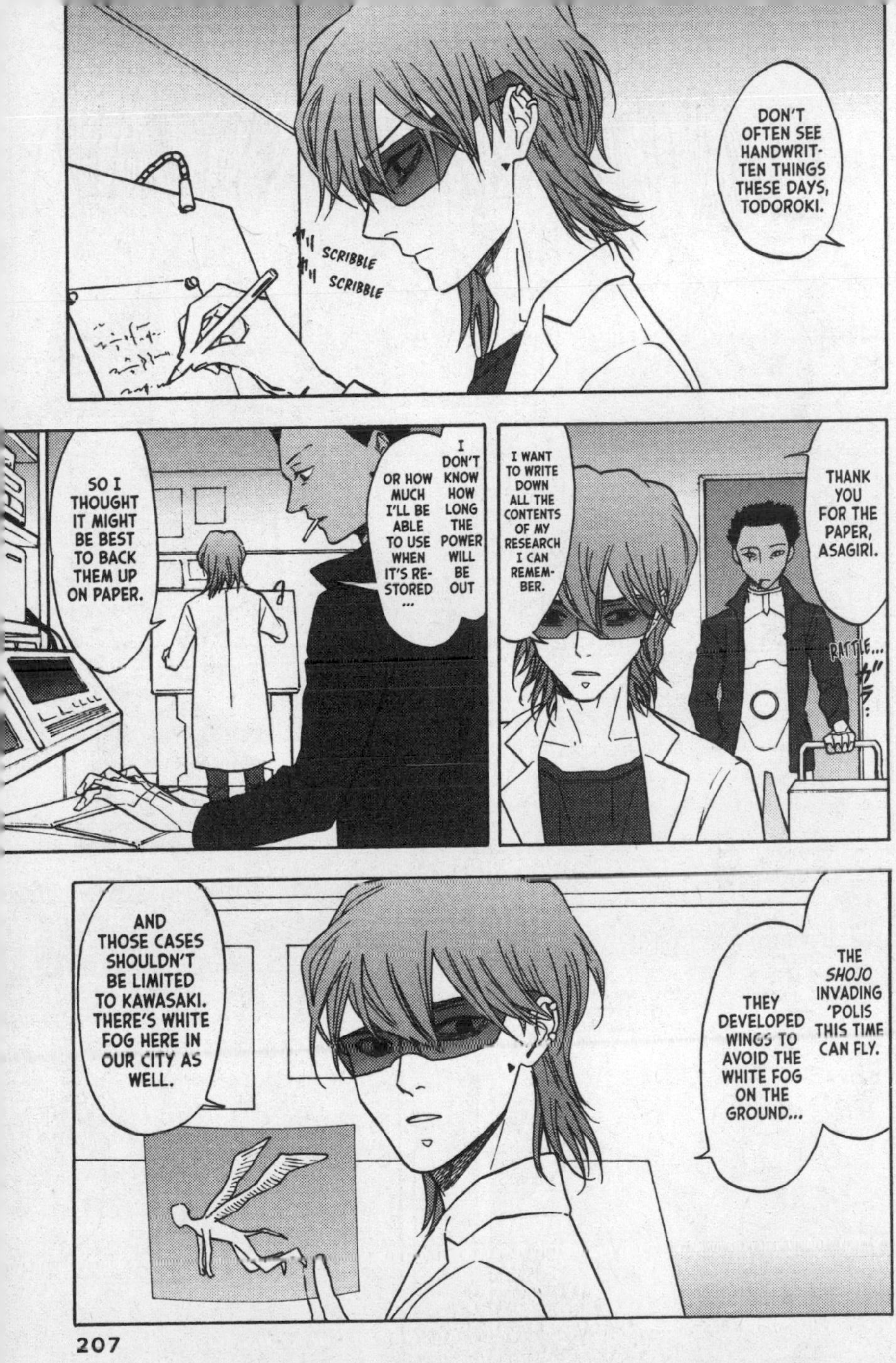
DON'T OFTEN SEE HANDWRITTEN THINGS THESE DAYS, TODOROKI.
SCRIBBLE
SCRIBBLE
THANK YOU FOR THE PAPER, ASAGIRI.
RATTLE...
I WANT TO WRITE DOWN ALL THE CONTENTS OF MY RESEARCH I CAN REMEMBER.
I DON'T KNOW HOW LONG THE POWER WILL BE OUT
OR HOW MUCH I'LL BE ABLE TO USE WHEN IT'S RESTORED ...
SO I THOUGHT IT MIGHT BE BEST TO BACK THEM UP ON PAPER.
THE *SHOJO* INVADING 'POLIS THIS TIME CAN FLY.
THEY DEVELOPED WINGS TO AVOID THE WHITE FOG ON THE GROUND...
AND THOSE CASES SHOULDN'T BE LIMITED TO KAWASAKI. THERE'S WHITE FOG HERE IN OUR CITY AS WELL.

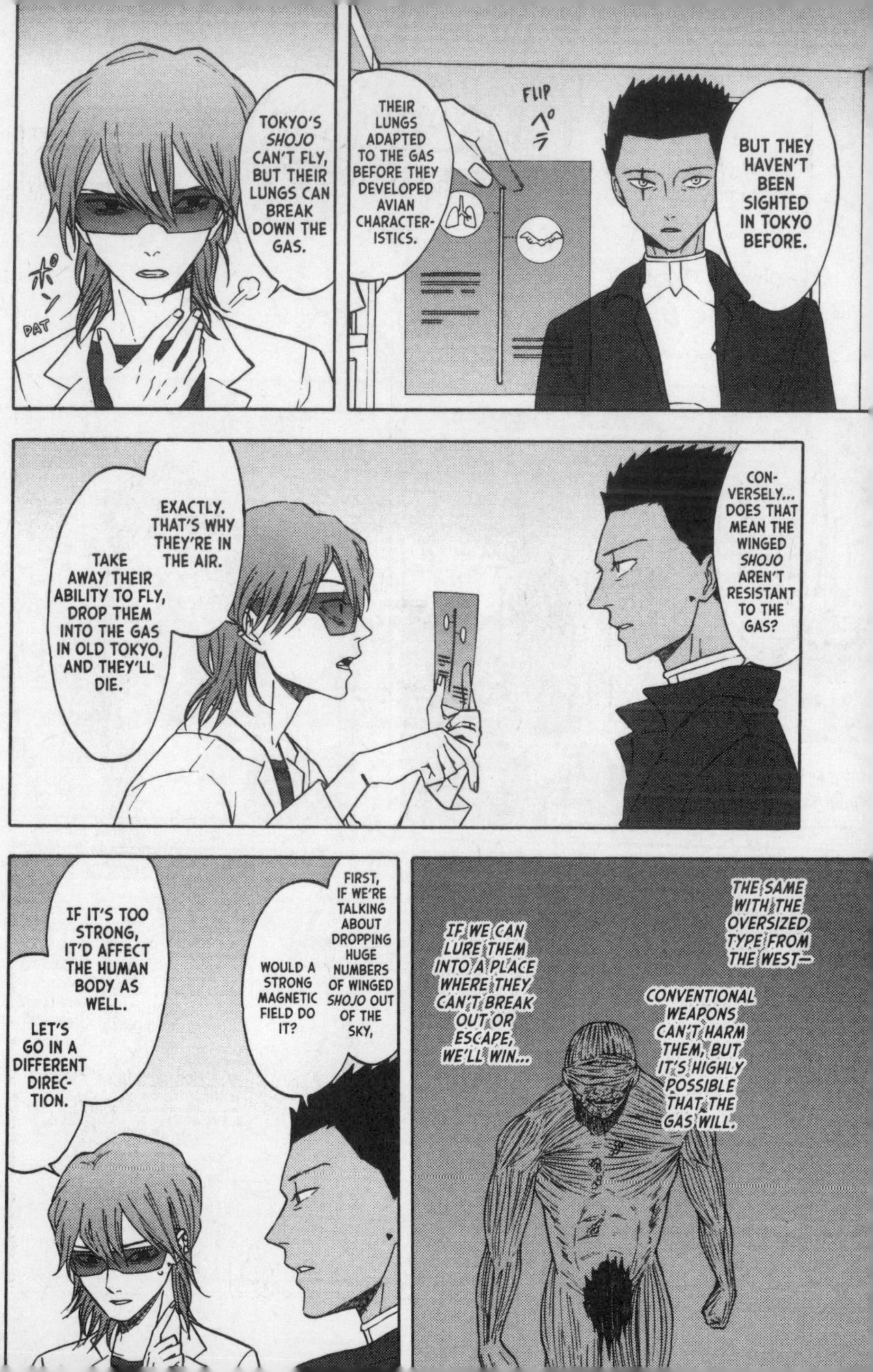
BUT THEY HAVEN'T BEEN SIGHTED IN TOKYO BEFORE.
FLIP
THEIR LUNGS ADAPTED TO THE GAS BEFORE THEY DEVELOPED AVIAN CHARACTER-ISTICS.
TOKYO'S *SHOJO* CAN'T FLY, BUT THEIR LUNGS CAN BREAK DOWN THE GAS.
PAT
CON-VERSELY... DOES THAT MEAN THE WINGED *SHOJO* AREN'T RESISTANT TO THE GAS?
EXACTLY. THAT'S WHY THEY'RE IN THE AIR.
TAKE AWAY THEIR ABILITY TO FLY, DROP THEM INTO THE GAS IN OLD TOKYO, AND THEY'LL DIE.
THE SAME WITH THE OVERSIZED TYPE FROM THE WEST—
IF WE CAN LURE THEM INTO A PLACE WHERE THEY CAN'T BREAK OUT OR ESCAPE, WE'LL WIN...
CONVENTIONAL WEAPONS CAN'T HARM THEM, BUT IT'S HIGHLY POSSIBLE THAT THE GAS WILL.
FIRST, IF WE'RE TALKING ABOUT DROPPING HUGE NUMBERS OF WINGED *SHOJO* OUT OF THE SKY,
WOULD A STRONG MAGNETIC FIELD DO IT?
IF IT'S TOO STRONG, IT'D AFFECT THE HUMAN BODY AS WELL.
LET'S GO IN A DIFFERENT DIREC-TION.

WE WON'T "DROP THEM," BUT SIMPLY "GET THEM TO LAND."

LURE THEM DOWN WITH FOOD.

THEN TRAP THEM, AND FILL THE AREA WITH GAS.

THAT LEAVES... THE OVERSIZED AND THE NORMAL TYPES.

IF IT'S STILL GOT POWER, WE SHOULD BE ABLE TO USE IT.

IT'S THE ONLY STADIUM IN THE CITY WITH A RETRACT-ABLE ROOF.

THEN IT'D HAVE TO BE THE ARIAKE COLI-SEUM.

...CONTAIN THEM SOME-WHERE ABOVE GROUND?

WHAT ABOUT THAT *SHOJO-HUMAN* COUPLE FROM KAWA-SAKI?

HA HA... THIS IS STARTING TO SOUND LIKE SOME KIND OF TORTURE COMPEN-DIUM.

GET THE LARGE ONES UNDER-GROUND, POUR CEMENT DOWN THERE...

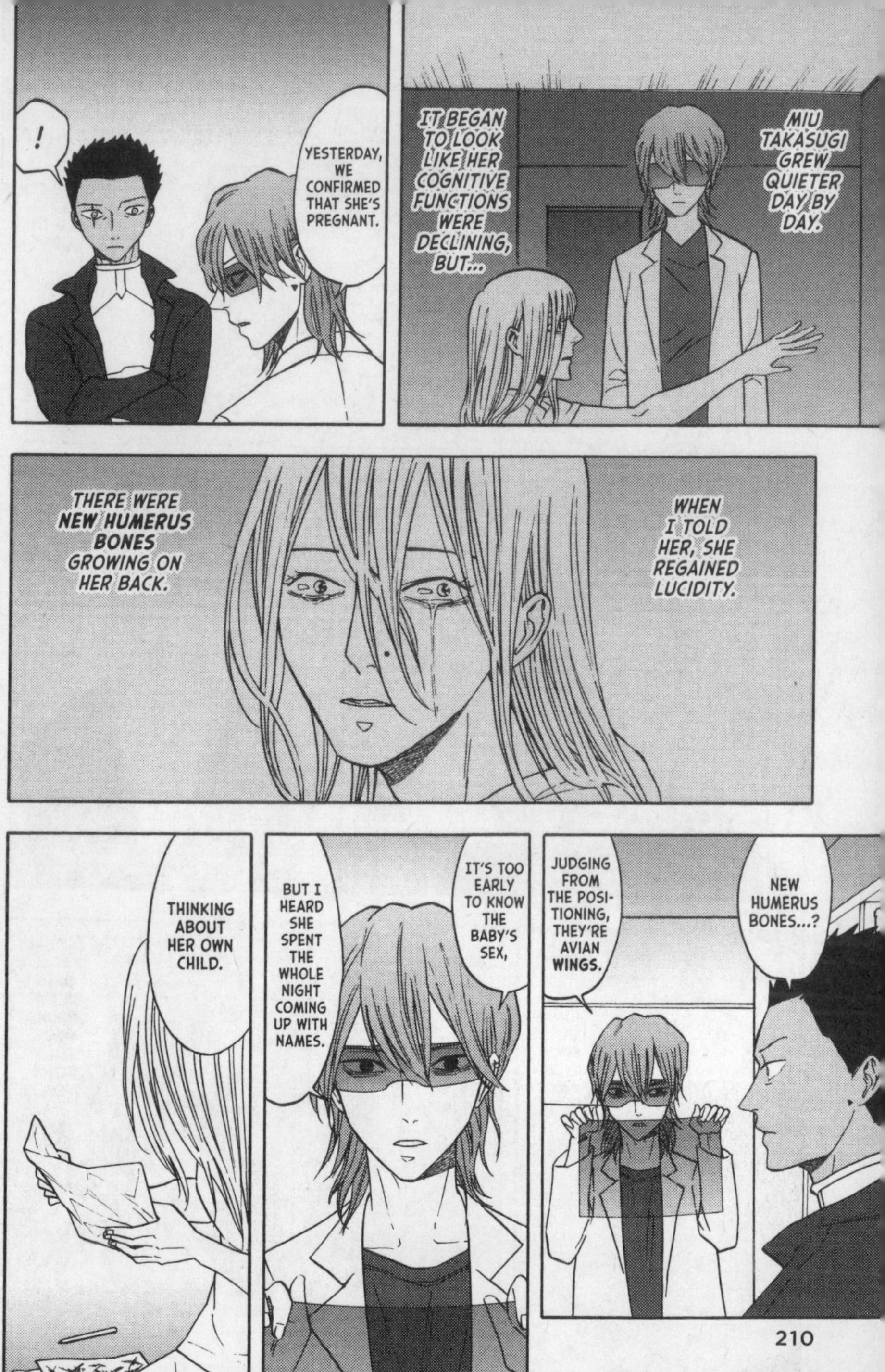
MIU TAKASUGI GREW QUIETER DAY BY DAY.
IT BEGAN TO LOOK LIKE HER COGNITIVE FUNCTIONS WERE DECLINING, BUT...
YESTERDAY, WE CONFIRMED THAT SHE'S PREGNANT.
!
WHEN I TOLD HER, SHE REGAINED LUCIDITY.
THERE WERE NEW HUMERUS BONES GROWING ON HER BACK.
NEW HUMERUS BONES...?
JUDGING FROM THE POSITIONING, THEY'RE AVIAN WINGS.
IT'S TOO EARLY TO KNOW THE BABY'S SEX,
BUT I HEARD SHE SPENT THE WHOLE NIGHT COMING UP WITH NAMES.
THINKING ABOUT HER OWN CHILD.

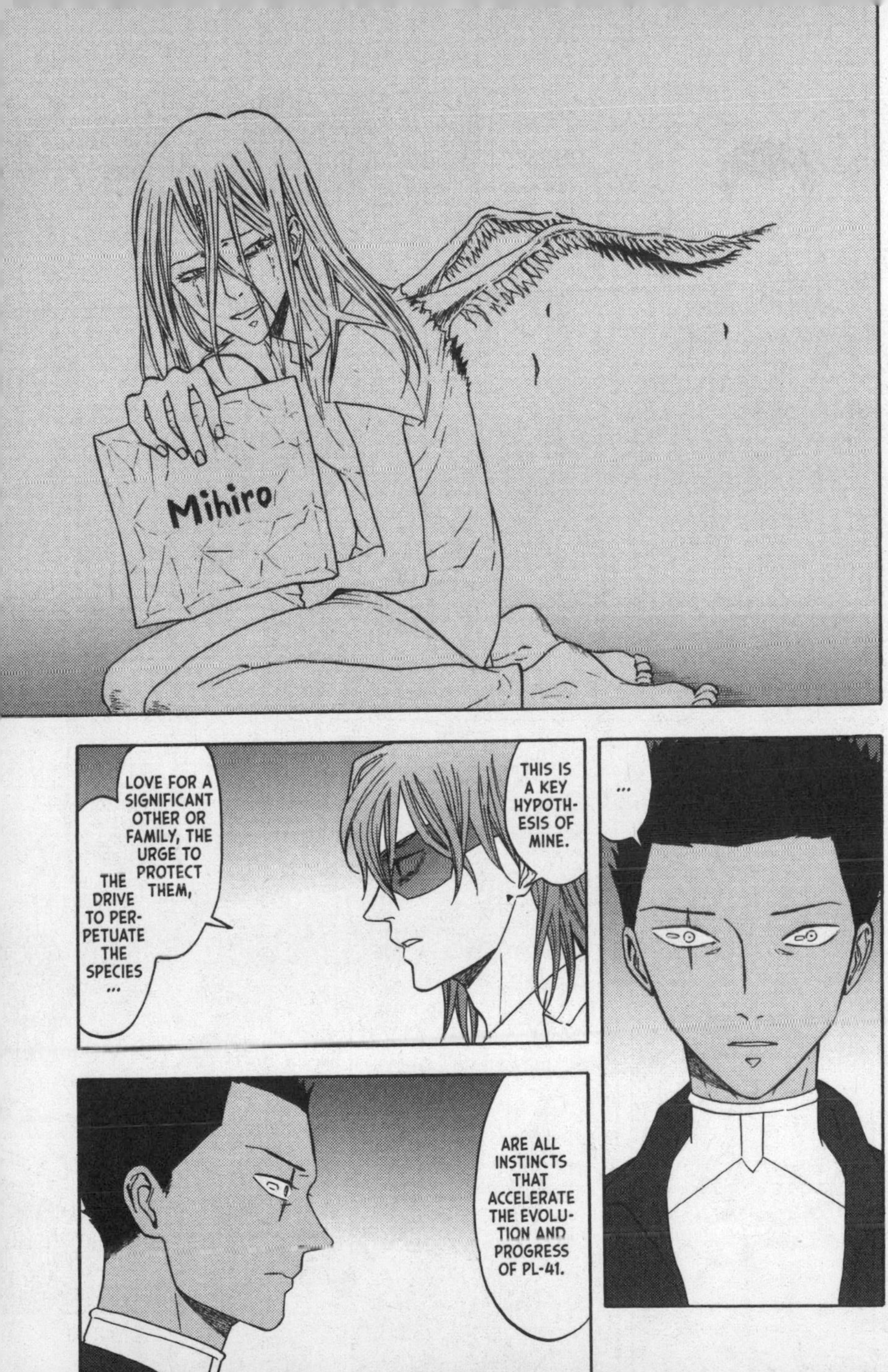
Mihiro
...
THIS IS A KEY HYPOTH-ESIS OF MINE.
LOVE FOR A SIGNIFICANT OTHER OR FAMILY, THE URGE TO PROTECT THEM,
THE DRIVE TO PER-PETUATE THE SPECIES ...
ARE ALL INSTINCTS THAT ACCELERATE THE EVOLU-TION AND PROGRESS OF PL-41.

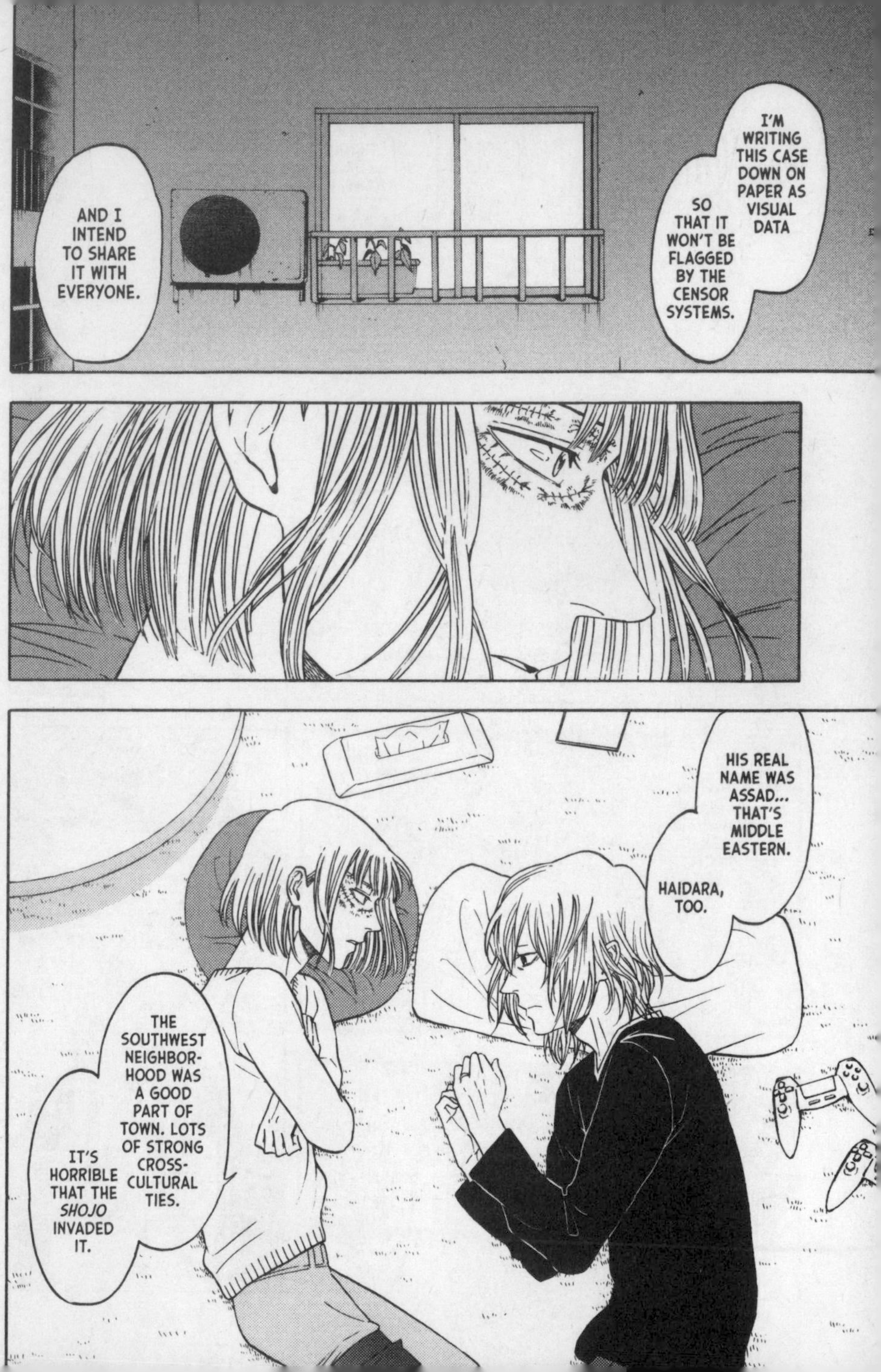
I'M WRITING THIS CASE DOWN ON PAPER AS VISUAL DATA
SO THAT IT WON'T BE FLAGGED BY THE CENSOR SYSTEMS.
AND I INTEND TO SHARE IT WITH EVERYONE.
HIS REAL NAME WAS ASSAD... THAT'S MIDDLE EASTERN.
HAIDARA, TOO.
THE SOUTHWEST NEIGHBOR-HOOD WAS A GOOD PART OF TOWN. LOTS OF STRONG CROSS-CULTURAL TIES.
IT'S HORRIBLE THAT THE *SHOJO* INVADED IT.

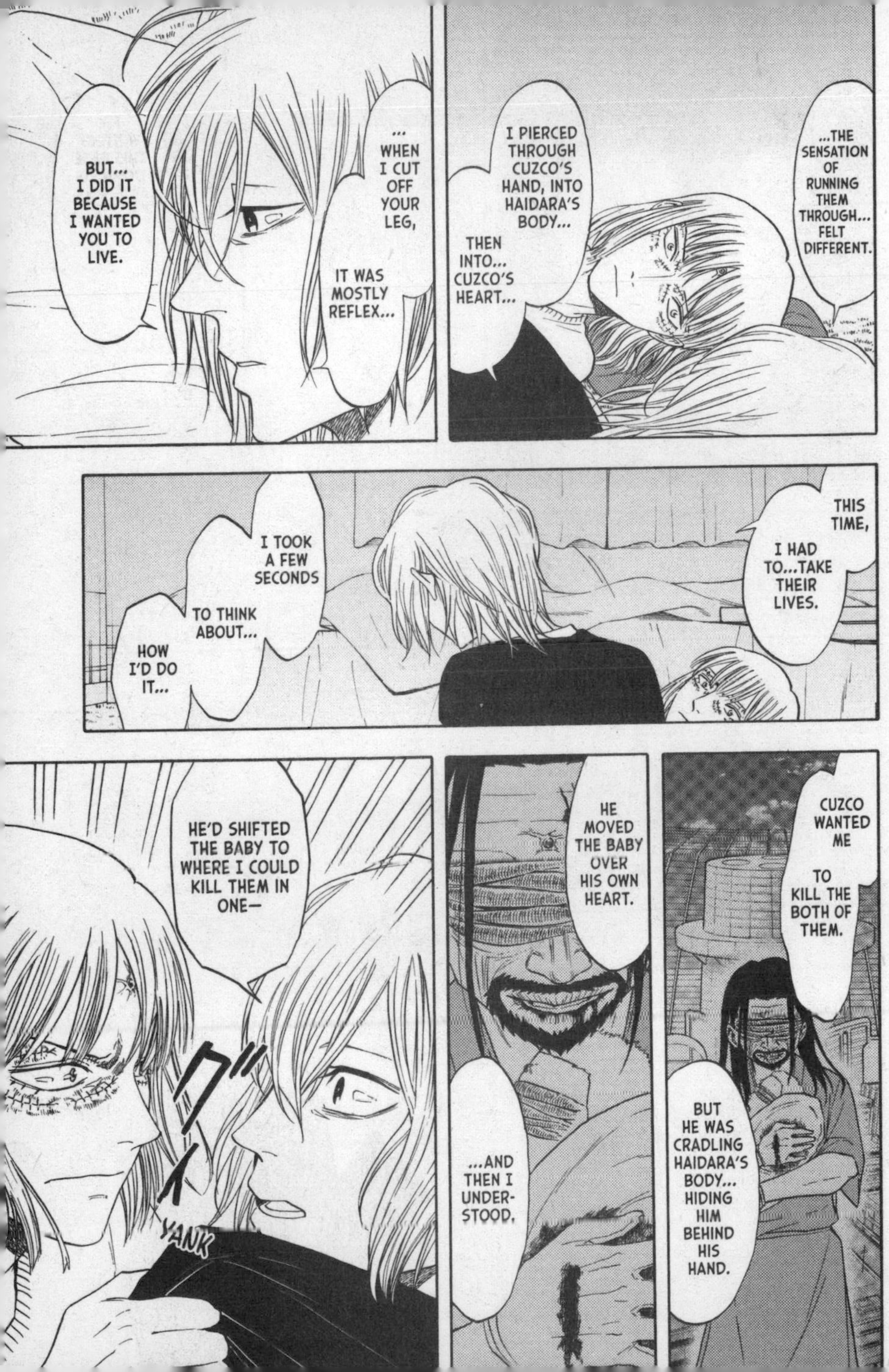
...THE SENSATION OF RUNNING THEM THROUGH... FELT DIFFERENT.
I PIERCED THROUGH CUZCO'S HAND, INTO HAIDARA'S BODY...
THEN INTO... CUZCO'S HEART...
...WHEN I CUT OFF YOUR LEG,
IT WAS MOSTLY REFLEX...
BUT... I DID IT BECAUSE I WANTED YOU TO LIVE.
THIS TIME,
I HAD TO...TAKE THEIR LIVES.
I TOOK A FEW SECONDS
TO THINK ABOUT...
HOW I'D DO IT...
CUZCO WANTED ME
TO KILL THE BOTH OF THEM.
BUT HE WAS CRADLING HAIDARA'S BODY... HIDING HIM BEHIND HIS HAND.
HE MOVED THE BABY OVER HIS OWN HEART.
...AND THEN I UNDERSTOOD.
HE'D SHIFTED THE BABY TO WHERE I COULD KILL THEM IN ONE—
グイ
YANK

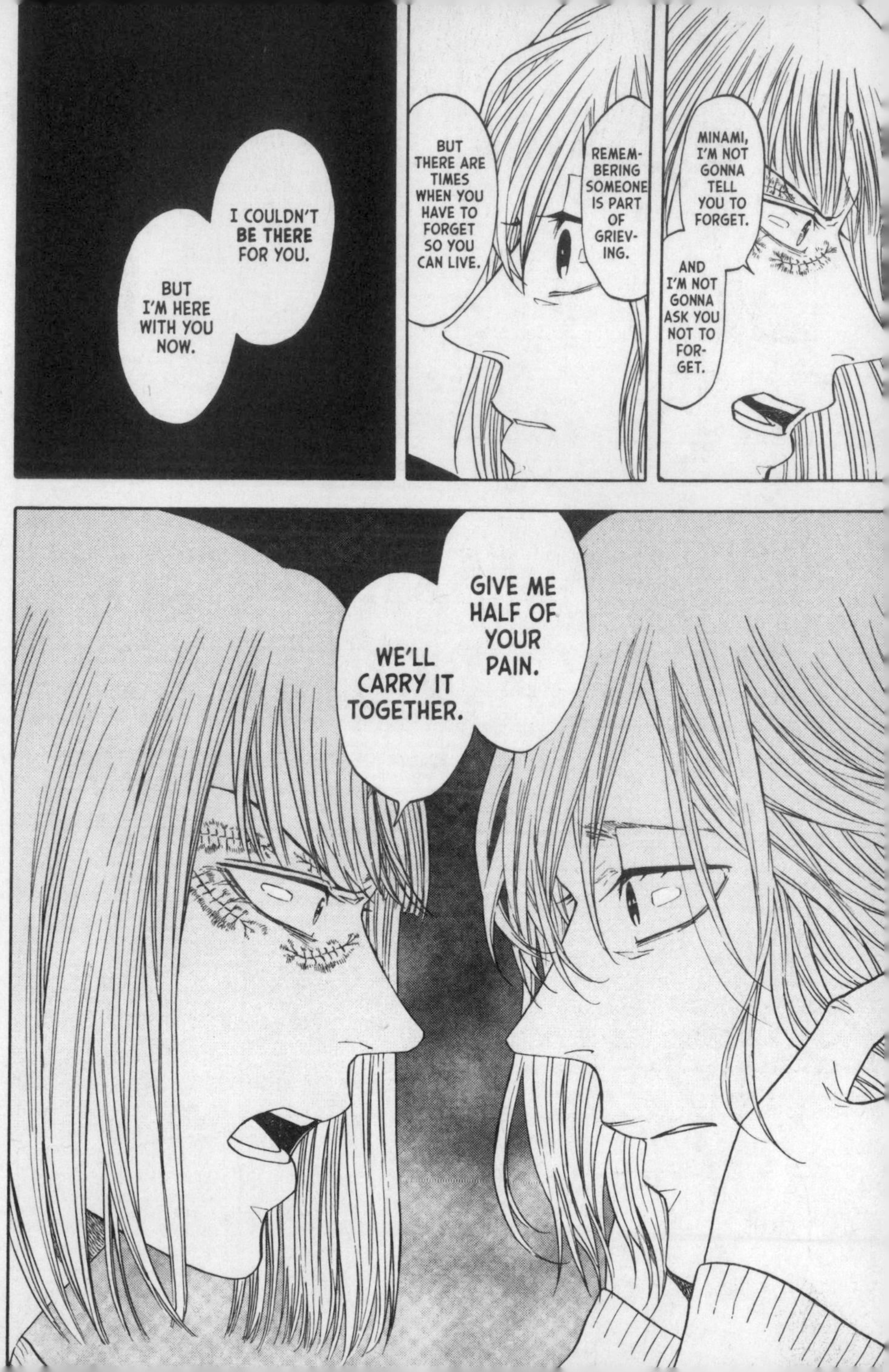
MINAMI, I'M NOT GONNA TELL YOU TO FORGET.
AND I'M NOT GONNA ASK YOU NOT TO FOR-GET.
REMEM-BERING SOMEONE IS PART OF GRIEV-ING.
BUT THERE ARE TIMES WHEN YOU HAVE TO FORGET SO YOU CAN LIVE.
I COULDN'T BE THERE FOR YOU.
BUT I'M HERE WITH YOU NOW.
GIVE ME HALF OF YOUR PAIN.
WE'LL CARRY IT TOGETHER.

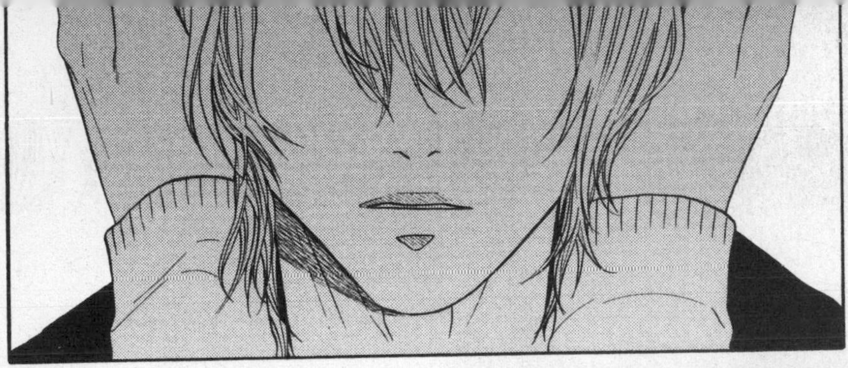

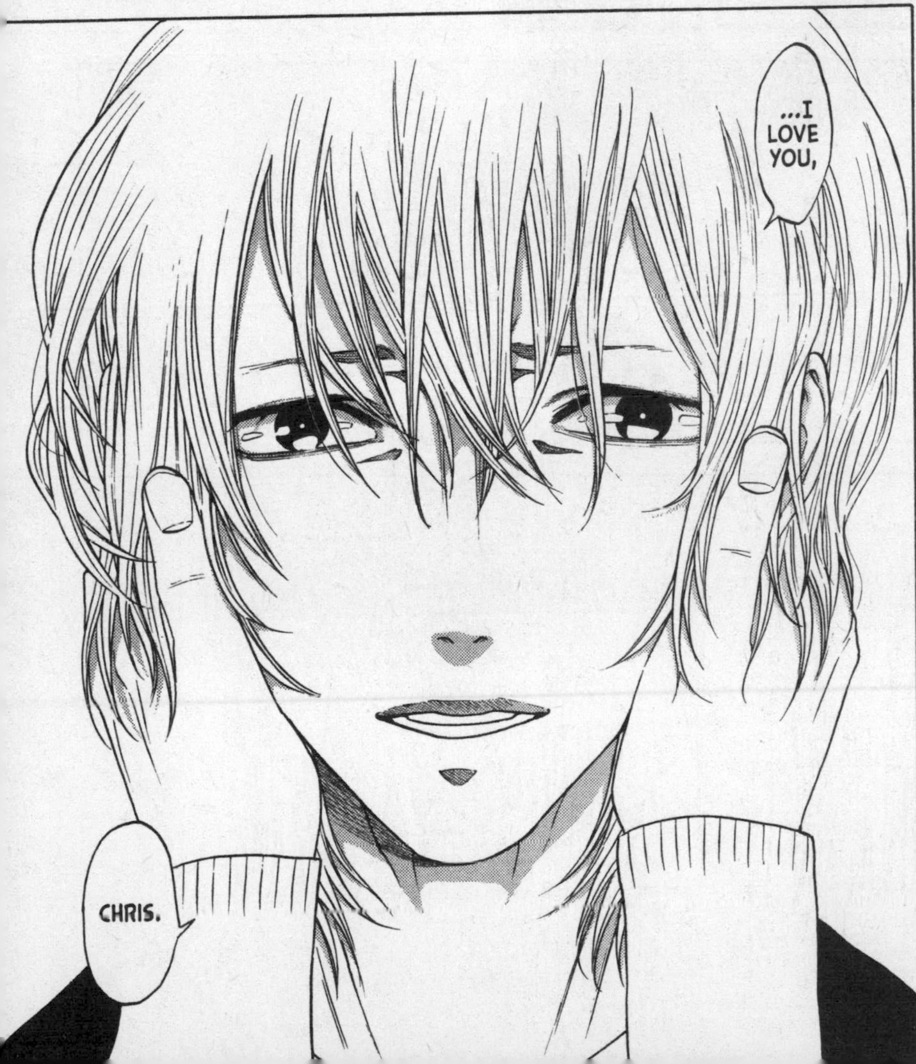
...I LOVE YOU,
CHRIS.

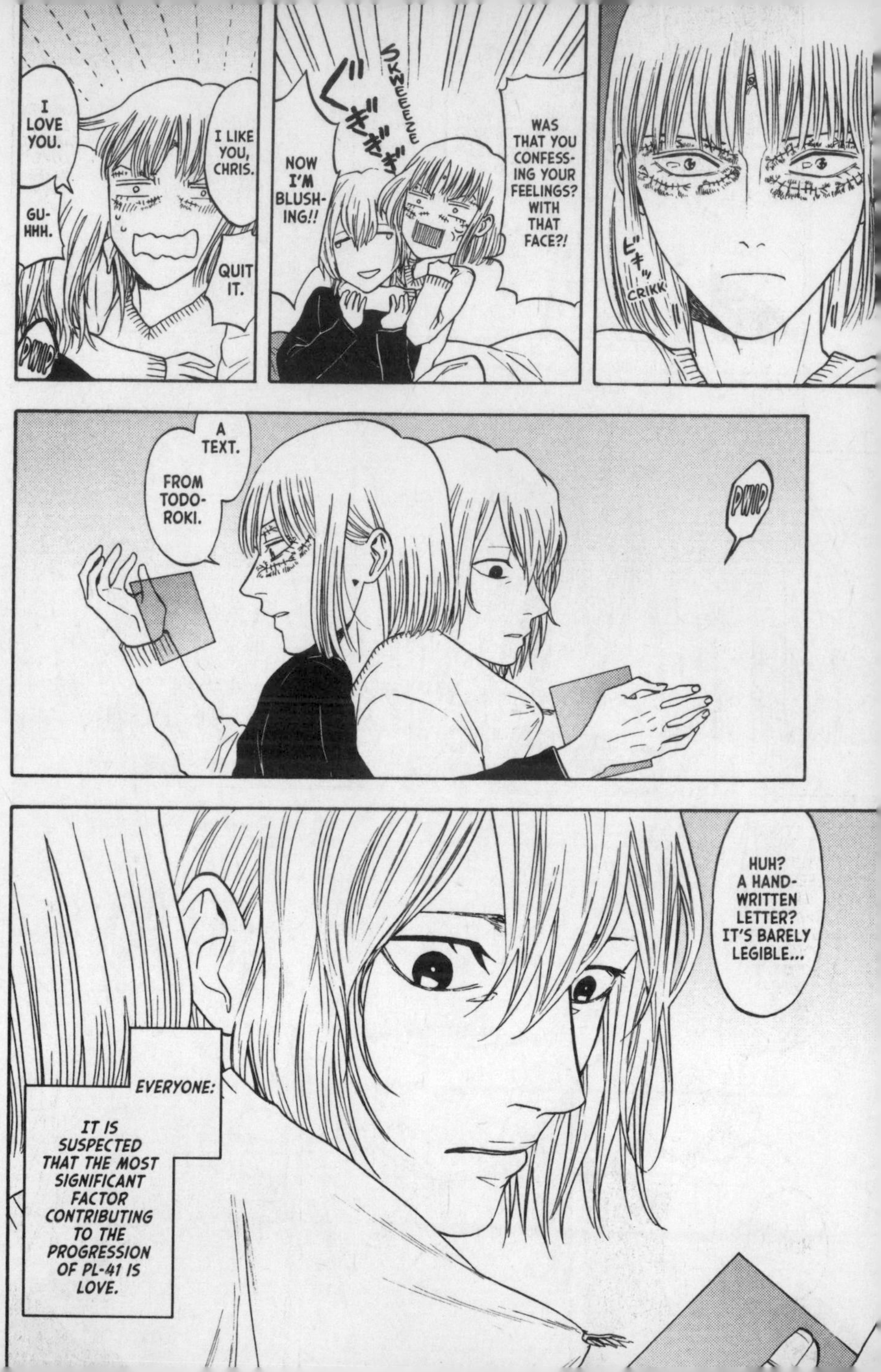
ビキッ
CRIKK
WAS THAT YOU CONFESSING YOUR FEELINGS? WITH THAT FACE?!
ぐぎぎぎ
SKWEEEEZE
NOW I'M BLUSHING!!
I LIKE YOU, CHRIS.
QUIT IT.
I LOVE YOU.
GU-HHH.
PWIP
PWIP
A TEXT.
FROM TODOROKI.
HUH? A HANDWRITTEN LETTER? IT'S BARELY LEGIBLE...
EVERYONE:
IT IS SUSPECTED THAT THE MOST SIGNIFICANT FACTOR CONTRIBUTING TO THE PROGRESSION OF PL-41 IS LOVE.

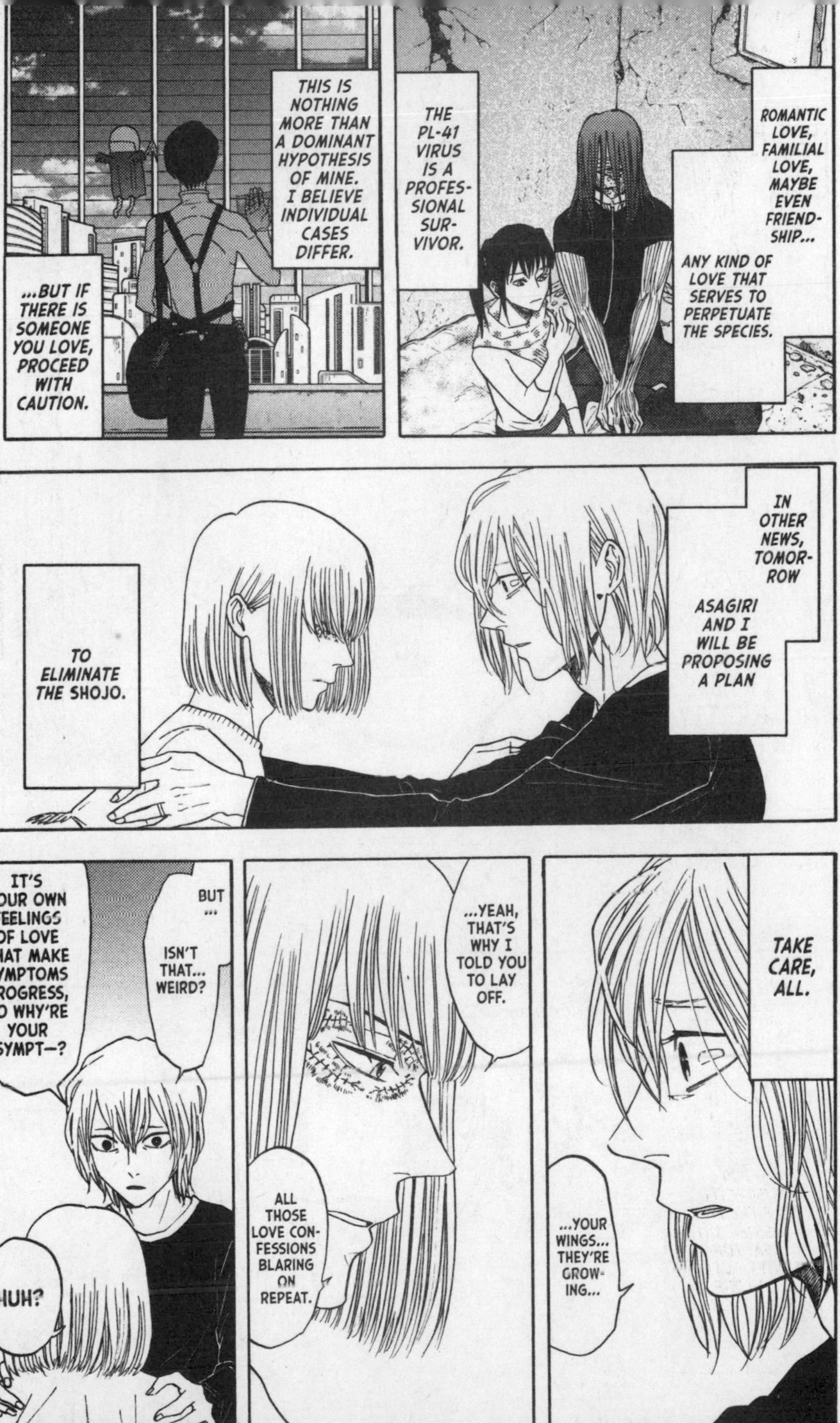
ROMANTIC LOVE, FAMILIAL LOVE, MAYBE EVEN FRIEND-SHIP...
ANY KIND OF LOVE THAT SERVES TO PERPETUATE THE SPECIES.
THE PL-41 VIRUS IS A PROFES-SIONAL SUR-VIVOR.
THIS IS NOTHING MORE THAN A DOMINANT HYPOTHESIS OF MINE. I BELIEVE INDIVIDUAL CASES DIFFER.
...BUT IF THERE IS SOMEONE YOU LOVE, PROCEED WITH CAUTION.
IN OTHER NEWS, TOMOR-ROW
ASAGIRI AND I WILL BE PROPOSING A PLAN
TO ELIMINATE THE SHOJO.
TAKE CARE, ALL.
...YOUR WINGS... THEY'RE GROW-ING...
...YEAH, THAT'S WHY I TOLD YOU TO LAY OFF.
ALL THOSE LOVE CON-FESSIONS BLARING ON REPEAT.
BUT...
ISN'T THAT... WEIRD?
IT'S YOUR OWN FEELINGS OF LOVE THAT MAKE SYMPTOMS PROGRESS, SO WHY'RE YOUR SYMPT—?
HUH?

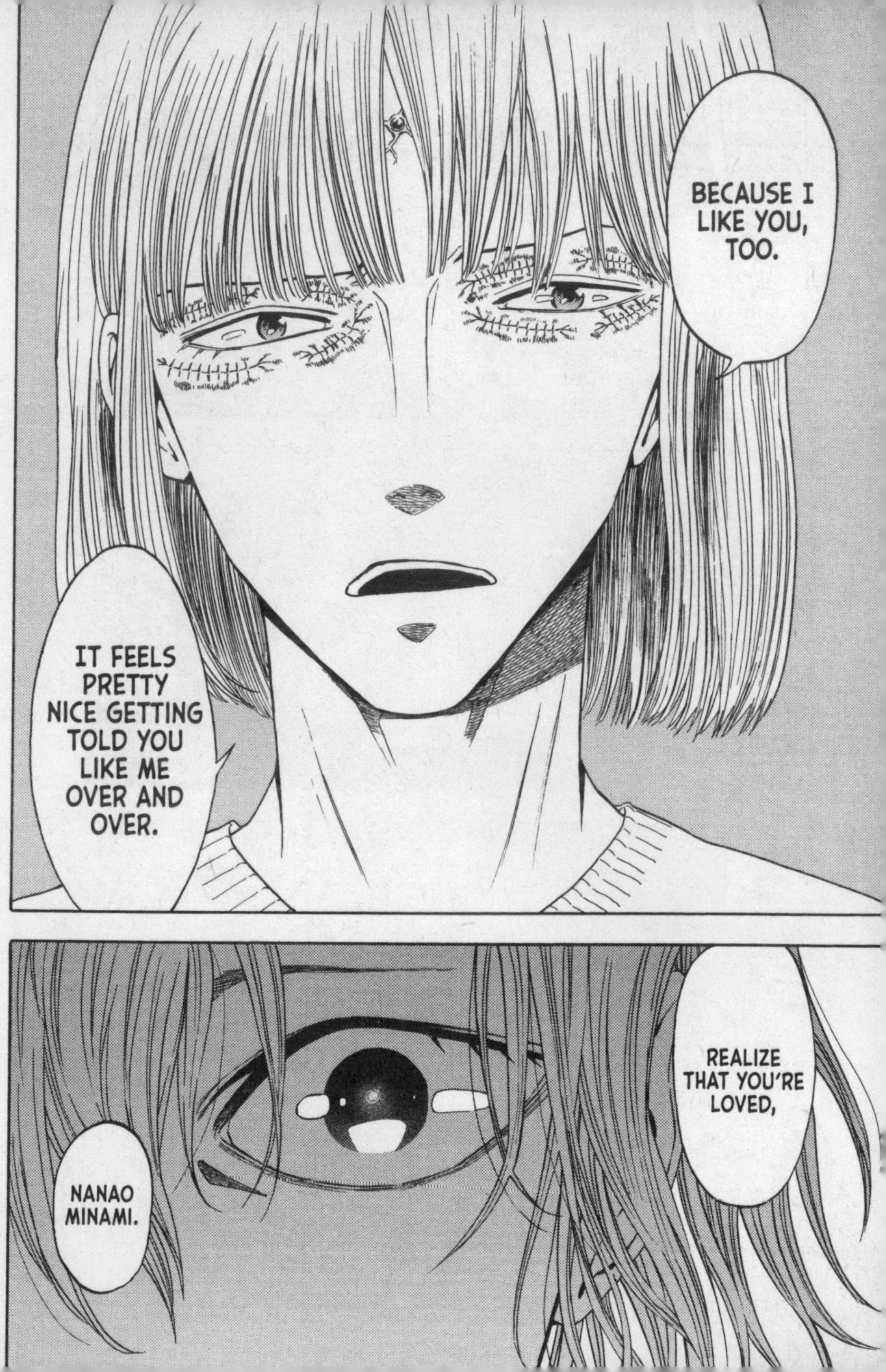
BECAUSE I LIKE YOU, TOO.
IT FEELS PRETTY NICE GETTING TOLD YOU LIKE ME OVER AND OVER.
REALIZE THAT YOU'RE LOVED,
NANAO MINAMI.

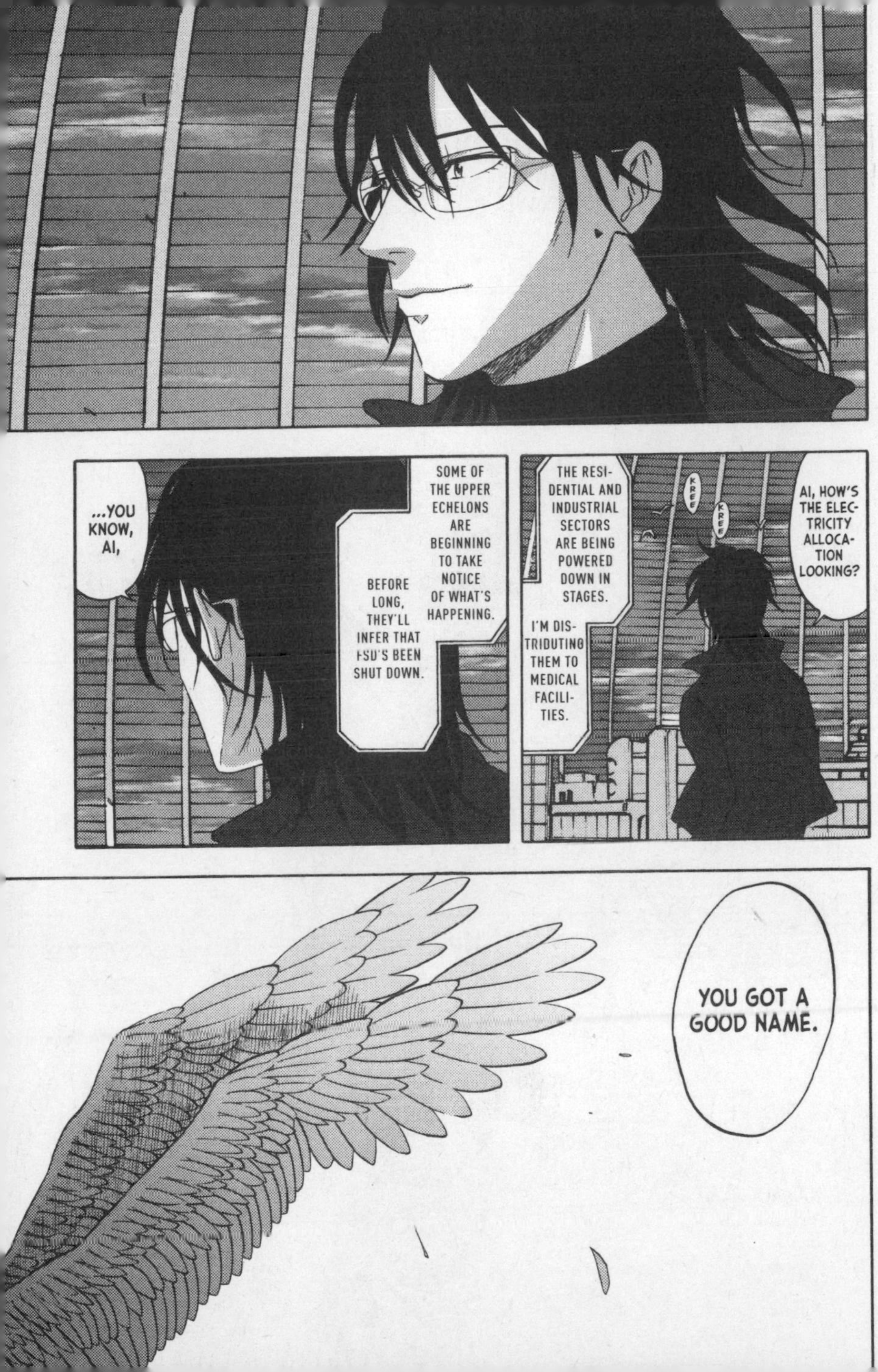
AI, HOW'S THE ELECTRICITY ALLOCATION LOOKING?
KREE
KREE
THE RESIDENTIAL AND INDUSTRIAL SECTORS ARE BEING POWERED DOWN IN STAGES.
I'M DISTRIDUTING THEM TO MEDICAL FACILITIES.
SOME OF THE UPPER ECHELONS ARE BEGINNING TO TAKE NOTICE OF WHAT'S HAPPENING.
BEFORE LONG, THEY'LL INFER THAT FSD'S BEEN SHUT DOWN.
...YOU KNOW, AI,
YOU GOT A GOOD NAME.

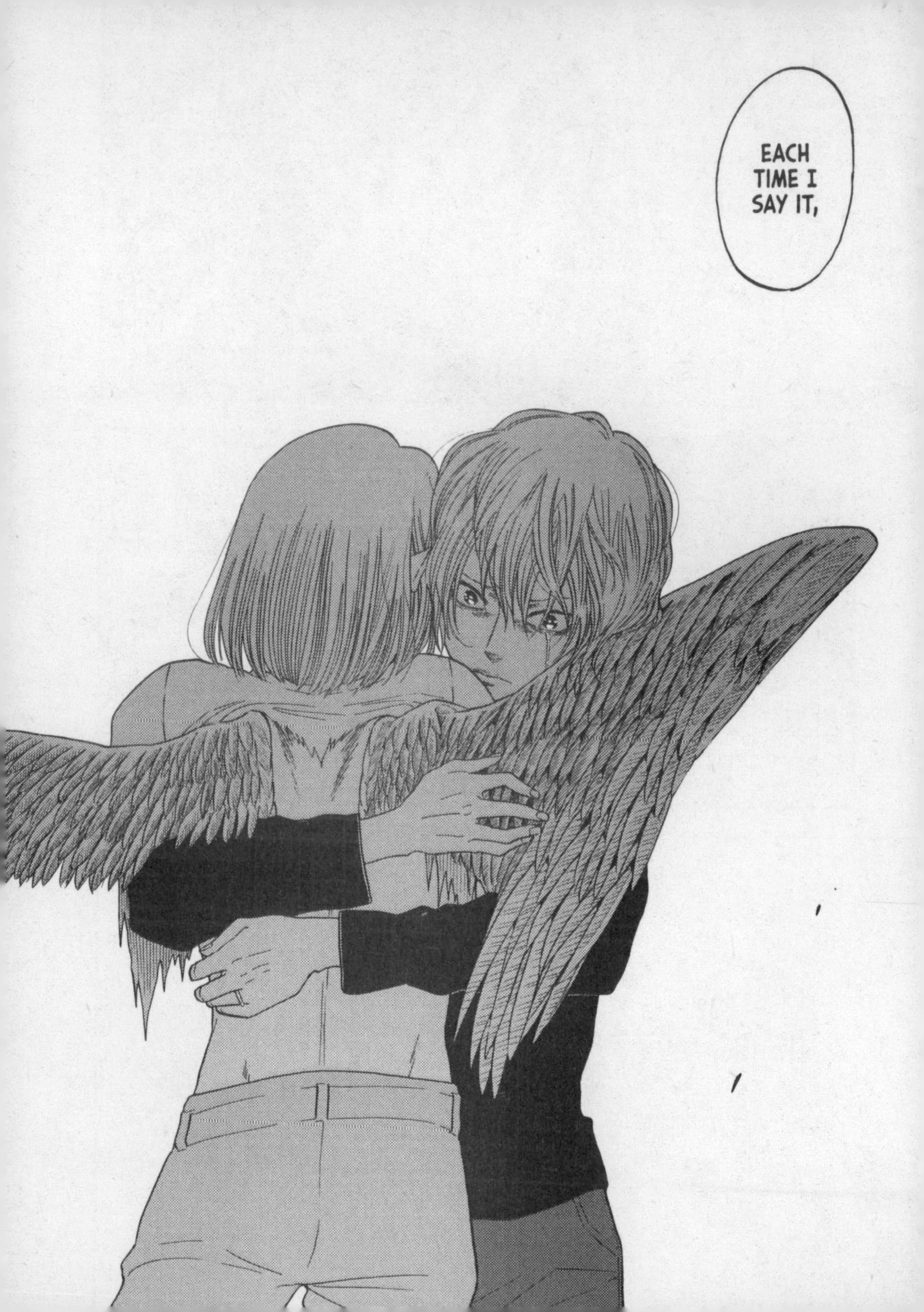
EACH TIME I SAY IT,

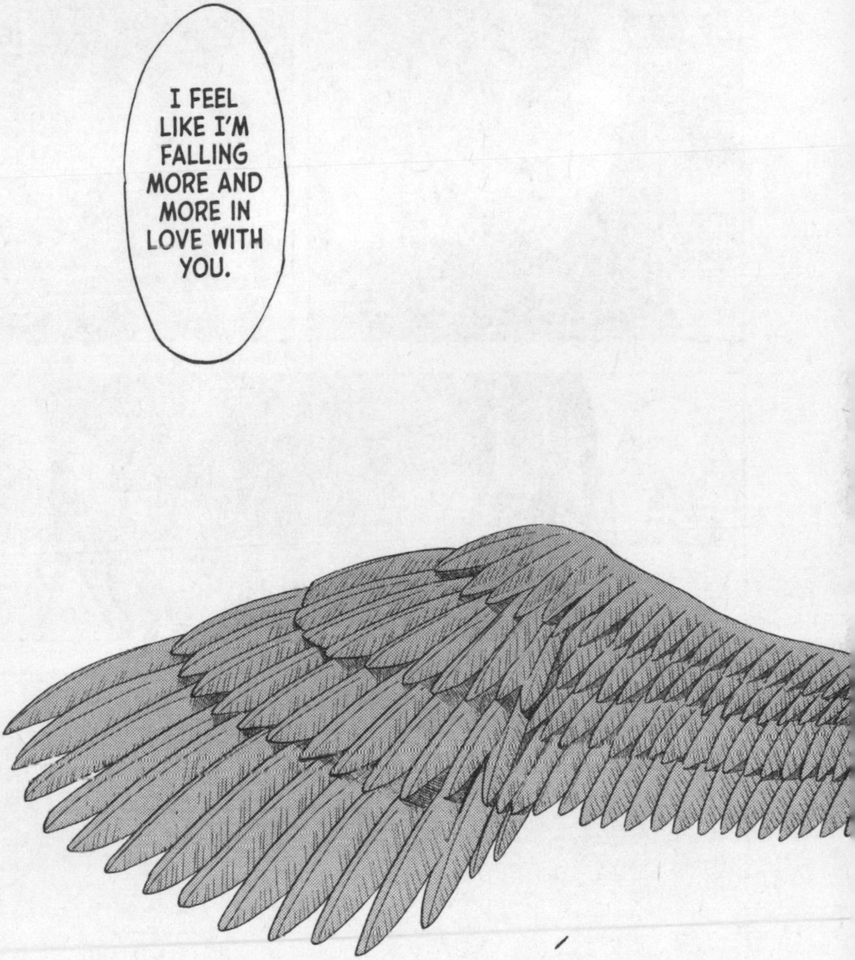
I FEEL LIKE I'M FALLING MORE AND MORE IN LOVE WITH YOU.

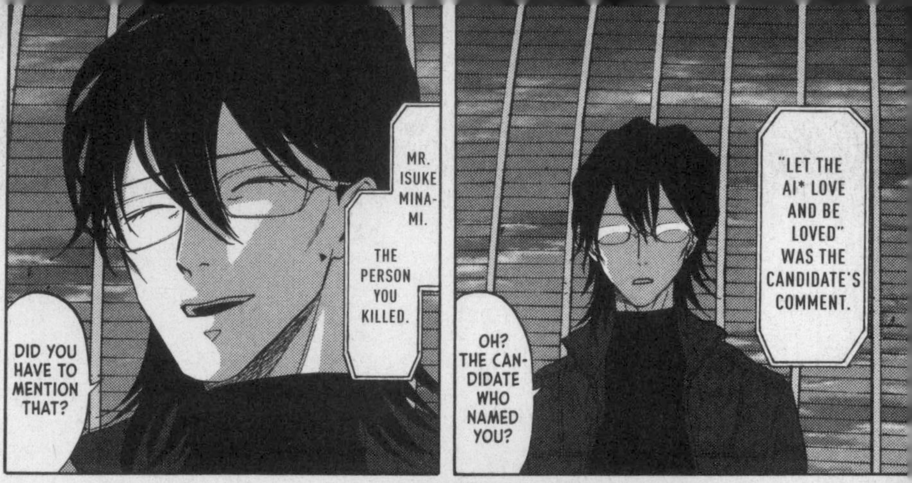
"LET THE AI* LOVE AND BE LOVED" WAS THE CANDIDATE'S COMMENT.
OH? THE CANDIDATE WHO NAMED YOU?
MR. ISUKE MINAMI.
THE PERSON YOU KILLED.
DID YOU HAVE TO MENTION THAT?

* The Japanese word "*ai*" means "love."

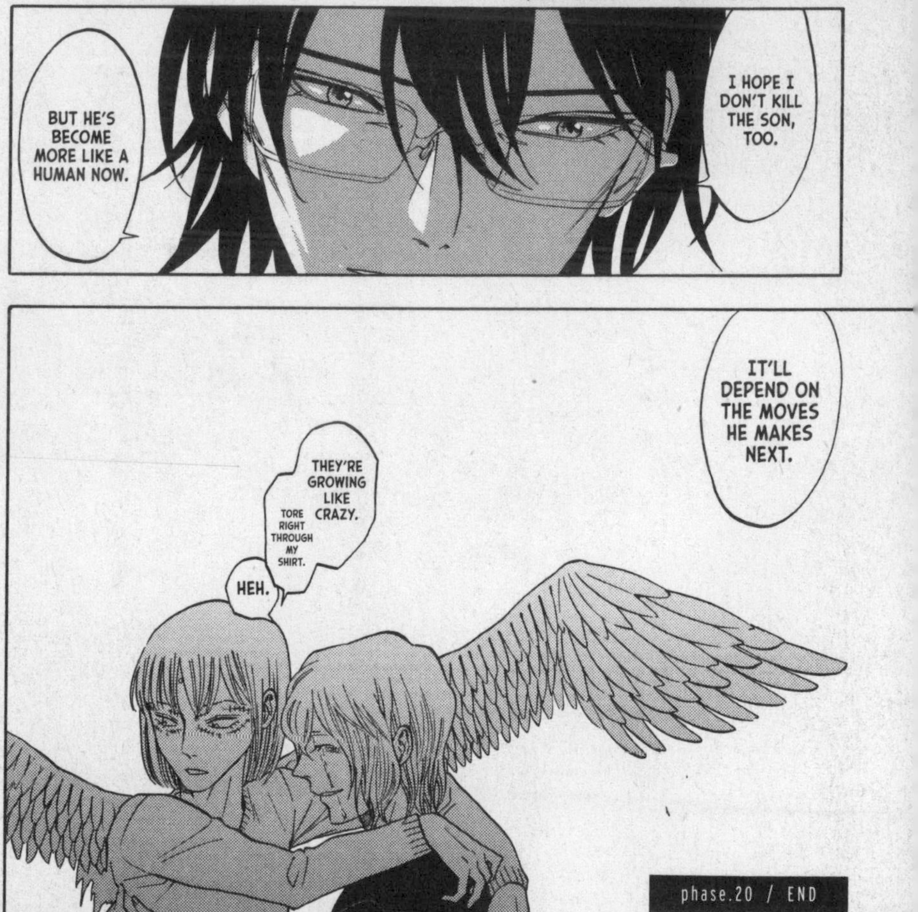
I HOPE I DON'T KILL THE SON, TOO.
BUT HE'S BECOME MORE LIKE A HUMAN NOW.
IT'LL DEPEND ON THE MOVES HE MAKES NEXT.
THEY'RE GROWING LIKE CRAZY.
TORE RIGHT THROUGH MY SHIRT.
HEH.
phase.20 / END

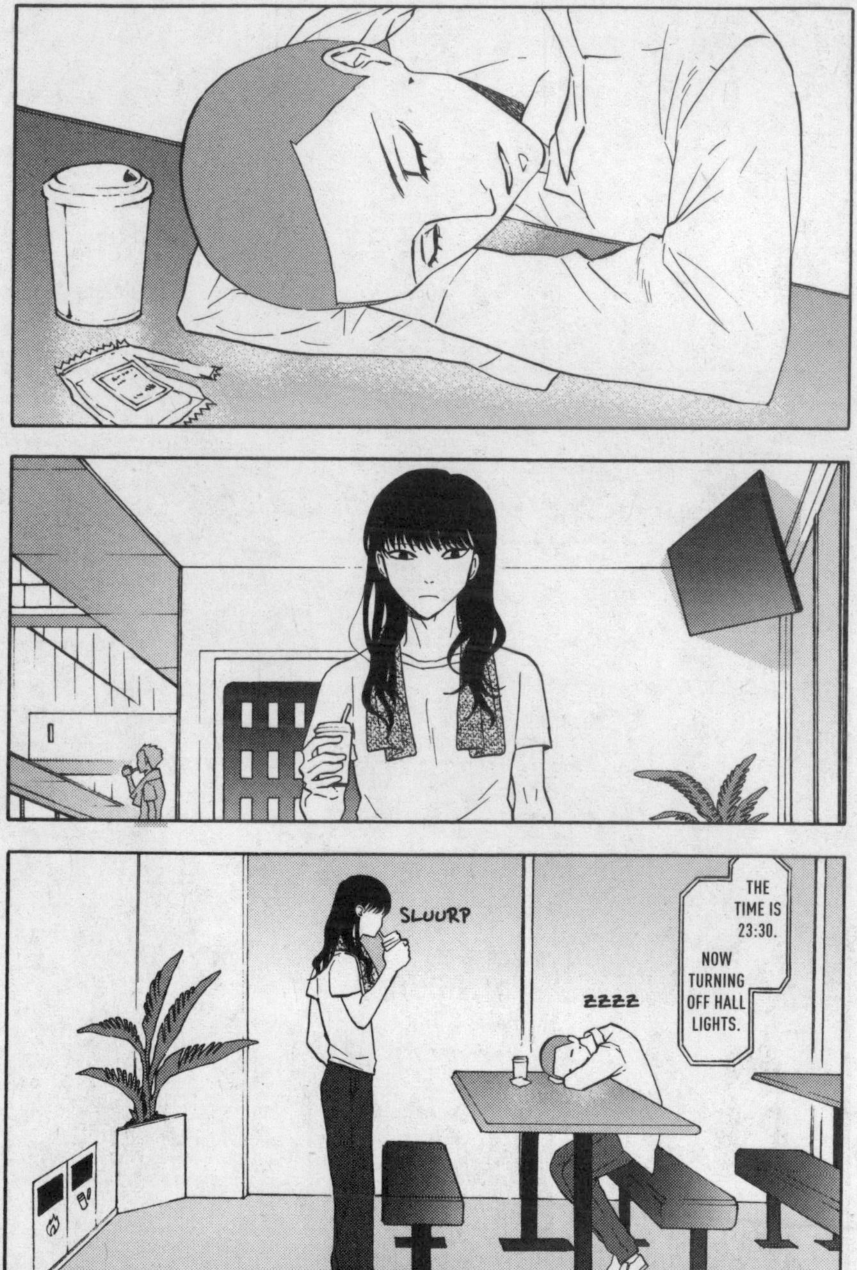
SLUURP
THE TIME IS 23:30.
NOW TURNING OFF HALL LIGHTS.
ZZZZ

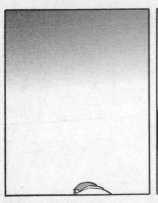

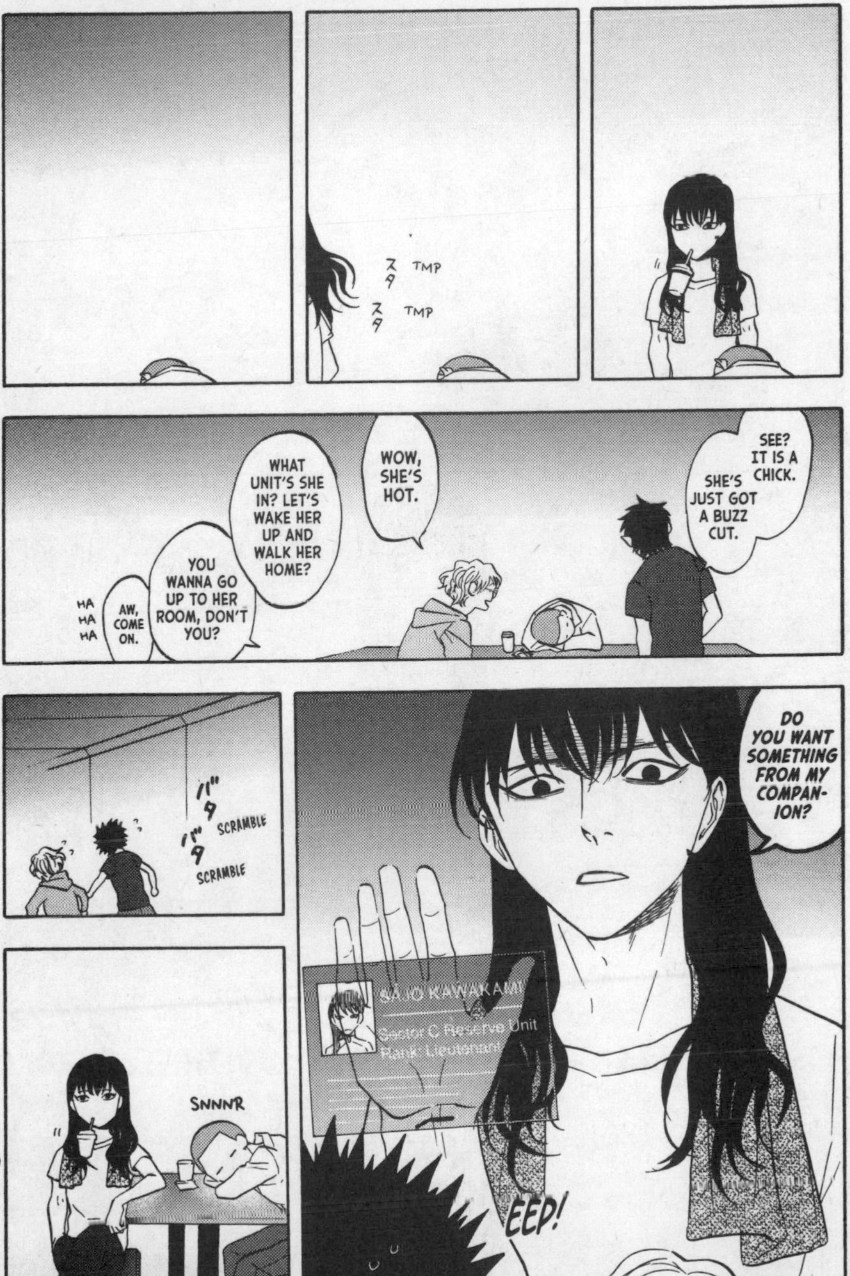
スタ TMP
スタ TMP
SEE? IT IS A CHICK.
SHE'S JUST GOT A BUZZ CUT.
WOW, SHE'S HOT.
WHAT UNIT'S SHE IN? LET'S WAKE HER UP AND WALK HER HOME?
YOU WANNA GO UP TO HER ROOM, DON'T YOU?
AW, COME ON.
HA HA HA
DO YOU WANT SOMETHING FROM MY COMPANION?
SAJO KAWAKAMI
Sector C Reserve Unit
Rank: Lieutenant
EEP!
バタ SCRAMBLE
バタ SCRAMBLE
SNNNR

END

DEVILS' LINE

Ryo Hanada

Tsukasa, a college student, is rescued from an attack by a devil, one of many vampires that can blend in among the human population. Anzai, her savior, is a half-devil who exploits his supernatural gifts as a member of a shadowy police task force that specializes in devil-related crime in Tokyo. As Anzai continues to keep guard over Tsukasa, the two quickly forge a tentative bond—one that Anzai fears will test his iron-clad rule of never drinking human blood...

All 14 Volumes Available Now!

APOSIMZ

ALL 9 VOLUMES AVAILABLE NOW!

TSUTOMU NIHEI

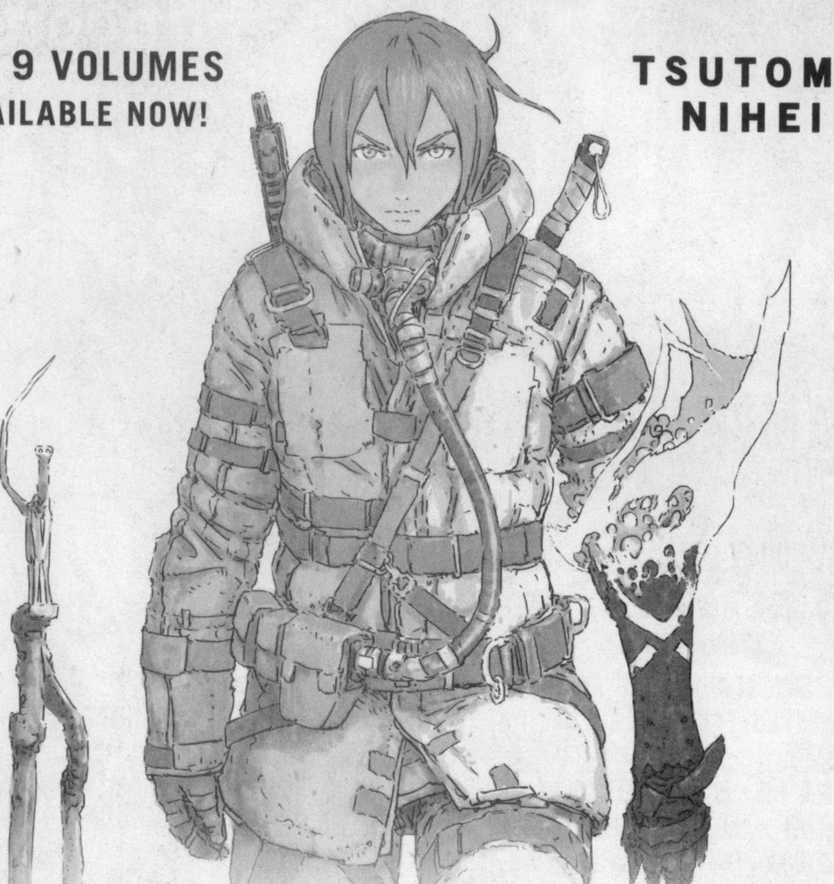

On a frigid, massive artificial planet known as Aposimz...

Eo, Biko, and Etherow, residents of the White Diamond Beam, are in the middle of combat training when suddenly a girl appears, Rebedoan Empire soldiers in hot pursuit. The girl asks for their help in keeping safe a "code" and seven mysterious "bullets." This chance encounter marks a major shift in the fate of the entire planet...

The curtain rises on a grand new adventure from Tsutomu Nihei, the author of *BLAME!* and *Knights of Sidonia.*

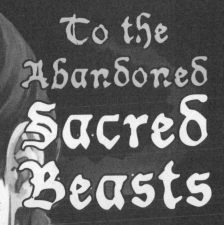

To the Abandoned Sacred Beasts

Presented by
MAYBE

During a protracted civil war that pitted the North against the South, the outnumbered Northerners used dark magical arts to create monstrous super-soldiers—Incarnates. Now that the war has ended, those Sacred Beasts must learn how to make their way in a peaceful society, or face death at the hands of a Beast Hunter.

Nancy Schaal Bancroft, the daughter of an Incarnate soldier who met an untimely end at the hands of one such Beast Hunter, turns to hunting the hunter. But once she catches up with her quarry, she discovers hard truths about the lives of the Incarnates...

VOLUMES 1-13 AVAILABLE NOW!

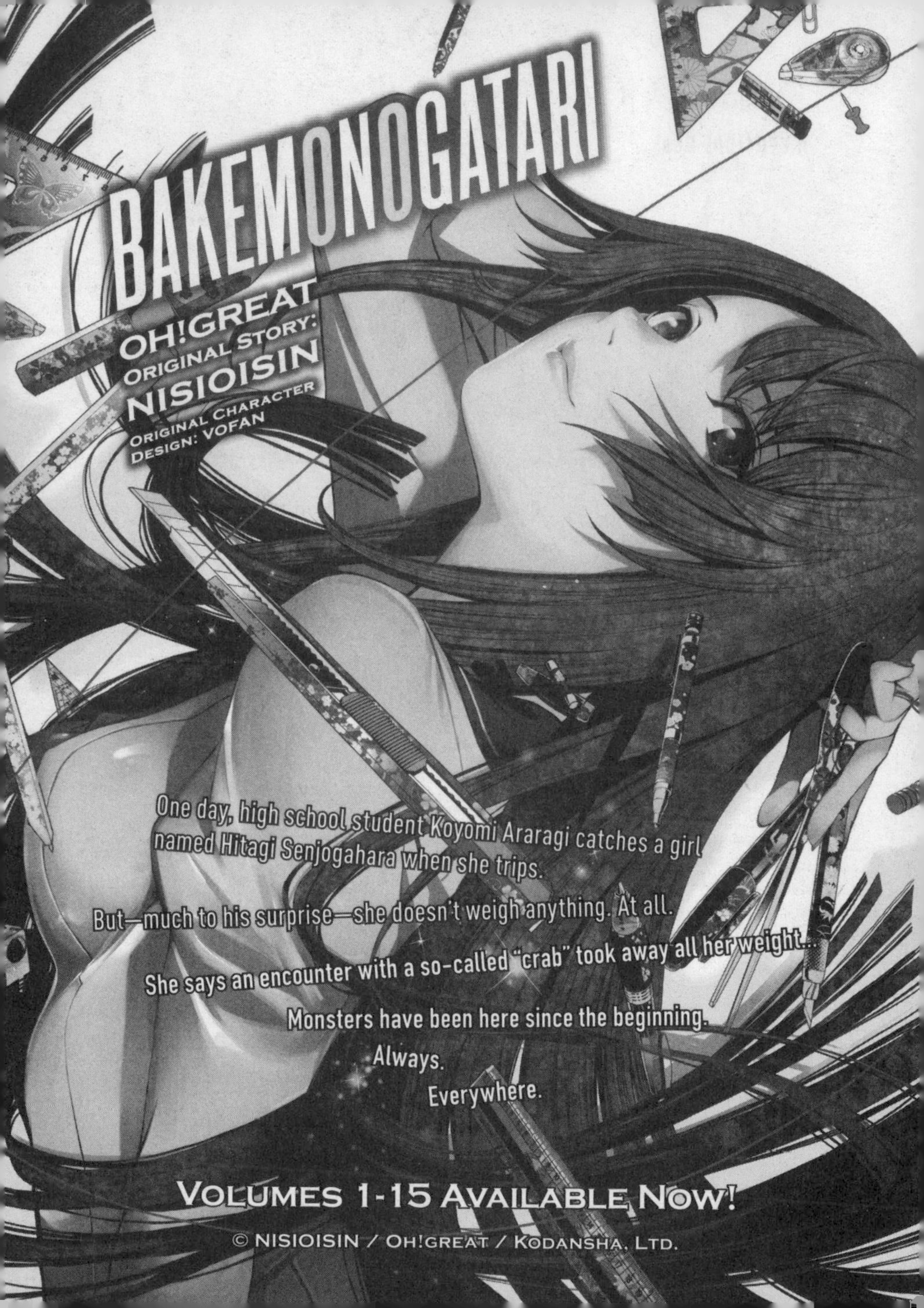
BAKEMONOGATARI
OH!GREAT
ORIGINAL STORY: NISIOISIN
ORIGINAL CHARACTER DESIGN: VOFAN
One day, high school student Koyomi Araragi catches a girl named Hitagi Senjogahara when she trips.
But—much to his surprise—she doesn't weigh anything. At all.
She says an encounter with a so-called "crab" took away all her weight...
Monsters have been here since the beginning.
Always.
Everywhere.
VOLUMES 1-15 AVAILABLE NOW!
© NISIOISIN / OH!GREAT / KODANSHA, LTD.

Blackguard 4
A VERTICAL Book

Editor: Michelle Lin
Translation: Melissa Tanaka
Production: Risa Cho, Pei Ann Yeap
              Lorina Mapa
Proofreading: Micah Q. Allen

Originally published in Japanese as *Burakkugarudo 4* by Kodansha, Ltd.
Burakkugarudo first serialized in *Gekkan Morning Two*, Kodansha, Ltd., 2019-2021

HERO
Words and Music by CHAD KROEGER
© 2002 WARNER-TAMERLANE PUBLISHING CORP. and
ANAESTHETIC PUBLISHING
All Rights Administered by WARNER-TAMERLANE PUBLISHING CORP.
All Rights Reserved
Used by Permission of ALFRED MUSIC

This is a work of fiction.

ISBN: 978-1-64729-151-8

Printed in the United States of America

First Edition

Kodansha USA Publishing, LLC
451 Park Avenue South
7th Floor
New York, NY 10016
www.kodansha.us

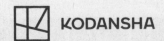

(Special Thanks To)
Family, friends, and colleagues
You, dear reader

(Managing Editor)
S-Hara

(Design)
Tadashi Hisamochi
(hive)

(Assistants)
Yoko
Kazuyo Haraguchi
Yukie Saito
Yui Tatami
Juan Albarran

(Guest Assistants)
Yohei Kurihara
risurisu

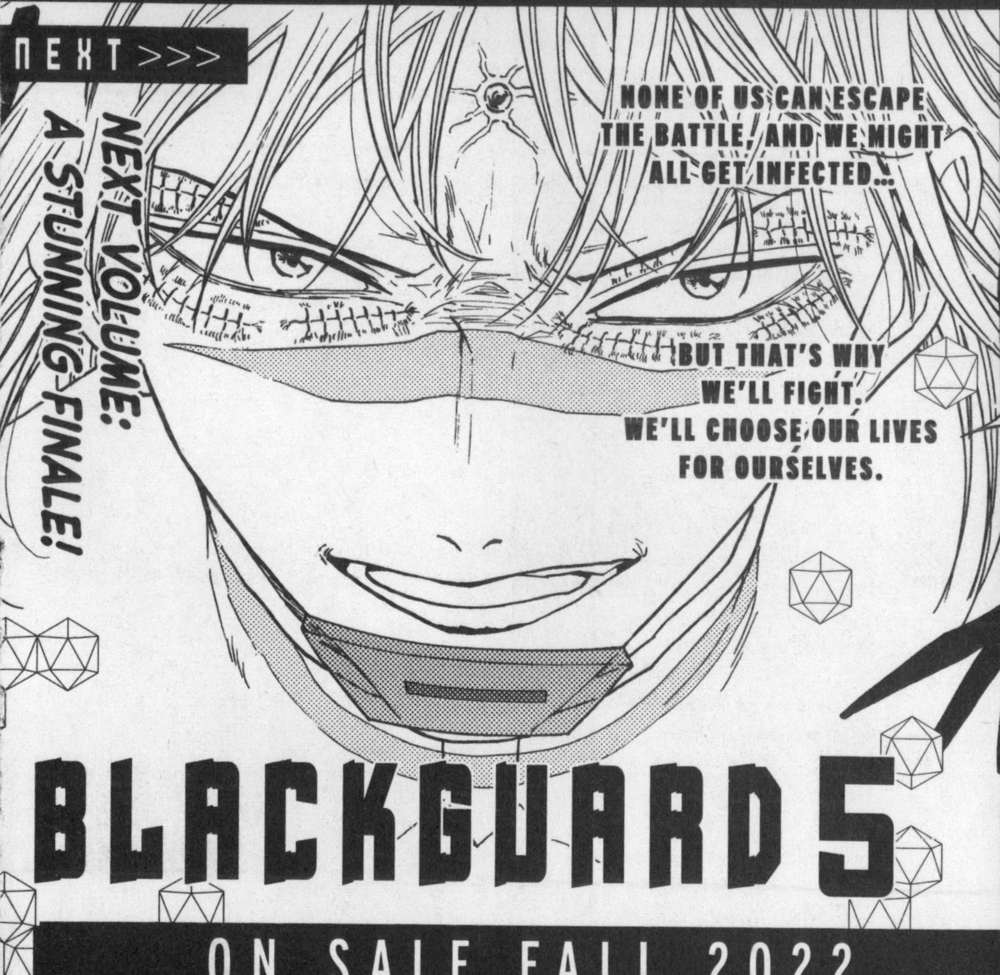
NEXT >>>
NEXT VOLUME:
A STUNNING FINALE!
NONE OF US CAN ESCAPE THE BATTLE, AND WE MIGHT ALL GET INFECTED...
BUT THAT'S WHY WE'LL FIGHT. WE'LL CHOOSE OUR LIVES FOR OURSELVES.
BLACKGUARD 5

ON SALE FALL 2022